나의

친애하는

적

허지웅 에세이

문학동네

컴퓨터 화면 위에 무질서한 점들이 있습니다. 점들은 규칙 없이 이동합니다. 이들은 멀리 있으면 서로를 끌어당깁니다. 그러나 너무 가깝게 다가가면 서로를 밀어냅니다. 완전히 겹쳐지면 둘 다 사라져버립니다. 이 프로그램은 점과 점 사이의 가장 완벽한 거리를 알아내려는 목적으로 만들어졌다고 합니다. 그러나 그토록 오랫동안 실행된 상태 그대로였음에도 불구하고, 점들은 여전히 움직이고 있습니다.

어른이 되면 사람과 사람 사이의 적절한 거리를 자연스레 알 수 있게 되리라 생각했던 것 같습니다. 그러나 마흔 살에 가깝게 된 지금에도 나는 그 거리에 대해 잘 알지 못합니다. 너무 다가가면 아픈 일이 생겼고 너무 떨어지면 외롭기 짝이 없었습니다.

가장 적절한 거리를 찾기 위해 겨우 떠올린 건 상대를 존경할 만한 적장처럼 대하는 것이었습니다. 처음에는 쉽지 않았습니다. 가까워지면 속을 모조리 내보여버리는 버릇이 쉽게 고쳐지지 않았습니다.

그러나 아주 조금씩 달라질 수 있었습니다. 서둘러 벽을 허물어 보이지 않는 것에 대해 상대가 서운해하고, 서운해하는 상대를 보며 내가 미안해하는 가장 어려운 순간만 견뎌내면 되는 일이었습니다. 나는 내가 사랑하는 모든 것들을 친애하는 적으로 바라보기 시작했습니다.

책임져야 할 것들이 많아질수록 가장 조심해야 할 건 나 자신에 지나치게 심취하는 일이라고 생각합니다. 자기에 심취하면 쉽게 뜨거워지고 자기 사정과 감정만이 특별한 것이라고 착각하게 됩니다. 그렇게 자기 사정에만 너그럽다보면 남의 사정은 나보다 덜한 별것 아닌 게 되고, 그러다보면 어느새 괴물이 되기 마련입니다. 그런 맥락에서 주변 세계를 친애하는 적으로 바라보는 태도는 확실히 도움이 되어주었습니다.

그제서야 나는 상대를 존중하면서 동시에 조심할 수 있는 방법을 아주 조금은 깨달은 것 같았습니다. 어쩌면 쉰 살이 되기 전에 사람과 사람 사이의 가장 완벽한 거리를 수식으로 완성할 수 있을지 모르겠습니다. 그럼 그 수식을 팔아 떼돈을 벌 생각입니다. 세상에는 의외로 나와 같은 고민을 하는 사람이 많기 때문입니다.

매일 쓰다보니 어느덧 한 권으로 만들 분량이 되었습니다. 내가 사랑한, 친애하는 적들에 관한 기록입니다. 〈한겨레〉와 〈씨네21〉에 연재한 글들과 새 글을 엮어 2년 만에 다시, 새 책을 펴냅니다. 여섯번째 책입니다. 좀더 부지런하게 쓰지 못해 죄송합니다.

내가 나를 차갑게 경계할 수 있도록 부디 언제까지나 도와주세요.
여러분은 나의 친애하는 적입니다.

2016년 11월
허지웅

1부 그럼에도 불구하고

2부 잊을 수 없는 얼굴이 있다

3부 끓는점

1부

그럼에도
불구하고

밖에 나서니 볕이 좋다.

좋은 빛들이 있다. 그리고 거기, 내게 특별히 좋은 빛이 있다. 다른 누군가에게는 별다를 거 없는 볕이다. 그런데 내게만 특별할 것만 같은 빛이다. 그런 빛을 찾는 일은 쉽지 않다. 정말 운좋은 누군가들은 그런 빛을 찾는다. 그리고 그것을 밝게 켜두어 나를 밝힌다. 그런데 별일 없이 그저 그런 어느 날 알게 된다. 느닷없이 알게 된다. 그 빛은 내 것이 아니라는 것을 말이다. 나 또한 그 빛을 그저 나를 밝히기 위해 이용했다는 걸 말이다. 그러고 나면 그 빛이 슬퍼 보인다. 슬프게, 보인다.

나와 상관없이 어느 누구에게나 따뜻하게 빛났을

그런 볕 아래 있는 나마저 슬프게 느껴진다.

그래서 그 빛을 꺼버렸다. 빛이 사라졌다. 그 빛 없이는 살 수 없을 것 같았던 내 삶을 돌아보았다. 명치가 쓰리다. 치사한 마음이 발톱부터 올라온다. 온몸이 뒤틀리고 가렵다. 그래서 가만히 누워보았다.

천장이 슬프다.

　모두가 누군가를 만나고 그중에 몇몇은 사랑에 빠진다. 그리고 운좋은 누군가들은 정말 만났어야 할 누군가와 만나 다시 없을 기억들을 남긴다. 가장 멋진 것과 가장 창피한 것들을 나눈다. 가장 훌륭한 것과 가장 추한 것을 교환한다. 나는 너에게 어울리는 사람이 되기 위해 노력하고 너는 나에게 어울리는 사람이 되기 위해 애쓴다. 거울 앞에 나란히 서서 우리가 얼마나 어울리는 사람들인지 감탄하고 좋아한다. 타인은 결코 이해할 수 없는 개그들이 오가고 그들끼리는 킥킥대며 좋아한다. 온전히 둘만이 누릴 수 있는 시간과 감정들이 쌓여간다. 서로가 서로에게 반드시 필요한 존재임을 믿고, 알고, 만족하고, 사랑한다. 비밀을 공유하고 서로의 비밀이 우리와 우리 밖의 세상 사이에 안전하기 짝이 없는 벽을 쌓아올린다고 생각한다. 벽은 갈수록 두터

워져가고 문밖에서 폭탄이 터져도 우리 둘은 안전할 것만 같다. 니 살이 내 살처럼 아프고 내 것 같다. 그리고 그렇게 사랑을 나누는 그들의 모습을 스스로 어여쁘게 여긴다.

그리고 헤어진다.

그렇게 한 가지 생각에 사로잡힌다. 밥을 먹고 똥을 싸고 출근을 하고 브레이크를 누르거나 액셀을 밟거나 좌회전을 하거나 유턴을 하거나 결재를 받거나 담배를 피우거나 잡담을 나누거나 소변을 보면서 눈앞에 붙은 '좋은 생각'류의 글귀들을 읽는 저 모든 순간들을 지배하는 단 한 가지 생각 말이다. 침대에 누워 그(녀)가 나를 사랑했던 시간들을 기억해내고 사소한 신호들을 되새기고 잘해주지 못했다는 죄책감과 속았다는 괘씸함과 대체 나는 얼마나 멍청한 것인가라는 자책감과 나와는 달리 그(녀)가 지금 누리고 있을 평안함을 상상하는 괴로움이 어우러져 범벅이 되다보면 뇌가 출렁거리며 조금씩 녹아 흘러내려 눈앞을 캄캄하게 덮어버리는 기분이다. 머리를 세게 흔들어 기합을 넣고 잠에 들 수 있는 최적의 자세를 찾아 숨을 고르고 나면 아까 했던 생각들이 똑같은 과정을 밟아 고스란히 반복된다. 그리고 삼천번째 눈앞이 캄캄해지고 나면 창밖으로 동이 트는 걸 발견하게 되겠지. 이불을 치우고 일어나 화장실로 걸음을 옮겨보지만 소용이 없다. 밤새 녹아내린 뇌가 온몸에 끈적하게 들러붙어 마음대로 움직일 수 없고 그냥 그 자리에 주저앉아버리고 싶

느닷없이 알게 된다.
그 빛은 내 것이 아니라는 것을 말이다.
나 또한 그 빛을 그저 나를 밝히기 위해 이용했다는 걸 말이다.
그러고 나면 그 빛이 슬퍼 보인다.
슬프게, 보인다.

나와 상관없이 어느 누구에게나 따뜻하게 빛났을

그런 별 아래 있는 나마저 슬프게 느껴진다.

천장이 슬프다.

을 것이다.

씨발 대체 얼마나 괴로운 일인가, 이별이란.

그래서 쓰러지듯 나는 다시 몸을 눕혀본다.

천장이 슬프다.

천장의 비어 있는 저 귀퉁이들을 나는 참을 수가 없다.

　비어 있는 귀퉁이들은 필연적으로 내려앉아 나를 누른다. 숨이 막히고 눈물이 새어나온다. 눈물이 무언가에 눌려 새어, 나온다, 는 것은 얼마나 안쓰러운 노릇인가. 울컥하고 시원하게 쏟아져 흘러준 것과 달리.

천장이 슬프다는 것은 그런 것이다.

하늘이 내려앉아 쥐어짰고,

나는 텅 비고 말았다.

좋은 어른

내게는 문신이 있다. 적지 않은 사람들이 오른팔에 쓰인 글귀가 무슨 뜻인지 물어왔고 나는 그때마다 비밀이라고 말했다. 혹은 '탕수육은 소스에 찍어먹는 게 아니라 소스를 부어먹는 것이다' 정도로 때에 따라 다르게 설명했는데, 그에 대해서는 굉장히 미안하게 생각하고 있다. 대단한 글귀라서가 아니다. 이런 종류의 말은 남에게 권할 것이 아니라 입다물고 내가 혼자 조용히 지켜야 하는 것이기 때문이다. 그래야 의미가 생긴다고 생각했다. 까먹지 않으려고 굳이 살 위에 써놓은 것인데 그 의미를 지키려고 노력하지 않는다면 거대한 낭비가 아니겠는가. 탕수육 이야기는 다시 한번 미안. 실은 현실주의자가 되자, 하지만 가슴속에는 불가능한 꿈을 간직하자.

라고 쓰여 있다. 68혁명 당시 체 게바라가 한 말이라고 대중에 알려진 글귀이지만 대개의 유명한 펀치라인이 그러하듯이 실제 화자와 일치하지 않을 가능성이 더 크다. 사실 내게는 그게 누가 한 말인지보다 문장 자체가 더 중요했다. 철저한 현실주의자로 상황을 판단하고 행동하되 결코 이루어질 리 없는 뜨거운 무언가를 그 기반에 두자는 것.

이 생각은 내게 참 소중했다. 내가 만난 많은 어른들은 정확히 그와 반대로 행동했기 때문이다. 그들은 겉으로 몽상가처럼 세상에 관한 따뜻하고 근사한 말을 늘어놓되 정작 중요한 순간에는 단 한 치의 손해도 용납할 수 없다는 뜨거움으로 그를 믿어왔던 주변의 많은 이들을 집어삼켰다. 그리고 지금의 나는 알고 있다. 그들이 그렇게 행동했던 건 딱히 남들보다 악해서가 아니라, 그렇게 행동하는 편이 세상을 살아나가는 데 훨씬 더 쉽고 편리하기 때문이라는 걸 말이다. 그게 내가 살아오면서 목격하고 학습한 이 세상의 '어른스러움' 혹은 '사회화'였다.

스물두 살이었다. 군대를 제대했지만 복학하지 않았다. 등록금과 집세와 생활비를 벌어야 했다. 건설현장에서 모래를 고르는 일부터 아무개 브랜드의 피팅모델까지 하루에 몇 개씩 닥치는 대로 일했다(나는 이 피팅모델 경력을 매우 자랑스럽게 생각하고 떠벌리는 경향이 있다. 나도 젊고 예뻤다……). 그러다 일확

현실주의자가 되자,
하지만 가슴속에는 불가능한 꿈을 간직하자.
까먹지 않으려고 굳이 살 위에 써놓은 것인데
그 의미를 지키려고 노력하지 않는다면
거대한 낭비가 아니겠는가.

천금의 부푼 꿈을 안고 시작한 일이 텔레마케팅이었다. 아무튼 나는 입으로 하는 일에는 뭐든지 자신이 있었다.

광화문의 큰 빌딩이었다. 사무실 문을 열고 들어갔더니 나와 비슷한 처지로 보이는 어린애들이 일렬로 앉아 있었다. 이 아이들보다 유능해 보여야 한다는 생각이 들었다. 앉지 않고 테헤란로 직장인의 각도로 비스듬히 서서 큰 소리로 전화를 해댔다. 머릿속으로는 계속 『슬램덩크』의 정대만 생각을 했다. 내가 당시 떠올릴 수 있는 가장 훌륭한 노력의 아이콘이었다. 면접을 보러 들어갔는데 하마터면 '감독님, 전화로 물건을 팔고 싶어요'라고 말할 뻔했다. 사흘 후에 합격했다는 전화를 받고 엄청나게 기쁜 마음으로 달려갔더니 그때 사무실 앞에 앉아 있던 애들 그대로 다 있더라.

사무실은 인사동의 작은 건물로 옮겨졌다. 일전의 큰 빌딩은 본부고, 이렇게 팀을 꾸려 다른 사무실로 분가하는 거라는 설명을 들었다. 팀장은 다소 비만 체형이었고 나이는 많지 않았다. 기껏해야 서른쯤으로 보였다. 부장은 바싹 말랐고 그보다 훨씬 나이가 많아 보였다. 물건을 팔기 위한 전화 통화 시나리오를 각자 써냈다. 내 것이 채택되었고 나는 곧장 부장의 신임을 얻었다. 육체노동이여 안녕, IMF 시대는 금 모으기가 아니라 오직 나 같은 인재를 발굴하는 일을 통해서만 이겨낼 수 있는 것이 아닌가, 그런 생각을 했다. 우리는 차량에 설치하는 GPS를 팔았다. 당시의 GPS는 화면 같은 게 없었고 그냥 과속카메라가 있을 때 음성으로 신호를 보내주는 역할을 했다. 나는 그걸 엄청나게 팔

왔다.

　부장과 인사동의 작은 민속주점에서 술을 마셨다. 그는 좋은 어른으로 보였다. 부장은 여러 가지 이야기를 들려주었다. 가족 이야기도 하고 정치 이야기도 하고, 무엇보다 우리 팀원들이 하나같이 자식 같고 가족 같은데 한창 공부해야 할 시기에 시대를 잘못 만나 이렇게 나와서 돈을 벌어야 한다는 게 안타깝다, 그래서 더 잘해주고 싶다, 그런 이야기를 했다. 아, 나는 엄청나게 감동했다. 그리고 저런 어른이 되어서 나중에 나보다 어린 청년들에게 똑같은 이야기를 해주어야겠다고 생각했다.

부장은 9월 25일 도망쳤다.

　정확한 날짜를 기억하는 건 그날이 월급날이었기 때문이다. 아침에 출근했더니 사무실 문은 잠겨 있었고 아이들은 그 앞에서 어쩔 줄 몰라하고 있었다. 나는 그들보다 한 살이 더 많다는 이유로 대책위원장 비슷한 것이 되었다. 팀장을 찾아가봤지만 자기도 피해자라는 말 이외에 별게 없었다. 부장은 사무실 집기와 직원들의 두 달 치 월급을 챙기고 사라졌다. 경찰서와 노동청을 방문해 이런저런 서류를 작성하면서 나는 참 마음이 복잡했다. 무엇보다 그 좋은 부장이 왜 이런 일을 벌이는 건지 알 수가 없었다.

　거의 두 달 후에야 부장을 만날 수 있었다. 그가 먼저 연락을 해왔다. 동대문 이대병원 앞에서 만났다. 부장은 자기를 그만 괴롭히라고 말했다. 돈이 있으면 주지 않겠느냐며 자기는 가족이 전부 흩어져서 고시원에서 힘들게 살고 있다고 했다. 나는 원래 고시원 살았다는 말이 자동적으로 튀어나오다가 목젖에 걸려 허우적대며 도로 들어갔다. 부장이 너무 낯설어 보였다. 나는 그게 무척 슬펐다.

이후로 많은 어른들을 만났다. 나는 불행하게도 좋은 어른을 많이 만나보지 못했다. 그것이 사회 일반의 반영인지 혹은 그저 나의 박복함의 결과인지 잘 모르겠다. 분명한 건 최악의 어른이란 늘 갱신되고 있다는 것뿐이었다. 상황은 내가 어렸을 때보다 더 나빠졌다. 아주 잠깐 불었던 20대 청년운동의 바람은 아프니까 청춘이라는 억박 아래 수렴되면서 자취를 감추었다. 세상 위로 첫발을 내딛는 사람들은 점점 더 불리해지고, 그 불리함은 더욱더 당연한 것으로 치부되었으며, 젊은이들은 거짓 위로로 가득찬 힐링 스폿들로 파편화되어 도피했다. 어른들이 만든 체계가 하나도 제대로 작동하지 않아 그걸 안전하다고 믿었던 아이들이 목숨을 잃었고, 이 명백한 죽음을 두고도 어른들은 좌와 우를 나누어대며 남겨진 자들을 능욕했다.

나도 이제 그들의 나이에 가까워졌다. 정말 무서운 건, 나도 그런 종류의 어른스러움에 너무나 익숙해졌다는 사실이다. 나는 늘 좋은 어른이 되고 싶었다. 내가 생각하는 좋은 어른이란 자기보다 어리고 경험이 없는 사람에게 양보할 줄 아는 사람이었다. 겉으로 냉정하되 속으로 상대를 이해하고 그에 기반해서 행동하는 사람이었다. 자기보다 젊은 이의 신념을 위해 내 신념을 포기할 수 있는 사람이었다. 그런데 내가 되고 싶은 어른으로 나이 먹어가는 일은 생각보다 훨씬 어려운 일이었다. 그날 멀어져가는 부장의 뒷모습을 바라보았던 20대의 내가 지금의 나를 만났을 때, 그가 나를 마음에 들어할지 잘 모르겠다. 나는 그게 너무 부끄럽고 슬프다.

살다보면
별일이 다 있다

살다보면 별일이 다 있어요.

나는 이 말을 좋아한다. 참 좋은 말이라고 생각한다. 어쩌면 가장 좋은 말인지도 모르겠다. 다른 그 어떤 말보다도 이 말은 가장 어른스럽게 세상을 포용하고자 하는 태도를 담고 있기 때문이다.

'살다보면 별일이'까지는 그것 참 내 기준에서는 도무지 용납하거나 이해할 수 있는 일이 아니라며 고개를 가로젓는 듯하지만, 이내 '다 있어요'라며 어찌됐든 앞의 말을 껴안아 어루만지며 화해하려 애쓰는 것 말이다. 세상은 이해할 수 없는 것투성이다. 그렇다고 내가 경험해보지 않았거나 이해할 수 없는 것이

곧 비정상을 의미하는 건 아니다. 왜냐하면 살다보면

별일이 다 있기 때문이다.

　오늘은 이 참 좋은 말이 가장 아름답게 쓰인 영화 가운데 하나를 골라보았다. 〈내겐 너무 사랑스러운 그녀〉다. 라이언 고슬링이 주연을 맡지 않았다면 훨씬 현실적이었을지 모른다. 하지만 이 영화 속의 라이언 고슬링은 대단히 망가져 있으니 대충 용납해보기로 하자.

　라스는 형과 형수와 함께 작은 마을에서 산다. 라스는 남들과 어울리는 데 문제가 있는 사람이다. 그는 타인이 접근하는 걸 두려워한다. 아니, 두려워하는 걸 넘어 누가 만지거나 안으면 말 그대로 '아파한다'. 형과 형수가 집에 살고 자신은 헛간을 개조해 살아간다. 누구와도 마주치고 싶지 않기 때문이다. 그런 라스를 형 내외는 안타까워한다.

　그러던 어느 날 라스가 여자친구를 집에 데려온다. 외국에서 와서 말도 하지 못하고 몸이 불편해 휠체어를 타야 한다고 소개한다. 아무래도 여자니까 자신과 함께 헛간에서 머무는 것보다는 빈방 하나를 내어주는 게 어떻겠냐고 형과 형수에게 묻는다. 그들은 뛸듯이 기뻐한다. 그리고 그녀를 저녁식사에 초대한다. 라스가 데려온 여자친구는 리얼돌이었다.

맞다. 리얼돌 말이다.

짐짓 태연한 척하지만 형과 형수는 크게 당황한다. 당연한 노릇이다. 식사 자리에서 라스는 리얼돌 '비앙카'와 아무도 알아듣지 못하는 대화를 나누며 즐거워한다. 형은 괴롭다. 라스가 급기야 미쳐버린 거라며 자책한다. 부부는 비앙카가 외국에서 왔고 몸이 좋지 않으니 아무래도 의사의 진찰을 받아보는 게 좋지 않겠느냐며 라스를 회유한다. 그를 진찰받게 하기 위해서다. 라스와 비앙카를 만나본 의사는 최대한 그들을 자연스럽게 받아들이는 게 일단 최선의 조치임을 설명한다. 형과 형수는 마을의 목사와 어르신들을 만나 도움을 요청한다. 비앙카를 실존 인물처럼 받아들여달라고 부탁하는 것이다.

말도 안 되는 일이야.

요즘 젊은이들은 도무지 약해빠졌단 말이야.

그만해요. 샐리, 당신 사촌은 고양이한테 옷을 입히죠. 헤이즐, 당신의 조카는 UFO클럽에 돈을 쏟아부어요. 어니, 게다가 당신의 죽은 부인은 도벽이 있었지요.

무슨 말이야, 그런 일 없어.

당신 부인 장례식 때 내 귀걸이를 하고 있더군요.

흠.

살다보면 별일이 다 있기 마련이에요.

그래도…… 설마 교회에는 오지 못하게 하실 거죠 목사님?

글쎄요, 이런 때일수록 먼저 생각해봐야 할 게 있지요. 예수님이라면 어떻게 했을까요.

한국의 대형 교회라면 있을 수 없는 일이겠지만. 그들은 라스와 비앙카의 관계를 받아들이기로 결정한다. 그렇게 비앙카는 이 마을의 일원이 된다. 처음에는 조금 어색해하던 사람들도 이내 비앙카를 자연스럽게 대하기 시작한다. 인사를 하고 파티에 초대하고 심지어 공동체를 위해 일을 부탁한다. 의상 모델이 되어달라 하고 소아암 환자들을 위해 책을 읽어달라고 하는 식이다(물론 실제 책을 읽는 건 녹음된 목소리다). 그렇게 거짓말처럼 비앙카는 '마을 사람'이 된다. 그냥 이웃이 아닌, 없어서는 안 될 공동체의 일원 말이다.

라스는 불만에 가득찬다. 비앙카가 마을의 대소사에 불려다니느라 자신이 그녀와 어울릴 시간이 줄어들었기 때문이다. 화가 잔뜩 난 라스에게 형수가 외친다. 마을 사람들이 비앙카에게 신경을 쓰는 건 당신을 염려하고 좋아하기 때문이에요. 어떻게 그걸 모를 수가 있어요?

그러는 와중에 라스는 다른 여자에게 관심을 갖는 자신을 발견하고 당황한다. 그녀는 늘 라스에게 관심을 갖고 잘 대해줬던 직장 동료다. 비앙카가 없는 틈을 타 라스는 그녀와 데이트를 한다. 그들은 볼링을 친다. 나오는 길에 라스는 죄책감을 느끼며 그녀에게 말한다. 저는 비앙카를 배신할 수 없어요. 알아요, 나 그런 나쁜 여자 아니에요.

라스는 그날 밤 비앙카와 함께 자기로 결심한다. 그러나 다음날 아침 비명을 지르며 형과 형수를 찾는다. 비앙카가 아프고 죽어간다는 것이다. 아니, 정확히 말하자면 라스가 비앙카를 떠나보내기로 결정한 것이겠지만.

<내겐 너무 사랑스러운 그녀Lars and the Real Girl>(2007)

그는 타인을 두려워한다.
사실은 누군가를 잃는 게 두려운 것이다.
그러나 누구나 언젠가는
무엇이든 잃게 마련이다.

이 영화는 라스가 어른이 되어가는 과정을 그리고 있다. 그는 타인을 두려워한다. 사실은 누군가를 잃는 게 두려운 것이다. 그러나 누구나 언젠가는 무엇이든 잃게 마련이다. 라스는 부모를 일찍 잃었기 때문에 그것을 잘 알고 있다. 그래서 애초 누구와도 관계를 맺고 싶어하지 않는 것이다. 그런 라스가 비앙카를 찾는다. 비앙카에게 누군가가 꽃을 주자 라스는 말한다. 이건 조화라서 시들지 않아 좋아.

그런 라스가 비앙카와 관계를 맺고, 그녀를 아끼고 사랑하고, 질투하고 징징대고, 안기고 치유받다가, 급기야 이별하고 그것을 받아들이기까지의 과정. 그게 〈내겐 너무 사랑스러운 그녀〉다.

나는 무엇보다 이 영화 속에 그려진 공동체의 선함에 관심이 갔다. 나는 그것이 애초 선함이었다고 생각하지 않는다. 자신이 손해 볼 일 없는 관심이고 가십이다. 그것에 참여하는 건 어느 정도의 오락거리다. 아마도 어느 정도는 스스로 좋은 사람이라고 판단할 수 있는 일탈이 생겨서 더욱 적극적이었을 것이다.

그러나 이후 그들이 비앙카를 찾고 그녀를 필요로 하는 것은 다른 문제다. 비앙카의 장례식에 모인 사람들을 바라볼 때 나는 비로소 엉엉 울었다. 그들은 진심으로 슬퍼하고 있다.

타인의 정상성을 의심하고 억지로 분류할 때 공동체의 정상성은 훼손된다. 반대로 타인의 정상성을 의심하거나 분류하지 않고 그럴 수 있는 삶의 일부로 받아들였을 때 공동체의 정상성은 굳건해진다. 부끄러운 벌칙 같은 일들이 우리 주변에서 일어난다. 내게도 일어난다. 그러나 내 고통을 내가 별일로 받아들이는 것보다 남들이 이해할 수 없는 누군가의 사연을 별일로 받아들이는 과정이 훨씬 더 힘들고 어렵다. 특히나 한국에서는 말이다. 극중의 누군가를 진심으로 응원하게 되는 영화는 드물다. 나는 라스를 응원하고 싶었다. 저 공동체는 염려되지 않았다. 저런 공동체는 알아서 잘 굴러갈 수밖에 없다. 라스는 얼마나 운이 좋은 사람인가! 그가 정말 행복해지기를 바란다.

살다보면 별일이 다 있어요. 나는 이 말을 좋아한다.

세상은 이해할 수 없는 것투성이다. 그렇다고 내가 경험해보지 않았거나 이해할 수 없는 것이 곧 비정상을 의미하는 건 아니다. 왜냐하면 살다보면

별일이 다 있기 때문이다.

살다보면 별일이 다 있어요.
나는 이 말을 좋아한다.
세상은 이해할 수 없는 것투성이다.
그렇다고 내가 경험해보지 않았거나
이해할 수 없는 것이 곧 비정상을 의미하는 건 아니다.
왜냐하면 살다보면
별일이 다 있기 때문이다.

<내겐 너무 사랑스러운 그녀>(2007)

선인장

사실 나는 아름다운 것에 대해 별 관심이 없다. 나는 미에 대한 기준이 뚜렷하다. 보통 그걸 미감이라 부른다. 하지만 내 미감은 대개의 취향을 포섭할 만한 아름다움을 거의 보지 못하고 지나치기 일쑤다. 나의 미감이란 그저 내가 강박적으로 좋아하는 것들을 다 더한 수를 나이로 나눈 값에 지나지 않는다. 맞다. 그건 엄밀히 말해 미감이라 불러선 안 되는 것이며, 심지어 해가 갈수록 그 수가 줄어들고 있다(감이 떨어지고 있다). 솔직히 말하자면, 아름다운 것을 사랑하는 일은 모든 동물이 다 할 수 있지만 아름답지 않은 것을 사랑할 수 있는 존재는 사람뿐이다. 아름답지 않은 것을 사랑하는 일은 인간을 사람답게 만드는 중요한 재능이라고 생각한다. 그렇다고 아름다운 것을 꼽아달라는 요청에 아름답지 않은 것을 사랑할 수 있는 게 어쩌고저쩌고라는 답을 하는 건 이 요청에 답을 보내온 다른 사람들에게도 무례한 짓이다. 그래서 고민해봤는데, 나는

선인장이 아름답다는 결정을 내렸다.

꼭 한 해 전에 처음 선인장을 샀다. 다른 이유는 없었다. 첫눈에 반해서 샀다. 굉장히 크고 화려하고 예뻤다. 선인장은 세 달 만에 죽었다. 과습 때문이었다. 물을 너무 많이 주었다. 살리려고 흙을 파서 말려보고 꽃집에도 가져가보았지만 허사였다. 선인장은 완전히 회생 불가라는 판정을 받기 전까지 거실 그 자리에 사흘 동안 있었다. 내 집안에서 생명이 꺼져가는 걸 며칠간 지켜보면서 나는 굉장한 죄책감에 사로잡혔다. 아끼고 사랑한답시고 익사시킨 것이다. 선인장이 죽어가던 모습을 빨리 머릿속에서 지워버리고 싶었다.

나는 곧바로 다른 선인장을 샀다. 그리고 이번에는 최대한 신경을 쓰지 않고 내버려두었다. 이따금 햇빛을 받아 반짝이는 선인장을 곁눈질로 보며 그 곧고 한결같은 생명력에 내심 경탄했다. 두어 달 전, 선인장이 하얗게 변해버린 걸 발견했다. 언제부터 그랬는지조차 알 수 없었다. 이전의 선인장이 떠올라서 나는 비명을 지르고 말았다. 반나절 동안은 빨리 포기해버리고 저번처럼 죽어가는 걸 지켜보지 말아야겠다고 생각했다. 너무 관심을 쏟아도 안 되고 너무 관심을 쏟지 않아도 안 된다니 나는 남은

생에 다시는 이런 걸 기르지 말아야겠다고 결심했다. 그러다 나머지 반나절 동안 마음을 고쳐먹었다. 열심히 수소문했다. 깍지벌레라는 병충해였다. 농약을 사서 일주일에 세 번씩 뿌리고 칫솔로 부지런히 닦아냈다. 병증은 쉽게 치유되지 않았다. 손에 가시가 박힌 상처들이 아물고 다시 다치기를 두 번 정도 반복했다.

지난 주말 아침에 일어나 거실 창문을 활짝 열었다. 녹색의 윤기를 되찾은 선인장이 햇빛을 받는 순간 꿈틀거리는 걸 본 것 같았다. 그건 내가 살면서 본 광경 가운데 가장 아름다운 것이었을지 모른다. 아무튼 나는 아름다움에 관한 감이 떨어지기 때문에 확신할 순 없다. 세상일이란 너무 다가가서도, 그렇다고 너무 멀리 떨어져서도 안 되는 모양이다.

첫눈에 반해서 샀다.
굉장히 크고 화려하고 예뻤다.
선인장은 세 달 만에 죽었다.
과습 때문이었다.
아끼고 사랑한답시고 익사시킨 것이다.

너무 관심을 쏟아도 안 되고
너무 관심을 쏟지 않아도 안 된다니
나는 남은 생에 다시는 이런 걸
기르지 말아야겠다고 결심했다.

지난 주말 아침에 일어나 거실 창문을 활짝 열었다.
녹색의 윤기를 되찾은 선인장이
햇빛을 받는 순간 꿈틀거리는 걸 본 것 같았다.
그건 내가 살면서 본 광경 가운데
가장 아름다운 것이었을지 모른다.

그럼에도
불구하고

밴크로프트가 침대에 앉아 셔츠를 벗었다. 더스틴 호프만은 안절부절못한다. 뭘 어떻게 해야 할지 모르는 눈치다. 하지만 우스꽝스러워 보이지 않기 위해 더스틴 호프만은 안간힘을 다한다. 앤 밴크로프트는 거침이 없다. 촬영장이 후끈하다. 더스틴 호프만은 앤 밴크로프트의 아들뻘이라는 설정이다. 심지어 극중에서 그녀는 그의 부모님과 친구다. 정확히는 그의 아버지의 동업자의 아내다. 더스틴 호프만이 남성으로서의 멀쩡함을 과시하기 위해 오른손으로 그녀의 젖가슴을 만진다. 그런데 이게 뭐랄까, 가슴을 만졌다, 라기보다 손을 가슴 위에 널어놨다고나 할까. 이모든 걸 지켜보던 감독 마이크 니콜스는 빵 터졌다. 촬영장이 떠나가라고 웃기 시작했다. 무단 투기를 했다가 걸린 사람마냥 가슴에서 손을 뗀 더스틴 호프만이 카메라를 등지고 방구석의 벽으로 향한다. 그리고 벽에 머리를 찧기 시작한다. "로빈슨 부인, 이건 옳지 못한 짓이에요." "내가 매력이 없니?" "아니요, 로빈슨 부인, 부인은 제 부모님 친구 중에 제일 멋진 분이에요." 하지만 더스틴 호프만이 벽에 머리를 박은 건 웃음을 참기 위해서였다. 어찌됐든 마이크 니콜스는 이 상황을 마음에 들어했다.

그래서 이 어마어마한 명장면이 탄생했다.

　　가장 좋아하는 영화가 뭐냐는 빤한 질문을 받을 때마다 나는 정말 힘들고 어렵다. 고를 수가 없다. 당연하잖아. 다만 그때 상황마다, 혹은 머릿속에 떠올린 기준에 따라 가장 좋아하는 영화가 다르게 떠오르기는 한다. 좋아하는 장면이 제일 많이 등장하는 영화라면 〈대부 2〉와 〈록키〉와 〈미드나잇 카우보이〉 중에서 갈등되긴 하는데, 아무래도 역시 〈졸업〉을 꼽을 수밖에 없다. 〈졸업〉은 정말이지, 아, 거의 모든 장면이 시퀀스 단위로 전부 다 좋다.

　　〈졸업〉은 아메리칸 뉴시네마의 시작을 알린 영화다. 아, 아메리칸 뉴시네마가 뭐냐 하면 글쟁이들과 영화사가들이 〈졸업〉 이전의 할리우드와 그 이후의 할리우드를 구분짓기 위해 규정한 개념인데, 천편일률적인 할리우드 시스템 안에서 베이비부머 세대들이 반항과 자유를 영화 문법과 제작 시스템 위로 가져와 발언하기 시작하면서 이전의 영화들과는 구분되었다는 의미로 만들어진 말이다. 〈졸업〉과 함께 아메리칸 뉴시네마를 본격적으로 선언한 영화가 〈우리에게 내일은 없다〉다. 이후 〈와일드 번치〉 〈미드나잇 카우보이〉 〈솔저 블루〉 〈작은 거인〉 〈어둠의 표적〉 〈대부〉 〈맨츄리안 캔디데이트〉 〈도청〉 등 수많은 뉴시네마 걸작들이 발표되었다. 서로 너무 다른 영화들처럼 보이겠지만 공통점이 있다. 이 영화들은 언뜻 봐도 좋은 놈 나쁜 놈을 가를 수 있는 기존 대중영화의 갈등 구조를 완강히 거부했다. 더불어 기존의 질서가 젊은 세대들에게 강요하는 것들, 요컨대 너도 이렇게 살아야 나처럼 될 수 있다는 논리를 조롱했다. 어차피 니들처럼 살아서 니들처럼 될 수 있는 시대도 아니었다. 지금처럼.

물론 노파심에 말을 더하자면, 이들은 무려 아메리칸 뉴시네마라는 걸 선언해놓고도 알량한 작가주의에 함몰되어 〈황무지〉같이 덩치 큰 졸작을 마지막으로 몰락해버리고, 스필버그와 루카스에게 바통을 넘겼다. 블록버스터라는 말도 그때 생겨났다. 이를테면 6월항쟁씩이나 해놓고 도로 노태우에게 표를 준 한국의 시민정신 같은 거랄까. 결국 애들은 애들일 뿐이었다는 말로 귀결될 수도 있는 건데, 나는 왜 '애 같은 애'들이 어른스러운 기민함과 능청스러움을 같이 누릴 기회를 다 놓쳐버리고 멍청하기 짝이 없이,

아무튼 그렇다는 이야기다.

요즘 같아서야 이 영화를 보지 못한 사람들이 대다수일 테

니 〈졸업〉에 대한 이야기를 더 하자면 전말은 이렇다. 주인공이 아버지 동업자의 아내에게 유혹을 당한다. 이제 막 대학을 졸업한 전도유망한 주인공은 기성세대의 질서에 억눌리고 기가 죽고 뭐가 옳은지 잘 모르겠고 어쩌고저쩌고, 어찌됐든 너무나 심란하고 궁지에 몰린 상황이다. 왜냐하면 앞으로 어떻게 살아야 할지 잘 모르겠으니까. 물론 그는 이런 거시적인 고민에 빠질 수 있을 만큼 여유로운 중산층 집안의 자제다.

그는 로빈슨 부인의 유혹에 결국 넘어간다. 그녀와 대화다운 대화를 하고 싶지만 그런 거 없다. 의미 없는 육체관계만 늘어간다. 그러던 와중에 속사정을 모르는 부모들(물론 여기서 로빈슨 부인은 제외된다)의 요구대로 로빈슨 부인의 딸과 소개팅을 강요받는다. 그는 매우 언짢다. 그래도 귀찮기 싫어서 억지로 만난다. 그런데 유레카! 만나고 보니 너무 좋은 거다. 이건 내 여자다, 싶은 거다. 그들은 서로 사랑하게 된다. 여기서 예상하다시피 로빈슨 부인의 방해가 시작되고 결국 주인공은 여자친구에게 털어놓는다. 내가 니 엄마랑 잤다. 그는 버림받는다.

이후 주인공은 정을 뗀 여자친구의 대학교를 찾아 무작정 떠난다. 그리고 결혼하려 한다. 아니 왜 갑자기 결혼을? 싶지만 이 영화가 67년도 영화라는 걸 감안하자. 계속되는 주인공의 구애에도 여자는 아랑곳하지 않고 다른 남자를 만난다. 상심한 주인공은 짐을 싸고 떠나기로 한다. 그런데 그날 새벽 그녀가 찾아온다. 자다 깬 주인공을 앞에 두고 그녀가 애매한 말들을 쏟아내기 시작한다. 그러더니 당장은 떠나지 말라고 말한다. 자기가 결정하기 전까지. 그녀가 방을 나선 후에 아닌 밤중에 홍두깨인 주인공이 외친다. 믿을 수 없어! 보는 나도 그랬다.

이야기는 익숙한 결말로 치달아간다. 그녀는 부모가 결정한 상대와 결혼을 하러 가고, 주인공은 필사적으로 그녀를 쫓아간다. 그리고 마침내 결혼식장에 당도한다. 이제 막 언약을 나눈 부부를 향해 주인공이 창문을 두드려대며 절망과 희망을 섞어 외쳐댄다. 일레인! 일레인! 일레인! 그걸 한참 바라보던 그녀도 마침내 소리친다. 벤!

그리고 우리가 다 아는 결말. 그는 웨딩드레스 차림의 그녀를 데리고 도망친다. 그리고 버스에 올라탄다. 그런데 우리가 다 아는 결말임에도 기억하지 못하는 마지막 장면이 있다. 많은 이들이 〈졸업〉의 결말을 해프닝으로 끝난 예쁘고 파릇파릇한 이야기로 기억하는 경향이 있다. 하지만 버스에 올라탄 그들의 표정을 보라. 처음에는 자신을 바라보는 승객들의 시선을 외면하며 기쁘고 흥분된 표정을 감추지 못한다. 그런데 시간이 지날수록 조금씩, 아주 조금씩 얼굴에서 빛이 빠져나간다. 급기야 표정이 사라지고 어두운 기색이 되고야 만다.

부모의 질서를 부정하고 맞서고 눈앞에서 깨부순 그들은 처음에는 기쁘고 흥분되었을 것이다. 그런데 그런 감정들은 이후에 그들이 짊어질 세상의 무게감과는 관계가 없는 것이다. 그들은 자신들이 직면한, 당장 짊어져야 할 삶의 무게감을 실감하고 표정이 어두워진 것이다. 나는 이 장면을 아이가 어른이 되는 순간이라고 생각한다. 그리고 이 영화는 아이가 어른이 되는 순간을 정확하게 포착한, 정말 얼마 되지 않는 희귀한 영화들 가운데 하나다.

그러나 그들이 부모의 요구를 따랐어야 했다고, 어른의 질서를 따르지 않았기 때문에 그들은 불행할 거라고 말하는 것에 대해서는 전혀 동의하지 않는다. 그들은 이후 혼란스러워하고 방황했을 것이다. 어렵고 당황스럽고 혼자 힘으로 많은 것을 증명해야만 했을 것이다. 그러나 나는 그들이 불행했을 거라 생각하지 않는다. 남의 말을 따르지 않았기 때문에 남 탓을 하지 않을 수 있는 사람들은 쉽게 불행해지지 않는다. 불행할 시간이 있으면 더 많은 걸 책임지고 노력한다. 어른스러운 길이란 건 없다. 다른 누구도 아닌 자기 자신의 선택과, 이후 어른스럽게 책임지는 것만이 있을 뿐이다. 나는 그들이 행복했을 것이라, 그리고 지금 이 시간에도 행복할 거라 확신한다. 〈졸업〉은 낭만이나 후회에 관한 영화가 아니다. 생의 다음 페이지를 넘길 때 느껴지는 단 한 장의 촉감과, 그것의 어마어마한 무게감과, 그럼에도 불구하고 그럴 만하다는 것에 관한 영화다. 그럼에도 불구하고 말이다.

남의 말을 따르지 않았기 때문에
남 탓을 하지 않을 수 있는 사람들은
쉽게 불행해지지 않는다.
불행할 시간이 있으면
더 많은 걸 책임지고 노력한다.

어른스러운 길이란 건 없다.
다른 누구도 아닌 자기 자신의 선택과,
이후 어른스럽게 책임지는 것만이 있을 뿐이다.

청소

무의식적으로 걸레를 왼쪽으로 비틀어 짰다. 짜고 나서야 매번 생각이 난다. 이걸 나는 걸레점이라고 부르는데 아무튼 오른쪽으로 비틀 때와 왼쪽으로 비틀 때의 점괘가 다르다. 무슨 내용인지는 비밀이다. 바닥과 선반, 책상과 책장 순으로 닦아낸다. 그리고 청소기에 전원을 넣어 그 반대 순서로 쓸어낸다. 걸레질을 먼저 하고 청소기를 나중에 돌려야 물기에 붙어 있는 먼지를 없앨 수 있다. 걸레질을 나중에 하면 여기저기 먼지를 발라놓는 꼴이 된다. 그렇게 물기와 함께 말라버린 먼지나 머리카락은 잘 떨어지지도 않는다. 청소기 브러시를 용도에 맞게 바꾸어 끼워가며 중력 방향으로 단계를 나누어 쓸어내다보면 대충 아침 청소가 마무리된다.

피규어나 장식품들에 묻은 먼지는 일주일에 두어 번 먼지떨이로 닦아낸다. '터는' 게 아니라 '닦는' 게 중요하다. 그러기 위해서는 먼저 먼지떨이에 정전기를 만들어주어야 하는데 창문 밖으로 세게 몇 차례 털어주고 시작하면 좋다. 먼지떨이에도 종류가 많다. 털 빠짐과 정전기, 기름기의 정도 따위가 전부 다르다. 정전기와 기름기는 서로 보완해주는 성격이다. 어느 한쪽이 지나치게 높으면 제대로 쓰지 못한다. 이건 영업비밀인데 타조털이 가장 훌륭하다.

청소보다 중요한 건 정리다. 배는 구획별로 구조를 나누어 침수가 되더라도 가라앉지 않게 만드는데, 집 정리도 그런 역할을 한다고 생각한다. 정리가 된 집에 들어갈 때는 단단하게 발을 디디는 기분이 들지만, 그렇지 않은 경우에는 어딘가 기분 나쁘게 스며들어가는 기분이 든다. 정리가 직관적으로 잘되어 있으면 매일 하는 청소에 드는 시간은 십 분이면 충분하다. 정리가 되어 있는 집은 청소를 하루이틀 하지 않아도 티가 나지 않는다. 정리의 묘는 얼마나 잘 감추느냐가 아니라 얼마나 잘 버리느냐에 달려 있다. 내게 쓸모가 없는 건 남들에게 필수품이라 해도 모으지 말아야 하고 일단 모았다면 버릴 수 있어야 한다. 여기에는 큰 지혜가 필요하다.

언제부터 주변을 정리하고 깨끗하게 유지하는 일에 강박을 느끼게 되었는지 잘 기억이 나지 않는다. 아마 별다른 계기가 있었던 것 같지는 않다. 스무 살 이후로 계속 혼자 살았으니 자연스레 그렇게 된 게 아닐까 싶다. 뭔가를 깨끗하게 만들어놓고 내심 기뻤던 첫번째 기억은 설거지를 했을 때였다. 초등학생이었다. 엄마가 외출한 사이 설거지를 해놓고 싱크대를 닦았다. 행주로 물을 훔쳐내자마자 생각보다 쉽게 광이 올라와서 정말 신이났다. 엄마가 기뻐해주어서 내심 흡족했다. 그뒤로 몇 시간 동안 싱크대 앞을 서성대면서 아버지나 동생이 사용하고 나면 곧바로 다시 닦아놓고는 생색을 냈다.

처음으로 완벽하게 청소를 했다, 는 실감을 한 건 대학생 때였다. 고시원 쪽방에 살면서 청소를 게을리하는 게 가능한 일인지 지금도 잘 모르겠다. 나는 코끼리를 냉장고에 넣는 방법에 대해 알고 있다. 냉장고를 고시원에 가져가면 된다. 대체 그 책상을 어떻게 방에 넣었을까. 문을 열자마자 정면에 보이는 책상이 방의 삼분의 일을 차지하며 한쪽 면을 완전히 가리고 있다. 잘 때는 의자를 책상 위로 올려놓고 다리를 그 안에 집어넣어야 한다. 두 팔을 벌리는 건 불가능하다. 옷이나 가방은 벽에 걸어둔다. 창문도 없다.

요컨대 남아도는 공간이 없다는 이야기다. 방이 조금이라도 더러우면 그건 다 내 몸에 묻는다. 아니 정확히 말하자면 옷에 묻는다. 세탁기가 공용이라 빨래를 자주 하는 것이 곤란해서 나는 옷 대신 방을 최대한 깨끗하게 유지하는 쪽을 택했다. 매일 두 번씩 천장까지 닦았다. 이후로 이사를 여러 번 다니며 환경이 많이 바뀌었다. 크고 쾌적해졌다. 하지만 고시원에 살 때만큼 내가 사는 공간에 대해 완벽하게 알고 있었던 적은 없다. 청소란 그 공간을 완전히 이해하게 만든다.

청소란 그 공간을
완전히 이해하게 만든다.

지금도 집청소는 내가 한다. 써놓고 보니 당연한 말이다. 나는 인류가 자기 혼자 힘으로 청소할 수 없는 크기의 집을 소유하면서부터 파멸을 향한 과잉이 시작되었다고 믿는 사람이다. 부동산 취득 자격면허 같은 걸 만들어서 시험장에서 혼자 청소할 수 있는 최대 평수를 측정해 딸 수 있게 하면 좋겠다. 사람의 욕심을 다스릴 수 있는 가장 기능적인 목적의 면허가 아닌가. 이 집을 사겠습니다. 아이고 사장님 안목이 역시 남다르십니다, 그럼 면허를 보여주세요. 아니 2급 보통이군요. 사실 수 없습니다. 나가주세요.

사정이 이렇다보니 청소에 관한 질문을 자주 받는다. 언제부터 그랬어요? 왜 그렇게 됐어요? 라는 질문에 말문이 막히는 경험을 몇 차례 했다. 나는 왜 청소를 할까. 결벽증이라고 매번 대충 둘러대지만 솔직히 그건 아닌 것 같다. 손은 자주 씻는 편이지만 그건 내가 만지는 물건들, 특히 키보드에 기름기가 남을까봐 그러는 것이다. 원고를 쓸 때 키보드가 끈적거리면 멀쩡한 문장도 비문이 된다. 키보드에 묻은 기름기는 키캡을 전부 분리해 닦아야 하기 때문에 골치가 아프다. 나는 남이 쓰던 숟가락으로도 잘 먹고 내 살보다는 남의 살을 훨씬 더 좋아하며 타인의 청결함을 두고 그 사람을 판단하지도 않는다. 깨끗하게 보이는 것보다는 어울리는 옷을 입는 게 더 좋아서 같은 옷을 여러 벌 사놓고 돌려 입는다. 그게 다 결벽증 증상이라고 하면 뭐 별로 할 말은 없지만.

나는 내가 무언가를 처음 상태로 되돌려놓는 일에 지나치게 매달린다는 결론을 내렸다. 조금 더 정확하게 말하자면, 나는 언제든지 눈앞의 이것을 본래의 상태로 복구시킬 수 있다는 생각으로부터 안정감을 찾는 것 같다. 그러나 여태 살아보니 본래 상태로 온전히 복구시킬 수 있는 거라고는 컴퓨터 백업파일과 청소밖에 없다. 그래서 나는 청소에 매달린다. 청소를 하면 회복이 되었다.

돌이켜보면 결코 되돌릴 수 없는 것들을 붙잡고 되돌려지지 않는다는 사실 앞에 늘 너무 오랫동안 분개했던 것 같다. 특히 인간관계가 그랬다. 거기에는 어떤 오해나 실수가 있더라도 어찌됐든 돌이킬 수 있어야만 진짜 우정이고 진짜 사랑이라는 생각이 있었다. 그러나 진짜 사랑과 진짜 우정이란 진짜와 가짜를 나누는 서로 다른 논리들 앞에서 유명무실해진다. 사실 언제든 돌이킬 수 있다는 믿음은 최선을 다해 노력하지 않게 하고 결과적으로 사람을 좀 비겁하게 만든다. 이제 와서 생각해보니 최소한 내가 실패한 관계들은 대개 그랬던 것 같다. 결국, 우리는 모두 순순히 누군가의 과거가 될 용기가 필요하다. 돌이키고 되돌리는 것에 대한 집착은 좀 느슨하게 내버려두고 말이다. 청소는 이제 좀 지겹다.

나는 내가 무언가를
처음 상태로 되돌려놓는 일에
지나치게 매달린다는 결론을 내렸다.
여태 살아보니 본래 상태로
온전히 복구시킬 수 있는 거라고는
컴퓨터 백업파일과 청소밖에 없다.
그래서 나는 청소에 매달린다.
청소를 하면 회복이 되었다.

A long time ago in a galaxy far, far away

미리 말해두지만 나는 〈스타워즈〉 광팬이다. 정상적인 범주를 넘어서 있다. 아주 오래전 우연히 돌려본 채널에서 〈스타워즈〉를 처음 보았다. 곧바로 제국군의 이미지에 압도되었다. 조금 큰 이후에는 제국군을 향한 열망이 내 안의 파시즘 성향을 드러내는 것이 아닌지 오랜 시간 고민하기도 했다. 전세대가 레니 리펜슈탈의 〈의지의 승리〉를 보며 내심 걱정했던 것들을 나는 〈스타워즈 에피소드 5: 제국의 역습〉을 보며 느꼈다.

밥벌이에 나선 이후로 〈스타워즈〉에 관련된 모든 것들을 사들이기 시작했다. 지금은 집 전체가 그냥 〈스타워즈〉 프랜차이즈 상점에 가깝다. 옆에 사람이 없을 때는 늘 다스 베이더의 숨소리를 따라하면서 걷는다. 나는 심지어 제다이를 종교로 믿는 사람들의 해외 그룹에도 가입되어 있다. 고백하기 어렵지만, 나는, 아 나는 아직도, 집에서 혼자 광선검을 가지고 논다! 입으로 소리를 내면서! 아흐흑! 스타워즈에 관한 한 나는 정상이 아니다. 그래서 미리 경고하는 거다. 이 글에는 객관성이 결여되어 있다. 그래서 일반적인 경우보다 더욱 건조하게 쓰려고 한다. 그러거나 말거나 어찌됐든,

나는 〈스타워즈〉에 관련된 이상 결코 객관적일 수 없다.

〈스타워즈: 깨어난 포스〉는 명확한 전략 아래 굴러가는 영화다. 이 영화는 시리즈 1편이라고 할 수 있는 〈스타워즈 에피소드 4: 새로운 희망〉의 구성과 감성을 그대로 복기하고 있다.

은하계 촌구석의 주인공이 거대한 사건에 휘말리고 중요한 데이터를 가진 드로이드를 만나게 되며 악당 세력의 추적을 받는다. 한솔로와 추바카는 도로 악명 높은 밀수업자가 되어 있고 주인공들을 만나 그들을 실어나른다. 그런 와중에 주인공은 자신의 피에 흐르는 포스를 직감한다. 주인공들은 악당들이 득실대는 은하계 구석의 바에 들어가 다음 단계로 넘어갈 준비를 한다. 악의 세력은 반칙에 가까운 어마어마한 무기를 가지고 있고 그것을 무고한 행성에 발사해 파괴한다. 주인공들은 가까스로 저항군에 합류해 악당들과의 대결에 나선다. 엑스윙 편대가 나서 이 얼티메이트 웨폰을 파괴한다.

다시 말하지만 〈스타워즈: 깨어난 포스〉는 얼개만 따져보았

을 때 〈스타워즈 에피소드 4: 새로운 희망〉과 완벽하게 똑같다. 이러한 서사 전략은 이 영화의 목적을 정확히 파악할 수 있게 한다. 〈스타워즈: 깨어난 포스〉는 에피소드 6 이후에 붙어나온 에피소드 7이 아니다. 〈스타워즈: 깨어난 포스〉는 스타워즈라는 거대한 세계관을 부활시키고 관객들과 재회하게 만드는 리부트 영화다. 리부트 영화이되 영화적인 모든 요소를 동원해 리부트가 아닌 척하는 것. 그것은 J. J. 에이브럼스가 〈스타트렉〉 시리즈를 리부트하면서 사용했던 전략과 정확히 일치한다. 다시 떠올리게 되는데 J. J. 에이브럼스의 〈스타트렉〉 리부트는 정말이지 다시없이 영리한 기획이고 이야기였다. 그 흔한 평행우주 콘셉트로 '미래의 과거'와 '오래된 현재'를 한 화면 안에 어울리게 만들다니. J. J. 에이브럼스는 트레키들에게 암살되지 않기 위해 대체 얼마나 많은 밤을 뜬눈으로 지새운 걸까.

자, 가장 중요한 질문. 관객들은 〈스타워즈: 깨어난 포스〉에 만족할 수 있을까. 일단 올드팬들은 무조건 만족할 수 있을 것이다. 한국에서의 첫번째 상영에서 기이한 현상이 목격되었다. 영화가 시작된 이후 타이틀 테마가 나오거나 올드 시리즈의 대사가 복기되거나 전설의 삼총사가 차례대로 등장하거나 밀레니엄 팔콘이 등장하거나 R2-D2가 나오거나 아무튼 거의 모든 서비스 요소들에서 환호성이 터져나왔다. 이러한 환호성은 미국에서는 자연스러운 것이다. 그러나 한국에서는 아무래도 주변의 이목을 신경쓰거나 왜 유난스럽게 미국 따라하냐는 눈총이 따르기 마련이다. 그럼에도 한국에서의 첫 상영 풍경은 놀라웠다. 이건

첫 상영에 기존 골수팬들이 대거 등판했다는 혐의를 감안하더라도 생경한 광경이다. 그만큼 〈스타워즈: 깨어난 포스〉는 모든 관객을 만족시킬 만한 구색을 갖추고 있고, 최소한 '이 영화는 이렇게 즐겨도 된다'는 공동의 합의를 이끌어내고 있다는 것이다.

그렇다면 이 새로운 3부작은 새로운 팬덤을 얼마나 영입할 수 있을까. 이건 미지수다. 관객들은 이 영화에 만족하고 즐거워할 것이다. 〈스타워즈: 깨어난 포스〉는 기존 〈스타워즈〉 시리즈를 통틀어서 가장 유머러스하고 비주얼 효과는 최고 수준이며 신인 위주의 캐스팅도 기가 막히고 연기의 합도 굉장히 뛰어나다. 그러나 새로운 관객들이 올드 시리즈의 관객들처럼 팬덤화될 것이냐를 따지고 보면, 나는 회의적이다. 일단 이 영화는 뛰어난 리부트이자 연작의 새로운 장이기는 하지만, 어쩌됐든 전작들의 위상과 잔상에 지나치게 기대고 있는 것 또한 사실이다. 밀레니엄 팔콘은 등장 자체만으로 오줌을 지리게 만들지만 처음 보는 사람들에게는 그냥 오래된 동그란 우주선일 뿐이다. 기존 시리즈를 영 모르는 사람들은 많은 대목에서 어리둥절할 수 있다. 올드 시리즈에 익숙한 사람들은 카일로 렌이 아버지를 살해하는 장면을 이해할 수 있지만, 새로운 관객들은 뜬금없이 괴상한 진행으로 인식할 여지가 큰 것이다.

가장 즐거웠던 부분은 퍼스트 오더가 가진 궁극의 무기, 스타킬러다. 스타킬러는 애초 루크 스카이워커가 루크 스카이워커라는 이름으로 결정되기 이전의 성이다. 루크 스카이워커는 루크 스타킬러였고 아나킨 스카이워커는 아나킨 스타킬러였다. 스타킬러는 올드 시리즈의 데스스타를 당연히 연상시킨다. 제국군은 데스스타를 두 번이나 건조했다. 그리고 두 번 모두 저항군에 의해 파괴당했다. 저 정도 규모의 공사를 두 번이나 했으니 제국군은 저항군에 박살나지 않았더라도 훗날 재정 파탄으로 몰락했을 것이다. 제국군의 유지를 물려받은 퍼스트 오더는 데스스타의 친환경 버전인 스타킬러를 건조했다. 통째로 만들기보다는 기존의 실패를 답습하지 않기 위해 행성을 개조했다. 대체 왜 악당들은 늘 대규모 공사 사업을 좋아하는 걸까. 데스스타랄지 스타킬러랄지 거 무슨 강이랄지.

SF라면서 왜 이리 물리 규칙을 거스르냐고 투덜거리지는 말자. 이건 하드 SF가 아니다. 스페이스 오페라다. 그것도 스페이스 오페라라는 SF 하위 장르를 설명할 때 대표격으로 소개되는 시리즈다.

가장 불만스러운 부분은 따로 있다. 주인공 레이의 능력치다. 나는 레이가 무척 마음에 든다. 영국식 발음도 좋고 얼굴도 너무 좋고 얼굴이 너무 좋다. 그런데 제아무리 뛰어난 포스를 가지고 있다 한들 아무런 제다이 수련 없이 포스를 사용하게 되고 심지어 광선검 결투로 카일로 렌을 이기는 대목은 용납하기 힘들다. 설정에 따르면 광선검은 굉장히 무거운 무기다. 〈스타워즈 에피소드 4: 새로운 희망〉에서 역사상 가장 긴장감 없는 결투로 손꼽을 수 있는 다스 베이더와 오비완 케노비의 대결을 떠올려보자. 하물며 충분한 수련과 지도 없이 자유로운 광선검 결투는 불가능하다. 그런데 여기서는 광선검을 처음 만져보는 핀이 그걸 막 휘두르고 심지어 카일로 렌에게 상처까지 입힌다. 이건 구 세계관을 감안할 때 설정 파괴에 가까운 진행이다.

　　개인적인 불만을 꼽자면 극중 루크 스카이워커의 광선검으로 등장하는 게 에피소드 4와 5에서 등장했던 버전 1이라는 점이다. 이건 애초 오비완 케노비가 직접 아나킨 스카이워커를 제압한 이후 죽어가는 그를 두고 수거해간 광선검이다. 그걸 오비완이 루크에게 주었는데, 에피소드 5에서 다스 베이더에게 손이 잘리면서 함께 잃어버렸다. 에피소드 6에서는 오비완 케노비의 광선검을 개조해서 루크가 직접 제작한 버전 2가 등장한다. 루크의 광선검이라면 버전 2가 등장해야 옳다. 영화를 보면 스스로를 베이더의 후예라고 여기는 카일로 렌이 '그건 내 것'이라며 탐을 내는데, 정확히 말해 베이더의 광선검은 다스 베이더로 거듭난 이후 전용으로 새로 제작된 것이다. 비슷하게 생겼지만 손잡이 윗부분이 다르다. 그러므로 〈스타워즈: 깨어난 포스〉에 등장하는 광선검을 베이더의 후예를 자처한다는 이유로 카일로 렌이 탐을 낼 이유가 없다(잠깐, 이거 아빠 떡밥인가?). 루크가 직접 제작했다는 점이나 미적으로 더 아름답다는 점에서 왜 루크의 광선검이 버전 2로 채택되지 않았던 것인지 안타깝다(내가 제작사를 가리지 않고 모으고 있는 광선검 레플리카가 버전 1이 아닌 버전 2이기 때문만은 아니다……)

　　〈스타워즈〉에는 자자 빙크스라는 슬픈 전설이 전해져내려온다. 〈스타워즈 에피소드 1: 보이지 않는 위험〉에 등장해 모든 팬덤을 충격과 공포에 몰아넣었던 최악의 캐릭터. 사람들은 〈스

타워즈: 깨어난 포스〉가 공개되기 훨씬 전부터 혹시 자자 빙크스가 살아 있는 게 아닌가 걱정에 휩싸였다. 자자 빙크스는 다행스럽게도 등장하지 않는다. 그런데 묘하게 자자 빙크스를 닮은 캐릭터가 등장하고, 심지어 이 영화에서 가장 관객들을 짜증나게 만드는 위력을 발휘한다. 나는 〈프란시스 하〉와 〈인사이드 르윈〉도 보았지만 애덤 드라이버가 이렇게까지 자자 빙크스를 닮았는지 처음 알았다. 카일로 렌은 왜 가면을 벗었는가! 자자 빙크스의 저주는 계속되고 있다.

　기계를 다루는 비정상적인 솜씨와 대놓고 깔아놓은 복선들로 미루어볼 때, 레이가 루크 스카이워커의 딸일 가능성은 '일단은' 당연해 보인다(그러나 이 시리즈가 가족관계 가지고 장난치기로 1세대 격인 막장의 뿌리라는 걸 잊지는 말자, 카일로 렌의 생부가 한솔로가 아닌 루크일 수도 있다는 심증도 간다). 만약 레이가 루크의 딸이라면 그 엄마는 누구일까. 혹시 포스의 궁극에 이른 루크 스카이워커가 파트너 없이 혼자 요도로 낳은 게 아닐까. 〈스타워즈: 깨어난 포스〉를 빌미로 내 덕질은 새로운 장을 맞았다. 앞으로 두 편의 정규 시리즈와 스핀오프들이 더 나오는 기간 동안 내 인생은 행복과 기대로 가득할 것이다. 아 너무 기쁘다. 너무너무 좋다.

구애

내가 가장 좋아하는 〈환상특급〉 에피소드 중에 이런 게 있다. 소년이 부모와 함께 놀이공원에 간다. 부모는 사이가 나쁘다. 부모가 또 다투는 동안 소년은 혼자 동굴 사파리에 들어간다. 어두컴컴한 길을 따라 유리벽으로 막힌 방들이 있다. 방안에는 부부가 한 쌍씩 들어가 있다. 소년이 지나가는 동안 그들은 소년에게 우리가 얼마나 좋은 부모가 될 수 있는지에 관해 구애하고 설득한다. 사랑받고 싶어 안달이 나서 큰 소리로 외친다. 마지막 방에 이르러 소년은 어느 소박해 보이는 부부를 발견한다. 이 부부는 소년에게 뭘 사줄 수 있는지 말하는 대신 사랑해주겠다고 말한다. 다음 장면에서 소년은 마지막 방에 갇혀 있던 부부의 손을 잡고 사파리를 떠난다. 처음으로 환하게 웃는 모습이다. 소년의 부모는 예의 그 방에 갇혀 있다. 그들은 떠나가는 소년의 뒷모습을 향해 애타게 절규한다.

한 편의 영화가 관객과 만나는 순간도 이와 같다. 대개의 영화들은 관객의 사랑을 얻길 갈구한다. 겉으로 짓고 있는 표정이 엄숙한지, 가벼운지, 시끄러운지, 우스운지, 근사한 몸짓으로 유혹을 하는지, 네가 나를 사랑해주든 말든 상관없다는 식인지와 전혀 무관하게 말이다. 모든 영화들은 관객이 자신을 선택해주길 바라고 또한 이해받기를 원한다.

유일한 차이는 영화가 관객에게 구애하는 태도로부터 발견된다. 많은 영화들이 우리가 얼마나 같은지, 얼마나 똑같은 코드를 가지고 있는지에 대해 큰 소리로 외치며 손짓을 한다. 그 결과 다수의 관객이 여태 수백 번 되풀이해서 봤던 똑같은 이야기를 선택하고, 극장을 나서면서 지루하다고 느끼거나 시간을 잘 때웠다고 안도한다.

반면 어떤 영화들은 우리가 얼마나 다른지에 대해 이야기한다. 나는 이렇게 다른 생각과 풍경들로 가득하다고 말이다. 소수의 관객이 이런 영화를 선택한다. 그리고 극장을 나서며 내 스타일이 아니라고 투덜거리거나 묘한 두근거림을 간직한 채 며칠 동안 가슴을 쓸어내리며 영화를 떠올린다.

사람이 사람과 만나는 순간도 결국 이와 같다고, 나는 생각한다. 닮은 점에 안도하는 사람들이 있고 다른 점에 흥분하는 사람들이 있다. 나는 대개 후자였던 것 같다. 우리는 서로 다르기 때문에 사랑했고, 너무 달라서 헤어졌다. '너무 달라서 정말 좋아!'가 '너무 다르니까 여기까지'로 돌변하기까지 우리들은 세상에서 가장 즐겁고 행복했다. 물론 그래서 모든 게 끝난 이후에는 더 많이 아프고 더 오랫동안 슬프다. 하지만 그렇다고 해서 그 두근거림을 포기할 수는 없는 노릇이다.

아니다. 잠깐. 포기할 수 없나?

　우디 앨런의 영화들은 '사랑이란 완전히 미친 짓이지만 그게 미친 짓이라는 걸 안다고 해서 사랑을 안 할 수도 없잖아?'라는 이야기를 여러 가지 뉘앙스로 변주해서 펼쳐놓은 동어반복이다. 그럼에도 불구하고 우디 앨런의 영화는 늘 새롭다. 우리가 이별을 겪을 때마다 했던 맹세를 매번 까먹어버렸기 때문이다. 다시는 사랑 안 한다는 맹세 말이다. 아! 담대해지고 싶다! 사랑 안 해. 사랑 안 한다고.

우리는 서로 다르기 때문에 사랑했고,
너무 달라서 헤어졌다.
'너무 달라서 정말 좋아!'가
'너무 다르니까 여기까지'로 돌변하기까지
우리들은 세상에서 가장 즐겁고 행복했다.
물론 그래서 모든 게 끝난 이후에는
더 많이 아프고 더 오랫동안 슬프다.

모두가 언젠가는
배운다

영화 〈이터널 선샤인〉에는 잠언집이 등장한다. 오랜 시간 동안 〈이터널 선샤인〉은 헤어진 연인을 그리워하는 모든 이들에게 바로 그 잠언집 같은 위력을 발휘해왔다. 수많은 이들이 '사랑하는 사람은 다시 만날 수밖에 없다'는 이야기에 위로받고 희망을 품었다.

이 영화를 보고 나서 연인과 다시 시작한 커플은 몇이나 될까. 아마도 그 선택을 저주하며 다시 헤어지기를 반복한 연인들의 수와 얼추 비슷할 것이다. 영화의 마지막, "지금은 당신의 모든 게 마음에 들어요" "지금은 그렇겠죠. 그런데 곧 거슬려할 테고 나는 당신을 지루해할 거예요" "괜찮아요" "괜찮아요"로 이어지는 마술같이 낭만적인 화해의 끝에서 나는 늘 당혹스러웠다. 괜찮아? 정말 괜찮은 걸까? 저렇게 쉽게? 하지만 생각해보면 당연한 노릇이다. 그들은 기억을 지웠으니까. 결론은 알고 있지만 그 결론에 이르렀던 모든 괴로움을 잊었으니까. 그래서 실감할 수 없으니까. 그러니까, 당장은 괜찮을 수 있다.

이 영화를 보고 괜찮지 않은 선택을 한 수많은 이들과는 달리 말이다.

이 빌어먹을 기억을 송두리째 지워버릴 수 있다면, 그래서 일상의 지루함을 되찾을 수만 있다면 고자가 되어도 상관없다는 사람들에게 〈이터널 선샤인〉은 달콤한 가정을 제시한다. 지울 수만 있다면. 심지어 이 영화처럼 그(녀)와 다시 시작할 수 있다면.

그런 달콤한 꿈을 꾸는 사람에게 내가 발견한 비밀 하나를 들려주겠다.

나는 항상 궁금했다. 이 영화가 그리는 시제에는 어떤 의미가 있는 걸까. 〈이터널 선샤인〉은 2004년에 나온 영화다. 그러나 이 영화에는 이 영화를 보고 있는 관객들의 호주머니 속에 들어 있는 그 흔한 휴대폰 하나 등장하지 않는다. 그뿐만 아니라 모든 게 90년대 초중반의 풍경이다. 도로 위의 차들, 기억을 지우는 장비들, 컴퓨터, 편지, 전화, 응답기. 모든 게 옛날 것들이다. 처음에는 그냥 복고풍이겠거니 생각했다. 그러나 반복해서 볼수록 확실해졌다. 〈이터널 선샤인〉이 그리는 풍경은 이 이야기를 들려주고 있는 사람의 기준에서 훨씬 이전의 것들이다. 최소한 10년 전 옛날 이야기라는 것이다. 그렇다면 궁금해질 수밖에 없다. 저 이야기가 회상되고 있는 시점, 그러니까 2004년의 조엘과 클레멘타인은 어떤 모습일까.

찰리 코프먼의 본래 각본에는 영화의 가장 처음과 마지막 시퀀스에서 좀더 나이든 조엘과 클레멘타인, 그러니까 영화가 만들어진 시점, 화자의 시점에서 그들이 등장한다. 클레멘타인은 방금 기억을 지웠으며 과거에도 이미 여러 번 기억을 지운 이력이 있다. 모두 조엘에 관련해서 말이다.

본래 원안대로였다면 이 영화에 대한 감상은 많이 달라졌을 것이다. 낭만은 덜어지고 판단은 선명해졌을 것이다. 우리는 언제나 다시 반복하고 싶어한다. 다를 수 있을 것이라 생각한다. 그것만 없었다면 우리는 우리로서 건재했을 것이라 상상한다. 그러나 이별은 그런 식으로 이루어지지 않는다. 방아쇠가 있었던 게 아니다. 그냥 그렇게 헤어진 것이다. 우리가 인생을 통틀어 확실하게 배우는 것 하나는, 언제나 실수는 반복되고 누구나 무언가를 잃게 된다는 사실이다. 어느 누구 하나 이 반복으로부터 도망칠 수 없다. 모든 것은 점멸하며 사그라든다. 후기 로마가 공화정 시대 로마처럼 눈부셨던가. 한심한 것들은 반복되고 좋은 것들은 기억에만 남는다. 조엘과 클레멘타인은 기억을 지 웠기 때문에 다시 시작할 수 있었다. 그리고 한심한 것들을 반복 했다. 그리고 다시 지웠다. 그리고 다시 반복했다. 그리고 다시 지웠다. 그리고 다시 반복했다…… 하느님 맙소사, 이런 글을 쓰 고 있는 내가 끔찍하다. 대체 왜 논리적으로 설명 가능한 것들은 하나같이 끔찍한 것들뿐인가.

그래서, 만약 내게 저런 기회가 주어진다면 어떻게 할까. 나 는 두 번 돌아보지 않고 기억을 지울 것이다. 그 모든 게 영원히 반복되리라는 걸 이미 모두 알고 있다 해도 말이다. 상관없다. 정말 사랑하는 사람들은 다시 만날 수 있다. 만약 그들이 기억을 모두 지운다면 말이다. 생각이 이즈음에 이르고 나니 〈이터널 선 샤인〉에 포함되지 않은 원안의 장면들이 크게 상관없어진다. 이 상상력이 허락된다면 우리는 모두 기억을 지우고 그 짧은 사랑 을 음주와 주정처럼 반복하는 걸 선택할 것이다. 우리는 특별하 지 않다. 우리는 한심하다.

영화의 시작과 끝에 벡Beck의 〈Everybody's Got to Learn Sometime〉이 흘러나온다. 그렇다. 모두가 언젠가는 배운다. 되 돌릴 수 없다는 것을.

방아쇠가 있었던 게 아니다.
그냥 그렇게 헤어진 것이다.
우리가 인생을 통틀어 확실하게 배우는 것 하나는,
언제나 실수는 반복되고
누구나 무언가를 잃게 된다는 사실이다.
우리는 특별하지 않다.
우리는 한심하다.
그렇다.

모두가 언젠가는 배운다.
되돌릴 수 없다는 것을.

친구를
보내는 방법

그는 수줍은 사람이었다. 그는 자신이 출연한 영화를 보지 않았
다. 불편했기 때문이다. 길을 다니다 그를 알아본 사람들이 이름
을 불러댈 때에도 마찬가지였다. 머리카락이 곤두섰다. 창피했
다. 어색한 미소가 흘러나올 뿐이었다. 그러나 어디선가, 누군가
그를 이렇게 부르면 이야기가 달라졌다.

"브라이언이다!"

묘한 일이었다. 그 이름이 들려오면 모든 게 달라졌다. 그
것은 그에게 많은 걸 환기시키는 이름이었다. 그는 그렇게 불리
는 걸 좋아했다. 멋지다고 생각했다. 그는 자신이 브라이언을 연
기한다는 사실을 자랑스러워했다. 이 역할로 최악의 배우에 노
미네이트되었던 기억 따위는 중요하지 않았다. 그는 브라이언

오코너를 사랑했다. 어쩌면 돔보다 더 말이다. 당장 닷지 차저
와 나란히 질주하는 닛산 GT-R의 배기음이 들려올 것만 같다.
2013년 11월 30일 토요일, 재능 있는 배우이자 훌륭한 레이서였
던 폴 워커가 차 위에서 세상을 떠났다.

누군가에게 〈분노의 질주〉는 그저 얄팍하고 시끄러운 할리
우드 프랜차이즈에 불과할지 모른다. 그러나 또한 누군가에게,
〈분노의 질주〉는 〈이니셜 D〉와 함께 늘 호명될 만큼 들끓는 낭만
과 청춘의 이야기다.

무려 일곱 번의 시리즈를 거치는 동안 주인공들은 많은 우
여곡절을 만났다. 동네 깡패 도미닉은 차나 훔치고 돌아다니다
어느새 거물급 국제 도망자가 되었다. 여자친구가 죽은 줄 알고
복수까지 끝냈는데 알고 보니 여자친구가 살아 있고 그전에 복
수한 사람에게 사과를 했는지 안 했는지 알 수 없지만 아무튼 중
간에 잠시 만난 새 애인을 걷어차고 구 애인을 되찾는 여정 끝에
이제 겨우 사면을 받아 고향에 돌아왔다. 동네 경찰 브라이언은
도미닉 패거리에 잠입했다가 마성의 도미닉에게 영혼을 사로잡
혀 인생이 영영 꼬였다. 도미닉을 도망치게 내버려둔 일로 경찰
에서 잘린 뒤 차덕후가 되어 보배드림에 상주하며 마이애미 스
트리트 레이싱계를 들쑤시고 인생을 낭비하다 겨우 복권되어
FBI에서 일했고, 그러거나 말거나 다시 한번 도미닉을 탈출시켜
역시나 국제 도망자가 되었다가 사면되었다. 도미닉을 탈출시키
는 건 브라이언의 성격이 되었다!

〈분노의 질주〉 시리즈는 크게 두 덩어리로 나눌 수 있다. 롭 코언의 1편과 존 싱글턴의 2편이 본래 이 시리즈의 정수를 담은 스트리트 레이싱 영화라면, 저스틴 린 3부작(〈더 오리지널〉〈언리미티드〉〈더 맥시멈〉)은 〈분노의 질주〉 출연진이 등장하는 '007'이나 '미션 임파서블'류의 액션물이라 할 만하다(〈패스트&퓨리어스: 도쿄 드리프트〉는 번외다). 사이즈가 훨씬 크고 화려하며 파괴적인 물량 공세를 자랑한다. 개인적으로는 존 싱글턴의 2편을 가장 좋아한다. 이후 저스틴 린의 3부작이 흡사 사운드 모듈을 장착해 언뜻 화려하지만 결국 인공적인 배기음에 가깝다면 2편의 액션이야말로 머플러팁이 까맣게 타들어가는, 중통을 떼어내고 아스팔트를 쪼갤 듯이 으르렁거리는 진짜배기 8기통 배기음이라는 생각이다.

일곱번째 시리즈인 〈분노의 질주: 더 세븐〉은 저스틴 린이 아닌 제임스 완이 연출했다. 〈쏘우〉의 신화적인 성공과 더불어 〈컨저링〉〈인시디어스〉의 홈런으로 모두가 주목하는 감독이다. 그러나 그런 그도 이 시리즈 안에서 뭔가 새로운 걸 할 수 있는 여지는 없었던 모양이다. 어찌됐든 〈분노의 질주: 더 세븐〉은 이야기 흐름상 저스틴 린 3부작의 관성 안에 있는 영화이기 때문이다. 화려하기 짝이 없는 액션이 이어진다. 그러나 이 시리즈와 제임스 완이라는 조합에서 상상해볼 수 있는 새로운 연출의 묘는 찾아보기 어렵다. 그리고 보면 저스틴 린이 이러니저러니 해도 정말 잘했던 거구나 싶기도 하고.

이야기는 전편의 악당이 식물인간이 되어 누워 있는 병실에서 시작된다. 그 악당의 형이 동생에게 복수를 약속하는 장면이다. 〈다이하드 3〉의 사이먼 그루버가 한스 그루버(1편의 악당)의 형이라는 설정이 떠오르는 대목이다. 그러나 사이먼 그루버는 제러미 아이언스다. 멋있지만 위협적이지 않다. 〈분노의 질주: 더 세븐〉에서 동생의 복수를 감행하는 건 제이슨 스태덤이라는 이름의 재앙이다. 오프닝 시퀀스의 마지막컷이 끝날 때까지 우리는 제이슨 스태덤이 동생이 입원한 병원에 저지르는 짓을 지켜볼 수 있다. 동생이 입원해 있는데! 저걸 다 부수면! 그리고 애스턴 마틴에 올라타 유유히 병원을 떠나는 제이슨 스태덤. 그렇다. 재수가 없으려면 이렇게도 없을 수 있는 것이다. 〈분노의 질주: 더 세븐〉은 시작하자마자 방어운전의 중요성을 관객에게 각인시킨다. 언제나 방어운전이 필수다. 블랙박스가 있어도 마찬가지다. 누가 끼어들었다고 구태여 그 차를 따라가 똥침하고 들이대고 상향등 올리고 빵빵대고 그러다 옆에 가서 창문을 열었다고 생각해보자. 그런데 저쪽 창문이 열리니 제이슨 스태덤이야. 아니면 그 사람 형이 제이슨 스태덤이야. 그렇다. 그런 일이 있을 수 있는 것이다. 무슨 일이 벌어질지 대체 누가 알 수 있단 말인가.

아무튼 이야기의 골격은 제이슨 스태덤의 복수다. 그런데 이 기본 골격이 후반으로 갈수록 좀 지저분해진다. 비밀요원이 끼어들고 해킹 디바이스를 찾아야 하고 다소 무의미하게 여러 나라를 돌아다니며 미션을 수행해야 한다. 무려 커트 러셀이 연기하는 비밀요원은 주인공들이 이 미션을 수행해야만 제이슨 스태덤을 찾을 수 있게 해준다고 한다. 그러거나 말거나 제이슨 스태덤은 주인공들이 이 모든 소동을 겪는 내내 수시로 나타나 사건에 개입한다. 요컨대 〈분노의 질주: 더 세븐〉의 이야기에는 '왜'가 빠져 있다. 맥락은 도려내지고 영화의 모든 구성요소는 오로지 강력한 '그림'을 보여주기 위한 수단으로 전락한다.

〈분노의 질주: 더 세븐〉은 수년 동안 무려 일곱 번에 걸쳐서 엄청난 튜닝에 튜닝을 거듭한 후륜구동차 같아 보인다. 처음에는 좋았다. 그런데 갈수록 차의 밸런스가 흐트러졌다. 매핑을 올리고 다운파이프를 바꾸는 동안 가장 중요한 안정화에는 신경을 쓰지 않았다. 게다가 후륜 특유의 오버스티어를 잡지 못했다. 일곱번째 튜닝에 이르러 마력과 토크는 엄청나게 늘어났다. 그러나 레이스를 펼치는 도중 결국 미션이 버티지 못하고 털려버렸다. 이 시리즈의 기획자들은 다음 여덟번째 속편을 만들기 전에 〈분노의 질주〉라는 텍스트가 가진 본연의 정수를 돌아보아야 할 필요가 있어 보인다. 다이노그래프 위에서만 의미가 있는 마력과 토크는 숫자일 뿐이다. 길 위로 돌아가야 한다. 튜닝의 끝은 언제나 순정이다.

어찌됐든 나는 이 영화를 보기 위해 아이맥스 상영관을 다시 찾을 계획이다. 엔딩 때문이다. 영화의 마지막에 이르러 폴 워커는 자신의 애마에 올라타 친구와 함께 도로를 달린다. 갑자기 두 갈래 길이 등장한다. 폴 워커와 그의 차는 친구와 헤어져 홀로 달려나가기 시작한다. 하늘에서 그들의 질주를 내려다보는 카메라의 시선은 폴 워커가 홀로 떠나가는 마지막 모습을 우아하고 아름답게 담아낸다. 이 영화의 엔딩은 붙여넣기한 듯 갑작스럽지만, 근래 들어 본 이별의 방식 가운데 가장 시적이다. 스크린이라는 공간을 매개로 고인이 된 배우와 관객이 만나고 헤어지는 그 모든 과정이 흡사 위령제와 같이 느껴졌다. 사고현장을 찾은 빈 디젤이 애도를 위해 몰려든 인파를 향해 말했다. "내 형제가 지금 여기 모인 여러분을 볼 수 있다면." 브라이언 오코너였던 남자. 그가 보고 싶다.

<분노의 질주: 더 세븐Fast&Furious 7> [2015]

길 위로 돌아가야 한다.
튜닝의 끝은 언제나 순정이다.

단추가 모두
채워져 있었다

이해할 수 없는 일들이 종종 벌어지곤 한다.

첫번째 이야기. 나흘 전 늦은 저녁이었다. 술약속이 있었다. 누구에게나 부담없이 입을 만한 외출복이 하나씩 있기 마련이다. 너무 무례한 것도, 그렇다고 지나치게 격식을 차린 것도 아닌 그런 옷 말이다. 내게도 그런 데님셔츠가 하나 있다. 좋은 기억도 나쁜 기억도 옷 위로 고스란히 쌓이다보니 어느 사이엔가 겨드랑이가 찢어져버렸지만 그거 입고 방송도 곧잘 한다. 며칠 전 마지막으로 입고는 벗어서 걸어두었던 셔츠를 집어들었다. 나는 순간 멈칫했다.

셔츠의 단추가 모두 채워져 있었다.

나는 한동안 그 자리에 서 있었다. 이 광경을 어떻게 해석해야 하는지 고민했다. 얼마 전 방송 스태프들이 이 방에 머문 적이 있는데 그때 누가 손댄 걸까. 아니다, 그 이후로 많이 입었다. 누가 들어와 만진 걸까. 아니다, 혼자 사는 집이고 이 집의 비밀번호를 아는 사람은 없다. 혹시 내가 잠근 걸까. 아니다, 어떤 사람들은 아침마다 새 옷 입는 기분을 내려고 세탁한 셔츠의 단추를 채워 보관하는 일도 있던데 무의미한 의식이나 절차를 좋아하지 않는 나는 단 한 번도 그런 적이 없다. 심지어 이 셔츠를 벗던 순간조차 생생하게 떠오른다. 이 데님셔츠의 단추는 똑딱이라서 벗을 때 들리는 소리나 손맛이 좋단 말이다. 주르륵 뜯어서 옷걸이에 걸어두었던 기억이 또렷하다.

두번째 이야기. 일 년 넘게 진행되어온 송사 하나가 마무리되었다. 인터넷 커뮤니티와 극우 사이트에 나에 대한 황당한 글을 지속적으로 올려온 사내가 있었다. 흔한 일이니 그냥 넘기려 했다. 그러나 글의 내용이 지나쳤고 내가 저질렀다고 주장하는 죄질도 사회에서 격리되어야 할 만한 악성이었으며 무엇보다 글을 꾸준히 올리는 게 문제였다. 한번은 경찰서에서 사내를 만난 적이 있다. 변호사는 대질할 필요가 없다고 했다. 하지만 나는 내 눈으로 꼭 한 번 사내를 보고 싶었다. 사무실에서 사내를 기다리면서 나는 사과를 받고 싶다, 사과를 받고 소송을 철회하자는 생각을 했다. 문이 열리고 사내가 들어왔다.

사내는 눈이 엄청나게 컸다.

키가 나만하고 시커멓게 탄 얼굴에 너무 큰 눈으로 두리번 거렸다. 나는 이런 일을 벌이는 사람은 의외로 평범하게 생겼을 것이고, 그런 평범한 의외성이야말로 삶의 원리라고 생각해왔다. 그런데 이 사내는 이토 준지 만화에서 튀어나온 사람 같았다. 아저씨가 나를 어디서 언제 봤다는 거냐, 이유가 뭐냐, 사과하고 싶은 마음은 들지 않느냐, 말을 다 하고 사내의 입이 열리기를 기다렸다. 남자는 그 큰 두 눈을 거의 깜박이지도 않았다. 마침내 입이 열렸다. 우리 봤잖아요.

그걸로 끝이었다. 나는 믿을 수 없다는 심정이 되어 사무실을 나섰다. 동시에 이상한 기분이 들었다. 남자의 태도가 너무 확고했기 때문이다. 혹시 내가 범죄를 저지르고 기억에서 지워버린 게 아닐까. 일어나지 않은 일에 대한 죄책감인지 공포인지 도무지 알 수 없는 감정이 밀려들었다. 사흘 전 사내가 10개월의 실형에 처해졌다는 통보를 받고 나는 참 복잡한 심경에 사로잡혔다. 사내는 왜 내게 사과하지 않았을까. 이 사내는 형을 살기보다는 병원에 보내져야 하는 게 아닌가. 10개월 후 세상 밖으로 나오면 나를 찾아오지 않을까.

세번째 이야기. 이틀 전 우연히 재벌 4세들과 술을 마시게 되었는데 심사가 뒤틀렸다. 꼴을 봐선 완연한 힙스터에 속물인데 되레 그들을 비웃으면서 자기들은 지상 위의 모든 고급, 하위 문화를 섭렵한 탈-재벌 4세들이며 무슨 대안 문화의 슈퍼전문가인 양 구는 게 취한 마음에 아니꼬웠다. 비아냥거리고 나와 집에 가면서 SNS에 자식이 스무 살을 넘기면 부모가 땡전 한푼 주지 못하게 법으로 막아야 한다는 요지의 글을 올렸다. 아침에 일어나서 지웠다. 술을 마시면 심사가 좀더 쉽게 뒤틀리고 치사해진다. 각자의 사정이 있는 건데. 그런데 새로 도착한 쪽지들 가운데 이상한 게 눈에 들어왔다.

니가 내 이야기를 하고 있다는 걸 다 알고 있다.

비겁하게 자신을 지목하지 않고 그런 글을 올려도 자신은 다 알고 있다. 우리 가족은 나를 비난할 수 있어도 너는 나를 비난할 수 없다. 비겁하게 숨어서 글이나 쓰지 말고 당당하게 만나서 붙자, 하는 요지의 이야기가 이어졌다. 뭔 소리인지 계정을 들여다봐도 깡통 계정이라 누군지 알 수 없었다. 내가 자신에게 방송이나 글로 특별한 신호를 보내고 있다고 주장하는 사람들을 보았으나 이렇게 증오에 찬 경우는 처음이었다. 어떤 경위로 이 사람이 그런 생각을 하게 된 건지 이해할 수 없었다.

　이해할 수 없는 일들이 종종 벌어지곤 한다. 대개의 이해할 수 없는 일은 체계를 모르기 때문에 벌어진다. 이를테면 방금 이

원고를 쓰면서 피우고 있던 전자담배의 배터리가 모두 닳았다. 무심코 일어났다가 충전기 앞에 가서야 불과 십 분 전에 이미 충전했다는 걸 생각해냈다. 이해할 수 없는 일이지만 사실 미스터리한 게 아니다. 접촉부위가 헐거우면 가끔 그런 일이 벌어진다. 배터리를 뺐다가 다시 끼웠고 전자담배는 다시 잘 작동했다. 이런 일은 체계를 알고 나면 더이상 이해할 수 없는 이야기가 아니다. 다만 셔츠의 단추가 채워져 있거나 엄청나게 눈이 큰 사내가 끝까지 사과하지 않았다거나 생전 처음 보는 사람이 네가 내 이야기를 하는 걸 알고 있다며 일대일 대결을 신청해오는 일 따위에는 체계도 없고 경위도 알 수 없다.

나는 조금은 진지하게 평행우주나 지구공동설에 대해 생각하게 되었다. 평행우주나 지구공동에 나와 똑같은 사람이 살고 있으며, 그들은 세간에 도플갱어라는 이름으로 알려져 있는데, 그 사람은 때로 우리집에 찾아와 셔츠의 단추를 잠그고 일상적으로 범죄를 저지르며 애꿎은 누군가를 SNS에서 괴롭히고 있다는 것이다. 이 세 가지 사건이 하루 차이로 연달아 벌어진 게 우연인지 징조인지 그저 내가 예민하게 받아들인 것인지 아직은 알 수 없다. 내가 아는 거라고는 요즘 아침에 일어나자마자 옷장 앞으로 걸어가 실눈을 뜨고 셔츠에 단추가 채워져 있는지 슬쩍 확인해본다는 것뿐이다. 그리고 혼자 웃는다. 이해할 수 없는 일을 이해할 수 없는 상태 그대로 내버려둘 수 있는 태도야말로 삶을 살아나가는 데 가장 중요한 재능 가운데 하나일지 모르겠다.

이해할 수 없는 일들이 종종 벌어지곤 한다.
내가 아는 거라고는 요즘 아침에 일어나자마자
옷장 앞으로 걸어가 실눈을 뜨고
셔츠에 단추가 채워져 있는지
슬쩍 확인해본다는 것뿐이다.
그리고 혼자 웃는다.
이해할 수 없는 일을 이해할 수 없는 상태 그대로
내버려둘 수 있는 태도야말로
삶을 살아나가는 데
가장 중요한 재능 가운데
하나일지 모르겠다.

내가 더 옳다는 사람들이
싸울 때

〈배트맨 대 슈퍼맨: 저스티스의 시작〉 보셨는가? 먼저 밝혀두지만, 나는 슈퍼맨이 엄마의 이름을 언급한 순간 배트맨이 주춤하고 결국 싸움을 관둔 것에 대해 별 불만이 없다. 이건 사실 꽤 말이 되는 설정이다. 배트맨이 슈퍼맨을 증오하는 표면상의 이유는 그가 인간이 아니기 때문이다. 인간이 아닌데 인간의 일에 끼어들고 신과 같은 권능으로 간단히 해결해버리기 때문이다. 그리고 그런 '신과 같은 권능'은 쉽게 타락할 수 있다고 생각하기 때문이다.

크립토나이트에 노출되어 배트맨 앞에 뒹굴며 최후를 맞이하는 순간 슈퍼맨은 마사를 외친다. 그리고 어디서든 끼어들기 좋아하는 로이스 레인이 뛰어와 그게 클라크의 엄마 이름임을 증언한다. 이때 배트맨은 생각했을 것이다. 아 너도 사람이구나. 그런 초능력을 가지고 있으면서도 엄마를 살리고 싶어서 렉스 루터 같은 놈의 협박에 따라 싸움을 하는, 아 너는 사람이구나. 즉, 배트맨이 슈퍼맨과의 결투를 포기한 건 '우리 둘은 엄마 이름이 같네?' 때문이 아니라, 슈퍼맨도 결국은 사람이라는 실감에 이르렀기 때문이다. 슈퍼맨을 없애버릴 수 있는 논리적 근거를 잃어버린 것이다.

다만 배트맨이 생각보다 빨리 싸움을 포기해 아쉽기는 했다. 욕을 퍼부으며 싸움을 포기해버리기는 하지만 빠른 결정이었다. 거기 로이스 레인이라는 증인이 없었어도 그랬을까. 이건 생각해볼 여지가 있다.

배트맨이 슈퍼맨을 증오하는 표면상의 이유는 신과 같은 권능을 경계하기 때문이다. 그러나 진짜 이유는 그런 권능을 질투하기 때문이다. 고담 시에서 가장 강하고 위험한 아이콘이 되기 위해 브루스 웨인은 평생을 통틀어 수련했다. 매일 밤 가면을 뒤집어쓰고 악당을 잡고 추적하고 추리했다. 가정을 일구지도 못했고 친구를 만들지도 못했다. 말 그대로 지옥같이 살아왔다. 그렇다고 자기 일을 사랑하느냐 하면 그것도 아니다. 사람들은 배트맨을 법 위에 군림하는 자경단이라고 손가락질하고, 배트맨 또한 스스로를 악당과 다름없다고 생각한다. 그는 스스로를 혐오한다.

그런데 어느 날 갑자기 하늘에서 나타난 외계인이 반나절 만에 도시 하나를 날려버리는 초월적인 능력으로 외계 악당을 가정을 일구지도 못했고 친구를 만들지도 못했다.
말 그대로 지옥같이 살아왔다.
그렇다고 자기 일을 사랑하느냐 하면 그것도 아니다.
사람들은 배트맨을
법 위에 군림하는 자경단이라고 손가락질하고,
배트맨 또한 스스로를 악당과 다름없다고 생각한다.

그는 스스로를 혐오한다.

<배트맨 대 슈퍼맨: 저스티스의 시작Batman v Superman: Dawn of Justice>(2016)

때려잡았다. 그 또한 법 위에 군림하는 게 명확해 보임에도 자기혐오에 빠져 있거나 이중 잣대로 괴로워하는 것 같지 않다. 그는 복면을 쓰지도 않는다! 심지어 사람들은 그를 사랑한다! 동상까지 세워줬다! 왜 너는 사실상의 자경단임에도 자경단 취급을 당하지도 않고 사랑까지 받는 거지? 왜 너는 나와 달리 정의를 실현하기 위해 아무것도 희생하지 않는 거지?

결정적으로 배트맨과 슈퍼맨의 첫 만남을 떠올려보자. 배트맨은 그날 밤 슈퍼맨에게 '형이 오늘 기분이 좋아서 봐준다, 영광으로 알아라'식의 선언을 듣는다. 또한 '법 위에 군림하는 자경단'이라는 이유로 슈퍼맨이 자신을 악당으로 생각한다는 걸 깨닫는다. 아 그러니까 너는 외계에서 온 타자인 동시에 객관적인 주체이니까 사람들 일에 마음대로 끼어들어도 되고 한낱 인간에 불과한 나는 안 된다? 도대체 무슨 수로 뒤틀리지 않을 수 있단 말인가. 배트맨이 슈퍼맨을 질투하고 싫어하지 않는다면 그건 정말 이상한 일일 거다.

말이 길어졌지만 이 영화의 패착은 배트맨과 슈퍼맨의 대결이 엄마 이름으로 끝나버렸기 때문이 아니다. 〈배트맨 대 슈퍼맨〉은 감독이 관객에게 어떤 이야기를 들려주어야겠다는 명확한 비전을 가지고 만든 '의도의 산물'이기보다, 일단 찍어놓고 허락된 상영시간 안에 최대한 말이 되게 열심히 끼워맞춘 결과물에 가까워 보인다.

시작부터 그렇다. 로이스 레인을 구하기 위해 슈퍼맨이 아프리카에서 벌인 일은 이 영화의 가장 큰 사건 가운데 하나다. 이

것 때문에 슈퍼맨은 청문회에 서기에 이른다. 그런데 스크린 밖의 누구도 대체 아프리카에서 무슨 일이 벌어졌다는 건지 알 수가 없다. 애초 보여주질 않았으니 당연한 노릇이다. 렉스 루터가 '하늘에서 그분이 온다'며 마지막에 지껄이는 독백은 다크사이드의 존재를 지각했다는 사실 위에 기반한다. 그런데 다크사이드의 심복 스테판 울프가 등장하는 장면은 '삭제 신'이라는 제목으로 나중에야 인터넷에 공개되었다.

배트맨이 원더우먼과 대화하며 저스티스 리그를 결성하겠다는 의지를 내비치는 건 꿈에서 다크사이드에게 세뇌된 슈퍼맨과 플래시의 경고를 봤기 때문이다. 이 꿈과 배트맨의 행동이 관객의 머릿속에서 직관적으로 연결되려면 배트맨이 그걸 단지 꿈이 아닌 실체를 가진 경고로 받아들일 이유가 추가되었어야 한다. 그러나 영화에선 CCTV에 목격된 플래시의 모습을 잠깐 보여주는 걸로 끝이다.

이 영화는 관객의 머릿속에서 거의 천 번쯤 재생되었을 웨인 부부의 총격사건 같은 걸 보여주는 데에는 아까운 시간을 평펑 써대면서 정작 필요한 최소한의 컷을 포함시키는 데에는 별관심이 없다. 이런 태도는 액션 시퀀스에서까지 이어진다. 시끄럽고 거대한 건 알겠지만 액션의 합이나 구체성이 보이지 않는다. 이렇다면 사운드를 최대로 켜둔 화면조정시간과 다를 게 없다. 잭 스나이더는 이후 공개될 감독판(확장판)을 기대해달라고 주문했다. 그러나 감독이 극장상영판에서 제대로 된 이야기의 꼴을 제시하지 못하고 '감독판을 기대해달라'고 이야기하는 건 무책임한 일이다. 〈왓치맨〉의 감독판이 훌륭했다는 점을 감안해도 마찬가지다. 감독이 이런 변명을 반복적으로 습관화하는 건 직무유기에 가깝다.

좋은 것도 있다. 나는 프랭크 밀러 버전에 가장 근접한 이번 배트맨이 영화화된 모든 배트맨 가운데 가장 마음에 든다. 떡밥도 많다. 플래시가 보여준 배트맨의 꿈속에서 다크사이드에 세뇌된 슈퍼맨이나 땅 위에 새겨진 다크사이드의 표식, 로빈이 조커에게 죽은 것인가 아니면 자신을 지켜주지 못한 배트맨에게 배신감을 느낀 로빈이 2대 조커가 된 것인가(코믹스에서 2대 로빈인 제이슨 토드는 조커에게 죽었다. 그러나 영화에서 잠시 노출되는 로빈의 코스튬을 보면 〈수어사이드 스쿼드〉의 조커와 같은 위치에 상처가 있는 걸 확인할 수 있다), 풀어나갈 단서들이 많다. 이런 것들을 찾아내고 상상하는 일은 언제나 즐겁다. 그러나 온몸을 던져 사랑할 준비가 되어 있는 영화에게 배신당하는 경험은 한 번으로 족하다.

덧붙이는 말

작가는 이 글을 쓰고 몇 달 후 〈배트맨 대 슈퍼맨〉이 그래도 〈수어사이드 스쿼드〉보다는 훨씬 더 훌륭한 영화였다는 걸 깨닫고 큰 충격에 빠졌다.

두 영화의
차이

여러분에게 〈판타스틱 4〉에 관련된 어마어마한 이야기 두 가지를 들려주겠다. 첫번째. 극 초반 소년 리드가 공간이동 기계를 발명하고 있던 창고는, 〈백 투 더 퓨처 2〉에서 비프가 자기 차를 주차해놓고 쓰던 차고와 같은 곳이다! 소오름! 두번째. 앞선 첫번째 이야기를 제외하고 나면 이 거대한 쓰레기 더미 같은 영화에 대해 더이상 언급할 만한 게 없다는 사실이다. 소오름!

정말 소름 끼치는 영화가 아닐 수 없다.

창작자의 과도하고 구체적이지 않은 비전은 때로 영화 제작 전반의 불확실성을 증가시킨다. 창작자의 머릿속에서만 성립하고 정작 밖으로 끄집어냈을 때 아무도 알아먹을 수 없는 비문 같은 영화들이 존재한다. 잘 통제된 비전과 그렇지 못한 비전의 차이는 크로넨버그와 타셈 싱의 영화를 비교해보면 알 수 있다. 자의식 강한 영화들의 스토리텔링이 종종 먹다 남은 과자 부스러기처럼 산산이 부서지는 건 그 때문이다. 지난 수십 년 동안 스튜디오 시스템은 그러한 불확실성을 감소시키는 방향으로 전개되어왔다. 의사 진행과 결정에 참여하는 주체들이 구체화되고 과정은 선명해졌다. 시스템이 견고해질수록 사고의 확률은 줄어들었다. 물론 그와 더불어 예상을 뒤엎는 예외적 영화들의 등장 또한 줄어들었다(본래 모든 종류의 시스템이란 특출난 것을 양산하는데 쓰이는 게 아니라, 전체적인 평균값을 끌어올리는 공식과 같은 것이다. 애초 '특출난' 것은 '양산'되지 않는다). 아무튼 결과적으로 대문 앞에 느닷없이 누군가 싸놓고 간 똥, 같은 영화는 거의 사라졌다. 그래서 〈판타스틱 4〉가 관객에게 선사하는 놀라움은 더욱 강력하다. 이러니저러니 해도

쌀 놈은 싼다는 것이다.

　〈판타스틱 4〉의 연출은 조시 트랭크다. 이건 언뜻 근사한 선택이었다. 그는 1인칭 시점 아이디어와 안티 히어로 이야기를 적절하게 배합한 영화 〈크로니클〉을 선보인 바 있다. 미국에서 만들어진 〈아키라〉처럼 보일 정도로 〈크로니클〉은 꽤 준수한 영화였다. 〈판타스틱 4〉의 리부트 기획에 조시 트랭크가 기용되었다

는 소식은 그래서 더욱 설렜다.

그런데 왜 이런 일이 벌어졌을까. 수 스톰이 제시카 알바가 아닌 케이트 마라이기 때문에? 닥터 둠의 후드가 컵라면 사발처럼 생겨서? 굳이 제이미 벨씩이나 캐스팅해놓고 더 싱을 연기시킨 까닭에? 〈위플래쉬〉의 마일스 텔러가 아직은 이런 대형 영화에 어울리는 배우가 아니기 때문에? 이도 저도 아니고 그냥 감독이 신인이라서?

디즈니-마블 스튜디오의 마블 코믹스 프랜차이즈가 죄다 흥행하면서 (역시 마블 코믹스의 대표적인 작품인) 『엑스맨』과 『판타스틱 4』 『데어데블』의 영화 판권을 가지고 있는 이십세기폭스는 조바심을 내고 있었다. 특히 폭스는 〈판타스틱 4〉의 리부트를 2015년까지 무조건 만들어야 한다는 부담감을 안고 있었다. 후속편을 만들지 않으면 〈판타스틱 4〉의 캐릭터들을 마블에 반환해야 하는 시점이었기 때문이다. 반환하는 게 훨씬 더 나은 선택이었겠지만 장사하는 입장에서 그런 결정을 하는 건 쉬운 일이 아니다. 폭스는 〈엑스맨〉과 〈판타스틱 4〉 프랜차이즈를 이어나가는 데 지원을 아끼지 않았다. 조시 트랭크가 작업한 〈판타스틱 4〉의 초기 시나리오는 호평을 받았고 캐스팅 열기는 뜨거웠다. 모든 게 순조로워 보였다.

문제는 조시 트랭크가 들고 온 편집본에 폭스가 전혀 만족하지 않으면서 벌어졌다. 폭스는 〈판타스틱 4〉의 두 시간 이십 분짜리 감독판을 길고 지루하다고 생각했다. 폭스가 원한 것은 단순 편집이 아니었다. 그들은 재촬영을 요구했다. 상당한 분량이었다. 당초 〈판타스틱 4〉 리부트는 2015년 3월에 북미 개봉을 예정에 두고 있었다. 폭스가 재촬영을 요구한 건 2015년 1월이다. 그들이 얼마나 조바심을 내고 있었는지 알 수 있는 대목이다. 개봉은 여름으로 미뤄지고 재촬영이 이루어졌다. 폭스의 생각에 수 스톰은 무조건 금발이어야 했고, 케이트 마라는 가발을 쓴 채 다시 연기해야만 했다. 재촬영과 편집을 거쳐 러닝타임 두 시간 이십 분짜리 영화가 한 시간 삼십 분으로 줄어들었다.

조시 트랭크의 두 시간 이십 분짜리 감독판이었다면 〈판타스틱 4〉에 대한 평가가 완전히 달라졌을까? 그건 누구도 알 수 없는 일이다. 누군가는 팔다리가 늘어나고 온몸이 불덩이가 되어 날아다니고 투명인간이 되고 돌덩이가 되는 슈퍼히어로는 영화 캐릭터로 더이상 별다른 매력이 없다고 말한다. 그러나 능력이라고는 그저 작아지는 것밖에 없는 슈퍼히어로 이야기가 얼마나 재미있는지 확인한 관객에게 그런 말은 별 설득력이 없다. 스튜디오의 개입이 늘 형편없는 결과로 이어지는 것도 아니다. 오히려 반대의 경우가 더 많다. 확실한 건 〈판타스틱 4〉 리부트가 2000년 이후 만들어진 슈퍼히어로 영화 가운데 확연히 덜떨어졌다는 사실뿐이다. 디즈니-마블 스튜디오가 벌여놓은 슈퍼히어로 유니버스 안에서 적어도 〈드래곤볼〉의 베지터 정도의 지분을 차지하길 바랐던 이십세기폭스는 이제 와 그냥 야무치가 되고 말았다. 영화가 공개된 이후 조시 트랭크는 이 모든 게 자기 탓이 아닌 폭스 책임이라는 요지의 글을 트위터에 올렸다가 지웠다가를 반복하고 있다.

디즈니-마블 스튜디오의 〈앤트맨〉이야기를 안 할 수가 없다. 앞서 언급했듯이 앤트맨은 코믹스팬이 아닌 이상 인지도가 떨어지는 캐릭터다. 〈판타스틱 4〉가 여타 마블 코믹스의 히어로들 가운데 인기나 인지도가 덜하다고들 하는데, 그걸 인정하고 보더라도 〈앤트맨〉에 비할 바는 아니다. 심지어 코믹스팬들조차 앤트맨을 그리 좋아하지 않는다. 코믹스팬들의 기억 속에 앤트맨-행크 핌은 그냥 '아내를 때리는 정신이 불안정한 천재'이기 때문이다. 〈앤트맨〉은 본래 기획을 이끌었던 에드거 라이트가 연출에서 하차하는 내분마저 겪었다. 실패할 조건을 고루 갖추고 있던 〈앤트맨〉은, 그러나 보기 좋게 흥행에 성공했다. 크기가 작아지는 것뿐인 슈퍼히어로의 단출한 능력을 조롱하면서도 그 매력을 다양한 액션의 합으로 극대화시켰다. 1대 앤트맨 행크 핌을 멘토 역할로 치워두고 2대 앤트맨 스콧 랭을 중심에 둘 만큼 영리하기도 했다.

　　그러나 〈앤트맨〉이 성공할 수 있었던 가장 큰 이유는 역시 이야기의 확장성에 있다. 관객은 〈앤트맨〉에서 〈어벤져스〉에 관련된 농담을 듣고, 아무렇지 않게 등장하는 어벤져스 본부와 팔콘을 목격하며, 〈캡틴 아메리카: 시빌 워〉로 이어질 다음 이야기를 상상할 수 있다. 〈아이언맨〉부터 시작된 디즈니-마블 스튜디오의 마블 유니버스는 이제 독립되고 단절된 이야기들을 넘어 하나의 유기적인 대체 역사가 되었다. 조금 과장하자면 코믹스에서 그러했듯 마블 영웅들의 이야기가 우리 시대에 존재하는 멀티 유니버스가 된 것이다. 스칼렛 위치가 정신분열을 일으켜

이 멀티 유니버스를 지워버리지 않는 이상, 다른 제작사의 마블 영화가 디즈니-마블 스튜디오의 마블 영화를 뛰어넘는 일은 없을 것이다. 그런 의미에서 마블 스튜디오가 스파이더맨 캐릭터를 사용할 수 있게 동의한 소니의 선택은 '매우' 옳다.

폭스에는 아직 〈엑스맨〉 프랜차이즈가 남아 있다. 이 시리즈는 매슈 본의 〈엑스맨: 퍼스트 클래스〉 이후 새로운 생명력을 얻었다. 〈엑스맨: 아포칼립스〉가 폭스에 "신에게는 아직 열두 척의 배가 남아 있습니다"가 될지 "브루투스 너마저"가 될지는 아무도 모른다. 그러나 〈엑스맨〉 시리즈 역시 향후 마블 유니버스에 편입되지 않는 이상 시간여행과 같은 아이디어만으로 연명하는 데는 한계가 있다.

덧붙이는 말

이 글이 쓰이고 얼마 후 〈엑스맨: 아포칼립스〉가 개봉했다. "브루투스 너마저"였다.

우리는
슬플 시간도 없다

슬픈 게 취미인 자들과 어울리지 말라.

우리는 슬플 시간도 없다.

시간여행

누구나 후회를 한다. 한 사람이 일생에서 겪는 후회의 총량을 무게로 느낄 수 있다면 인류는 중력 없이도 땅에 붙어 있을지 모른다. 어쩌면 나이가 들수록 쪼그라드는 이유가 거기 있을지도 모른다. 후회의 무게를 이기지 못해 어깨도 쑤시고 등도 구부러지고 점점 더 작아지다가 마침내 대지로 스며드는.

그때 그렇게 하지 않았다면 어땠을까, 라는 필연적인 질문. 거기서 수없이 많은 시간여행 이야기들이 태어났다. 시간여행 이야기가 주는 재미의 팔 할은 과거로 돌아가 무언가를 바꿨을 때 그 결과가 시간여행자의 현재에도 영향을 끼친다는 설정에서 출발한다.

과연 그럴까. 마티가 과거의 아버지에게 용기를 불어넣어

비프의 얼굴에 주먹을 날리게 했을 때, 현재 시점의 아버지 또한 변모해 더이상 루저가 아닌 성공적인 작가로 거듭나는 게 가능한 걸까(〈백 투 더 퓨처〉). 날짜가 바뀌지 않고 하루가 끊임없이 되풀이되었을 때 그 하루의 양상은 기본적으로 똑같이 반복되는 걸까(〈사랑의 블랙홀〉).

비만으로 고생하는 누군가가 있다. 그가 과거로 돌아가 자신이 그간 먹었던 저 수많은 야식을 먹지 못하게 만들고 돌아왔다고 가정해보자. 그는 야식을 먹지 않은 행동의 결과로 만들어진 새로운 현실로 돌아오게 되는 걸까, 아니면 과거로 갔다가 돌아왔을 뿐 여전히 비만인 타임라인에 존재하게 되는 걸까. 그는 비만이 아닌 상태로 살아온 기억과 비만이었던 본래의 기억을 둘 다 가지고 있게 되는 걸까, 하나만 가지고 있게 되는 걸까.

해답은 없다. 아무도 모른다. 빛보다 빨리 여행했을 경우 미래여행은 가능하지만 과거로의 여행은 불가능하다는 것부터 대체된 타임라인 이론의 평행우주에 이르기까지, 시간여행의 구체성은 규정되는 게 불가능하다. 누구도 시간여행을 실제로 해본 적 없기 때문이다. 시간여행 이야기의 포인트가 여기 있다. 아무도 '정말' 해본 적은 없다. 그러니까 이야기 안에서 설정만 잘 만들어내면 얼마든지 이걸 가지고 이야기가 잘 굴러가게 만들 수 있다. 향이 다 타들어가는 것을 지켜보며 관객이 발을 동동 구르게 만들 수 있는 것이다(〈나인: 아홉 번의 시간여행〉). 누구도 입증한 적이 없는, 세상에 존재하지 않는 규칙을 이야기 안에서 논리적인 장치로 활용해 서스펜스를 만들어낼 수 있다. 멋지기 짝이 없는 일이다. 시간여행 이야기야말로 유물론자들의 지옥인 동시에 길티 플레저다.

드라마 〈시그널〉은 잘 만들어진 시간여행 이야기의 가장 최근 사례다. 주인공은 특정 시간에만 작동해 과거와 통신할 수 있는 무전기를 손에 넣게 되고, 이를 통해 미제 사건들을 해결한다. 아이디어 자체가 새로운 건 아니다. 가깝게는 〈더 폰〉이 있었고 대표적으로는 〈프리퀀시〉가 있으며 레퍼런스라면 역시 그레고리 벤퍼드의 소설 『타임스케이프』가 있었다. 〈프리퀀시〉는 『타임스케이프』에서 아이디어를 가져왔다. 이후 수많은 영화들이 〈프리퀀시〉를 따라했다. 그러나 아무도 〈프리퀀시〉가 『타임스케이프』를 도용했다고 말하지는 않는다. 어디에도 완전무결하게 새로운 것 따위는 없다. 중요한 건 아이디어 자체가 아니라 그 아이디어를 어떻게 운용하는지에 달려 있다. 과거와의 통신을 통해 현실을 바꾼다는 아이디어를 가지고 어떻게 이야기를 잘 꾸려나갈 것인가가 중요한 것이다. 그리고 〈시그널〉의 김은희 작가는 이를 성공적으로 수행해냈다.

〈시그널〉이 한국 시장에서 성공할 수 있었던 가장 큰 이유 가운데 하나는 화성 연쇄살인사건과 같은 한국의 대표적인 미제 사건들을 다수 다룬다는 점이다. 즉 주인공들이 갖는 안타까움과 절박함이 관객에게도 충분히 공유된다. 이는 최근 대중문화 콘텐츠가 대부분 과거로의 회귀나 복기에 매달리는 현상과 맞물려 있다. 요즘은 거의 모든 채널에서 과거를 이야기한다. 과거와 현재를 교차해서 보여주며 주인공의 남편이 누구인지 궁금하게 만들거나 과거의 노래를 새로 부르며 경쟁한다. 개인적으로는 대중문화 전 분야에 걸친 이와 같은 유행이 경쟁이라는 형식과 만나면서 과거에의 집착을 넘어 퇴행에 이르는 것 같아 썩 내키지 않는다('이기기 위한' 노래를 듣는 데 정말 지쳤다). 여기에 〈시그널〉이 더해졌다. 지금의 한국 소비자들은 과거를 그리워하는 동시에 바꾸고 싶어한다. 흥미로운 일이다.

〈시그널〉에도 미흡한 점은 존재한다. 과거와의 통신을 이야기의 주요한 동력으로 사용하면서도 정작 이 통신 자체를 극적 장치로서 제대로 활용해내지는 못했다. 가까운 예로 드라마 〈나인: 아홉 번의 시간여행〉을 떠올려보자. 여기서 시간여행은 향을 태우는 것으로 이루어진다. 거기 명확한 제약을 설정해둔다. 시간여행은 향이 타는 시간 동안만 가능하다. 시간여행은 정확히 현시점에서 20년 전으로만 가능하다. 향은 아홉 개가 있다. 그러므로 시간여행도 아홉 번만 가능하다. 향에 대해 아는 사람은 주인공과 악역을 막론하고 바뀐 타임라인과 본래의 타임라인을 둘 다 인식할 수 있다. 과거를 바꿔 현재에 대한 새로운 기억이 심어지는 동안 뇌에 과부하가 걸린다. 반복되면 건강에 영향을 끼친다. 이와 같은 제약들은 그대로 이야기에 갈등을 만들어내는 장치로 활용된다.

그러나 〈시그널〉의 무전기는 이야기의 진행에 그리 큰 갈등이나 서스펜스를 만들어내지 못한다. 특정 시간대에만 작동한다는 점 정도를 제외하면 별다른 제약이 없다. 이 통신이 어떻게 시작되었는지에 관한 설명은 그냥 시간여행의 패러독스에 느슨하게 떠넘겨버렸다. 누가 듣고 가서 써먹지도 않는다. 시간여행이라는 구심축을 빼버려도 별문제 없는 회차마저 존재했다. 앞서도 설명했듯이 시간여행 이야기의 가장 큰 장점은 그걸 아무도 해본 적이 없다는 데 있다. 그러니까 뭘 어떻게 설정하든 이야기 안에서 일관성만 있으면 된다. 이런 종류의 이야기에서 서스펜스는 무전기로 뭘 할 수 있느냐가 아니라 뭘 할 수 없느냐로부터 조성된다. 〈시그널〉은 시간여행 이야기만이 가질 수 있는 장점을 고루 성취하는 데에는 실패했다.

다행스러운 건 〈시그널〉이 다음 이야기로의 길을 활짝 열어두었다는 점이다. 이 정도면 열린 결말이 아니라 작가가 명확하게 다음 이야기를 의도하고 있다고 봐야 한다. 김은희 작가는 그간 꾸준히 장르물을 시도하며 평균 이상의 완성도를 보여주었지만 늘 후반부가 아쉽다는 지적을 받아왔다. 이번에는 달랐다. 언제나 좋았던 초반부 이후에도 중반부에서 여간해선 집중력을 잃지 않았고 결말 또한 완결성과 지속 가능성 사이에 근사한 무게중심을 찾는 데 성공했다. 이 정도면 〈시그널〉 시즌 2가 무척 재미있으니 꼭 보라는 미래로부터의 무전을 받지 않더라도 기대해볼 만하다.

책

그것을 쓴 자가 집중력을 발휘해서 자기 딴에 가장 중요하다고 생각하는 아이디어와 문장, 정확한 단어들을 탈탈 털어넣은 기록이다. 탈탈 털어넣었기 때문에 작가 입장에서 이것은 매우 친절한 텍스트다. 그러나 독자 입장에서는 그렇지 않다. 작가가 정말 이야기하고자 했던 비전은 한 번에 눈에 들어오지 않기 마련이다. 작가에게 쉽고 당연한 명제가 독자에게는 생소하고 어려운 것일 수 있기 때문이다. 작가가 이야기하고자 하는 정수에 가닿기까지는 독자가 직접 채워넣어야 하는 구멍이 많다.

나는 그 구멍을 채워나가는 과정이 독서라고 생각한다. 이 구멍을 채우기 위해서는 그간 독자가 경험했던 것들, 읽었던 것들, 잠시 스치고 지났던 사소하고 별것 아니었던 기억과 지식들이 동원되어야만 한다. 혹은 삶의 어느 순간 정말 중요한 것이라고 가슴을 치며 깨달았으나 살면서 금방 잊어버렸던 어떤 것들이 환기되어야만 한다.

한 권의 책을 만나 읽어내려가며 문장과 문장 사이의 빈 공간을 나만의 단서들로 채워나가는 이 과정이야말로 그 무엇과도 바꿀 수 없는 보물이다. 흡사 웹상의 하이퍼링크처럼 머릿속에서 단어와 단서들이 꼬리를 이어 나만의 사유를 만들어가는 자극은 독서 이외에서 얻어내기 어려운 경험이다. 만화책이든 소설책이든 인문학책이든 전문 서적이든 빨간 책이든 파란 책이든 관계없이 말이다.

©김지윤

전에 살던 연남동 집 거실 사진을 보고 팬분이 그려준 수채화.

한 권의 책을 만나 읽어내려가며
문장과 문장 사이의 빈 공간을
나만의 단서들로 채워나가는 이 과정이야말로
그 무엇과도 바꿀 수 없는 보물이다.

지금 모래를
퍼내고 계십니까

오랫동안 아끼고 좋아해왔던 작품을 다시 꺼내 보는 일은 늘 즐겁다. 이야기를 따라가느라 정신없었던 처음과는 달리 집중할 수 있다. 관련된 주제나 근거들을 따로 찾아볼 기회도 가질 수 있다. 무엇보다도 다르게 기억하고 있는 대목이 많다. 그렇다면 무엇 때문에 내가 그걸 다르게 기억하고 있는지 고민해본다. 그 과정이 가장 즐겁다. 내가 그것을 그렇게 기억하고 싶었던 건지, 아니면 지금의 내가 그때의 나와 다르기 때문인지 판단해볼 기준이 생기기 때문이다. 우리는 대개 우리가 기억하고 싶은 대로 무언가를 기억하고, 그것을 근거로 엉뚱한 일을 벌이기 마련이다.

아베 고보의 『모래의 여자』는 1962년에 출판된 소설이다.

처음 읽은 건 10년 전쯤 강화도 여행을 갔을 때다. 저자에 관한 지식이라고는 일본 전후 세대를 대표하는 작가 가운데 오른쪽에 미시마 유키오, 왼쪽에 아베 고보가 있다는 것 정도였다. 미시마 유키오는 읽어봤어도 아베 고보는 처음이었다. 숙소에 도착하자마자 틀어박혀 이 책을 읽었다. 새벽 무렵 다 읽고 밤새 잠을 못 이룬 채 해변을 계속 걸었던 기억이 난다. 기회가 된다면 꼭 읽어보길 추천한다. 실존주의에 기반한 내용이지만 우화에 가깝고 중편 분량이라 쉽게 읽을 수 있다. 굉장한 소설이다. 영화 〈모래의 여자〉를 찾아본 건 당연히 원작에 매료되었기 때문이었다. 아베 고보가 직접 각본을 썼고 칸 국제영화제 심사위원 특별상을 수상했다.

이야기는 남자가 희귀한 곤충을 채집하기 위해 사막을 찾아가면서 시작된다. 마을 전체에 사막화가 진행중이다. 바닷바람에 실려 내륙으로 끝없이 모래가 밀려온다. 남자는 여기서 희귀한 곤충을 찾아 곤충도감에 이름을 올리길 희망하고 있다.

차편이 끊기자 촌장은 남자에게 하루 묵고 갈 것을 권한다. 남자는 고맙다며 좋아한다. 촌장은 그를 함정처럼 깊게 파인 커다란 모래 구덩이로 데려간다. 모래 구덩이 안에는 쓰러져가는 집이 하나 있다. 남자는 밧줄에 매달린 채 구덩이 안으로 안내된다. 집안에는 여자가 한 명 살고 있다. 어둑한 밤이 되자 여자가 집밖으로 나선다. 그러더니 모래를 퍼내기 시작한다. 모래가 끊임없이 밀려내려와 쌓이기 때문에 파묻히지 않으려면 끊임없이 퍼내야 한다는 것이다. 그렇게 퍼낸 모래는 밧줄에 매달린 통에 담겨 구덩이 밖으로 끌어올려진다. 마을 사람들은 모래를 모아 인근 마을의 공사장에 팔고 있다.

아침이 밝고 집을 나서려던 남자는 크게 당황한다. 밧줄이 사라진 것이다. 남자는 모래를 퍼낼 일꾼으로 납치된 것이며, 이런 식으로 구덩이 안에 갇혀 노동하는 게 자신이 처음이 아니고, 이것이 마을을 지탱해온 원동력임을 알게 된다. 남자는 모래 구덩이를 끝없이 기어오른다. 그러나 번번이 밀려내려오는 모래에 휩쓸려 굴러떨어지고 만다.

이건 말도 안 되는 일이야. 모래가 문제면 과학적으로 해결해야지 사람을 납치해서 모래를 퍼내게 하다니.

그것도 생각해봤어요, 하지만 이 방법이 가장 돈이 덜 들어요.

며칠을 그러다 자포자기한 심정이 든 남자는 화가 나 집을 때려부수기 시작한다. 여자가 말리다가 둘이 부둥켜 얽힌다. 그들은 섹스를 한다. 이 시퀀스는 대단하다. 얼굴 위주로 클로즈업된 컷과 모래로 뒤덮인 살을 보여주는 게 대부분이지만 그 모든 게 엄청나게 절박하고 동물적이다. 그리고 길다.

남자는 탈출하기 위한 시도를 멈추지 않는다. 남자는 여자에게 술을 먹여 잠들게 하고 그물을 엮어 만든 밧줄을 구덩이 밖으로 던진다. 그리고 몇 번의 시도 끝에 탈출에 성공한다. 남자는 달리고 또 달린다. 그러나 곧 쫓기게 된다. 도망가던 남자는 모래늪에 빠진다. 남자는 결국 구덩이 안에 다시 처박힌다.

3개월이 지났다. 남자는 매일 밤 여자와 함께 모래를 퍼올리는 일을 한다. 노동에 찌들어 제대로 생각하기조차 힘들다. 그러나 아직 포기하지 않았다. 집 앞에 구멍을 파고 빈 물통 하나를 파묻는다. 까마귀 덫을 설치하는 거라고 설명한다. 까마귀 다리에 구출해달라는 편지를 달아 날려보낼 작정이다. 그런데 어느 날 덫을 열어보니 물통에 물이 가득차 있다. 남자는 소스라치게 놀란다. 어떻게 물이 생긴 거지? 남자는 모래가 펌프 역할을 해 모세관현상으로 물이 모였다는 사실을 깨닫는다. 식수가 해결되었음을 기뻐하던 남자는 이 사실을 비밀로 한다.

어느 날 여자가 산통을 느낀다. 남자가 소리를 질러 마을 사람들을 부른다. 구덩이 안으로 들어온 사람들이 여자를 데리고 나간다. 집밖을 서성이던 남자는 마을 사람들이 여자를 끌어올릴 때 사용한 밧줄을 그대로 두고 갔다는 것을 발견한다. 남자는 구덩이 밖으로 올라간다. 올라가서 경치를 구경한다. 다시 내려온다. 그리고 통 안에 물의 양이 늘었음을 확인하고 만족스러워한다. 남자는 당장 이 유수장치를 발명한 것에 대해 마을 사람들에게 설명하고 싶은 마음으로 가득하다. 탈출은 그 이후에 생각해도 늦지 않아. 남자는 생각한다.

소설의 한 구절은 이 이야기의 어떤 측면을 친절하게 안내해준다.

"과연 노동에는, 목적지 없이도 여전히 도망쳐가는 시간을 견디게 만드는, 인간이 기댈 언덕 같은 것이 있는 모양이다."

남자의 일상은 밖에 있었다. 그러나 이제 그의 일상은 모래 구덩이 안에서 삽질하는 것이 되었다. 그게 그의 밥벌이다. 끝이 없는 일이다. 무의미한 일이다. 그럼에도 이제는 여기가 그의 우주다. 처음에 곤충도감에 이름을 싣고 싶어서 사막을 찾아왔던 남자는, 마을 사람들에게 유수장치를 소개하고 인정받기 위해 구덩이 안에 남는다. 결국 남자는 구덩이 밖의 삶과 안의 삶 사이에 큰 차이를 느끼지 못하게 된 것이다.

아마도 사람들은 엄청난 부가가치를 만들어내고 있다고 스스로 자부하면서 구덩이 안에서 모래를 퍼내는 일을 매일같이 반복하고 있는지 모른다. 그 지루하고 의미 없는 반복에 염증을 느끼던 사람조차 마침내 길들여지고 익숙해져 아무런 문제를 느끼지 못하고 심지어 자아를 성취하며 만족하게 되는 것이다. 문제의식을 가지고 분투하는 사람보다 일상에 침몰된 사람이 더 행복해 보인다. 다시 꺼내볼 때마다 전율한다. 마침내 구덩이 밖으로 나설 기회를 가지게 되었음에도 다시 들어가 당장의 목적에 만족하고 설레어하는 풍경을 자꾸 떠올리게 된다. 어느 쪽이 더 옳은 선택일까. 더 권할 수 있는 삶일까. 이 이야기를 처음 읽었을 때는 남자를 비웃었다. 지금은 쉽게 판단하지 못하겠다.

<모래의 여자>(1964)

남자의 일상은 밖에 있었다.
그러나 이제 그의 일상은
모래 구덩이 안에서 삽질하는 것이 되었다.
그게 그의 밥벌이다.
끝이 없는 일이다.
무의미한 일이다.
그럼에도 이제는 여기가 그의 우주다.
문제의식을 가지고 분투하는 사람보다
일상에 침몰된 사람이 더 행복해 보인다.
어느 쪽이 더 옳은 선택일까.
더 권할 수 있는 삶일까.

공간을
이해하는 법

오래전 고시원에 관한 글을 쓴 적이 있다. 그 글의 마지막은 다음과 같았다.

"고시원에서 원생으로 2년을 살고 총무로 2년을 더 산 뒤 주변에 반지하 전세방을 얻어 나왔다. 벌써 3년째인데 퇴근해서 현관문을 열 때마다 매번 어색하다. 고시원으로 부러 돌아가고 싶은 마음은 없다. 하지만 그때만큼 살고 있는 공간의 모든 걸 이해하고 있는 것 같지는 않다. 어른이 된다는 건, 어쩌면 주변 세계를 향한 애정을 조금씩 잃어가는 과정일지도 모르겠다."

내게 집은 부동산이 아니다. 집은 살아가는 공간이다. 또한 반드시 이해해야 할 과제다. 대학생 때부터 누구의 도움도 받지 않고 서울 한복판에서 몸뚱이만 가지고 시작해 내 힘으로 마련한 공간이다. 누우려면 의자를 책상 위에 올려두어야 했던 고시원부터 혼자 살기 딱 좋은 크기의 지금 집에 이르기까지 나는 늘 내가 살아가는 공간에 대해 이해하려고 최선을 다했다. 문을 열고 들어서면 시야에 들어오는 천장부터 바닥까지 전부 온전한 내 힘으로 쌓아올린 것들이다. 이 안에서 나는 먹고 자고 씻으며 밥벌이를 한다.

청소를 하는 건 그래서 중요하다. 청소를 하다보면 공간을 이해할 수 있다. 뭐를 어떻게 두어야 어울리고 어울리지 않는지 알게 된다. 어디는 훌륭하고 또 어디는 부족한지 그래서 어떻게 해야 보완할 수 있는지 알 수 있다. 내가 혼자 청소할 수 없는 크기의 집을 소유하는 건 괴상한 일이다. 직접 청소하지 않으면서 그 공간을 이해하고 있다고 말하는 사람들을 나는 믿지 않는다. 내 집 마련하려고 그토록 오랜 기간 고되고 살벌한 비용을 지불했으면서 공간을 꼭 이해해야 하냐고 되묻는 사람들도 나는 좀처럼 신뢰하지 못하겠다.

잊을 수 없는
얼굴이 있다

살다보면, 삼루에서 태어난 주제에 자신이 흡사 삼루타를 쳐서 거기 있는 것처럼 구는 사람들을 만나기 마련이다. 아무튼 삼루에 누가 있다는 건 좋은 일이다. 재수가 없어도 내버려둔다. 심지어 삼루 말고는 어디도 가본 적이 없는 그를 향해 응원을 한다. 그가 홈으로 무사히 들어와 점수를 낼 수 있도록 편의와 우선권을 제공한다. 어찌됐든 그는 삼루에 있으니 말이다.

마침내 기회가 온다. 평생 삼진 아니면 파울만 쳐대던 무명의 노력파 타자가 이루타를 쳐냈다. 아마도 그것은 그의 인생에 허락된 단 한 번의 완벽한 안타일 것이다. 이루타를 쳐낸 무명의 타자는 아깝게 태그아웃당한다. 그러거나 말거나 점수만 만들어준다면 상관없다. 모두의 시선이 삼루로 모인다. 지금이다! 뛰어! 점수를 내줘! 삼루에서 태어나 평생 삼루타를 친 것처럼 굴었던 자가 느지막하게 뛰기 시작한다. 그런데 조금 뛰는가 싶더니 도로 삼루에 돌아와버린다. 다소간의 야유가 있었으나 삼루에 주자가 있다는 게 중요한 거 아니겠냐는 집단 지성에 의해 소동은 금세 잦아든다. 경기가 끝난 후, 평생 단 한 번의 완벽한 이루타를 쳐낸 동료에게 미안하지 않냐고 묻는 기자를 향해 그가 말한다.

아프니까 이루타죠. 천 번을 흔들리면 언젠가 그도 저처럼 삼루타를 칠 수 있지 않을까요(엄지 척).

이런 우사인 볼트 척추기립근 염려해주는 세상을, 우리는 살아왔다. 나는 평생 그런 사람들을 경멸해왔다. 그런데 요즘 들어서는 내가 그런 사람들과 결과적으로 다른 게 뭔지에 대해 자꾸 생각하게 된다.

한번은 아버지를 찾아간 적이 있다. 새벽에 일어나서 똥을 싸다가 문득 그래야겠다는 생각을 하고 연락을 했다. 문자를 보냈고, 와도 된다는 허락을 받았다. 아버지와는 중학생 때 이후로 왕래가 없었다. 그날 아침 내가 왜 갑자기 찾아갈 생각을 했던 건지 잘 모르겠다. 다만 아버지를 만나 대답을 들어야 할 것들이 있었다. 그 대답을 듣지 않으면 앞으로도 잘 살아나갈 수 없을 거라는 생각을 했다.

원주는 추웠다. 아버지는 원주에 있는 대학교에서 오랫동안 교수를 하고 있었다. 터미널 앞에서 만났다. 중학교 시절에 멈춰 있는 내 기억 속의 아버지 차는 언제까지나 하얀색 엑셀이었는데 다른 차를 보니 기분이 이상해졌다. 만남은 뜨겁지도 차갑지도 않았다. 그저 우리 둘 다 이런 종류의 만남에 익숙하지 않다는 것 정도는 알 수 있었다. 차로 이동하는 동안 나는 아버지가 이 만남에 대해 내심 꽤 감동하고 있으며, 내게도 같은 종류의 감동이 전해지길 원하고 있다는 느낌을 받았다. 나는 뜨거운 화해를 하러 거기 간 것이 아니었다. 정신을 똑바로 차려야겠다는 생각을 했다.

아버지 사무실에 앉아서 이런저런 이야기를 했다. 아버지 전공분야에 관한 아무짝에도 쓸모없는 이야기들이 대부분이었고 그마저도 어색하고 거대한 구멍을 메우기 위한 용도였지만, 놀랍게도 유익한 시간이었다. 하지만 내가 물어보고 싶은 건 따로 있었다.

군대를 전역한 뒤 돈이 없어서 복학을 하지 못하고 하루에 아르바이트를 세 개씩 하다가 탈진을 해서 쓰러진 날이 있었다. 그날 밤 나는 고시원 앞에서 소주 두 병을 억지로 한꺼번에 털어넣었다. 그리고 아버지에게 전화를 했다. 신호음이 가는 동안 입술을 얼마나 깨물었는지 정말 피가 났다. 도움을 구걸한다는 게 너무 창피했다. 모멸감이 느껴졌다. 아버지 도움 없이도 잘살 수 있다고 언제까지나 보여주고 싶었는데 이렇게 백기를 들고 전화를 한다는 게 끔찍했다. 그 와중에 소주는 알코올이니까 이 상처가 소독이 되어서 덧나지 않겠지라는 생각을 하고 있던 찰나 아버지가 전화를 받았다.

나는 아버지가 교수로 있는 대학교에서 자녀 학비가 나온다는 사실을 알고 있었다. 지금 너무 힘들어서 그러는데 나중에 전부 갚을 테니까 제발 등록금을 내주면 안 되겠느냐고 부탁했다. 월세와 생활비는 내가 벌 수 있다, 당장 등록금만 어떻게 도와달라고 말했다. 예상되는 상대의 답변이 있을 때 나는 그 답변을 듣기 싫어서 최대한 이야기를 길게 늘어놓는 버릇이 있다. 그날도 그랬다. 등록금도 갚고 효도도 하겠다는 이야기를 한참 하고 있는데 등록금과 효도 사이의 어느 지점에서 아버지가 대답을 했다.

그날 원주의 사무실에서 나는 아버지에게 물었다. 왜 능력이 있으면서도 자식을 부양하지 않았는지 물었다. 왜 등록금마저 주지 않았느냐고 물었다. 후회하고 있다고, 아버지는 말했다. 아버지 입에서 후회라는 단어를 들은 건 그때가 처음이자 마지막이었던 것 같다. 후회하고 있다, 는 말은 짧은 문장이다. 그러나 놀랍게도 나는 만족스러웠다.

내가 확인하고 싶었던 건 왜 내가 아버지에게 미움받아야 하는지였다. 대체 내가 뭘 잘못해서 학교에서 공짜로 나오는 학비 지원금마저 주고 싶지 않을 만큼 미웠는지 하는 것 따위 말이다. 부모에게조차 사랑받지 못하는 사람이라는 게 나는 반평생 슬프고 창피했다. 그래서 타인에게 사랑받기 위해 노력하는 건 일찌감치 포기했다. 남의 눈치 보면 지는 거라고 위악적으로 노력하다보니 쿨병이니 뭐니 안 좋은 말이 쌓여갔지만 중요하지 않았다. 남에게 결코, 다시는 꼴사납게 도움을 구걸하지 않고 오

부모에게조차 사랑받지 못하는 사람이라는 게
나는 반평생 슬프고 창피했다.

그래서 타인에게 사랑받기 위해 노력하는 건
일찌감치 포기했다.
남에게 결코, 다시는 꼴사납게 도움을 구걸하지 않고
오로지 혼자 힘으로 버텨 살아내는 것만이 중요했다.

로지 혼자 힘으로 버텨 살아내는 것만이 중요했다. 구체적이지 않았지만 후회하고 있다는 말로 내게는 충분했다. 삶이란 마음먹은 대로 안 되기 마련이다. 아버지도 잘해보고 싶었을 것이다. 후회하고 있다면 그것으로 된 것이다. 후회하고 있다는 그 말에 나는 정말 태아처럼 안도했다.

아버지가 그래도 네가 그렇게 어렵게 산 덕분에 독립심이 강한 어른이 되어서 혼자 힘으로 잘살고 있으니 다행이라고 말하기 전까지는 말이다.

그날의 만남은 그걸로 끝이었다. 아버지를 본 건 그게 마지막이었다. 나중에 연락이 몇 번 왔지만 받지 않았다. 돌아가는 버스 안에서 자신도 어렸을 때는 나중에 자식을 낳으면 친구 같은 부모 자식 사이가 되고 싶었다는 아버지의 말을 계속해서 곱씹었다. 아, 자신이 원하는 어른으로 나이 먹어가기란 얼마나 어려운 일인가.

살다보면 삼루에서 태어난 주제에 자신이 흡사 삼루타를 쳐서 거기 있는 것처럼 구는 사람들을 만나기 마련이다. 나는 평생 그런 사람들을 경멸해왔다. 그런데 이제 와 돌아보니 내가 딱히 나은 게 뭔지 모르겠다. 나는 심지어 삼루에서 태어난 것도 삼루타를 친 것도 아닌데 아무도 필요하지 않고 여태 누구 도움도 받지 않았으니 앞으로도 혼자 힘만으로 살 수 있다 자신해왔기 때문이다. 나는 그런 자신감이 건강한 것이라고 생각했다. 요즘에 와서야 그것이 착각이라는 걸 깨닫고 있다.

어떤 면에선 아버지 말이 맞았다. 그게 누구 덕이든, 나는 독립적인 어른으로 컸다. 아버지에게 거절당했듯이 다른 누군가에게 거절당하는 게 싫어서 누구의 도움도 받고 싶지 않았다. 그래서 누구에게도 도움을 구하거나 아쉬운 소리를 하지 않고 멀쩡한 척 살아왔다. 시간이 흘러 지금에 와선 도움이 필요할 때 도움이 필요하다고 말할 수 있는 능력도, 타인의 호의를 받아들일 줄 아는 능력도 잃어버리고 말았다. 이제는 혼자서밖에 살 수 없는 사람이 되어버린 것 같다. 좋은 어른은커녕 이대로 그냥 독선적인 노인이 되어버릴까, 나는 그게 너무 두렵다.

평생을 흔들어놓는
영화가 있다

하루를 흔들어놓는 영화가 있다. 카페에 앉아 뭔가 정리해보려 하지만 아무것도 손에 잡히지 않고 가슴이 텅 비어 자그마한 진동에도 천둥이 치듯 쿵쾅거릴 것이다. 그런 영화들이 있다. 그런 영화들은 하루가 지나고 이틀이 흘러야 비교적 선명한 사실관계들이 수면 위로 떠오르기 시작한다. 사실과 기분이 적당히 분리되고 나면 준비가 된 것이다. 그때 그 영화에 관한 글을 쓸 수가 있다.

문제는 하루가 아니라 평생을 흔들어놓는 영화가 있다는 것이다. 그런 영화는 프레임과 컷이 아닌 냄새와 질감으로 기억되고, 구체적인 서사가 아닌 뭉쳐진 이미지 그 자체로 동공 저 안쪽에 조각칼로 새겨지듯 각인된다. 그런 영화들에 관해서는 좀체 글을 쓰기 어렵다. 썼더라도 나중에 읽어보면 한심하기 이를 데 없다. 대개 인생을 흔들어놓을 수 있는 것들이란 구체성이 결여되어 있기 마련이다. 그렇게 불투명하기 때문에 '삶'을 뒤흔들어놓을 만큼 강력할 수 있는 것이다.

1999년 여름, 종로2가의 (지금은 없어진) 코아아트홀을 찾은 건 순전한 의무감 때문이었다. 당시에는 대학교 영화동아리에 반드시 봐야 할 영화 리스트 같은 것들이 존재했다. 국내에 정식으로 수입되지 않았거나 단종된 것들이 대다수였기 때문에 비디오테크나 황학동 풍물시장 같은 곳을 이용해 영화를 구해 보았다. 어렵게 구한 영화들의 정보를 연합동아리 연락망을 통해 공유하곤 했는데 지금도 그런 게 있는지는 잘 모르겠다.

아무튼 그 리스트 안에 토드 헤인스의 〈포이즌〉이 있었다. 선배가 구해온 것을 암굴 같은 동아리방에 모여 작은 비디오비전으로 보았다. 안 그래도 좋지 않은 화질이 담배 연기 때문에 더 뿌옇고 암울했다. 테이프의 상태가 나빠 중간에 비디오클리너를 세 번 정도 돌리고 데크를 네 번 정도 내리쳤던 것 같다. 대체 얼마나 끊어 보았는지 거의 스톱모션애니메이션이라 해도 될 정도였다. 아무튼 나는 〈포이즌〉에 완전히 매료당했다. 며칠 동안 영화의 잔영에서 헤어나오지 못했다. 그러던 중 토드 헤인스의 신작이 코아아트홀에서 상영한다는 소식을 듣고 찾아갔다. 그게 〈벨벳 골드마인〉이었다.

나는 그날 수업을 다 째고 혼자 〈벨벳 골드마인〉을 두 번 내리 보았다.

극장을 나서 깜깜해진 하늘을 올려다보는데 완전히 다른 세상 같더라. 아직도 그때 맡은 공기의 냄새를 잊을 수가 없다. 그런데도 당시의 기분을 '완전히 다른 세상 같았다'는 말 이외에 다른 무엇으로도 표현할 수가 없다. 이상한 노릇이다.

〈벨벳 골드마인〉은 70년대 글램록의 시대를 조명한다. 오스카 와일드의 이야기에서부터 100년 후 글램록이 영국을 점령하기까지 쉴새없이 이야기를 쏟아내던 영화는 80년대의 차가운 풍경으로 점프한다. 한때 글램록의 열렬한 팬이었으나 글램록 스타 브라이언 슬레이드의 거짓 암살소동 이후 염세적으로 돌변한 기자 아서 스튜어트가 주인공이다. 브라이언 슬레이드의 거짓 암살소동 10주년을 맞이해 기획기사를 쓰라는 데스크의 요청에 아서는 난감해한다. 취재를 시작하고 아서는 브라이언 슬레이드, 커트 와일드, 수많은 글램록 스타들, 그들 주위를 맴돌았던 10년 전의 자기 자신을 힘들게 다시 마주하게 된다. 그리고 마침내 브라이언 슬레이드가 맥스웰 데몬으로, 그리고 다시 토미 스톤으로 둔갑하기까지의 모든 사실을 알아낸다. 그러나 달라지는 건 아무것도 없다.

이 영화는 내게 일종의 해방구 같았다. 극장 밖의 세상은 허물어져가고 있었다. IMF라는 이름의 부도수표를 우리가 갚아야 한다는 사실에 당혹스러웠고, 대학생은 면제해줄 수 없냐고 손을 들어 질문하고 싶지만 소시민들의 주머니 깊은 곳 금붙이들이 나라 살리는 데 쓰시라며 카메라 앞에 전시되는 저 거대한 서사 안에서 개인의 사정과 생계 따위는 긁으면 까맣게 드러나는 금박마냥 별게 아니었다. 그리고 나는 학비와 집세를 벌어야 했다. 99년에는 또 무슨 영어 이름의 광풍이 도착할지 모르는 일이었다. 군대를 가자! 군대를 가자! 나는 그때 술만 마시면 외쳤다. 군대로 튀자! 군대로 도망쳐봤자 나쁘면 나빴지 나을 게 없다는 걸 곧 겪게 되었지만, 아무튼 모든 것이 시대를 강타한 1800원짜리 대패삼겹살처럼 혼돈 그 자체였다.

〈벨벳 골드마인〉이 그리는 풍경 또한 혼란스러웠다. 이 영화는 뜨겁고 역동적인 글램록의 70년대와 건조하게 말라붙은 팝의 80년대를 교차해서 보여주면서 점멸 끝에 사라져버린 모든 것들과 거짓말들, 변화한 것들, 변하지 않은 것들을 비춘다. 그 속도와 화려함에 몸을 싣고 가다보면 먹먹하고 슬퍼진다. 변한다는 건 슬픈 일이다. 그러나 단순히 변했기 때문만은 아니다. 반역과 반동, 뜨거운 것과 차가운 것이 결국 동류의 혼돈으로부터 빚어진다는 사실을 깨닫기 때문이다. 그리고 그 혼돈은 영원히 지속된다. 그래서 슬픈 것이다. 그런 어쩔 수 없는 반복이 슬픈 것이다. 그렇게 혼이 나가버릴 즈음 커트 와일드가 말한다. 우리는 세상을 바꾸려 했어. 그런데 우리가 바뀌어버렸지.

이제 와 떠올려보면 〈벨벳 골드마인〉은 이후 겪게 될 그 모든 혼란과 혼돈의 서막과 같았다. 그리고 이 영화는 내가 그 모든 혼돈에 휩쓸려 익사하지 않고 한발 물러서서 관찰할 수 있게 만들어주었다. 삶과 혼돈은 결코 유리되거나 결별할 수 없는 것이기에, 매번 마냥 슬퍼하고 분노하기보다 껴안아 아우를 수 있어야 한다는 필요를 알려주었다. 실천하기는 어렵지만 마음속에

그 속도와 화려함에
몸을 싣고 가다보면
먹먹하고 슬퍼진다.
변한다는 건 슬픈 일이다.
커트 와일드가 말한다.
우리는 세상을 바꾸려 했어.
그런데 우리가 바뀌어버렸지.

간직하고 있다보면 의외의 순간에 도움이 된다. 언젠가는 나도 커트 와일드처럼 그렇게, 브로치를 누군가에게 건네주고 싶다.

2016년 1월 10일, 데이비드 보위가 사망했다. 본인이 싫어했기 때문에 영화 제목 외의 다른 곳에 그의 음악을 쓸 수는 없었다. 그러나 〈벨벳 골드마인〉은 데이비드 보위의 이야기다. 브라이언 슬레이드는 데이비드 보위이고, 커트 와일드는 이기 팝이다. 맥스웰 데몬은 지기 스타더스트이고 비너스 인 퍼스는 더 스파이더스 프롬 마스인 것이다.

본인이 그토록 좋아하지 않았던 영화이지만, 그럼에도 불구하고 〈벨벳 골드마인〉만큼 데이비드 보위를 기억하고 떠나보내는 데 어울리는 건 없다고 생각한다. 앞서도 말했듯이 이 영화는 브라이언 슬레이드를 모욕하기 위한 것이 아니라 변화와 혼돈, 그리고 그것을 감당해내는 태도에 관한 영화이기·때문이다. 이 글을 쓰려고 〈벨벳 골드마인〉을 다시 보는데 UFO가 하늘을 가르는 장면이 등장하자마자 심장이 툭, 하고 바닥을 굴렀다. 그동안 눈이 부시게 반짝거리며 빛나셨습니다. 이제 고향별로 돌아가서 재미있게 사세요. 안녕히.

엄마,
나의 가장 친애하는 적

4절지 갱지를 가로로 세 번 접고 세로로 두 번 접는다. 접힌 면을 따라 자른다. 이걸 몇 차례 반복한다. 잘린 종이들을 모아 한쪽 면에 스테이플러를 박는다. 스테이플러를 박는 과정에서 정렬이 흐트러질 수 있으니 최대한 체중을 실어 종이가 움직이지 못하게 눌러야 한다. 그리고 그 위에 연필로 이야기를 썼다. 구상한 건 없었다. 그냥 되는대로 썼던 것 같다. 그게 내가 처음으로 쓴 소설이다.

　그때는 '드라큘라'나 『프랑켄슈타인』의 괴물 같은 고딕 호러소설의 주인공들과 웰스의 『우주전쟁』 같은 SF소설에 사로잡혀 있었다. 당연히 '드라큘라'와 『프랑켄슈타인』의 괴물이 등장해서 싸우는 이야기를 썼다. 정확히는 '드라큘라'와 『프랑켄슈타인』의 괴물이 싸우다가 지구를 침략한 외계인에 맞서 협력하는 내용이었다. 쓰는 것과 제본의 순서가 거꾸로 된 것 같지만 변명을 하자면 나는 열 살이었다. 방학이 오면 내내 그런 걸 여러 편 썼다. 여러 편을 썼지만 독자는 늘 한 사람이었다. 엄마였다.

그때는 엄마가 참으로 거대한 사람이었다. 이걸 써서 엄마에게 읽어주고, 엄마가 재미있다고 말해주는 걸 듣는 게 세상에서 가장 중요한 일이었다. 그리고 엄마는 늘 재미있게 들어주었다. 마지막으로 쓴 건 〈터미네이터 2〉를 보고 깊은 감명을 받아서 썼던 〈터미네이터 3〉였다. 기체 터미네이터가 등장하는데 화산으로 끌고 가서 증발시킨다. 이미 기체인데 어떻게 증발시키는지에 관한 과학적 검증 과정은 없었다. 나중에 고쳐 쓸 법도 했지만 당시 아버지와 다투고 난 직후였던 엄마가 내 소설에 심드렁한 반응을 보여 너무 큰 충격을 받고 소설 쓰는 일을 집어치웠다. 아마 이건 엄마도 모를 거다.

다시 말하지만 그녀는 내게 정말 거대한 사람이었다. 사춘기가 오기 전까지는 감히 대적할 엄두를 내지 못했다. 아주 어렸을 때는 장난감을 사달라 졸랐고 조금 크고 나서는 책을 사달라 졸랐고 너는 왜 만날 똑같은 옷만 입고 다니냐는 놀림을 당한 이후에는(픽 더 8학군) 옷을 사달라 졸랐지만 한 번 안 된다는 말을 듣고 나면 속만 상하지 뭘 어찌할 방도가 없었다.

엄마가 책을 사주지 않을 때가 가장 서러웠다. 사실 따지고 보면 내가 책 없이 살지 못하는 아이가 된 건 엄마 탓이기 때문이다. 정확한 나이가 기억나지 않을 만큼 어렸을 때 엄마가 '이야기 성서'라는 걸 몇 권 사왔다. 그런데 그걸 아버지랑 상의하지 않고 산 모양이었다. 아버지는 상의하지 않고 뭔가를 사는 걸 싫어했다. 몇 번 큰소리가 오고간 이후 엄마는 장롱 안 깊숙이 책을 숨겨두었다. 그리고 아버지가 없을 때만 읽으라고 신신당부했다. 학교를 마치고 돌아와 아버지가 퇴근하기 전까지만 읽을 수 있었기 때문에 내게 책을 읽는다는 건 늘 큰 일탈이었다. 해선 안 되는 일이었고 가슴이 콩닥콩닥 뛰는 일이었다. 초인종 소리만 나면 후다닥 책을 치워 장롱에 집어넣고 현관으로 뛰어나갔다. 게다가 내용도 만날 신이 화를 내고 벌을 내리고 멀쩡한 남의 아들을 제물로 내놓으라 하고 그걸 진짜로 하나 안 하나 간을 보면서 애정투쟁을 하지를 않나, 사람들을 싹 다 잡아 죽이니 신명이 났다. 그뒤로 나는 내내 책에 미쳐 살았다.

언젠가 한번은 엄마 지갑에 손을 댔다. 그걸 엄마가 알았다. 엄마는 아무 말도 하지 않았다. 바로 나갈 채비를 하더니 나를 붙잡고 터미널 앞 파출소로 끌고 갔다. 그리고 파출소에 들어가 자수를 하라고 말했다. 자수를 하라니. 그 사람 많이 오가는 광장의 파출소 앞에서 나는 설마 그냥 겁만 주는 거겠지, 생각하고 그냥 서 있었다. 그러다 장난이 아니라는 걸 깨닫고 울기 시작했다. 나는 그날 거기 네 시간 동안 서서 울다가 간신히 엄마의 용서를 받고 은촛대를 받은 장발장의 심정이 되어 집으로 돌아갔다. 지금도 고속버스터미널 앞에는 겁이 나서 잘 가지 못한다.

그렇게 엄마는 늘 거대했다. 두 형제를 혼자 맡아 키우게 되면서 그녀는 더 커지고 강해졌다. 그러다 대학교에 들어가고 독립하면서 엄마의 거대함이 희미해졌다. 군대를 다녀오고 졸업을 하고 취직을 하면서 더욱 그렇게 되었다. 나는 가족끼리 서로 폐 끼치지 않고 살면 그게 최고라고 생각했다. 그래서 왕래도 없었다. 연락도 잘 받지 않았다. 더이상 엄마는 거대하지 않았다.

지난 정권, 촛불집회가 한창이던 어느 날 나는 광장 위에 있었다. 밤이었다. 그날은 집회 규모가 꽤 컸다. 나는 혼자였다. 당시 촛불집회의 쉼터 같은 역할을 했던 광화문 앞의 프랜차이즈 카페 앞에 서서 휴대폰을 들여다보고 있었다. 그때 누가 뒤에서 내 팔을 꽉 움켜잡았다. 나는 깜짝 놀라서 돌아보았다. 그건 내가 살면서 경험한 것 중에 가장 현실 같지 않은 순간이었다.

엄마가 웃으면서 서 있었다.

엄마는 하도 뭐가 문제라고 하길래 한번 나와봤다고 말했다. 누가 들으면 요 앞에 사는 사람이 작은 집회 구경 나온 줄 알겠지만 사람들은 종로를 가득 메울 만큼 많았고 엄마는 수원에 살았다. 나를 어떻게 찾았냐고 물었더니 그냥 보이길래 잡았다고 말했다. 기가 막혔다. 그때 기억을 되짚어보면 엄마는, 엄마는 작았다. 엄마는 작고 나이들고 약했다. 나는 화를 냈다. 아직 택시 할증 안 붙었으니까 빨리 집으로 돌아가라고 말했다. 그리고 엄마를 두고 내 갈 길을 갔다. 왜 그랬는지 잘 모르겠다. 지금 생각해보면 나는 내가 어딘가에 기고한 글을 읽고 여기 나온 것이 분명한 엄마를 보는 게 고통스러워서 도망쳤던 것 같다. 어쩌면 그냥 작고 나이들고 약한 사람이 여기 있는 게 싫었던 것인지도 모르겠다. 나는 엄마가 그렇게 작은 줄 그때 처음 알았다.

큰일은 그다음에 벌어졌다. 청계천을 가운데 두고 빌딩 뒤쪽으로 돌아가는데 함성이 크게 들리고 난리가 났다. 진압이 시작된 것이다. 사람들이 쓰러지고 개중에는 다치는 사람도 보였다. 엄마는 전화를 받지 않았다. 건물 사이를 이잡듯이 뒤지고 다녔다. 진압이 소강 상태에 이르렀지만 엄마는 여전히 전화를 받지 않았다. 주저앉아서 기계적으로 통화버튼을 누르고 있었다. 수신음 소리가 뚝 끊기더니 엄마 목소리가 들렸다. 나는 반사적으로 소리를 빽 질렀다. 엄마는 하도 시끄러워서 전화 온 줄 몰랐다고 말했다. 그리고 집에 들어가는 중이라고 했다. 나는 화가 나서 바로 전화를 끊어버렸다. 이후로 많은 시간이 흘렀지만 그날 일이 종종 떠오른다. 엄마가 너무 작았다.

그녀는 한때 세상에서 가장 거대한 사람이었다. 그러나 지금은 내가 아는 이들 가운데 가장 작고 약한 사람이다. 이런 변화를 어떻게 받아들여야 하는지 나는 아직도 잘 모르겠다. 엄마 앞에서 어떻게 행동해야 하는지, 어떤 표정을 지어야 하는지도 잘 모르겠다. 엄마 생각을 하면 나는 늘 조금 울고 싶어진다. 그렇다면 엄마 무릎 위에서 울고 싶다. 하지만 나는 엄마 앞에서 울지 못한다.

치명적인
얼굴

잊을 수 없는 얼굴이 있다. 오래전 일이다. 자정이 넘도록 잠이 오지 않아 TV를 틀었다. 다이얼을 돌려 채널을 맞추다 2번에 가서 시선이 멈추었다. 여자인지 남자인지 가늠할 수 없는 누군가가 거기 있었다. 얼굴 가득 두껍게 분칠을 하고 빨갛다못해 검정에 가까운 립스틱을 칠한 채 엄청나게 큰 두 눈과 입을 껌벅이며 화면을 가득 메우고 있었다. 그가 노래를 부르며 춤을 추었다. 그렇게 생긴 사람은 처음 보았다. 그런 목소리도 처음 들었다. 게다가 자꾸만, 브라운관 너머의 나를 정면으로 바라보았다. 영화 속 인물이 왜 상대역을 보지 않고 내 쪽을 바라보며 말을 하고 윙크를 하는지 알 수가 없었다. 주인공뿐만이 아니었다. 그 영화를 이루고 있는 모든 것들이, 이상했다. 이상했다, 라는 말 이외에 저 모든 광경을 표현할 수 있는 단어란 존재하지 않았다.

아마 내 또래가 90년대 초반에 이 영화를 봤다면 그 경로가 대개 이와 비슷할 것이다. 〈록키 호러 픽쳐 쇼〉였다. 처음에는 신기해서 지켜보았다. 제목도 내용도 장르도 이게 과연 영화이긴 한지도 알지 못했다. 심야에 AFKN에서 포르노를 보았다는 도시 전설이 떠올랐다. 그래서 보는 걸 그만둘 수 없었다. 그런데 갈수록 기분이 좀 이상해졌다. 그러니까 그게 이를테면 뭐랄까, 불온했다. 인류가 봐선 안 되는 걸 보고 있다는 본능적인 두려움 같은 것이었다. 미군이 현관문을 박살내고 들어와 이 영화는 실수로 송출된 것이며 한국의 청소년이 0시 이후 미군 방송을 볼 경우 사살한다고 외칠 것만 같았다. 그러거나 말거나. 영화 내내 거의 한마디도 알아듣지 못했지만 멈출 수가 없었다. 프랭크 박사가 죽음을 맞이하고 영화가 끝났다. 시간이 한참 더 흘러 창을 통해 볕이 스미기 시작하는데 나는 여전히 소파 위에 박혀 있었다. 꼼짝할 수 없었다. 가슴이 저릿한 게 명치 주변에 쥐가 난 것 같았다. 사랑에 빠진 것이다! 이후로 오랫동안 이 영화에 사로잡혀 살았다. 모두가 흉물스럽다고 기겁하는 포스터를 방안 가득 붙여놓고 노래를 외우고 타임워프 춤을 따라 추었다. 그리고 프랭크 박사를 흠모했다. 〈록키 호러 픽쳐 쇼〉는, 프랭크 박사는 그렇게 내 인생을 뒤흔들어놓았다.

잊을 수 없는 얼굴이 있다. 역시 오래전 일이다. 교실마다 칠판 옆의 상단 모서리에 작은 TV가 달려 있었다. 그냥 TV도 아니고 무려 비디오데크가 붙어 있는 비디오비전이었다. 시청각 교육을 위해 전격 설치되었다는 최첨단의 교보재였으나 막상 교육을 위해 이 첨단의 교보재가 활용된 일은 거의 없었다. 시험이 끝나거나 학기 마지막날이 되면 우리는 대여점에서 영화 비디오를 빌려와 선생님의 허락을 구한 뒤 단체관람을 했다. 나는 그렇게 모두 다 같이 한 공간에서 영화를 보는 일이 너무나 즐거웠다. 도서 부장이라는 감투를 쓰고 있다보니 비디오를 빌려오는 일은 대개 내 몫이었고 나는 막중한 사명감을 짊어진 채 영화를 고르는 일에 한 시간 두 시간씩 공을 들이고는 했다.

　　그날 내가 빌려온 영화는 〈피의 피에로〉였다. 무서운 영화를 여럿이 함께 보는 일이 얼마나 즐거운지 알고 있었다. 제목이 너무 마음에 들었다. 원제는 다른 것 같았으나 중요하지 않았다. 학교를 향하는 내내 이 영화를 빨리 함께 보고 싶어 견딜 수가 없었다. 흡사 내가 만든 영화처럼 말이다.

　　숨죽인 50명의 소년 소녀들이 교실 천장 한쪽의 작은 브라운관을 노려보는 가운데 영화가 시작되었다. 'Stephen King's It'이라는 원제가 화면 가득 붉은색으로 빵, 하고 떴다. 그 아래에는 작게 '피의 피에로'라는 자막이 따라왔다. 나는 원제와 출시명이 다른 영화들이 대놓고 대담하게 뻥을 치는 이 순간이 늘 즐거웠다. 제목이 그게 아닌데 뭐가 피의 피에로람 헤헤헤헤헤헤. 화면이 밝아지고 소녀가 등장했다. 작은 세발자전거를 타고 놀고 있었다. 곧이어 집마당의 풍경. 소녀가 기척을 느끼고 어딘가를 바라본다. 이불 빨래들이 가득 널려 있는 공간 너머로 목소리가 들려온다. 누군가 소녀에게 말을 걸고 있다.

광대였다. 대머리에 붉은색 뒷머리가 무성하고 얇은 눈썹과 큰 두 눈, 빨간 코와 주름 너머로 새하얗게 무고해 보이는 웃음이 드러났다. 광대를 보고 소녀가 웃음지었다. 그런데 다음 순간, 달콤한 말을 속삭이던 광대의 입이 커지는가 싶더니 상어 같은 이빨이 드러났다. 광대의 얼굴이 화면 가득 차올랐다. 표정을 가로지르는 그늘이 생겨났다. 눈도 입술도 잔인하게 일그러졌다. 소녀가 비명을 질렀다. 광대의 이빨이 교차되었다. 목젖까지 클로즈업! 50명의 비명이 교실을 채웠다. 전에도 이런 일이 있었다. 그러나 달랐다. 이번에는 나도 같이 놀랐기 때문이다. 저 광대의 얼굴. 어디서도 본 적이 없는 종류의 표정이었다. 영화 내내 광대가 등장할 때마다 기겁을 했다. 급기야 우리 분단 맨 앞줄의 여자아이가 울기 시작했다. 평소에도 잘 울던 애이긴 했지만, 아무튼 나는 당혹감과 미안함, 그리고 광대에 대한 충격으로 거의 가위가 눌린 듯 웅크린 채 영화를 지켜보아야 했다. 광대의 이름은 페니와이즈였다. 이 영화를 몇 번 더 보았다. 원작소설도 읽었다. 가장 좋아하는 책 가운데 하나가 되었다. 그러나 이후로도 영화 버전의 페니와이즈를 볼 때마다 공포에 떨어야만 했다. 무서움을 잘 타지 않는다. 그런데 페니와이즈만은 달랐다. 저런 건 본 적이 없었다. 이후로도 그랬다.

내가 가장 사랑했던 캐릭터와 내가 가장 무서워했던 캐릭터가 모두 한 사람의 배우였다는 걸 알게 된 건 훨씬 나중의 일이었다. 〈록키 호러 픽쳐 쇼〉의 프랭크 박사와 〈피의 피에로〉의 페니

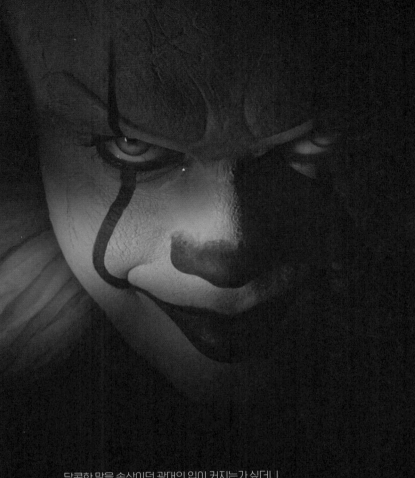

달콤한 말을 속삭이던 광대의 입이 커지는가 싶더니
상어 같은 이빨이 드러났다.
광대의 얼굴이 화면 가득 차올랐다.

<피의 피에로Stephen King's It>(1990)

표정을 가로지르는 그늘이 생겨났다.
눈도 입술도 잔인하게 일그러졌다.
저 광대의 얼굴.
어디서도 본 적이 없는 종류의 표정이었다.

와이즈를 연기한 건 같은 사람이었다. 팀 커리였다.

　이 남자가 배우를 하지 않았다면 대체 무엇을 할 수 있었을까. 어렸을 때 즐겨 읽었던 탐정소설의 캐릭터 가운데 '니주멘소'라는 괴도가 있었다. 에도가와 란포의 소년탐정단 시리즈에 등장하는 '이십면상二十面相' 말이다. 변장의 귀재로 너무 많은 얼굴을 가지고 있어, 심지어 그 자신조차 원래 자신의 얼굴을 잊어버렸다는 이십면상. 내게는 팀 커리야말로 이십면상 그 자체다. 그는 〈록키 호러 픽쳐 쇼〉로 영화에 데뷔한 이래 셀 수 없이 많은 무대와 스크린을 들쑤셔왔다. 그는 단 한 번도 슈퍼스타가 되지는 못했다. 그러나 내게, 또 누군가에게 팀 커리는 할리우드 셀러브리티나 명망 있는 배우 이상의 무언가였다.

　눈동자가 세 개는 있어도 될 법한 큰 눈과 자유자재로 움직이는 안면 근육, 거기에 길게 찢어진 입이 만들어내는 표정은 어느 옷을 입혀놓아도 압도적이고 독보적이며 유일무이한 것이었다. 그래서인지 팀 커리의 얼굴에는 어딘가, 아무래도 보호자와 함께 보면 안 될 것 같은 아슬아슬함이 새겨져 있다. 밑도 끝도 없이 음란하다가도 치명적으로 일그러져 소름끼치는 얼굴이다. 여기에 훌륭한 노래 실력까지(그는 가수이기도 하다). 마성의 아무개라는 식상한 수사는 오로지 팀 커리에게만 허락되어야 마땅하다. 형, 나를 마음대로 해도 좋아, 라고 말하게 만드는 단 한 사람이다.

　물론 그런 게 늘 도움만 되었던 건 아니다. 팀 커리는 팀 버튼 버전의 〈배트맨〉(1989)에서 조커 역할을 하기로 되어 있었

이 남자가 배우를 하지 않았다면
대체 무엇을 할 수 있었을까.
변장의 귀재로 너무 많은 얼굴을 가지고 있어,
심지어 그 자신조차 원래 자신의 얼굴을 잊어버렸다는 이십면상.
내게는 팀 커리야말로 이십면상 그 자체다.

<록키 호러 픽쳐 쇼The Rocky Horror Picture Show>(1975)

다. 그러나 너무 소름 끼친다는 이유로 반려되었다. 외부에는 그가 2순위였으며 본래 잭 니콜슨이 1순위였다고 알려졌다. 대신 영화가 히트한 이후 기획된 TV애니메이션 시리즈에서 조커의 목소리를 맡게 되었다. 그런데 이마저 엎어지고 마크 해밀이 조커 역할에 낙점됐다. 이번에도 이유는 같았다. 목소리가 너무 소름 끼쳐서. 또! 두 번씩이나! 소름끼쳐서 영원히 고통받는 팀 커리! 어찌됐든 〈배트맨〉이 개봉한 이듬해 〈피의 피에로〉로 사람 죽이는 광대 역할을 했으니 미련이 남지는 않을 듯.

2015년 4월 19일은 팀 커리의 69번째 생일이었다. 내가 너무나 사랑했던 고전 게임 '가브리엘 나이트'에서 가브리엘 나이트의 목소리를 형이 연기했다는 걸 얼마 전에야 알았어요. 내 취향을 미친듯이 관통하는 형, 사랑합니다. 생일 축하해요. 날 가져……

커튼은 언뜻 보기에도 축축했고 나는 거기 손을 댈 만큼 젊고 거리낄 것이 없었다. 커튼을 걷자 10평 남짓한 방이 드러났다. 어둡고 습했다. 얼마나 어둡고 습했냐 하면 어느 누구 하나 손을 뻗어 전등불을 켤 엄두를 내지 못할 정도였다. 불을 켜면 어둡고 습한 방의 구석에 그게 뭐가 됐든 아무튼 뭐라도 죽어 자빠져 있을 것만 같았다. 방안 가득 사람들이 앉아 있었다. 대화는 거의 없었다. 이 방의 공기를 조금이라도 덜 마시기 위해서가 아닐까, 나는 생각했다. 나도 자리를 찾아 앉았다. 앉자마자 한쪽 벽이 밝아졌다. 프로젝터가 달구어지는 소리가 났다.

컬트영화 정기상영회였다. 90년대 말에는 그런 게 많았다. 누군가 비디오테이프 하나를 보물 다루듯 꺼내더니 데크에 집어넣었다. 영화가 시작되었다. 이 방의 공기와 너무나 잘 어울리는 풍경이 펼쳐졌다. 차갑게 젖어 있는 영국의 전원이었다. 빨간 우비를 뒤집어쓰고 있는 소녀가 뛰어놀고 있었다. 얼마 지나지 않아 소녀가 물에 빠졌다. 이야기가 이어졌다. 영화가 상영되는 내내 내가 어떤 자세였는지 불편했는지 옆에 누가 있었는지, 그딴 건 하나도 기억나지 않는다. 아까 그 축축한 커튼에 둘둘 말려 눈만 빼꼼히 내밀고 있었던 것 같기도 하고. 영화가 끝나자마자 인사를 나눌 겨를도 없이 정거장까지 한달음에 내달려 시내버스의 맨 뒷좌석에 앉자마자 창문을 열고 그때 들이켰던 걸로 지금까지 호흡하고 있는 게 아닐까 싶을 만큼 깊은숨을 몰아 마셨던 것만은 확실히 기억이 난다. 그걸 뭐라고 설명하면 좋을까. 검고 빨갛고 묵직한 액체가 위치를 가늠할 수 없는 수챗구멍 안으로 영원히 빨려들어가는 것 같은 영화였다. 마술에 걸린 것 같았다.

그게 〈쳐다보지 마라〉였다. 니콜라스 뢰그의 〈쳐다보지 마라〉는 만들어진 지 수십 년이 지난 영화임에도 불구하고 영화광들의 입을 통해 여전히 회자되는 작품이다. 영국 영화 베스트를 꼽는 차트에서는 늘 상위권을 차지한다. 그 영화의 섹스 신은 연출이 아니라 실제 삽입섹스였다느니, 그게 아니고 실제 섹스를 하기는 했는데 그 컷은 감독만 보관하고 있다느니 하는 식의 논란이 있을 때도 언제나 가장 먼저 언급되는 레퍼런스 가운데 하나이기도 하다. 저 영화 속의 섹스로 낳은 아이가 바로 키퍼 서덜랜드라고 말하는 사람을 보기도 했는데 키퍼 서덜랜드는 66년생이다 이 멍청아! 아무튼 그 장면 이야기는 뒤에서 하기로 하고.

영화의 이야기는 이렇다. 뜻하지 않은 사고로 딸이 집 앞의 연못에 빠져 죽는다. 상심한 부부는 남편의 새로운 일터가 베니스로 결정된 차에 함께 그곳에서 머물기로 한다. 베니스에서의 일상이 펼쳐진다. 남편은 오래된 성당을 복원중이다. 아내는 소일을 하며 남편의 곁을 맴돈다. 둘 다 가족의 비극은 가슴 깊은 곳에 묻어두었다. 어느 날 아내는 낯선 할머니 자매를 만난다. 이들 자매는 주인공 부부를 유심히 지켜보던 중이었다. 할머니 자매 중 동생은 눈이 보이지 않는다. 언니는 자신의 동생을 이곳에서 꽤 유명한 심령술사라고 소개한다. 심령술사 동생은 아까 그들 부부의 모습을 유심히 지켜본 데 이유가 있었다고 말한다. 그들 부부 사이에 죽은 딸이 있었다는 것이다. 더불어 남편에게는 <u>스스로 부정함에도 불구하고 영적인 것을 볼 수 있는 힘이 있다</u>고도 말한다. 아내는 자매의 말에 빠져든다. 그리고 딸의 영혼이 그들 부부를 보살피고 있다고 믿는다. 남편은 시큰둥할 뿐이다.

이후 남편은 자꾸 이상한 모습을 목격하게 된다. 골목에서, 사진 속에서, 뜻하지 않은 곳들에서 빨간 우비를 입은 작은 소녀가 보이는 것이다. 남편은 이를 이상하게 생각하지만 아내에게 말하지는 않는다. 이 와중에 아내는 심령술사 동생으로부터 "당신의 딸이 지금 당장 베니스를 떠나라고 말하고 있다"는 이야기를 전해 듣고 불안을 느낀다. 그때 영국에서 비보가 전해진다. 하나 남은 자식인 아들이 작은 사고를 당해 진찰을 받고 있다는 것이다. 아내는 서둘러 영국으로 떠난다. 홀로 남은 남편은 일터로 향하던 중 검은 옷을 입은 아내가 예의 심령술사 자매와 함께 배를 타고 가는 모습을 목격한다. 안 그래도 심령술사 자매를 불신하고 있던 남편은 그들이 아내를 유괴했다고 믿게 되어 수사를 의뢰한다. 그러나 아내는 영국에 있었고 남편은 자신의 착각으로 심령술사 자매가 불편한 일을 겪게 된 것을 미안해한다. 수사당국에 구류되어 있던 심령술사 동생을 집에 데려다준 남편은 밤길을 걷던 중 다시 한번 빨간 우비를 입은 소녀를 목격한다. 남편은 소녀를 쫓아간다. 남편의 뒤를, 이제 막 베니스에 도착한 아내가 뒤쫓는다. 숨바꼭질 같은 추격이 이어진다. 그리고 마침내 충격적인 결말.

〈쳐다보지 마라〉가 지금 이 시점에서도 여전히 새롭게 느껴지는 이유는 특유의 편집 때문이다. 이 영화의 편집은 그 호흡이 대단히 묘하다. 이 영화에서는 꽤 많은 양의 몽타주가 등장한다. 서로 연관이 없는 컷들이 빠른 호흡으로 교차편집되어 있다. 기본적으로 이 영화의 몽타주는 진실에 기반하지 않는다. 사실을 보여주는 것이 아니라 불안과 혼돈에 기반하고 있다. 이를테면 어떤 영화의 주인공이 상념에 젖어 있는 컷을 상상해보자. 다음 컷은 바닥에 있는 작은 가방 하나를 비춘다. 다시 주인공을 보여주는 컷으로 돌아온다. 일반적인 경우 이와 같은 편집에서 관객은 주인공이 지금 어딘가에 놓여 있는 저 가방에 대한 생각을 하고 있다고 여기게 된다. 혹은 주인공은 모르고 있지만 가방 안에 폭탄이 들어 있으며 이것이 곧 폭발할 것이기 때문에 아무 조치 없이 그저 생각에만 빠져 있는 주인공을 바라보며 초조함을 느끼게 될 것이다. 〈쳐다보지 마라〉에서 그런 일반적인 형태의 몽타주는 찾아볼 수 없다. 감독은 순전히 관객의 오해와 착각을 만들어내기 위해 컷을 이어붙인다. 아예 존재하지 않고 순전히 주인공의 상상 속에서만 존재하는 가방을 보여주며 그것이 실제하는 것마냥 관객마저 주인공의 혼돈 속으로 유도하는 것이다. 즉, 이 영화는 컷과 컷의 논리적인 연결을 통해 관객의 불안과 착각을 생산해내지 않는다. 이 영화 자체가 불안과 착각이다.

이 영화가 유명해지는 데 결정적인 기여를 한 저 섹스 장면에 대해 이야기해보자. 나는 도널드 서덜랜드를 너무나 좋아한다. 미드 〈24〉의 잭 바우어 캐릭터를 사랑하지만 그 역할을 연기한 키퍼 서덜랜드를 애정하는 것의 곱절 이상으로 그의 아버지에 심취해 있다. 도널드 서덜랜드는 수없이 많은 영화에서 다양한 역할을 연기해왔다. 그 대부분이 주연보다는 조연이었고 또한 악역이었다. 개인적으로 법칙 같은 것을 만들어낸 게 있는데 도널드 서덜랜드 비중의 법칙이라고. 그가 나오는 영화는 일단 재미있다. 그리고 그가 나오는 분량이 많으면 많을수록 '정말' 재미있다. 그렇게 좋아하는 배우다. 그럼에도 불구하고 딱히 도널드 서덜랜드의 알몸을 보고 싶지는 않다. 나와 같은 생각을 가진 관객에게 불행한 일이지만, 〈쳐다보지 마라〉에서는 도널드 서덜랜드의 알몸이 정말 오랫동안 등장한다. 얼마나 긴 시간 동

<쳐다보지 마라Don't Look Now>(1973)

이 영화는 컷과 컷의 논리적인 연결을 통해
관객의 불안과 착각을 생산해내지 않는다.
이 영화 자체가 불안과 착각이다.

안 자세히 나오는지, 도널드 서덜랜드 자신보다 이 영화의 관객이 그의 몸에 대해 더 잘 알게 될 것이다. 그뿐만이 아니다. 줄리 크리스티의 알몸 또한 그렇다(이 부분에 대해선 불만이 없다). 둘의 정사 장면은 너무나 현실적이라 도무지 연기라고 믿을 수 없는 수준이다. 이 섹스 장면은 영화의 촬영 첫날 기습적으로 이루어졌다. 원래 대본에 없었다. 그런데 영화 속 부부의 대화가 거의 논쟁뿐이라 감독이 순간적으로 떠올린 아이디어였다. 줄리 크리스티는 본래 일정에 없었던 섹스 장면을 주문받고 경악했다. 그렇게 정사 장면이 촬영되었고, 이게 다음날 아침 부부가 나갈 채비를 하고 집밖으로 나서기까지의 과정과 교차편집으로 구성되면서(벗고-입는 컷들의 조화) 그 분량이 엄청나게 길어졌다. 논란은 길었고 답변은 지체되었다. 도널드 서덜랜드는 21세기 들어서야 그것이 실제 성교가 아니었다고 해명했다.

최근 〈쳐다보지 마라〉의 리메이크 소식이 전해졌다. 나는 이 영화가 가지고 있는, 그 믿을 수 없이 강력한 마술적인 기운이 리메이크된 영화에서 재현될 수 있으리라 도무지 상상할 수 없다. 어떤 영화는 굳이 돈을 들여 복기하기보다 그저 원전을 다시 한번 꺼내어 관람하는 게 비교할 수 없이 더 나은 경우가 있는 법이다. 나는 이 리메이크에 반대한다.

불온하다

감독은 자신의 말을 신뢰하지 않는 자에게 꽤 오랫동안 시달린 게 틀림없다. 그렇지 않다면 믿어주지 않은 사람들에게 이토록 큰 벌을 내리는 영화를 만들지는 않았으리라. 〈곡성〉은 믿음에 관한 영화다.

　마을에 이유를 알 수 없는 살인사건들이 잇따라 벌어진다. 가해자들은 범죄를 저지르기 직전에 하나같이 피부병을 앓고 귀신에 들린 것 같은 행동을 했다. 주인공은 경찰이다. 얼마 전부터 마을에 일본에서 왔다는 정체불명의 사내가 출몰한다. 일본인에 관한 좋지 않은 소문이 많다. 주인공은 이 일본인이 사건과 관련이 있을 것이라는 심증을 갖는다. 그러다 주인공의 딸이 피부병과 귀신 들림 증상을 보이기 시작한다. 주인공은 다급해진

감독은 자신의 말을 신뢰하지 않는 자에게
꽤 오랫동안 시달린 게 틀림없다.
그렇지 않다면 믿어주지 않은 사람들에게
이토록 큰 벌을 내리는 영화를
만들지는 않았으리라.
<곡성>은 믿음에 관한 영화다.

<곡성> [2016]

다. 주인공은 일본인을 찾아가 마을을 떠나라고 협박한다. 딸을 구하기 위해 용하기로 소문난 박수무당이 마을에 도착한다.

〈곡성〉은 다 보고 나서도 꽤 많은 수수께끼를 남기는 영화다. 황정민이 돈벌이를 위해 악령을 불러들인 것인가, 아니면 같은 미놀타 카메라를 사용하고 훈도시를 입는 둘이 처음부터 협력한 것인가, 왜 곡성 지킴이 천우희는 일본인을 귀신으로 단정지으면서도 주인공에게 죄 없는 사람을 의심해서 죽게 만들었다고 말했나.

주어진 상황만 가지고 판단할 때 딸을 해한 건 일본인이 아니라 황정민이며 굿판 대결은 편집이 그렇게 되어 있을 뿐 서로 다른 대상을 향한 굿이었다는 것, 딸을 해함으로써 주인공이 일본인에 대한 증오를 폭발시키게(미끼를 '삼키게') 황정민이 의도했다는 것, 일본인과 황정민은 같은 종류의 수련을 받은 것인지는 몰라도 어찌됐든 동일한 방식으로 영을 수집하는 악행을 저지르고 있고 황정민은 주인공의 영을 확보하고 일본인은 끝내 악마로 각성하는 데 성공한다는 것 정도로 정리할 수 있겠다. 그러나 〈곡성〉에서 이와 같은 사실관계를 정리하는 작업은 관객의 사후 유희를 제외하면 별 의미가 없다. 이것은 모두 애초 감독이 의도하고 의뭉스럽게 흩뿌려놓은 이야기다. 결국 어떻게 생각하든 상관없다는 태도의 결과물인 것이다. 이 영화를 만든 사람의 비전이 집중력 있게 주력해서 보여주고자 하는 건 오로지 곡성 지킴이 천우희의 말을 믿지 못하고 정황에 현혹되어 잘못된 판단을 내리는 주인공의 선택이다. 그리고 주인공은 되돌릴 수 없는 파국적 결말을 맞는다. 가혹하다.

믿음에 관련해 이 영화는 시작부터 끝까지 기독교 인용을 꽤 많이 하는 편이다. 예수가 죽음에서 부활한 후 제자들이 의심하자 이를 꾸짖는 대목을 직접적으로 인용하고 악마로 각성해 부활한 일본인이 성흔을 드러내면서 사제를 희롱하며 천우희는 닭이 세 번 울 때까지, 라는 조건을 달아 상대의 믿음을 시험대에 올린다. 그러나 보지 않고도 믿을 것을 종용하고, 또 그것을 받아들이는 건 인간에게 너무 버거운 일이다. 그런 의미에서 볼 때 〈곡성〉이 보여주는 비극은 선택의 문제라기보다 인간에게 애초에 내재된 한계로부터의 어쩔 수 없는 결말에 가깝다.

〈곡성〉에서 배우들의 연기는 곽도원부터 김환희에 이르기까지 균질하고 흠잡을 데가 없다. 현장에서 잘 조율된 결과물이라는 티가 많이 난다. 구니무라 준의 존재감은 각별하다. 원안대로 기타노 다케시였다면 더 좋지 않았을까 생각해보았으나 끝까지 보고 생각을 고쳤다. 그중에서도 황정민이 대단하다. 이건 기록될 만한 연기다. 역할 때문에 그저 밖으로 내지르는 장면들이 먼저 눈에 들어오겠지만 영화가 진공 상태에 빠졌을 때마다 디테일을 채워주는 건 거의 다 황정민이다. 영리한 배우다. 분량과 상관없이 말이다. 〈죠스〉에도 정작 상어는 몇 분밖에 나오지 않는다.

영화를 보면서 오컬트 한일전, 조선 〈컨저링〉 같은 우스개를 몇 가지 떠올렸지만 금방 지워버렸다. 〈곡성〉은 장르적 소재를 다루면서도 기존 관객에게 익숙할 만한 장르적 해법으로 이야기를 풀어나가는 대신 상황의 현실적인 면모와 일상성을 강조하기 때문이다. 〈곡성〉은 살인과 영적 능력, 귀신, 귀신 들림, 엑소시즘, 살아 있으면서도 죽은 사람, 위악적일 정도로 많은 성경 인용, 샤머니즘 등의 장르적인 소재를 엄청나게 쏟아낸다. 그러나 이 영화를 본 사람들 가운데 누구도 같은 종류의 소재를 다룬 호러영화를 본 것 같은 느낌을 〈곡성〉에서 받지는 못했을 것이다. 이를테면 〈컨저링〉과 〈곡성〉은 유사한 갈등 양상을 보여주지만 구조와 분위기는 완전히 정반대를 향하고 있다는 이야기다.

즉 이 영화에서 공포의 순간은 관객이 예상할 만한 순간에 예상할 만한 방식으로, 그러니까 장르적인 공식 안에서 운용되기보다 극중 현실 안에 그냥 '발생되어' 있다. 나는 악이 어떤 사연과 이유를 가지고 탄생하는 게 아니라 그냥 발생하는 것이라는 생각을 가지고 있다. 내가 꽤 좋아하는 괴담의 마지막에서 "대체 왜 나냐"는 희생자의 절규 앞에 귀신은 이렇게 말한다. "그냥." 그런 종류의 우연과 무작위성이야말로 공포를 배가시킨다. 아귀가 딱 들어맞는 설명은 음모론이나 꾸며낸 이야기 속에서만 존재하지, 대개의 경우 현실은 그렇지 않기 때문이다. 기껏 쌓아올린 서스펜스와 공포를 마지막에 설명 가능한 사연을 통해 스스로 허물어버리는 영화들을 수없이 많이 보아왔다.

〈곡성〉이 장르적인 소재들을 일상의 맥락 위에 별 이상할 것 없다는 식으로 포섭하는 태도는 60~80년대 한국 공포영화 혹은 구로사와 기요시 영화의 공기와 닮아 있다. 구로사와 기요시 영화에서 악은 공포를 만들어내기 위한 장치가 아니라 그냥 영

나는 악이 어떤 사연과 이유를 가지고
탄생하는 게 아니라
그냥 발생하는 것이라는 생각을 가지고 있다.

<곡성>(2016)

내가 꽤 좋아하는 괴담의 마지막에서
"대체 왜 나냐"는 희생자의 절규 앞에
귀신은 이렇게 말한다.
"그냥."

화 속 현실 안에 스며들어 있고, 그렇기 때문에 별다른 무대장치나 효과 없이 귀신이나 살인이 등장해 영화의 분위기를 묘하게 정적으로, 그러나 참을 수 없이 무섭게 만든다. 〈곡성〉은 우리에게 익숙한 지방색과 배우들의 탈장르 연기를 통해 일상성을 구축하면서 그 위로 초현실적인 이미지들을 아무렇지 않게 배치하여 구로사와 기요시 영화에서 보았던 효과들을 폭발적으로 배가시킨다.

그래서 〈곡성〉은 시종일관 매우 이상한 공기를 뿜어낸다. 이건 매우 이상한 영화다. 지금이라서 더욱더 이상한 영화다. 한국 영화가 급속하게 산업화되고 어느 정도 예측 가능한 시장적 면모를 갖추면서 2000년대 중후반 이후로 사라졌던, 바로 그 불온하고 기이한 에너지가 고스란히 발견된다. 이러한 에너지를 계속 가지고 작업할 수 있는 감독은 지금 한국에 몇 명 남아 있지 않다. 이 '불온하고 기이한' 영화가 평단과 관객으로부터 꽤 많은 지지를 이끌어낸 현상이야말로 〈곡성〉과 관련해 벌어진 가장 이상한 일임에 틀림없다. 거기에는 여러 가지 이유가 있겠으나, 최근 수년째 서로 크게 별다를 것 없는 기획성 영화들이 한국 영화의 팔 할을 차지하고 있다는 피로도와 그에 대한 반작용이 낳은 결과라고 생각한다. 무언가 같은 영화를 보고 그것의 이상하고 불온하며 무시무시한 지점에 관해 갑론을박하고 왁자지껄하게 떠드는 즐거움을 우리는 너무 오래 잊고 살았다.

밤이었고 나는 소파 위에 무너져 있었다. 전화가 왔다. 매니저였다. 면회를 올 수 있느냐는 이야기였다. 나는 바로 채비를 하고 병원으로 향했다. 가는 내내 차 안에서 마음이 복잡했다. 면회를 오라는 건 면회를 할 수 있을 만큼 상태가 호전되었다는 의미일까, 아니면 마지막 인사를 준비하라는 걸까. 전자일 것이다. 형이 쓰러진 이후 나는 단 한 번도 그의 회복을 의심해본 일이 없었다. 그렇게 벌떡 일어나 이 모든 게 촌극으로 기억되리라 믿어 의심치 않았다.

병원에 도착했다. 매니저가 나타났다. 안 그래도 가냘픈 사람인데 눈자위가 함정처럼 파여 있었다. 그녀는 형에게 차도가 있다고 말했다. 혈압이 올라갔다는 것이다. 나는 그럴 줄 알았다고 대답했다. 중환자실의 형은 수없이 많은 튜브들에 연결된 채 힘없이 누워 있었다. 거짓말처럼 벌떡 일어나 농담이라고 말할 것 같아 몇 번을 움찔했다. 며칠 못 본 사이에 얼굴이 작아져 있었다. 형 퇴원할 때는 살 확실히 빠져 있겠다고 농을 건넸다. 매니저가 형 옆으로 다가가 앉았다. 이전 병원에서 의식 있을 때 내 이야기를 했다며 여기 왔으니 눈떠보라고 말을 건넸다. 형은 미동조차 하지 않았다. 베개맡에서는 계속해서 형의 노래들이 재생되고 있었다. 나는 그의 얼굴 가까이 다가갔다. 그대로 귀에 대고 몇 마디를 했다. 형이 깨어나면 두고두고 나를 놀려먹을 수 있는 이야기였다. 다음날 형은 세상에서 영영 모습을 감추었다.

형은 곧잘 철 지난 농담을 길게 늘어놓고는 했다. 나는 그런 그를 무척 구박했다. 구박하는 재미가 있는 형이었다. 구박을 하면 소녀같이 부끄러워했다. 그게 보고 싶어 더 구박한 적도 있다. 솔직히 정말 재미는 없었다. 서로 닮은 점이 많았다. 형이 말하기 전에도 내심 알고 있었다. 그래도 형이 그렇게 말할 때는 싫은 기색을 냈다. 괜히 그랬다. 형의 방송 복귀작에 게스트로 다녀왔다. 나는 형에게 무조건 여기서 망가져야 사는 거라고 말했다. 녹화 내내 놀려먹었다. 재미있었다. 그렇게 놀려먹은 게 형을 마주한 마지막이었다. 그렇게 놀려먹은 게 말이다.

끝나고 나오는 길에 형이 1차 체중 감량 끝나는 날 양꼬치를 먹으러 가자고 했다. 그러다 중간에 문자를 보내왔다. 킹크랩으로 메뉴를 바꾸자고 했다. 나는 그러자고 했다. 형은 문자를 보내고 다음날 쓰러져 입원했다. 그는 약속을 지키지 않았다. 며칠 전 꿈을 꾸었다. 형이 사람들 앞에서 내게 면박을 주었다. 왜 전화하고 문자하고 오버냐며 소리를 질렀다. 사람들이 막 웃었다. 나는 얼굴이 달아올라 부풀리지 말라고, 전화한 적 없고 문자만 하지 않았냐고, 그러게 왜 나이 먹고 사람 걱정시키냐고 또 구박을 했다. 아침에 일어나서 나는 형이 금방 일어나겠거니 낙관했다.

오래전 형이 결혼식 축가를 불러주었다. 〈일상으로의 초대〉였다. 형은 노래를 부르는 동안 몇 번이고 음이탈을 했다. 나는 그걸 가지고 두고두고 놀려먹었다. 부끄러웠다고 말했다. 사실이 아니었다. 나는 여태 단 한 번도 그렇게 아름다운 노래를 들어본 적이 없다. 내내 그걸 흥얼거렸다고 말해주지 못했다. 목덜미를 잡아쥐듯 굵고 낮은 저음으로 시작하던 재미없는 농담들이 자꾸 귀에 걸려 떠오른다. 나는 절대 울지 않을 거다. 나는 결코 울고 싶지 않다. 구박을 하고 싶다. 다시 한번 형에게 구박을 하고 싶다. 그러나 이제는 더이상 그럴 수가 없다. 구박을 하고 싶어도 그럴 수가 없다니 너무 폭력적이라 막 얻어맞은 것같이 뺨이 얼얼하다. 친애하는 친구이자 놀려먹는 게 세상 최고로 재미있었던 나의 형 신해철이 세상을 떠났다. 음악을 하는 사람으로서, 남편으로서 부모로서, 그리고 무엇보다 한 사람의 시민으로서 누구보다 충실했던 우리 형 신해철이 세상을 떠났다. 그 또한 다른 사람들과 같이 모순적이었으나 그 모순과 싸워 이기려 끝내 분투하며 스스로를 소진했던 예민한 영혼의 소유자 신해철이 세상을 떠났다.

　　형에게 미처 말하지 못했다. 누구나 쉽게 입에 올릴 수 있는 말인데 그걸 하지 못했다. 형이라서 말하지 못했다. 나라서 말하지 못했다. 간지러워서 하지 못했다. 어리석었다. 해야 할 말을 제때 하지 않고 미루는 일이란 대체 얼마나 한심한가.

　　형 사랑해. 언제까지나 사랑해. 형 사랑한다.

* 이 글은 신해철 유고집 『마왕 신해철』에 수록된 추모 원고이다.

형에게 미처 말하지 못했다.
누구나 쉽게 입에 올릴 수 있는 말인데 그걸 하지 못했다.
형이라서 말하지 못했다.
나라서 말하지 못했다.
간지러워서 하지 못했다.
어리석었다.
해야 할 말을 제때 하지 않고 미루는 일이란
대체 얼마나 한심한가.

형 사랑해. 언제까지나 사랑해. 형 사랑한다.

두 손으로 얼굴을 가리고
우는 사람들

나는 사람들이 우는 건 하나도 슬프지 않은데, 울면서 두 손으로 얼굴을 가리는 모습은 너무 슬퍼서 견딜 수가 없다.

신해철에
관하여

안녕하세요, 신해철입니다.

뭔 소리야. 나는 생각했다. 누구라고요? 신해철이라고요. 그러고 보니 목소리가 닮은 것 같다. 그런데요? 만나서 해야 할 이야기가 있어서요.

그래서 우리는 만났다. 추운 날이었다. 식당에서 만났다. 그를 태운 검정색 차가 도착했다. 우리는 좀 쑥스러웠던 것 같다. 누가 먼저랄 것도 없이 술을 마셔댔다. 둘 사이의 빈 공간을 술로 메우려는 것 같았다. 정작 해야 할 이야기는 거의 하지 못했다. 그는 먼저 취해버렸다. 몸이 전 같지 않다고 말했다. 그를 태운 검정색 차가 떠났다. 뒤늦게 취기가 올라온 나는 그러니까 오늘 뭐 때문에 만난 것이었더라, 생각하면서 집으로 비틀비틀 걸어갔다.

다음날 다시 전화가 왔다. 야 난데, 그러니까 우리가 만나서 해야 할 이야기가 있어서, 여기까지 하고 말하는 사람이나 듣는 사람이나 둘 다 웃음이 터져버렸다. 나는 주소를 받아들고 그가 운영하는 실용음악학원을 향했다. 오래된 책들이 빼곡하게 들어찬 그의 어둡고 음험한 사무실에서, 우리는 하루 만에 다시 만났다. 이후 저 어둡고 음험한 사무실에서 참 많은 일이 있었다. 농을 하고 울고 화를 내고 대개는 별 시답지 않은 이야기들로 밤을 꼬박 새웠다. 이상한 인연이다.

요는 같이 일을 해보자는 것이었다. 『맥심』이라는 잡지가 라이선스 문제로 재창간을 하면서 자신이 편집장을 맡게 되었는데 나보고 수석에디터를 하면서 부편집장 노릇을 해달라고 했다. 경력관리 측면에서 좀 생각해보아야 할 문제였지만 별로 고민하지 않고 그렇게 하자고 했다. 거절하기에는 너무 빨리, 너무 깊게 친해져버렸다.

결과적으로는 좋지 않은 선택이었다. 새벽 2시에 빨리 와달라는 연락을 받고 갔다. 그는 화가 머리끝까지 나 있었다. 편집권이 있는 편집장인 줄 알고 애초 승낙한 것이었는데 알고 보니 그렇지 않았다고 했다. 일종의 항명이 있었고, 이게 대체 무슨 일인지 알아보다가 뒤늦게 얼굴마담이라는 걸 깨달았다는 것이다. 그는 곧 잡지를 그만두었다. 이 사건의 좀더 정확한 경위를 알아보고 싶었지만 관두었다. 내막이 어찌되었든 그가 그만두었으니 나로서도 더 있을 이유가 없었기 때문이다. 그래서 나도 그만두었다.

한동안 소송을 하겠다고 분개하던 그는 금방 평정을 되찾았다. 내 결혼식에 와서 그는 〈일상으로의 초대〉를 불렀다. 노래 중간에 음이탈을 했다. 가뜩이나 성당이라 엄중한 분위기인데 나는 그만 웃음을 터뜨리고 말았다. 그리고 두고두고 그걸 놀려먹었다. 내가 신혼여행 내내 저 목소리의 질감을 떠올리며 노래를 흥얼거렸다는 건 미처 말하지 못했다. 나중에 이야기할 수 있을 거라 생각했던 것 같다. 그건 내가 태어나서 들어본 노래 가운데 가장 아름다운 것이었다.

그리고 어느 날, 그가 사라졌다. 말 그대로 잠적해버렸다. 그가 칩거에 들어간 십수 개월 동안 나는 방송생활을 시작했다. 자주 그가 궁금했다. 그러나 그럴 만한 이유가 있을 거라 생각했다.

그에게 전화가 걸려온 건 늦은 저녁이었다. 통화버튼을 눌렀다. 너 이혼했다며, 이 거지같은 새끼야. 타박을 해야 할 건 이쪽인데 뜻밖의 공격을 받고 나는 그만 더듬거리고 말았다. 그리고 그가 나를 너무 잘 안다는 사실을 떠올렸다. 십수 개월의 시간차가 사라지고 이음매 없이 맞춰졌다.

우리는 동네의 양꼬치 집에서 재회했다. 그는 굉장히 건강해 보였다. 새 앨범이 나올 것이라며 녹음파일을 들려주었다. 실험적인데 대중적이다, 라고 나는 말했다. 실험적인데 대중적이다. 그가 따라 말했다. 그리고 크게 기뻐하며 덧붙였다. 그게 내가 잘하는 거지.

며칠 후 늦은 밤 그가 다시 찾아왔을 때 나는 우리가 처음 만났을 때가 떠올라 굉장히 즐거웠다. 그는 늘 차를 타고 우리집 앞에 와서 나를 싣고 어디론가 떠나고는 했다. 우리는 분당의 그의 집으로 갔다. 형수님과 아이들이 집을 비운 터라 우리는 밤새 술을 마셨다. 그가 칩거하는 동안 했던 개인적인 고민들, 사랑스럽기 짝이 없는 그의 아이들, 내 이혼 이야기, 세상 돌아가는 풍경, 사후세계와 외계인 식민지, 사람들은 그의 친구라고 알고 있지만 사실은 겉 다르고 속 달라 싫어한다는 아무개, 우리가 오해받는 것들, 그럼에도 불구하고 해야만 하는 것들, 야 너는 내가 젊었을 때랑 굉장히 닮았다, 어디 가서 그런 이야기 하지 말어 내가 훨씬 더 잘생겼어, 그런 도무지 초점 없는 대화들을 하다가 다음 날 오후 1시가 되어서야 기절해버렸다.

겨우 술을 깨고 침대에서 일어났을 때 나는 한동안 여기가 어디인지 몰라서 당황했다. 뛰어내리듯이 침대를 벗어나 방문을 열고 나갔다. 형이 등을 보이고 서 있었다. 거기 기둥에 붙어 있는 아이들 사진을 보고 있었다. 그 모습이 이상하게 잘 지워지지 않는다.

의식이 있는 그를 마지막으로 본 건 〈속사정쌀롱〉 촬영장이었다. 같이 촬영을 마치고 나가면서 그는 나흘 뒤에 킹크랩을 먹으러 가자고 했다. 다음날 그는 쓰러졌다. 건강에 이상이 있는 사람이 술약속을 할 리가 없기 때문에 나는 별일이 아닐 거라 낙관했다. 병원을 찾았을 때 그는 의식이 없었다. 매니저의 말로는 중간에 잠깐 의식이 있었고, 나를 찾았다고 했다. 그 와중에 약속을 떠올린 것이었는지 모르겠다. 귀에 대고 몇 번이고 속삭였다. 나 찾았다며, 나 왔어. 나 왔다고. 그러나 그는 다시는 일어나지 못했다.

그의 부고를 듣고 썼던 짧은 글 이후 나는 내가 그에 대한 이야기를 글로 쓸 수 있을 거라 생각하지 않았다. 그것은 갑작스럽고 느닷없으며 앞뒤가 맞지 않는, 옳지 않은 죽음이었다. 그를 떠올리는 건 내게 너무 고통스러운 일이었다. 가끔 그에 대한 이야기가 나올 때면 나는 자리를 피하거나 억지로 다른 생각을 했다. 때마침 다른 일들이 맞물리면서 나는 심각한 우울증을 앓았다. 소중한 사람들이 모두 나를 떠나가려고 작정한 것만 같았다. 침대에 누우면 잠이 오지 않고 천장이 내려앉았다. 그렇게 2년이 지나갔다.

며칠 전 형의 2주기를 맞아 혼자 술을 마셨다. 그리고 그의 트위터 계정을 들어가보았다. 그의 말투가 묻어나는 짧은 글들이 여전히 거기 그대로 있었다. 그 마지막 몇 개월 동안 계속해서 언급되는 내 이름을 발견하고 나는 마음이 내려앉았다. 그리고 그 말들과 대화를 했다.

나는 이제 괜찮은 것 같다.

　누군가에게 신해철은 투사였다. 누군가에게 신해철은 광장의 음악이었다. 누군가에게 신해철은 이제 다시 오지 않을 젊은 시절의 섬광이었다. 누군가에게 신해철은 논객이었으며 누군가에게 신해철은 늦은 밤 이어폰을 통해 울려퍼지던 굵고 낮은 목소리였다. 신해철은 어쩌면 그 모든 것과 무관한 무엇이었다. 그는 그저 마음 약하고 대책 없이 따뜻하며 아이들을 거짓말처럼 사랑하는 아버지였다. 내게 그는 좋은 친구였다. 나도 그에게 좋은 친구였기를 바란다. 형이 보고 싶다. 우리 형이 너무 보고 싶다.

어느 밤,
형의 집에 놀러갔다가 찍은
아이의 그림.
그는 그저 마음 약하고 대책 없이 따뜻하며
아이들을 거짓말처럼 사랑하는 아버지였다.
내게 그는 좋은 친구였다.

질병 같은
남자

늘 헛갈리는 게 있다. 빤한 사실인데도 헛갈린다. 뭐 그런 게 다
들 한두 개씩은 있지 않던가. 나는 언제나 〈페드라〉가 〈싸이코〉
보다 먼저 나온 영화라고 생각해버린다. 히치콕의 〈싸이코〉가
줄스 다신의 〈페드라〉보다 2년 먼저 나왔는데도 말이다. 그래
〈싸이코〉는 1960년이고 〈페드라〉는 1962년이지, 그런데 〈페드
라〉가 〈싸이코〉보다 먼저야, 이런 식이다.

　　앤서니 퍼킨스 때문이다. 〈페드라〉와 〈싸이코〉의 주연은 모
두 앤서니 퍼킨스다. 〈페드라〉에서 앤서니 퍼킨스는 새엄마 페
드라와 사랑에 빠진 아들을 연기한다. 모든 게 망가져버린 그 순
간 앤서니 퍼킨스는 은빛 애스턴 마틴에 몸을 싣고 그리스의 해
변도로를 달리며 바흐의 〈토카타와 푸가 D단조〉를 미친듯이 홍

얼거리고 새엄마의 이름을 비명 지르듯 외치다가 끝내 절벽에 떨어져 죽는다.

문제는 여기서부터다. 내 머릿속에서 앤서니 퍼킨스는 신에게 다시는 엄마를 사랑하지 않겠다고 맹세하고 다시 태어나는 걸 허락받는다. 그래서 다시 태어났는데 이런 씨발, 하필이면 〈싸이코〉의 노먼 베이츠야. 엄마가 베이츠 부인이야. 알고 보니 베이츠 부인도 페드라가 다시 태어난 거야. 결국 페드라의 망령에 사로잡힌 앤서니 퍼킨스는, 아니 노먼 베이츠는 엄마의 수족이 되어 베이츠 모텔을 운영하며 조용히 살아간다. 그리고 어느날 마리온이라는 이름의 금발 여성이 찾아오는데…… 내 머릿속에서 그렇다는 이야기다.

앤서니 퍼킨스라는 이름의 저 배우가 부자연스러울 정도로 긴 팔과 긴 다리를 대기중에 허우적대며 우아하기 짝이 없는 길고 흰 손가락으로 페드라를 만질 때 나는 잠시나마 그녀를 질투했다. 어린 눈으로 보기에도 앤서니 퍼킨스는 아름답고 매혹적이며 어딘가 병적이었다.

어딘가 질병 같은 사내였다. 열이 끓어오르고 고통을 자아내는 질병이 아니라, 별다른 징후나 증상 없이 찾아와 사람을 죽음에 이르게 만드는 질병 같았다. 〈페드라〉에서 자신을 사랑하는 새엄마를 두고 분투하는 알렉시스를 연기할 때도, 〈싸이코〉에서 이미 죽고 없는 엄마에 빙의되어 자신에게 접근하는 여성들을 도살하는 노먼 베이츠일 때도, 〈심판〉에서 인간이라는 자기한계에 부딪혀 자폭할 수밖에 없는 케이를 연기할 때도, 앤서니 퍼킨스는 늘 창백하고 유약하지만 치명적인 공기로 관객을 집어삼켰다. 그러고 보면 앤서니 퍼킨스는 줄스 다신의 〈페드라〉에서 그리스 비극적인 인간형을, 히치콕의 〈싸이코〉에서 프로이트적인 인간형을, 오선 웰스의 〈심판〉에서 카프카적 인간형을 모두 눈부시게 연기해냈다. 이토록 위대한 배우의 전성기가 짧았다는 건, 그리고 〈싸이코〉의 후속편들에 출연해 스스로의 커리어를 갉아먹었다는 건 너무나 안타까운 일이다.

〈페드라〉는 앤서니 퍼킨스가 등장하는 영화 가운데 내가 가장 좋아하는 작품이다. 〈페드라〉는 그리스 신화의 파이드라(이하 영어식 표기 '페드라'로 통일) 비극을 각색한 영화다. 줄스 다신 감독의 아내이기도 한 멜리나 메르쿠리가 페드라를 연기했다. 메르쿠리는 어디까지나 아름답고 훌륭한 배우지만, 페드라 역할로 적합했는지는 의문이다. 아무튼 감독이 아내를 캐스팅하는 일은 법으로 막아야 한다.

페드라 비극은 팜므파탈의 원형으로 손꼽힌다. 그리스 신화에서 페드라는 아테네의 영웅 테세우스의 두번째 아내다. 신화 속 페드라와 에우리피데스의 페드라와 라신의 페드라가 서로 내용이 조금씩 다르다. 골자는 페드라가 테세우스의 아들 히폴리토스에게 사랑을 고백한다는 점이다. 히폴리토스는 새엄마의 구애를 단박에 거절한다. 히폴리토스가 아버지에게 이 사실을 털어놓을까봐 페드라는 전전긍긍한다. 그러다가 남편에게 "당신 아들에게 추행당했다"며 거짓을 고한다. 분노한 테세우스는 아들을 저주하고 추방한다. 히폴리토스는 전차를 몰고 떠나다가

어딘가 질병 같은 사내였다.
열이 끓어오르고 고통을 자아내는 질병이 아니라,
별다른 징후나 증상 없이 찾아와
사람을 죽음에 이르게 만드는 질병 같았다.

〈싸이코Psycho〉(1960)

앤서니 퍼킨스는
늘 창백하고 유약하지만
치명적인 공기로
관객을 집어삼켰다.

절벽에 떨어져 죽는다. 에우리피데스와 라신의 버전에서는 페드라도 자살한다.

영화 〈페드라〉는 무대를 현대의 그리스로 옮겨왔다. 남편은 선박왕이다. 전처와의 사이에서 태어난 아들 알렉시스는 영국에서 유학중이다. 남편은 알렉시스를 그리스로 불러들여 사업을 물려주고 싶어한다. 그래서 아내 페드라를 시켜 알렉시스를 그리스에 돌아오도록 종용하게 만든다. 영국에서 조우한 페드라와 알렉시스는 아무래도 어색하다. 그러나 금방 친숙해진다. 어렸을 때 새엄마 페드라를 미워했던 알렉시스도 지금은 더이상 그렇지 않다. 아니 오히려 아름다운 페드라에게 끌린다. 둘은 사랑에 빠진다. 불같이 사랑에 빠졌던 둘은 다시 현실로 돌아오고 알렉시스는 상처를 받는다. 알렉시스가 그리스에 돌아오자 아버지는 크게 기뻐하며 사업상 정략결혼을 시켜 사업을 물려주려 한다. 그러나 알렉시스를 포기하지 못한 페드라는 이에 반대하며 남편에게 모든 사실을 털어놓는다. 그리고 모두가 비극적인 결말을 맞는다.

신화 속의 페드라는 남편에 대한 공포와 자신의 사랑을 받아주지 않은 아들을 향한 분노로 치명적인 선택을 하는 인물이었다. 영화 속의 페드라는 신화 속의 인물과는 다르다. 영화 속 페드라는 이미 예견되어 있는 파멸에도 불구하고 안락한 미래를 내팽개치며 사랑을 위해 불구덩이 속으로 뛰어드는 인물이다. 그녀는 영화 중반 이후 계속해서 망설이고 고민하고 조금씩 미쳐간다. 그러나 알렉시스가 자신을 여전히 사랑한다는 걸 확인한 이후 조금도 망설이지 않고 세속적인 영락을 포기하며 자기 선택을 실행에 옮긴다. 유감스럽게도 그런 일은 현실에서 잘 벌어지지 않는다. 그런 관점에서 볼 때 영화 〈페드라〉의 페드라는 악녀가 아니라 신념이 있는 캐릭터다. 영화 〈페드라〉를 팜므파탈 영화의 카테고리 안에 두는 건 이치에 맞지 않는 일이다.

　이 영화를 다시 볼 때마다 신경쓰이는 건 앤서니 퍼킨스가 연기하는 알렉시스가 마지막 질주를 위해 은색 애스턴 마틴을 차고에서 끌어내는 순간이다. 얼마 전 아버지가 사준 새 차다. 영화에서 차가 그리스에 도착했을 때 딱 한 번 몰았다. 그런데 차고에서 후진으로 빠져나오는 차를 잘 보면 운전석 쪽 문이 찌그러져 있다. 이토록 아름다운 차의 문이 찌그러져 있다니 볼 때마다 가슴이 아파 솜씨 좋은 덴트 가게를 소개해주고 싶어진다. 대체 어느 틈에 찌그러뜨린 걸까. 그러고 보면 알렉시스가 죽음을 맞이한 건 아버지의 저주 때문도 아니고 포세이돈의 복수 때문도 아니고 페드라의 폭로 때문도 아닌, 그냥 알렉시스가 운전을 잘 못해서일지도 모르겠다. 〈페드라〉를 다시 꺼내보고 나면 마지막 순간 알렉시스가 입이 찢어져라 흥얼거리던 바흐의 〈토카타와 푸가 D단조〉를 반복해서 몇 번이고 듣게 된다. 누구나 그럴 거다. 오리지널 트랙에는 '안녕 요한 세바스찬'이라는 제목으로 수록되어 있다. 좋은 제목이다. 안녕 바흐, 안녕 페드라, 안녕 알렉시스. 안녕.

결혼을
해부하는 남자

아버지는 감독이고 어머니는 각본을 썼다. 누나는 배우다. 대부
는 저 위대한 폴 뉴먼이고 대모는 비명의 여신 제이미 리 커티스
다. 그 자신은 히스 레저의 딸인 마틸다의 대부다. 민주당원이
다. 토비 맥과이어가 〈씨비스킷〉을 찍다가 허리를 다치고 〈스파
이더맨 2〉에서 하차하게 되었을 때 피터 파커 역할을 대신 하기
로 되어 있었다. 내가 그를 처음 본 건 〈도니 다코〉에서였다. 몇
번을 돌려 봤는지 셀 수 없을 정도로 훌륭한 영화였다. 당시 그를
보며 너는 지구에서 애늙은이 역할을 가장 잘 연기하는 배우다,
라고 생각했다. 놀란 건 〈투모로우〉에서였다. 이 빤한 영화에 혼
자 열심히 활기를 불어넣고 있었다. 무엇보다 나보다 한 살밖에
어리지 않은데 2004년도 영화에서 고등학생 역할을 하고 있었

다. 이런 젠장,

제이크 질렌할 이야기다.

제이크 질렌할은 정말 잘생긴 배우다. 속눈썹은 우리집 빗자루로 써도 괜찮을 것 같고, 주워 담을 수 없는 말은 잘 뱉지 않을 것 같은 크기의 입술을 가졌으며, 적당히 좁은 미간은 이 사람의 집중력에 돈을 걸어도 괜찮겠다는 믿음을 갖게 한다. 그런데 그는 정말 그렇게 빤하게 잘생긴 배우의 길을 걷지 않았다. 필모그래피 관리가 잘된 배우다. 인디영화 작업을 게을리하지 않으면서 (그가 인디영화 작업을 일종의 셀러브리티 면피용 트로피 정도로 느슨하게 생각하지 않는다는 건 영화를 보면 금방 알 수 있다) 스스로의 배우 함량을 시험해보기 좋은 장르영화들에 많이 참여했다.

누군가 제이크 질렌할의 필모를 관찰하다가 이런 질문을 던졌다. 이렇게 잘생긴 배우가 왜 로맨스 영화를 많이 찍지 않았을까? 무슨 소리, 그건 〈브로크백 마운틴〉을 떠올리지 않아서 하는 말이다. 〈브로크백 마운틴〉은 그저 그런 로맨스 영화 천 편의 박력을 가진 영화다. 잭 트위스트는 비명에 갔어도 그의 데님셔츠와 에니스의 젖은 눈빛은 우리 마음속에 영원히 남아 있을 것이다. 아이 스웨어.

그의 영화 가운데 가장 좋아하는 영화를 꼽는 건 어려운 일이다. 나는 언제나 가장 좋아하는 무언가, 별점은 몇 개, 이따위 질문이나 작업에 대해 곤란함을 느껴왔다. 그러나 제이크 질렌할이 나온 영화 가운데 단 한 편만 다시 보는 게 허락된다면 답변이 좀 쉬워진다. 나는 두 번 생각하지 않고 〈조디악〉을 볼 거다.

연출과 촬영, 이야기의 짜임새, 주역부터 단역에 이르기까지 더할 나위 없이 훌륭하게 조율된 연기톤, 일생에 한 번 먹을까 말까 한 굉장한 상찬 같은 영화인 〈조디악〉에서 제이크 질렌할은 주인공 로버트 그레이스미스를 연기했다. 〈조디악〉에서 배우로서 가장 큰 기량을 보여준 건 마크 러팔로와 로버트 다우니 주니어다. 그러나 '대체 왜 저렇게까지 필사적으로 범인이 누군지 알아내야만 하는가?'라는 관객의 질문—조디악이라는 이야기의 목적에 합당한 답을 안겨주는 건 제이크 질렌할의 연기다. 이 보이스카우트 같은 인물은 반드시 범인을 찾아내 그와 눈을 맞춰봐야만 자기 인생이 낭비되지 않았음에 안도할 수 있는 것이다.

제이크 질렌할의 2015년작 〈데몰리션〉은 흥미로운 영화다. 일단 준수한 웰메이드다. 만듦새가 도발적이지 않되 깔끔하기 짝이 없다. 누가 보더라도 아 참 잘 만들었다. 이쯤에서 이렇게 저렇게 해서 마무리되겠구나, 하고 마음 푹 놓고 무장해제할 수 있게 만든다. 다만 이 이야기가 관객의 저마다 다른 삶과 만났을 때 자아내는 감회란 결코 빤하지 않을 것이다. 이 영화는 무언가를 자꾸 돌아보게 만든다.

주인공은 아내와 함께 차를 타고 가던 중 사고를 당한다. 주인공은 살아남았지만 아내가 죽었다. 그런데 이상하다. 주인공은 도무지 슬픔을 느낄 수 없다. 아내의 죽음보다는 병원의 자판기가 돈을 먹고 초콜릿을 뱉어내지 않은 것에 대해 더 문제의식을 느낀다. 장례식장에서도 슬픈 표정을 만들어보려고 거울 앞에서 노력해보지만 잘 되지 않는다. 사람들은 그런 그를 보며 그저 충격이 커서 그렇겠거니 생각한다. 그러나 그게 아니라 정말 슬프지 않은 것이다. 이후부터 주인공의 행동이 좀 이상해진다. 그는 주변의 물건들을 분해해보기 시작한다. 그의 논리를 따르자면 '무언가를 고치기 위해서는 일단 전부 분해한 다음 뭐가 중요한지 알아내야 하기' 때문이다. 동시에 주인공은 자판기 회사 고객센터 앞으로 자기 심정이나 근황을 편지에 써 보내기 시작한다.

주인공이 슬프지 않은 이유는 아내의 죽음 이전에 그들의 관계가 이미 죽어 있었기 때문이다. 이미 관계가 끝난 상태에서 관계가 지속되다가 아내의 죽음으로 물리적인 관계가 끝이 났다. 그러자 비로소 이 관계가 이미 예전에 끝나 있었다는 걸 실감하게 되는 것이다. 주인공이 이해할 수 없는 건 '왜' 그들의 관계가 틀어지고 잘못되어 끝나 있었냐는 점이다. 그래서 그는 하나씩 주변의 물건들을 분해하기 시작한다. 수사적인 의미에서의 분해가 아니라 정말 말 그대로 물건을 분해한다. 큰 틀에서 볼 때, 그는 그의 결혼을 분해하고 있다. 다 분해하고 나면 대체 뭐가 잘못되었던 건지 발견할 수 있을 것 같아서다. 그리고 놀랍게도, 주인공은 무엇이 문제였는지 발견하기에 이른다.

이 영화의 주인공이 삶을 이해하고 받아들이는 태도는 보기 드물게 솔직하다. 대개 사람은 어떤 상황을 맞이했을 때 학습된

<데몰리션Demolition>(2015)

대개 사람은 어떤 상황을 맞이했을 때 학습된 대로 행동한다.
슬픈 일이 생기면 이렇게, 기쁜 일이 생기면 저렇게 한다.
그렇게 행동하는 게 타인의 감정을 불편하게 하지 않고
상황을 빠르게 무마하기 좋기 때문이다.

그런데 주인공은 학습된 대로 행동하지 않고
자기 기분이 왜 이런지 무엇이 문제였는지
찾아내길 바라고 또 끝내 규명해낸다.

그에 따르는 수많은 타인들의
오해와 편견에도 불구하고 말이다.

대로 행동한다. 슬픈 일이 생기면 이렇게, 기쁜 일이 생기면 저렇게 한다. 그렇게 행동하는 게 타인의 감정을 불편하게 하지 않고 상황을 빠르게 무마하기 좋기 때문이다. 그런데 주인공은 학습된 대로 행동하지 않고 자기 기분이 왜 이런지 무엇이 문제였는지 찾아내길 바라고 또 끝내 규명해낸다. 그에 따르는 수많은 타인들의 오해와 편견에도 불구하고 말이다. 소란이 따랐음에도 더 많은 사람들이 행복해진 건 주인공의 용기와 끈기 덕분이다.

시끄럽게 만드는 것을 겁내지 말아야 한다.

내려놓기 위해
필요한 것들

동네 한적한 골목에 안마하는 집이 있다. 들어가보면 흐릿한 한약 내음이 듬성듬성 박혀 있다. 가만 보면 어떤 향을 쑤셔박아놓은 듯한 공간이 있고 자리와 함께 향도 같이 나이를 먹은 것 같은 공간이 있는데 이곳은 후자라서 마음에 든다. 막상 그리 오래된 집은 아니라서 비결이 무엇인지 궁금하기도 하다. 여기저기 몇 번 쿡쿡 눌러보고는 사촌이 땅을 사셨군요? 할 것 같은 한의사 선생님도 있다.

처음 이사 왔을 때 한두 번 갔다가 시간이 영 마땅치 않아 가지 못했다. 요즘 몸이 많이 불편해져서 다시 오가는 중이다. 뒷목과 어깨가 단단하게 굳었다. 누군들 그렇지 않겠느냐만 좀 심각한 수준이다. 일종의 직업병이다. 안마를 해주는 선생님과 이런저런 이야기를 나누었다. 고백하는 건데 나는 그녀를 존경한다. 내가 하지 못하는 걸 할 줄 아는 모든 이가 내게는 선생님이다. 그래서 나는 그녀를 선생님이라고 부른다. 선생님은 고향이 광주인데 지방 곳곳 다녀보지 않은 곳이 없다. 지역에서 자기 가게를 운영하다가 지금은 여기서 일을 하는 중이다. 나를 안마하다보면 땀이 많이 나는데 시술자가 땀이 나면 안마받는 사람에게 기를 빼앗기는 거라고 한다. 나는 유물론자라서 그런 거 안 믿는다고 했더니 하긴 자기 자신만 믿으면 되죠, 라는 대답이 돌아온다. 아이고 선생님, 실은 저는 저를 제일 믿지 못합니다.

목과 머리가 연결되는 어느 한 부분을 누르니 거의 불알을 차인 것처럼 아파서 비명을 질렀다. 아픔이 가시고 나서 나는 불알이 목 뒤에 달렸더라면 체위는 어떻게 달라졌을 것인지에 관해 궁금해졌다. 아무튼 선생님은 아픈 게 당연하다는 투다. 스트레스가 모이는 곳이라고 한다. 궁금해져서 여기를 아프지 않아하는 사람도 있었냐고 물어보았다. 여지껏 그리 많은 사람들을 만났는데 이곳이 아프지 않은 사람은 단 두 사람이었다고 한다. 한 사람은 말해줄 수 없고 다른 한 사람은, 너무 빤해서 말하기가 좀 그렇지만, 스님이었다. 분명히 아플 텐데 전혀 아프지 않아서 의아했단다. 결혼을 할 수 있는 스님이었다. 같이 온 분이 아내였는데 남편이 스님이라고 해서 뒤늦게 아 어쩐지 대머리, 했다고.

나는 너무나 궁금해졌다. 나는 스트레스 때문에 오만 가지가 힘들고 어려운데 스트레스를 옵션에서 끄고 144Hz 모니터에서 60프레임을 고정하고 인생을 돌릴 수 있다면 얼마나 근사할까. 이건 다른 이야기인데 최근 촬영 때문에 병원에 가서 남성호르몬수치 검사를 했다가 깜짝 놀랐다. 내가 연애라는 단어조차 피곤해하고 만사 무기력한 건 선택이 아니라 필연이었다. 아무튼 그래서 그 스님은 어떻게 스트레스를 받지 않고 사는 거냐고 물어보았다.

스님은 이렇게 말했다고 한다. "내가 어떻게 할 수 없는 건 그냥 내려놓으면 됩니다." 나는 이와 유사한 문장을 여러 번 보았다. "해는 동쪽에서 떠서 서쪽으로 진다." "똥을 싸면 똥이 마렵지 않다." "설탕을 넣으면 달고 소금을 넣으면 짜다." "밥을 먹으면 배가 부르다."

내가 궁금한 건, 그래서 어떻게 하면 내려놓고 싶은 것들을 내려놓을 수 있느냐는 것이었다. 선생님은 노력하면 된다고 말씀하셨다. 처음에는 잘 되지 않았는데 에이 내가 어떻게 할 수 없는 건데 뭐, 그리고 여러 번 생각하고 나니 이제는 꽤 괜찮아졌다고 말했다. 흠 글쎄. 안마를 받을 때 압이 들어가는 순간 숨을 내쉬며 억지로라도 이완해야 몸이 풀린다. 그런데 나는 더이상 안마에 집중할 수 없이 이 문제에 골몰하게 되어버렸다. 어떻게 하면 내려놓고 싶은 것들을 내려놓을 수 있는 걸까.

마음속에 눌러 담아놓은 것들을 하나둘 떠올려보았다. '2억이면 뭐도 하겠다'고 나는 SNS에서 말한 적이 있다. 나를 싫어하는 사람들은 내 이야기가 나오면 만사를 제쳐두고 반드시 그 말을 언급한다. 돈이면 뭐든 괜찮다는 사람이라고 주장하고 싶어서일 거다.

그런데 그 글은 그런 게 아니었다. 그건 당시 곽노현 교육감이 상대후보에게 후보 사퇴를 대가로 2억을 주었던 사건에서 비롯되었다. 그때 곽노현 교육감이 문제의 2억을 두고 "대가성이 없었다"고 말한 게 나는 이해가 되지 않았다. 그걸 가지고 정말 대가성이 없었다고 편을 드는 나꼼수 팬덤이 가장 문제였다. 안 그래도 '나꼼수 팬덤은 선거를 앞두고 문제를 야기할 소지가 크다'는 칼럼을 시사인에 썼다가 팬덤과 한창 갈등을 빚고 있었다. 이걸 문제없다고 말하는 순간 선거에서 결정적인 위력을 발휘할 중간층은 떠난다. 조바심이 났다. 근본주의자들의 폭력을 진영의 이름으로 감싸안는 운동은, 언론은, 정당은 필연적으로 망한다. 세상을 간편하게 절대선과 절대악으로 나누어버리고 무조건 내 편 감싸고 보는 진영논리라는 게 얼마나 허무하게 판을 일그러뜨리고 망쳐버리는지에 관해 그때 당시보다 바로 지금 훨씬 잘 이해할 수 있으리라 생각한다.

나는 대가성 없는 2억이라는 게 말이 되느냐, 그런 말을 진영논리로 감싸안는 게 정상인가, 나는 2억이면 뭐도 하겠다고 썼다. 결국 남은 건 뒤의 말뿐이었다. 맥락은 결코 기록되지 않는다. 과격한 말이었다. 어쩌면 과격하고 선정적인 나중의 말만 남은 게 당연한 노릇인지도 모르겠다. 요즘에는 그렇게 생각한다. 어찌됐든 이후 나는 140자 단위로 말의 맥락이 절단되어 기록되는 트위터를 가능한 한 멀리했다.

〈국제시장〉은 비교적 최근의 일이다. 〈한겨레〉에서 진중권 교수와 한 해 결산 대담을 했다. 나는 반성하지 않는 어른들에 관한 이야기를 하면서 지금의 지옥도는 외면하고 군사독재 경제개발 신화를 떠올려 자위할 기성세대의 정신승리가 토할 거 같다고 말했다. 이는 TV조선에 의해 '허지웅이 영화 〈국제시장〉을 보고 토할 거 같은 영화라고 말했다'고 왜곡되었다.

내가 〈국제시장〉이 토할 것 같은 영화라고 말했다며 노이즈 마케팅이 꽤 오랫동안 계속됐다. 내가 아니라고 해봤자 내가 그랬다는 기사가 하루에 오백 개씩 올라오니 이미 난 그렇게 말한 사람이 되어 있었다. 영화에 천만 관객이 들자 '허지웅씨, 괜.찮.아.요?'라는 제목으로 감독 인터뷰 기사가 났다. 나는 모 방송사의 출연금지 블랙리스트에 올랐다. 처음에는 좀 이상하다고 생각했다가 경로를 거쳐 팩트를 확인한 후에야 알게 되었다. 화가 났다. 그러나 이제 와 떠올려보면 아예 이해할 수 없는 일도 아니었다. 감독은 별 악의 없이 일종의 화해의 제스처로 그렇게 말했을 수 있고 모 방송사는 당시 여러모로 기득권층에 밉보이지 말아야 할 이유가 있었기 때문이다.

전에는 뭔가를 내려놓기 위해 가장 필요한 건 쉽게 까먹을 수 있는 능력이라고 생각했다. 그러나 살아보니 마음에 들지 않는 일을 까먹기 위해 열심히 노력하다보면 까먹지 말아야 할 중요한 것까지 함께 잊어버리기 마련이더라. 그리고 그렇게 까먹은 중요한 것들은 너무 중요하고 소중해서, 반드시 훗날 가슴을 치고 후회하게 된다. 어쩌면 뭔가를 내려놓기 위해 필요한 건 망각이나 체념이 아니라 이해하는 태도일지 모르겠다는 생각을 했다. 내가 그 입장이었으면 그럴 수도 있었겠다는 이해 말이다.

내가 생각한 것에 대해 동의를 구하기 위해 선생님을 올려다보았다. 이마의 땀을 닦아내고 있길래 나는 얼른 시선을 돌려버렸다. 그럴 때는 늘 미안해진다. 스트레스가 모이는 곳이라는 저 뒷목 어딘가가 전혀 아프지 않을 그런 날이 과연 올지 모르겠다.

마음에 들지 않는 일을
까먹기 위해 열심히 노력하다보면
까먹지 말아야 할 중요한 것까지
함께 잊어버리기 마련이더라.
그리고 그렇게 까먹은 중요한 것들은
너무 중요하고 소중해서,
반드시 훗날 가슴을 치고 후회하게 된다.
어쩌면 뭔가를 내려놓기 위해 필요한 건
망각이나 체념이 아니라
이해하는 태도일지 모르겠다는 생각을 했다.

위대한
무표정의 사내

버스터 키튼입니다. 성룡이 말했다. 가장 좋아하는 배우를 꼽으라는 질문에 0.5초 만에 돌아온 답변이었다. 버스터 키튼이 누구인지 모르는 리포터가 까르르 웃었다.

30년이나 늦게 도착한 박수군요. 노인이 말했다. 회고전 자리였다. 30년 전 만들어졌으나 당대에는 외면당했던 〈제너럴〉이 상영중이었다. 관객이 박수를 치고 발을 구르며 웃음을 토해내는 소리를 극장 밖에서 들은 뒤였다. 〈사이트 앤드 사운드〉 기자가 열심히 받아 적었다.

노인은 이듬해 세상을 떠났다. 1966년 2월 1일. 일흔한 살이었다. 그것은 본인의 영화와 무척이나 닮은 해피엔딩이었다. 영화에서 그는 시종일관 주변으로부터 폄훼당하고 멸시당하며 무시되고 간과된다. 혹은 아예 잊힌다. 그럼에도 그는 누구도 알아주지 않는 선의를 포기하지 않는다. 그리고 마침내 러닝타임의 마지막 일 분여를 남기고 우연한 기회를 통해 복권된다. 〈셜록 주니어〉에서 할머니의 돈을 찾아주기 위해 자기 돈을 내밀고 정작 자신은 도둑으로 몰리는 것처럼. 〈카메라맨〉에서 자신의 실력과 선의를 입증받고 사랑하는 여인과 함께 박수갈채를 받으며 도로 한복판을 걷는 것처럼. 그러니까 흡사 하루종일 폭풍우가 몰아치다가 해 지기 직전 그것이 0.5초든 30년이든 아무래도 상관없을 만큼 평생에 단 한 번도 본 적이 없는 미친듯이 맑고 밝은 노을이

아 몰라, 저런 인생은 사양이다.

　조셉 프랭크 키튼 주니어가 버스터 키튼이 된 까닭에 대해서는 본인이 여러 번 설명한 바 있다. 요컨대 어렸을 때부터 어디서 굴러떨어져도 뼈가 부러지거나 다치지 않았다는 것이다. 실제 키튼이 처음 무대에 올랐던 보드빌쇼(라고 쓰고 아동학대쇼라고 읽는다)가 인기 있었던 이유는 키튼의 아버지가 아들을 멀리 집어던지고 떨어뜨려도 어느 한구석 다치지 않기 때문이었다. 키튼에게 버스터라는 이름을 붙여준 것이 마술사 해리 후디니인지 아니면 그의 유모였는지에 대해서는 자료마다 진술이 다르다. 다만 키튼이 알려진 것처럼 정말 뼈가 부러지지 않는 아이였던 건 아니다. 그는 어렸을 때 공연중 오른손에 골절을 입어 평생

왼손으로 글을 써야만 했다. 버스터 키튼의 전설은 타고난 것이 아니었다. 믿을 수 없는 연습량과 시행착오, 그리고 끝까지 버티어낸 결과물이었다.

버스터 키튼은 대개 찰리 채플린과 함께 거론된다. 혹은 찰리 채플린, 해럴드 로이드, 버스터 키튼 이 세 명이 함께 언급된다. 당대 슬랩스틱 코미디의 스리 아미고three amigos다. 채플린은 감정을 중요시했다. 로이드는 재미를 우선시했다. 키튼은 그 가운데 가장 장인에 가까웠다. 채플린이 감정과 메시지를 전달하기 위해 영화를 활용했다면, 키튼은 영화라는 매체가 사실은 언제나 영화 그 이상일 수 있음을 증명하기 위해 몸을 활용했다. 버스터 키튼이 자기 몸을 어떻게 활용하는지에 관해서는 문자를 통해 전달할 수 없다. 오로지 영화를 통해 가능하다. 오로지 영화를 통해서 말이다.

〈캐논볼〉 촬영현장의 어느 스태프는 재키 챈이라는 이름의 낯선 동양 배우에게서 버스터 키튼의 바로 그런 측면을 엿보았다. 그래서 그에게 버스터 키튼을 추천한 것이었다. 키튼의 영화를 본 이후 성룡의 영화관映畵觀은 영영 바뀌었다. 〈스팀보트 빌 주니어〉나 〈제너럴〉에서의 저 놀라운(아마도 결코 앞으로는 가능하지 않을) 아날로그 액션 시퀀스들은 성룡뿐만 아니라 몸을 쓰는 모든 배우들로 하여금 버스터 키튼이라는 인간의 놀라움에 경탄을 바치게끔 만들었다.

그러나 버스터 키튼의 진면목은 위험을 무릅쓴 슬랩스틱 액션에만 있는 게 아니다. '영화라는 매체가 사실은 언제나 영화 그 이상일 수 있음을 증명'해내는 데에는 영화라는 매체 자체에 관한 충분한 성찰과 고민이 필요했다. 이것은 단지 앞에 보이는 것을 기록하는 도구인가, 아니면 그 이상의 새로운 무엇을 만들어낼 수 있는 마술인가. 영화 초창기 역사의 모든 선지자들이 그러했듯, 키튼은 어떤 의미에서 마술사였다. 그는 〈셜록 주니어〉에서 이미 지금 시대의 감독들이 쓰는 거리두기 트릭을 선보였으며, 영화를 보고 있는 관객에게 영화 속의 다른 영화를 보여주며 액자식 구성 속의 내러티브가 상호 영향을 끼치는 장치들을 상업적으로 성공시켰다. 영화를 사랑하는 사람들에게 저 모든 장면은 평생 충족할 수 있는 미감의 어느 극한이다. 무성영화 전성기인 1920년대 키튼은 채플린과 굳이 견주지 않아도 저 홀로 독보적이었다.

버스터 키튼의 몰락은 20년대 후반 유나이티드 아티스트와 결별한 이후 MGM과 계약하면서 시작되었다. 〈제너럴〉이 흥행에 실패하면서 키튼은 경제적인 어려움에 직면한다. 그는 사업적인 수완이나 깜냥이 부족한 사람이었다. 키튼이 자신의 스튜디오를 MGM에 매각하고 그 또한 소속 배우로 들어가겠다고 말했을 때 가장 반대했던 것은 찰리 채플린이었다. 제작과 편집에 관련된 일체의 권리를 내놓는 일이었다. 이것은 버스터 키튼의 영화에서 극약 처방에 가까웠다. 채플린은 키튼이 너무나 쉽게 거대 제작사의 부속품으로 전락해 소모되리라 예상했다.

그러나 키튼은 결국 MGM으로 들어갔다. 〈카메라맨〉과 〈홧김에 한 결혼〉을 MGM에서 내놓았다. 그것이 버스터 키튼 인생

<제너럴The General>(1926)

영화 초창기 역사의
모든 선지자들이 그러했듯,
키튼은 어떤 의미에서 마술사였다.
영화를 사랑하는 사람들에게
저 모든 장면은
평생 충족할 수 있는
미감의 어느 극한이다.

의 마지막 무성영화였다. 키튼 본인은 유성영화 환경에서도 자신이 생명력을 이어나갈 수 있으리라 생각했다. 무대 공연을 통해 다져진 실력이기 때문이다. 그러나 문제는 유성이냐 무성이냐에 있지 않았다. 채플린의 예상이 맞았다. 권한의 문제였다. 키튼은 더이상 필요 이상의 위험한 촬영을 할 수 없었다. MGM이 그것을 감당하려 하지 않았다. 하고 싶은 것도 할 수 없었다. 모든 것을 스튜디오와 상의하고 결재를 얻어야 했다. 조율과 협업을 통해 더 나은 것을 만들어내는 위대한 감독들이 있다. 그러나 홀로 고군분투하며 고집스레 하고 싶은 것을 할 수 있어야만 무언가를 성취해내는 감독들 또한 존재한다. 버스터 키튼은 여실히 후자였다. 그는 MGM으로 들어간 결정을 두고두고 후회했다. 이후 그는 여태 쌓아놓은 커리어가 먼지가 되어 날아가고 또 그 먼지가 앉아 있던 희미한 자취마저 남김없이 지워져버리는 모멸의 시간을 묵묵히 겪어내야만 했다. 뒤늦게 복권되기 전까지.

키튼의 전성기 영화를 보면 그가 전혀 웃지 않는다는 걸 금방 알 수 있다. 그는 웃지 않는다. 차라리 울상에 가까운 무표정이다. 무대 공연 시절 자기가 웃지 않으면 않을수록 관객의 웃음이 더 커진다는 경험치를 발휘한 결과물이었다. 그래서 그는 여태 '그레이트 스톤 페이스Great Stone Face'로 불린다. 그러나 그가 패티 아버클과 연기했던 1910년대 영화들을 보면 이야기가 다르다. 영화에서 키튼은 크게 웃고, 슬프게 울며, 소스라치게 놀란다. 그 표정들을 보고 있으면 마음이 복잡해진다. 이 위대한 무표정의 사내에게는, 그의 안에는, 남에게 주고 싶은 감정들이

<스팀보트 빌 주니어Steamboat Bill, Jr.>(1928)

이 위대한 무표정의 사내에게는,
그의 안에는,
남에게 주고 싶은 감정들이
그렇게도 많았던 것이다.

그렇게도 많았던 것이다.

10년 전 버스터 키튼에 관해 썼던 글의 마지막을 다시 옮기고 싶다. 그는 한때 완전히 잊힌 듯 보였으나 실제로는 한 번도 지워진 적이 없었던, 그 자체가 전설로 완벽하게 산화된 존재다. 그가 떠난 후 50년이 지났으나 그의 영화는 여전히 새롭고 재기발랄하며, 그를 능가하는 배우는 아직 도래하지 않았다. 이것이 무표정의 위대한 희극배우 버스터 키튼의 전모다.

악취미의
제왕

이상한 우연이다. 〈쳐다보지 마라〉에 관해 쓰면서 이 영화를 떠올렸다. 로빈 하디의 〈위커맨〉 말이다. 〈쳐다보지 마라〉와 같은 해에 만들어졌다. 둘 다 영국산 컬트영화를 대변하다시피 하는 작품이다. 미국 개봉 때에는 두 영화가 묶여서 동시상영으로 배급되었다. 두 편 모두 해괴하고 불균질하며 상영 내내 꿈을 꾸고 있는 듯한 질감을 가진, 아무튼 도대체가 이상하기 짝이 없는 영화다. 〈쳐다보지 마라〉에는 도널드 서덜랜드가 나온다. 〈위커맨〉에는 크리스토퍼 리가 나온다. 두 사람 공히 해괴한 취향을 가진 영화광들에게 어딘가 사연 있는 동네 국밥집 아저씨 같은 배우다. 그런데 지난주 갑자기, 그러니까 집에 돌아와 바지를 벗다가 다른 한쪽 다리가 채 빠져나오지 않은 상태에서 너를 체포한다

는 말을 듣는 것처럼 갑작스럽게

크리스토퍼 리가 죽었다.

크리스토퍼 리가 죽었다, 는 문장은 흡사 "오늘 우리 회사 구내식당 점심 메뉴는 김치찌개에 낙타 고기야" "아니 또?"라는 대화처럼 이상하다. 참을 수 없이 괴상하다. 드라큘라에 사루만에 두쿠 백작에 서머아일 영주였던 사람이 죽을 수도 있는 것인가. 크리스토퍼 리는 1958년 〈드라큘라〉에서도 늙었었고 1973년 〈위커맨〉에서도 늙었었고 1974년 〈007 황금총을 가진 사나이〉에서 007과 싸울 때도 역시 늙었으며 2000년대 〈반지의 제왕〉과 〈스타워즈〉 시리즈에서도 꾸준히 늙었는데 이제 와 새삼 늙었다는 게 세상을 떠날 이유로 합당한 것인가. 아 나는 모르겠다. 우리는 때로 어떤 배우가 영원히 살겠거니 하고 착각하는 모양이다. 아무튼 그래서 나는 〈위커맨〉을 추억하며 크리스토퍼 리를 떠나보내기로 했다.

위커맨은 고대 드루이드교 사제들이 인신공양을 하는 의식을 펼칠 때 사용했던 구조물로 알려져 있다. 거대한 사람 모양의 우리를 만들고 그 안의 칸마다 제물을 가둔 채 통째로 불태워버리는 것이다. 위커맨이 실재했느냐에 관한 논쟁은 무척 오래됐다. 『갈리아 전쟁기』에 언급만 될 뿐 가공의 신화적 가십에 불과하다는 말도 있다. 그러나 그냥 상상의 산물로만 생각하기에는 문헌 속에서의 묘사가 구체적이고 일관되어 있다. 일단 역사 속

인신공양 그 자체는 확정적인 증거들이 넘쳐난다.

영화는 시작하자마자 주인공의 성격을 유추할 수 있게 하는 몇 개의 컷들을 연달아 보여준다. 에드워드 우드워드가 연기하는 경찰관 하위는 독실한 기독교인이다. 완고하고 독선적이며 보수적이고 종교적인 신념과 확신으로 가득찬 인물이다. 그는 얼마 전 약혼을 했다. 이후 언급되다시피 그는 아직 동정의 몸이다. 이 동정의 꼰대가 영화의 주인공이다. 그가 동정의 꼰대라는 사실은 농담거리라기보다 이 영화가 다루는 이야기의 매우 중요한 지점이다. '왜 그여야만 했는가'라는 질문에 대응하는 설정이기 때문이다.

하위가 어느 소녀의 실종사건을 수사하기 위해 서머아일이라는 이름의 섬을 찾으면서 비로소 본격적인 이야기가 시작된다. 항구에서부터 일이 삐걱댄다. 항구에서 만난 노인들 가운데 어느 누구도 하위가 찾고 있는 소녀를 알지 못한다고 말한다. 그러나 노인들의 평온한 얼굴 사이로 문득문득 삐져나오는 불쾌한 웃음은 이들이 거짓말을 하고 있다는 걸 쉽게 감지하게 만든다. 실종된 소녀의 어머니도 그런 소녀는 알지 못한다고 말한다. 숙박을 위해 찾은 펍에서도 마찬가지다. 하위는 자신이 이 섬의 사람들에게 기만당하고 있다는 걸 간파한다. 사실 모를 수가 없다. 정교한 거짓말이라기보다 참기 어려운 웃음을 눌러가며 늘어놓는 빈정거림에 가깝기 때문이다.

문제는 여기서 그치지 않는다. 하위는 섬을 둘러본 후 얼마 되지 않아 엄청난 문화 충격에 휩싸인다. 이 섬은 기독교를 믿지 않는다. 대신에 고대의 자연신들을 섬긴다. 그뿐만 아니라 아이부터 어른에 이르기까지 모두 다 성교에 관련된 말과 행동을 한다. 밤이 되면 들이며 길 위에서 너도나도 자연스레 뒤엉켜 섹스를 하고 있다. 아이들이 부르는 동요의 주제가 섹스다. 아이들은 남근상 주변을 빙빙 돌며 춤을 추고 뛰어논다. 이 섬에서 공공연한 섹스는 금기가 아니다. 자연의 풍요와 연관된 것이기 때문에 되레 학습과 사회화를 통해 권장된다. 그 모든 풍경을 바라보며 진격의 기독교인 하위는 거의 통증에 가까운 분노와 환멸을 느낀다.

하위의 증오심은 이 섬을 다스리는 서머아일 영주를 만나면서 극에 달한다. 크리스토퍼 리가 연기하는 서머아일 영주는 우아한 몸짓으로 낡은 종교 대신에 채택한 자연신 숭배가 이 섬의 풍요로움과 평화에 어떻게 기여했는지 설명한다. 하위와 서머아일 영주의 종교적 가치관이 격돌하는 이 장면에서 크리스토퍼 리의 연기는 과연 압도적이다. 온화하고 부드럽지만 단호하고 확정적이다. 그 발음 하나하나가 음악처럼 관객의 귀를 휘감아 적신다. 시를 읊듯 뱉어내는 서머아일 영주의 웅변은 장엄하다. 그러나 그것은 설득될 준비가 되어 있지 않은 자에게 구역질을 불러일으킬 뿐이다. 하위는 혐오와 증오로 가득차 영주의 집을 나선다. 이교도 나부랭이들에게 질릴 대로 질린 하위는 이 섬어딘가에 소녀가 살아 있으며 마을축제 날 인신공양의 제물로 바쳐질 것이라는 확신을 갖게 된다. 그리고 마침내 5월 1일 축제날. 가면을 쓰고 축제 행렬에 숨어든 하위는 드디어 섬의 비밀과 마주한다.

〈위커맨〉에서 하위와 서머아일 영주는 종교적 신념에 근거하여 상대를 쉽게 판단하고 행동하며 비이성적인 결론으로 치닫는다는 점에서 서로를 투영한 거울상과도 같다. 그러나 이 영화에서 좀더 유효하게 꼬집고 있는 것은 기독교인 하위의 억압되고 비틀린 욕망이다. 자연스레 하위에게 자신을 동일시하고 있던 당대의 관객은 극 후반 하위의 눈앞에 위커맨이 등장한 순간 겁을 집어먹고 비명을 질러댔다. 이 순간은 이야기를 전부 다 알고 영화를 다시 보는 관객에게도 여전히 섬뜩하다. 이상하게 주눅이 들고 빨려들어가는 듯한 장면이다. 그것은 이성이나 종교관으로 간파할 수 없는, 너무나 상스럽고 압도적으로 거대한 고대로부터의 불온함이다. 한없이 견고하게만 느껴졌던 기독교 세계관이 저 불온한 풍경 앞에 속절없이 허물어지는 경험, 이것이야말로 저 흔한 신체훼손 장면 하나 없는 〈위커맨〉이 가장 무시무시한 영화의 목록들 가운데 영원히 회자되고 언급되는 이유다.

〈위커맨〉에서 가장 재미있는 대목은 사실 마을의 기이한 풍경을 다룰 때마다 펼쳐지는 노래들이다. 정서적으로 그 위력이 커서 〈위커맨〉을 뮤지컬영화로 생각하게도 만든다. 이 괴상하고 기발한 노래들은 꿈인지 환영인지 농담인지 연극인지 알 수 없는 이 영화의 비틀린 현실감에 활력을 불어넣는다. 그 가운데 크리스토퍼 리가 피아노를 치며 묵직한 저음으로 부르는 노래가 있다. "주전자가 많이 깨졌군요, 우리 예쁜 아가씨. 못을 많이 박아서 그렇게 된 거랍니다. 성할 리가 없지요." 이 괴상하기 짝이 없는 노래를 자꾸 다시 듣게 되는 밤이다. 나의 위대한 암흑의 군주, 저 모든 악취미들의 제왕. 부디 편히 잠드시길.

<위커맨The Wicker Man>[1973]

나의 위대한 암흑의 군주,
저 모든 악취미들의 제왕.
부디 편히 잠드시길.

멜 깁슨에
관하여

한 남자가 외딴 도로에 서 있다. 경찰이다. 차를 손보는 중이다.
옅은 하늘색 반팔티셔츠에는 기름때가 요란하다. 걸음을 내딛을
때마다 무릎 바로 아래까지 꽉 찬 가죽부츠의 주름이 보기 좋게
접혔다 펴지기를 반복한다. 차 안에서는 무선통신이 요란하다.
동료들이 폭주 범죄자 나이트라이더를 추격하는 중임을 알리는
경찰 통신이다. 남자가 가죽재킷을 걸쳐입고 차에 올라탄다. 선
글라스를 착용하고 백미러를 살짝 흘긴다. 동료들은 전멸했다.
경찰들을 따돌린 나이트라이더의 8기통 엔진이 괴성을 지르며
도로를 가른다. 마침내 남자의 차가 출발한다. 차체에 새겨진 인
터셉터Interceptor라는 글자가 크고 선명하다. 나이트라이더와 길
한가운데서 마주한다. 서로를 향해 질주하는 두 대의 차. 충돌

의 순간, 나이트라이더가 먼저 핸들을 틀어 아찔하게 피해나간다. 여전히 운전대를 잡고 질주하는 나이트라이더. 그러나 그가 흐느끼기 시작한다. 이제 다 끝났다며 울부짖는다. 무엇 때문일까. 아마도 상대의 압도적인 무게감을 감지했기 때문이리라. 나이트라이더는 얼마 더 가지 못하고 결국 전복사고로 목숨을 다한다. 마지막 폭발의 순간, 멈춰선 인터셉터에서 남자가 내린다. 선글라스를 벗고 도로 위에 선다. 먼지가 되어 사라지는 나이트라이더를 안타깝게 바라본다. 차에서 내리는 순간부터 선글라스를 벗기까지 굵고 신속하게 이어지는, 여러분 여기 이 영웅의 근심을 보시오, 라고 외치는 듯한 세상에서 가장 근사한 클로즈업. 처음으로 온전한 모습을 드러낸 남자의 전신.

그렇게 세상은 멜 깁슨과 만났다.

〈매드 맥스〉 시리즈는 인류의 대중문화에 엄청난 영향을 끼쳤다. 핵전쟁 이후의 디스토피아를 다룬 텍스트들 가운데 〈매드 맥스〉의 영향권으로부터 완전히 자유로운 것 따위는 존재하지 않는다. 요는 스타일이다. 이전에는 존재하지 않았다. 조지 밀러는 〈매드 맥스〉를 통해 완벽하게 새로운 스타일을 창조해냈다(물론 그조차 돈 존슨의 〈소년과 개〉로부터 엄청난 영향을 받았다. 이를테면 제록스와 스티브 잡스의 관계랄까). 조지 밀러가 시도한 것은 서부극의 무대를 핵전쟁 이후 사막화된 지구로 바꾸어놓고 피 한 바가지를 쏟아부은 것뿐이었으나 그가 성취한 것은 그

여러분 여기 이 영웅의 근심을 보시오,
라고 외치는 듯한 세상에서 가장 근사한 클로즈업.
처음으로 온전한 모습을 드러낸 남자의 전신.
그렇게 세상은 멜 깁슨과 만났다.

<매드 맥스Mad Max>(1979)

보다 훨씬 놀랍고 뿌리깊은 것이었다. 그리고 이 스타일은 당대의 수많은 창작자들에게 도무지 베끼지 않고서는 견딜 수 없는 충동을 이끌어냈다. 〈매드 맥스〉가 없었다면, 맥스 로카탄스키가 없었다면 우리는 〈북두의 권〉의 켄시로도 〈폴아웃〉도 〈보더랜드〉도 〈더 로드〉도, 하다못해 〈워터월드〉마저 만날 수 없었을 것이다(여기 왜 〈워터월드〉가 끼냐고 불평하는 독자가 분명 있을 것이다. 그러나 두고두고 영원히 놀려먹을 수 있는 영화가 내 인생에서 사라진다는 건 너무 가슴 아픈 일이다).

바로 그 〈매드 맥스〉의 중심에 맥스 로카탄스키, 멜 깁슨이 있다. 애초 멜 깁슨은 맥스 로카탄스키가 될 생각이 없었다. 단지 친구의 오디션에 따라갔을 뿐이다. 대개 '친구의 오디션에 따라갔을 뿐'인 전설이 그러하듯, 조지 밀러는 친구 대신 멜 깁슨에게 홀딱 반하고 말았다. 조지 밀러는 괴짜를 찾고 있었고, 멜 깁슨은 바로 전날 바에서 난투극을 벌인 덕분에 사람이라고 볼 수 없는 몰골을 하고 있었다. 조지 밀러는 이런 꼴로 찾아온 배우의 정신세계에 동물적으로 끌리고 말았다. 그는 멜 깁슨에게 상처가 다 나은 이후 다시 한번 찾아와달라고 요청했다. 멜 깁슨은 몇 주 후 그를 다시 찾았고, 그렇게 맥스 로카탄스키가 되었다.

〈매드 맥스〉 이후 멜 깁슨의 경력은 우리 모두 알고 있듯 화려하기 짝이 없다. 그는 세 편의 〈매드 맥스〉 시리즈가 끝나자마자 〈리셀 웨폰〉 시리즈의 마틴 릭스가 되었다. 80년대는 멜 깁슨의 것이었다. 90년대라고 다르지 않았다. 〈브레이브 하트〉의 윌리엄 월레스가 되었고 직접 연출했으며 아카데미 작품상과 감독상을 수상했다. 실존 인물을 스크린 위로 가져온 영화 가운데 역사 왜곡 면에서 전무후무하다 할 만한 〈브레이브 하트〉가 과연 작품상과 감독상을 수상할 만한 작품인가에 관한 시비가 있었다. 그러나 곧 잊혔다. 〈컨스피러시〉나 〈싸인〉과 같은 오래도록 기억될 영화에서 더욱 오래도록 기억될 연기를 해냈다. 2000년대 들어는 〈패션 오브 크라이스트〉와 〈아포칼립토〉를 만들어냈다. 그리고 '연출도 하는 배우'가 아니라 우리 시대 가장 빼어난 감독들 가운데 하나가 되었다. 온통 좋은 일뿐이다. 이토록 성공적인 인생은 드물다. 그러나 결코 누구에게도, 삶이란 그리 호락호락하지 않다.

〈브레이브 하트〉는 역사 왜곡 논란이 있었다. 〈패션 오브 크라이스트〉는 고증의 문제가 아니었다. 이 영화는 오랫동안 기획된 만큼 고증에도 더없이 많은 노력이 들어갔다. 문제는 이 영화에 투영된 연출자의 가치관이었다. 〈패션 오브 크라이스트〉는 유대인을 욕먹이기 위한 영화라고 손가락질당했다. 〈아포칼립토〉는 원주민을 너무 잔혹하게 묘사했다는 여론의 십자포화를 받았다. 특히 〈패션 오브 크라이스트〉를 전후하여 그의 반유대주의 정서가 도마 위에 올랐다. 그의 아버지는 홀로코스트를 부정하는 사람이었다. 독실한 가톨릭교도인 멜 깁슨은 유대인을 자극하는 발언으로 이전에도 논란에 휩싸이는 일이 잦았다. 〈패션 오브 크라이스트〉로 그는 유대인들과의 전쟁을 선포한 셈이었다.

나는 〈패션 오브 크라이스트〉 속에 묘사된 유대인과 당대 유력 사제들의 행동이, 실제 우리가 보고 읽는 성경에 기록된 것 이상, 이하도 아니라고 생각한다. 기록된 바에 따르면 예수는 예루살렘에 도착하자마자 교회를 신랄하게 비판하였고, 성전의 웅장함에 매료된 제자들을 꾸짖었다. 예수는 사실상 유대 사제들에 의해 정치범으로 몰려 살해당한 것이나 마찬가지였다. 자신들의 민족주의 성향에 거슬린다는 이유로 상대의 가치관을 공격하고 역사 왜곡을 운운하는 건 곤란하다. 〈패션 오브 크라이스트〉를 단지 유대인을 욕먹이기 위해 만든 영화라고 말하는 건 2차대전 다큐멘터리를 히틀러 욕먹이기 위한 선전물이라고 폄훼하는 것이나 다를 바 없는 공격이다.

어찌됐든 할리우드에서 유대 권력을 무시한다는 건 관자놀이에 대고 방아쇠를 당기는 것보다 훨씬 빠르고 효과적인 퇴장의 지름길이다. 실제 〈패션 오브 크라이스트〉 이후 멜 깁슨의 필모그래피에는 별다른 게 없다. 직접 각본을 쓰고 제작하고 연출한 〈아포칼립토〉 정도를 제외하면 기억에 남을 만한 작품이 존재하지 않는다. 여기에 멜 깁슨의 알코올중독 문제와 가정사까지 겹쳤다. 이제 와 멜 깁슨은 연예 가십난에나 가끔 등장하는 잊힌 추억 속 배우 취급을 받는다. 이제는 늙고 쇠락한 사고뭉치 80년대 액션 영웅 말이다. 이런 상황에 〈익스펜더블 3〉에 나오는 그를 보고 있는 건 곤혹스럽다.

멜 깁슨은 전통적인 공화당 지지자 정도로 여겨져왔다. 그가 단 한 번도 자신의 정치 성향에 대해 발언한 일이 없음에도 말이다. 그러나 멜 깁슨은 부시의 이라크 전쟁에 대해 공개적으로 반대하고 비판한, 몇 안 되는 할리우드 배우 가운데 하나였다. 그는 (평소 마음에 들지 않았을 것이 확실한) 마이클 무어의 〈화씨 9/11〉을 지지하기도 했다. 멜 깁슨에게 필요 이상의 과한 뉘앙스로 자기 의견을 밝히는 문제가 있다는 건 부정할 수 없는 사실이다. 그는 부주의하다. 때로 사려 깊지 못하다. 그로 인해 쓸데없이 너무 많은 오해를 사고 말았다. 나는 멜 깁슨이 클린트 이스트우드와 함께 기록될 만큼 위대한 감독이라 생각한다. 그리고 그렇게 되리라 믿는다. 그가 만들 영화들을 상상하고 기다린다. 그때까지는 맥스 로카탄스키의 '마지막 8기통 인터셉터', XB 포드 팔콘 쿠페를 타고 달리는 꿈이나 실컷 꾸어야겠다.

끓는점

도움을 청할
자격이 없는 사람들

아저씨는 늘 새까맣게 취해서 인사동 입구에 널브러져 있었다. 아니면 오가는 사람들을 붙잡고 뭔가 한참 동안 하소연하고는 했다. 편의점에 들어와 소주 한 병과 종이컵을 계산대 위에 올려 놓고는 십 원짜리와 백 원짜리 동전을 쏟아내 그중에서 제일 더러운 걸로 계산을 치르고는 했다. 비교적 깨끗한 동전은 다시 아저씨 주머니 속으로 사라졌다.

가끔씩은 행패를 부리기도 했다. 소주를 그냥 가지고 나가는 걸 말리느라 실랑이가 커지는 일도 있었다. 아저씨는 보통 늦은 밤에 나타났지만 이른 저녁에 편의점을 찾는 경우도 있었다. 출근했더니 이전 근무자가 아저씨를 붙잡고 힘겹게 씨름을 하고 있었다. 그런 와중에도 그 친구는 아저씨를 향해 꼬박꼬박 존대를 하며 웃어 보이려 애쓰고 있었다. 나는 그런 그 친구의 옆모습을 보며 잠시 동안 참 예쁘다는 생각을 했다.

가끔 그 친구가 생각난다.

인사동에서 편의점 야간 아르바이트를 할 때였다. 전역을 하고 복학하기 전까지 열심히 돈을 모았지만 등록금을 내고 월세와 생활비를 빼고 나니 큰일이다 싶었다. 다음 학기 등록금도 모으기 시작해야 해서 수업을 전부 오후로 밀어넣고 일과가 끝나면 편의점에 나갔다. 새벽 6시에 퇴근하면 고시원에 돌아와서 쪽잠을 자고 11시에 일어나 학교를 갔다. 한 학기를 그렇게 보내고 방학 동안 열심히 벌어 다음 학기 등록금을 낼 수 있었다. 98학번이었기에 망정이지 요즘 학번이었다면 하루가 48시간이었더라도 결국 등록금과 월세를 내지 못하고 대출을 받았을 거다. 나는 대출이 너무너무 싫다.

그 친구는 오후 근무자였다. 이 편의점은 세 명의 근무자가 여덟 시간씩 돌아가며 일을 했다. 내가 출근을 하면 그 친구는 내게 인수인계를 하고 퇴근했다. 딱 한 번 세 명이 모여 밥을 먹었다. 밥 먹는 내내 점장 욕만 했던 것 같다. 그 친구는 휴학을 하고 학비를 벌고 있다고 했다. 내심 형편이 이해가 돼서 장하다고 말해주었다. 내가 제일 연장자라 자연스레 계산을 하려는데 그 친구가 옆에 와서 만 원짜리 한 장을 보탰다. 괜찮다고 말하는데 씩 웃고 나가버렸다. 좋은 아이였다.

어느 날 수업을 듣고 있는데 점장에게서 문자가 왔다. 한 시간 먼저 출근해달라는 내용이었다. 편의점에 갔더니 그 친구는 없고 점장이 계산대를 지키고 있었다. 그 친구가 일을 그만두게 되었고 당분간은 점장이 오후 근무를 설 텐데 자기가 9시까지밖에는 있을 수 없으니 앞으로 한 시간씩 일찍 와달라는 이야기였다. 갑작스러웠지만 무슨 일이 생겼나보다 싶었다. 자정 무렵 그 친구가 찾아오기 전까지는 그랬다.

누군가 편의점 문을 열고 들어왔다. 까만 옷을 입고 하얗게 질린 얼굴을 한 그 친구였다. 느닷없이 더이상 나오지 말라는 통보를 받았는데 그만두는 건 상관없지만 너무 억울하다고 말했다. 무슨 일인지 물어보았다. 요전 날 일을 하는 도중 점장 남편이 편의점에 와서 계산대에서 30만 원을 가져갔고, 그래서 따로 메모까지 해두었는데 그걸 점장은 자기가 가져갔다고 생각한다는 것이었다. 그러고 보니 그런 메모를 본 일이 기억났다. 그래서 그날 정산도 30만 원을 빼고 했다. CCTV에 녹화가 되어 있지 않느냐고 물었다. 점장 남편이 창고에 들어갔다 나왔는데 그때 녹화를 잠시 멈추었던 것 같고, 알바 세 명 근무시간 가운데 CCTV가 멈추었던 건 그때밖에 없으니 네가 가져간 게 확실하다고 점장이 말했다는 것이다. 월급 정산도 30만 원을 제하겠다고 말했다며 억울해서 어떻게 해야 할지 모르겠다고 말했다.

다음날 점장에게 이 이야기를 했다. 전에도 남편분이 돈을 가져간 적이 있지 않느냐. 남편과 이야기를 더 해보시는 게 맞지 않느냐. 점장은 남편과는 이미 이야기가 끝났고 그런 일이 없다고 말했다. 그렇다면 차라리 경찰에 신고해서 조사하는 게 낫지 않겠느냐, 그 친구가 저렇게 억울하다는데 경찰에 신고를 하든지 아니면 노동청에 부당해고로 진정을 제기하도록 도울 수밖에 없다, 다시 한번 남편과 이야기를 해봐주시라 부탁했다. 점장은 순순히 그렇게 하겠다고 말하더니 서슬 퍼런 눈을 하고 나가버렸다. 비상연락망에서 아직 지워지지 않은 그 친구의 전화번호를 찾아 문자를 보냈다. 그 친구는 고맙다는 짧은 답을 보내왔다.

사흘 후에 출근했더니 점장이 없고 새로 뽑은 근무자가 일하고 있었다. 창고에 옷을 갈아입으러 들어갔다가 점장의 메모를 발견했다. 30만 원을 빼지 않고 그 친구에게 정산을 다 마쳤고 오해가 풀려 일이 잘 마무리되었으니 그렇게 알라는 내용이었다. 인수인계를 받고 계산대에 들어가 자리를 잡았다. 새 근무자가 유통기한이 지난 삼각김밥 하나를 집어들어 비닐을 뜯더니 한입 가득 입에 물었다. 그리고 그 친구 이야기를 꺼냈다.

점장님한테 원래 일하다가 잘린 여자애 이야기 들었어요. 전에 술집에서 일했었다면서요?

나는 한참 가만히 서서 새로 온 근무자의 얼굴을 들여다보았다. 잠시 당황스러웠다. 처음 듣는 이야기였다. 그러나 전에 술집에서 일했든 청와대에서 일했든 그게 이 문제랑 무슨 관계가 있다는 건지 알 수가 없었다. 그런데 그게 그거랑 무슨 상관이에요? 새 근무자는 조금 당황하더니 인사를 하고 나가버렸다. 상황을 보아하니 그 친구가 점장에게 어떤 모욕적인 이야기를 들었을지 짐작이 되었다. 그 친구에게 잘 해결된 게 맞냐는 문자를 보내보았지만 답은 오지 않았다. 나는 한 달을 더 일하고 편의점을 그만두었다.

그뒤로 나는 그 친구를 보지 못했다. 그러나 그 친구는 여러 가지 모습으로 계속해서 내 앞에 나타났다.

배를 타고 가던 아이들이 사고를 당해 구조를 기다렸으나 어른들이 시키는 대로 하다가 어른들이 만들어놓은 시스템이 하나도 작동하지 않아서 목숨을 잃었다. 그 아이들의 아버지는 광장 위에 섰고 철저하고 공정한 조사를 요구했다. 그러나 본래 가정에 소홀한 아버지였다, 보상금을 노리고 그러는 것이다 등의 이야기들이 쏟아져나오면서 위로는커녕 모욕을 당했다. 경찰의 물대포를 맞고 쓰러진 남자가 오랜 혼수상태 끝에 사망했다. 남자의 가족은 아버지의 존엄을 지키기 위해 분투했다. 그러나 아버지의 임종 순간을 지키지 않고 해외에 있었다는 이야기가 쏟아져나오면서 위로와 지지 대신 비아냥과 손가락질을 당했다.

순백의 피해자.

나는 이걸 순백의 피해자라고 이름 붙였다. 사람들은 순백의 피해자라는 판타지를 가지고 있다. 피해자는 어떤 종류의 흠결도 없는 착하고 옳은 사람이어야만 하며 이러한 믿음에 균열이 오는 경우 '감싸주고 지지해줘야 할 피해자'가 '그런 일을 당해도 할말이 없는 피해자'로 돌변하는 것이다.

그러나 순백의 피해자란 실현 불가능한 허구다. 흠결이 없는 삶이란 존재할 수 없다. 설사 흠결이 존재하지 않을 경우에도 얼마든지 인과관계를 만들어내 낙인찍을 수 있다. 나쁜 피해자 착한 피해자를 나누고 순수성을 측정하려는 시도들의 중심에는 의도가 있다. 피해자의 요구나 피해자가 상징하는 것들이 강자의 비위에 거슬리는 것이라면, 그런 피해자는 언제 어디서 어떤 방식으로든 너무나 손쉽게 나쁜 피해자로 전락할 수 있는 것이다.

사람들은 간과한다. 순백의 피해자라는 요건을 충족할 수 있는 사람은 아무도 없으며, 그 자신 또한 언젠가 피해자가 되었을 때 순백이 아니라는 이유로 구제받지 못할 것이라는 사실을 말이다. 나는 그 친구를 더 열심히 돕지 못했다는 이유로 종종 참을 수 없이 부끄러워진다. 우리가 제대로 지켜주지 못했던 그 많은 피해자들을 떠올려보자. 어쩌면 우리는 어느 누구에게도 도움을 청할 자격이 없는 사람들인지도 모르겠다.

순백의 피해자.
사람들은 순백의 피해자라는 판타지를 가지고 있다.
우리가 제대로 지켜주지 못했던
그 많은 피해자들을 떠올려보자.
어쩌면 우리는 어느 누구에게도 도움을 청할
자격이 없는 사람들인지도 모르겠다.

세월호

아이들이 사고를 당했는데

어른들이 만들어놓고 지키라 했던 장치들이 하나도 작동하지 않았고

그래서 수 시간 동안 아이들이 죽어가는 걸 무능하기 짝이 없이 지켜보기만 했는데

이후 이 죽음을 두고 어른들은 반성하는 대신 네 편과 내 편을 갈라 지겹게 싸웠고 희생자들을 모욕했다. 어른스럽지 못하고 무책임하고 몰염치했다.

　세월호는 한국 사회윤리의 아우슈비츠다. 창피하고 부끄럽고 참담해서 세월호만 생각하면 도망치고 싶다.

"한국은
나쁜 나라입니다"

최승호의 〈자백〉은 국가정보원의 간첩조작사건을 다루는 다큐다. 소셜 펀딩과 40개월에 가까운 취재 과정을 통해 완성되었다. 보통 이렇게 정치적 소재를 다루는 다큐를 볼 때면 조금 더 긴장한다. 소재의 민감성 때문이 아니다. 내가 편들고 싶어하는 이야기라 해서 은연중에 영화의 함량에 대해 호의적인 평가를 내리지는 않을까 걱정되기 때문이다. 그래서 다른 때보다 좀더 정신을 바짝 차리고 보게 된다.

정치적 입장과 진영에 따라 영화를 보기도 전에 이를 지지해줄 준비가 되어 있는 팬덤 관객이 예정된 작품들이 존재한다. 책임감 있는 연출가라면 그런 경우일수록 작품의 함량을 끌어올리기 위해 분투할 것이다. 그러나 불행하게도 그렇지 않은 사례가 많았다. 어떤 소재를 다루어냈다는 용맹함과 연출가의 영웅 심리만 남을 뿐 본질을 향한 사유는 정작 낡거나 얇고 초라하기 이를 데 없는 일이 더 많았던 것이다. 이게 다 마이클 무어 탓이다. 선정성과 어긋난 비아냥만 가지고 다큐를 이끌어가는 잘못된 풍조를 유행시켰다. 그건 예능이지 다큐가 아니다. 그런 유행을 좇는 한국의 연출가들은 마이클 무어가 과거의 지나친 자기확신과 쇼맨십을 일정 정도 덜어내고 〈식코〉 이후 명백하게 보여주고 있는 발전상에 대해선 무관심하다. 알 수 없는 일이다.

좋은 다큐는 반드시 자신이 전달하고자 하는 진실에 관해 스스로 한번 더 의심한다. 그리고 그런 의심의 사유를 통해 관객이 영화를 찬양하게 만드는 대신 관객이 영화에 당황하게 만든다. 그런 종류의 당황은 필연적으로 관객의 고민과 깊은 울림을 이끌어낸다. 송두율 교수의 간첩사건을 다루었던 〈경계도시 2〉나 용산 참사를 다룬 〈두 개의 문〉을 떠올려보자. 〈경계도시 2〉는 이 사람이 진짜 간첩이면 어떻게 하지, 라는 연출자 자신의 레드콤플렉스와 진보 좌파 진영 내부의 허영, 비뚤어진 욕망을 노출함으로써 좋은 다큐가 될 수 있었다. 〈두 개의 문〉은 피해자뿐만 아니라 가해자의 목소리에 주목해 용산 참사를 둘러싼 다양한 시각을 입체적으로 조명하는 방식으로 사건의 실체를 '강요'하는 대신 '규명'해낸 좋은 다큐였다.

무엇을 다루었느냐가 중요하지 작품의 함량이 뭐가 그렇게 중요하냐 이 엄혹한 세상에, 라고 말하는 사람들과 나는 별로 대화할 필요를 느끼지 못한다. 그것은 다큐 〈자백〉에서 과거 군부 독재 시대를 비판하는 등장인물의 대사처럼 '목적을 위해서라면 어떤 수단이든 상관없다'는 태도다. 내가 편들고 싶은 것을 위해서라면 프로파간다라도 상관없다는 사람들은, 결과적으로 그들이 비판하고자 하는 이들과 동업자다. 그뿐만 아니라 정치적 소재를 다루는 다큐들을 모두 통쳐서 함량 미달이라는 편견을 만들어내고 결과적으로 좋은 다큐가 빛을 보지 못하게 만든다. 세상을 망치는 건 그런 사람들이다.

자, 그렇다면 최승호의 〈자백〉은 좋은 다큐인가.

나는 〈자백〉이 좋은 다큐라고 생각한다. 〈자백〉은 잘 만들어진 탐사보도 다큐 필름의 조건을 비교적 잘 갖추고 있다. 그리고 그런 성취를 이끄는 눈부신 순간들을 포착해내는 데 성공했다. 아쉬운 점이 없는 건 아니다. 작품의 응집력을 고려할 때 국정원 간첩자살사건 대목은 빼는 게 나았다. 아이가 위험할 수 있는 상황인데도 피해자의 자녀와 스피커폰으로 통화하며 아버지의 죽음을 알리는 부분은 이 작품의 윤리성에 대해 고민하게 되는 지점이기도 하다. 원세훈 전 국정원장의 멘트를 얻기 위해 그와 대화하려 노력하는 시퀀스도 그리 유의미한지 모르겠다. 물론 어떤 사람들에게는 우산 밑으로 목격된 원세훈의 웃음이 통쾌하게 느껴지겠지만 〈자백〉이 좋은 다큐가 되는 데 그런 장면은 그다지 위력을 발휘하지 못한다.

〈자백〉이 관객의 정신을 바짝 차리게 만드는 장면은 후반부다. 조작된 증거와 강요된 자백만을 가지고 재판에 임했던 검사들이 너무나 편안한 자연인의 모습으로 퇴근하며 낄낄대는 풍경은 매우 눈부신 포착이다. 그러나 그보다 강력하게 관객을 압도하는 장면은 다음에 나온다. 과거 군부독재 시절 간첩조작사건으로 억울하게 고초를 겪은 피해자들이 있다. 격리되고 고문당하고 무참하게 찢어발겨졌다. 그리고 수십 년 만에 비로소 대법원에 의해 무죄판결을 받아낸 사람들이다.

그 가운데 현재 일본에 거주중인 간첩조작사건 피해자 김승효씨가 있다. 그는 서울대 재학 시절 북한의 지령을 받아 학생운동을 주도했다는 혐의로 체포돼 극심한 고문을 당했다. 그 결과 그는 정신분열 환자가 되고 말았다. 이제 초라한 백발의 노인이 된 김승효씨가 당시의 기억을 띄엄띄엄 일본어로 이야기한다. 그 기억은 참혹하고 끔찍하다. 인터뷰 도중 김승효씨는 혼잣말을 하기도 하고 우리 눈에 보이지 않는 누군가와 대화를 하기도 한다.

그러다 정신을 번쩍 차린 김승효씨가 카메라를 바라보고 한국말로 이야기하기 시작한다. 그가 수십 년 만에 처음 꺼낸 한국말은 "한국은 나쁜 나라입니다"다. 한국은 나쁜 나라입니다. 그는 이 말을 두 번 반복한다. 목적을 위해서는 수단을 가리지 않습니다. 한국은 나쁜 나라입니다.

이 순간 〈자백〉은 국가가 개인에게 어떤 짓을 할 수 있는지, 어떤 짓을 실제로 했는지, 그리고 그것이 시간을 초월하여 어떤 상흔을 남기는지 명백하게 보여준다. 거기에는 더할 것도 뺄 것

<자백>(2016)

정신을 번쩍 차린 김승효씨가 카메라를 바라보고
한국말로 이야기하기 시작한다.
그가 수십 년 만에 처음 꺼낸 한국말은
"한국은 나쁜 나라입니다"다.
한국은 나쁜 나라입니다.
그는 이 말을 두 번 반복한다.
목적을 위해서는 수단을 가리지 않습니다.
한국은 나쁜 나라입니다.

도 없다. 수많은 이들의 삶이 말 그대로 그냥 어그러진 것이다. 한국의 사회통합을 위해 '사용'되고 '폐기'된 것이다. 이 지점의 처연한 문제의식은 그런 끔찍한 일이 수십 년 전에 끝난 것이 아니라 바로 지금 이 시간에도 아무런 반성 없이 벌어지고 있다는 본래의 이야기로 자연스레 확장된다.

〈자백〉이 끝나고 나면 지금까지 간첩 혐의로 체포되었다가 최종 무죄판결을 받은 사람들의 인명 목록이 스크롤된다. 목록은 끝을 모르고 이어진다. 흥미로운 건 목록의 마지막이다. 1997년을 마지막으로 끊겼다가 2011년부터 다시 시작되고 있다. 간첩 조작사건은 1997년을 마지막으로 과거의 불우한 기억에 그치는 것 같았으나 2011년부터 다시 시작되었다. 1997년과 2011년이라는 글자에 음영효과를 다르게 넣었으면 좋지 않았을까 생각하며 탄식했다. 이 숫자는 〈자백〉이 다루고 있는 어떤 장면들보다 더 많은 것을 드러내고 있다.

소년은 부엌칼을
가방 안에 집어넣었다

똑같은 아침이었다. 소년은 창밖을 올려다보았다. 하늘은 아직 어두웠다. 어제처럼 구름이 많았다. 하루종일 흐릴 것 같았다. 가방을 챙겼다. 교과서 몇 권을 빼고 몇 권을 더했다. 하지만 이제 곧 가방은 어제보다 훨씬 더 무겁게 느껴질 것이다. 소년은 부엌칼을 가방 안에 집어넣었다.

소년은 초조했다. 소년은 가방 안에 손을 뻗어 칼을 만져보았다. 나는 이 칼을 쓸 것이다, 반드시 쓸 것이다, 소년은 다짐했다. 하지만 그러면 어떻게 되는 거지. 녀석은 어떻게 되는 거고 나는 또 어떻게 되는 걸까. 소년은 혼란스러웠다. 분명한 건 더이상은 이렇게 살 수 없다는 것뿐이었다. 소년은 마지막으로 한번만 더 어른들을 믿어보기로 했다. 소년은 담임선생님에게 면담을 요청했다.

면담이 끝났다. 소년은 문을 닫고 나왔다. 군이 보복에 대한 이야기를 꺼냈다. 막아주길 바랐던 것 같다. 그러나 돌아온 건 '보복은 나쁘다'는 원론적인 대답뿐이었다. 녀석을 학교폭력위원회에 회부하겠다는 말 같은 건 귀에 들어오지 않았다. 더이상은 단 한 대도 맞고 싶지 않았다. 디디고 있던 한 뼘의 바닥마저 사라져버린 기분이었다. 어른들은 믿을 수 없다. 결국 내 힘으로 해결할 수밖에 없는 것이다.

1교시가 끝나자마자 녀석이 소년을 찾아와 머리와 뺨을 때렸다. 미처 준비해왔던 걸 꺼내들지는 못했다. 아직은 그럴 수가 없었다. 2교시 수업 내내 소년은 가방 안의 칼만 생각했다. 다른 건 떠올릴 수가 없었다. 수업이 끝나자마자 녀석이 다시 찾아왔다. 화장실로 따라오라고 했다. 소년은 비로소 결심이 섰다. 가방 안에서 칼을 빼들어 단단히 움켜쥐었다. 소년은 칼을 들고 화장실로 갔다.

경찰이 물었다. 지금도 동급생이 죽었으면 좋겠니. 소년은 대답했다. 아니요, 죄송합니다.

2016년 9월 26일 벌어진 이 일은 원주 중학생 칼부림사건으로 세상에 알려졌다. 피해자는 10여 곳이 넘는 자상을 입었다. 학교폭력 피해자에서 살인미수 가해자가 된 소년은 이틀 후 구속되었다.

왕따를 검색해보면 연관검색어로 가장 먼저 뜨는 건 왕따를 당하지 않는 방법이다. 왕따를 당하고 있을 때 알려야 할 곳이나 해결할 수 있는 과정을 다루는 대처법 같은 건 검색어에 없다. 예방법은 찾아보되 해결책은 포기한 병증. 그것이 지금 한국의 왕따 문제다.

한국에서 왕따 문제를 다루는 방법은 내부고발자를 다루는 모습과 묘하게 닮아 있다. 어떻게든 내부에서 조용하게 해결하길 바란다. 부조리 자체에 관심을 기울이기보다는 내부고발자 개인의 성향을 들어 조직에 어울리지 못하는 부적응자의 문제로 바꾸어버린다. 남들도 그러는데 왜 우리 뭐만 가지고 그러냐는 옹호성 관전자들이 생겨난다. 그마저도 관심은 잠깐이고 내부고발자는 결코 보호받지 못한다.

왕따라는 말이 세상에 등장한 지도 거의 20년 가까이 되었다. 이지메라는 일본어를 쓰다가 내가 대학에 진학하던 해에 처음 왕따라는 말이 나왔으니 그즈음 되었을 것이다. 그 오랜 세월 동안 실효성 있는 해결책은 나오지 않았다. 폭력의 강도는 날이 갈수록 사악하고 강력해졌다.

원주의 사건이 처음 알려졌을 때 나는 작은 옷가게를 하는 동네 동생과 술을 마시고 있었다. 좀 여성스러운 친구다. 술을 마시다가 마침 이 사건 이야기가 나왔다. 그가 말했다. 이제 며칠 동안 전국에서 왕따당하고 있는 애들은 더 많이 두들겨맞겠네요. 내가 생각했던 것과 달랐다. 이런 일이 벌어지면 왕따를 시키던 가해자들도 적어도 당분간은 조심하게 되는 게 아닐까. 그게 무슨 말이냐고 물어보았다.

그는 자신도 고등학생 때 왕따를 당했다고 했다. 그런데 당시 마침 비슷한 칼부림사건이 옆 학교에서 벌어졌다. 하루종일 그 일로 학교가 뒤숭숭했다고. 그날 밤 이 친구를 괴롭혀왔던 패거리가 다시 그를 불러냈다. 빵셔틀이나 시키고 그저 비굴한 웃음을 지어주면 몇 번 쥐어박고 끝내던 아이들이었다. 그런데 그날따라 어딘가 격양돼 있었다. 그들은 "너도 나 칼로 찌를 거냐" "해봐, 해봤자 너도 전과자밖에 더 되냐"라는 말을 내뱉었다. 그리고 그날 이 친구는 여지껏 경험해보지 못한 수준으로 험하게 맞아야만 했다.

"이런 사건은 학교나 지역 차원에서 쉬쉬하고 덮어서 그렇지 여지껏 셀 수 없이 많이 있었던 일이에요. 저 아이는 사람을 찔렀으니 처벌을 받겠죠. 이제 학교폭력에 대항하면 어떻게 되는지 또하나의 사례가 등장한 셈이에요. 사람들이 이런 건 또 안 까먹거든요."

나는 늘 이기는 경험의 중요성에 대해 이야기해왔다. 이겨본 사람이 이길 의지를 가지고 다음에도 이길 수 있는 것이다. 그러나 내부고발자도 학교폭력의 피해자도 비극적인 결말만 쌓여왔다. 이러한 경험치는 가해자들에게 매우 잘못된 신호를 보내기 마련이다. 계속 그렇게 해도 된다는 신호 말이다. 물에 빠져 구조를 기다리던 아이들이 어른 시키는 대로 했다가 떼죽음을 당했다. 학교폭력으로부터 구해달라고 자기 발로 찾아간 어른과의 면담에서 어떠한 희망도 찾을 수 없었다. 어른들은 언제나 면피만 할 뿐 해결의 의지가 없다. 그런 세상이다. 구제받는 것이 불가능하다는 걸 깨달은 개인이 선택할 수 있는 건 자력구제뿐이다. 대체 이 아이들에게 칼을 쥐여주는 건 누구인가.

술을 마시고 집으로 돌아가는 길 내내 마음이 복잡했다. 어쩌면 왕따 문제에 대해 이토록 오랫동안 우리 사회가 미온적인 태도를 보이는 것은, 우리 가운데 상당수가 이 문제에서 심정적인 가해자이기 때문이 아닐까 생각했다. 괴롭힘을 당하는 사람들은 그럴 만한 이유가 있기 때문에 괴롭힘을 당하는 것이고 그렇게 조직의 결속력에 해를 끼치는 사람들에게는 왕따라는 것도 일종의 사회화 과정일 수 있다고 여기는 것이다.

문득 중학교 때 같은 학급의 친구 한 명이 떠올랐다. 왕따라는 단어가 존재하지 않을 때였지만 그건 명백한 왕따였다. 속눈썹이 무서울 정도로 길었던 그 친구는 옷을 갈아입지 않고 잘 씻지도 않았다. 괴롭힘을 당해도 그는 늘 웃을 뿐이었다. 아이들은 쉬는 시간마다 그 친구를 둘러싸고 왜 안 씻냐고 왜 옷을 안 갈아입느냐고 손가락질했다. 누군가 발을 걸어 그 친구가 넘어지면 조소를 보냈다. 그 친구와 몸이 스치면 더럽다고 외치며 수돗가로 달려갔다.

그 가운데는 나도 있었다. 나도 그리 옷을 자주 갈아입던 형편은 아니었고, 그래서 그 친구가 독박을 쓰는 게 내심 다행이라 생각했던 기억이 난다. 그래서 괴롭힐 일이 있으면 더 크게 웃었고 더 크게 욕을 했다. 나는 세상에 면목이 없다. 어른이 만든 세상에서 어른이 하라는 대로 했다가 경계로 내몰린, 교복을 입고 있는 세대 앞에 어떤 표정을 지어야 할지 모르겠다. 다 우리가 이렇게 만들어버렸다.

어른들은 언제나 면피만 할 뿐 해결의 의지가 없다.
나는 세상에 면목이 없다.
어른이 만든 세상에서
어른이 하라는 대로 했다가 경계로 내몰린,
교복을 입고 있는 세대 앞에
어떤 표정을 지어야 할지 모르겠다.
다 우리가 이렇게 만들어버렸다.

내부고발자

대개의 변화는 경험치로부터 나온다. 경험들이 쌓여야 하는 것이다. 화제가 되는 사안부터 내부고발자가 보호받고 다른 길을 보장받을 수 있도록 '지켜봐'주어야 한다. 고발당한 자들은 이 모든 게 잊혀 복수할 수 있게 되기만을 느긋하게 낙관하며 기다리는 중이다.

4등

〈위플래쉬〉는 죽여주는 영화였다. 관객 가운데 이 영화가 재즈 플레이어를 다루고 있다는 걸 기억하는 사람이 얼마나 되려나 모르겠다. 플레처가 호통치는 장면은 〈풀 메탈 자켓〉 같았고 연습 장면은 〈취권〉 같았으며 연주 장면은 〈블랙 호크 다운〉 같았다. 그 모든 호흡이 잘빠진 난도질 영화 같아서 마지막 시퀀스에 이르고 나면 주인공 아버지처럼 동공이 확장되고 호흡이 가빠지다 마침표를 딱, 하고 찍는 순간 아드레날린이 폭발해 상영관의 의자를 잡아빼 던져버리고 주차장까지 걸어가는 내내 극장 벽을 더블타임 스윙의 빠르기로 두드려 치고 싶을 지경이었다. 촬영한 컷들을 가지고 '편집'을 했다기보다 '조율'을 했다는 표현이 어울릴, 그야말로 호흡의 호흡에 의한 호흡을 위한 영화였다. 엄청나게 매혹적인 영화다.

　그리고 그렇게 매혹적인 영화들은 때때로 정작 말하고자 했던 비전과는 전혀 달리 엉뚱한 감상을 관객에게 전달하곤 한다. 이를테면 〈대부〉를 보고 마피아가 되고 싶다든지, 〈기동전사 건담〉을 보고 군인이 되고 싶다든지, 〈위플래쉬〉를 보고 역시 천재는 다그쳐서 계발되고 만들어지는 거라고 생각한다든지 말이다. 플레처 같은 능력은 없으면서 플레처처럼 행동하는 것만 좋아하는 통제 환자들이 차고 넘치는 사회에서는 더욱 그렇다.

　사실 〈위플래쉬〉는 전혀 반대의 이야기를 하는 영화다. 천재 소년이 기존의 규칙을 대변하는 악당 스승을 만나 그의 규칙을 따르고 닮아가다가 파멸할 뻔한다. 권위 있는 시니어가 '이기기 위해선 이렇게 저렇게 해야 하고 그걸 가르치려고 노력하면서 손가락질을 당하는 나는 영웅이고 남들은 다 위선자다'라는 식의 말을 내뱉으면 누구나 혹하기 쉽다.

　그러나 이 천재 소년은 정면 대결 안에서 스승의 룰을 부정하고 그것과 결별하는 방식으로 끝내 각성해 판을 뒤집어엎는다. 이게 〈위플래쉬〉의 이야기다. 〈위플래쉬〉는 〈죽은 시인의 사회〉가 아니라 〈매트릭스〉에 가까운 영화다. 천재를 각성시킨 건 그 자신이지 매타작이나 자기계발서나 강박적인 동기부여가 아니다(물론 플레처는 자기 패배를 인정하고 천재가 탄생하는 순간을 목격하는 자체를 즐길 만큼 성숙한 악당이다. 잘 만들어진 악당 캐릭터들이 그렇듯. 플레처는 그래서 매혹적이다).

　물론 〈위플래쉬〉는 천재 이야기다. 공감할 수 있는 여지가

<위플래쉬|Whiplash>(2014)

천재 소년은 정면 대결 안에서 스승의 룰을 부정하고
그것과 결별하는 방식으로 끝내 각성해 판을 뒤집어엎는다.
천재를 각성시킨 건 그 자신이지
메타작이나 자기계발서나 강박적인 동기부여가 아니다.

적을 수 있다. 그렇다면 우리에게 조금 더 친숙하고, 그래서 우리 자신과 주변을 돌아볼 수 있는 공간을 확보해줄 만한 영화를 찾아보자. 정지우 감독의 〈4등〉이다. 나는 이 영화가 너무 좋다.

주인공은 수영에 재능이 있는 소년이다. 자기가 그걸 알고 있다. 엄마에게는 꿈이 있다. 아들이 1등을 하는 것이다. 그래서 극성이다. 자식이 재능을 발견하게끔 길을 모색해주기보다 없는 재능을 발명하게 하려고 자식에게 온갖 수고를 아끼지 않는 대다수 한국의 부모들이 그렇듯. 그런데 문제가 있다. 정작 소년은 1등에 별 관심이 없다. 만날 4등을 한다. 엄마는 복장이 터진다. 아들이 패배자로 성장할 것 같아 조마조마하다.

어느 날 교회에서 정보를 입수한 엄마는 과거 학생 때 천재적인 수영 선수였다는 코치를 소개받는다. 엄마는 코치에게 아들을 맡긴다. 코치는 처음에는 심드렁하다. 그러나 곧 소년에게 재능이 있다는 걸 눈치챈다. 코치는 진심으로 소년을 가르치기 시작한다. 그리고 드디어 대회. 언제나 4등만 하던 소년이 간발의 차이로 2등을 한다. 엄마는 떨듯이 기뻐한다. 그날 밤 집에서 파티가 벌어진다. 너무 옭아매지 말고 그냥 취미로 즐기게 놔두라던 아버지도 정작 2등을 했다니까 기분이 좋은 눈치다.

그때 고기를 먹다 말고 동생이 말한다. 정말 맞고 하니까 잘한 거야? 예전에는 안 맞아서 늘 4등 한 거야?

영화 〈4등〉은 우리에게 익숙한 풍경을 펼쳐놓는다. 극성맞은 부모와 고통받는 아이. 그러나 이 영화의 진심은 그런 부모 몇 사람 타박하는 것에 가닿아 있지 않다.

관객은 코치가 학생 시절 '감독이 너무 때린다'는 이유로 전도유망한 수영 선수의 길을 때려치운 걸 영화 초반부 시퀀스를 통해 알고 있다. 그런 코치가 지금은 이렇게 이야기한다. "그때 감독님이 나를 더 때리고 강하게 키웠으면 내가 더 많이 성공했을 텐데." 혹은 이렇게도 이야기한다. "네가 열심히 안 하니까 때리는 거지, 열심히 하면 때리겠냐." 관객은 또한 아들이 맞으면서 수영을 배우고 있다는 걸 엄마가 눈치챘다는 사실을 알고 있다. 엄마는 이렇게 이야기한다. "나는 우리 애가 맞는 것보다 1등 못할까봐 더 무서워."

수영이 아니라 다른 무엇으로 바꾸어도 마찬가지다. 매를 든 선생님이든 군대 선임이든 회사 선배든. '폭력이 동원되더라도 강하게 통제하고 억압할수록 개인에게 동기가 생기고 세상은 더 잘 굴러간다'는 걸 겉으로 주장하는 사람은 요즘 드물다. 그러나 그게 내심 불편한 진실이라고 생각하는 태도는 우리 사회 깊숙이 자리잡고 있다.

〈4등〉의 호쾌한 점은 소년이 이 모든 걸 이겨내는 과정에 있다. 〈위플래쉬〉의 주인공처럼 스승에게 압도되고 그를 닮아가기도 한다. 그러나 소년은 결국 경쟁 자체를 부정하지도 않으면서 경쟁에서 이기고 성장하는 방법을 스스로 터득해낸다. 이 소년에게 재능이 있고 자신이 그걸 알고 있다는 점은 이 이야기가 성립하기 위한 핵심이다. 만약 이 이야기가 경쟁이 왜 필요해 재능 없이도 1등 할 수 있어 따위의 히피 같은 이야기였으면 굉장히 싫었을 것 같다. 중요한 건 자기 능력을 객관화할 줄 아는 소년의

<4등>(2014)

엄마는 이렇게 이야기한다.
"나는 우리 애가 맞는 것보다 1등 못할까봐 더 무서워."
'폭력이 동원되더라도 강하게 통제하고 억압할수록
개인에게 동기가 생기고 세상은 더 잘 굴러간다'는 걸
겉으로 주장하는 사람은 요즘 드물다.
그러나 그게 내심 불편한 진실이라고 생각하는 태도는
우리 사회 깊숙이 자리잡고 있다.

태도와 그에 반해 열등한 수준에 매몰되어 있는 주변의 계발 심리다.

보통 부조리한 세상과 이상을 좇는 개인을 연결할 통로가 되어준답시고 대단한 현자처럼 구는 사람들은 무슨 굉장한 진리를 설명하듯이 이런 이야기를 들려주고는 한다.

"너 힘들고 좆같은 거 알아, 그런데 이게 세상이야, 나라고 나쁜 사람 되고 싶어서 이러겠니? 니 눈에는 한심한 어른으로 비치겠지, 하하하(고개를 약간 기울인 쓴웃음)…… 너는 잘될 거야, 일단 영리하게 굴자."

소년은 그런 플레처의 논리, 앞선 세대의 노하우, '세상의 태도'와 타협하지 않는다. 그리고 자기 힘으로, 자기만의 동기를 가지고 결과를 만들어낸다.

그런 점에서 영화 〈4등〉의 가장 빛나는 순간은 마지막 장면이 아니다. 이 영화의 가장 빛나는 순간은 코치가 남긴 선물을 소년이 집어들지 않는 장면이다. 소년은 부조리한 질서로부터 어떠한 유산도 이어받기를 거절한 것이다.

<4등> (2014)

소년은 플레처의 논리,
앞선 세대의 노하우,
'세상의 태도'와 타협하지 않는다.
그리고 자기 힘으로,
자기만의 동기를 가지고 결과를 만들어낸다.

우리에게 필요한 건 노블레스 오블리주 따위가 아니라 모두에게
한 치의 오차도 없이 엄정하게 적용될 원칙과 약속이다.

착한 주인, 착한 임금, 착한 지배계급에 대한 판타지는 쓸모
없고 오래된 노예근성에 불과하다. 그런 걸 요구할 이유도 없다.
왕조가 아닌 이상 우리가 채택한 시스템에서는 모두에게 공히
적용되는 엄정한 원칙과 약속이야말로 가장 소중한 가치다.

'착한 주인'에 대한 전근대적 판타지를 없애야만 '모두에게
똑같은 원칙과 약속'이라는 당연한 헌법적 질서가 뿌리내릴 수
있다. 그러나 현실은 어느 지배계급의 스캔들을 다른 지배계급
의 미담으로 덮는 식의 과정이 영원히 반복되는 세상.

실패하기에는
너무 거대한

〈머니 몬스터〉는 외연이 화려한 영화다. 조디 포스터가 연출을 맡았다. 조지 클루니와 줄리아 로버츠가 연기한다. 이야기 또한 관객의 마음을 잡아끌기 충분해 보인다. 꽤 잘나가는 경제예능 쇼가 진행되는 도중에 이 쇼에서 추천한 금융상품에 투자했다가 전 재산을 날린 소시민이 난입하여 진행자를 인질로 삼고 폭주한다.

이야기는 실제 쇼가 진행되는 것처럼 거의 실시간으로 흘러가고 관객은 흡사 이 사건이 진짜로 벌어지고 있다는 느낌을 받을 만하다. 그뿐만 아니라 단지 인질극과 실시간 흐름에서 오는 서스펜스를 넘어 결코 처벌받는 법이 없는 경제사범을 단죄해내는 쾌감마저 존재한다. 리먼 브러더스 사태를 비롯한 일련의 금

융 환란 이후를 살아나가는 미국 관객에게 이는 꽤 각별한 대리만족일 것이다. 요컨대 당대의 요구를 담고 있다는 이야기다. 그런데 이상한 일이다. 〈머니 몬스터〉는 외연부터 이야기에 이르기까지 언뜻 갖출 것을 다 갖추고 있음에도 불구하고 결국 아무것도 성취해내지 못하는, 초라한 완성도를 드러내고 만다. 어떻게 된 일일까.

이야기는 주인공이 진행하는 경제예능쇼 〈머니 몬스터〉의 촬영과 함께 시작된다. 주인공 리 게이츠는 프로그램의 여전한 인기에도 불구하고 전과 같지 않은 위상 탓에 다소 신경질을 부린다. 프로듀서는 이번 생방송을 마지막으로 프로그램을 떠날 작정이다. 누구 하나 입 밖으로 꺼내지는 않지만 다들 지쳐 있는 느낌이다.

쇼가 시작된다. 주인공이 여느 때처럼 오늘의 추천상품을 소개하려는 찰나 카메라의 시선 구석에 낯선 남자가 포착된다. 택배 기사다. 아니나 다를까 촬영장으로 난입한 택배 기사는 주인공을 인질로 잡고 그에게 폭탄조끼를 입힌다. 인질범은 이 쇼에서 추천한 상품에 투자했다가 알거지가 된 소시민이다. 주인공은 당신이 손해 본 액수를 보상하겠다고 제안하지만 인질범은 거절한다. 그가 원하는 것은 완벽해 보였던 이 상품의 주가가 왜 휴지 조각이 되었는지, 외부에 알려진 공식 성명이 아닌 실제 거기서 무슨 일이 벌어진 건지에 관한 진실이다. 카메라는 계속해서 돌아가고 인질범의 요구는 생중계로 미국 전역에 방송된다.

방송을 보고 있던 시민들은 되레 인질범을 응원하게 되고 주인공은 시간이 갈수록 초조해진다. 주인공은 진실을 밝히기로 마음먹는다.

경제범죄는 할리우드 영화의 주소재 가운데 하나였다. 이 방면의 레퍼런스라고 할 만한 〈월스트리트〉는 오래도록 사랑받으며 수많은 유사 영화들을 양산해냈다. 경제범죄 영화는 기본적으로 사기극이었다. 잘 빼입은 엘리트들이 어떤 방식으로 합법적인 사기를 쳐서 판돈을 긁어가는가에 관한 이야기였다. 지나치게 심각하지 않으면서 쿨해 보이는 소재였고 관객은 〈스팅〉이나 〈오션스 일레븐〉을 보듯이 경제범죄 영화를 소비했다.

리먼 브러더스 사태를 전후한 미국의 경제 환란 이후 모든 것이 바뀌었다. 이 경제 환란은 미국인의 삶을 근원부터 송두리째 뒤흔들어놓았다. 이제 경제범죄 영화는 할리우드에서 만들어지는 영화들 가운데 가장 진지하고 구조적이며 지능적인 동시에 관객의 영혼을 잡아 흔드는 장르가 되었다.

〈마진 콜: 24시간, 조작된 진실〉(이하 〈마진 콜〉) 〈투 빅 투 페일〉 〈빅 쇼트〉 〈인사이드 잡〉 같은 수작들이 등장했고, 〈라스트 홈〉 같은 평범한 영화조차 앞선 수작들의 자장 안에서 특별해 보일 지경에 이르렀다. 이 영화들은 더이상 '경제'와 '범죄'를 따로 구분지어 설명하기 어려워진 현실의 문제를 다루었다. 잠시 다른 이야기이지만, 〈마진 콜〉 〈투 빅 투 페일〉 〈빅 쇼트〉 〈인사이드 잡〉을 아직 보지 못한 독자가 있다면 반드시 한꺼번에 몰아서 보길 추천한다. 동시대성이라는 사명감을 제외하더라도 관객의 영혼을 위해 반드시 봐야만 하는 영화들이다. 〈인사이드 잡〉은 다큐니까 제일 마지막에 보는 게 감상의 흐름을 위해 좋을 것 같다.

〈머니 몬스터〉는 앞서 언급한 영화들의 연장선 위에 있는 영화다. 그러나 이 영화는 〈마진 콜〉이나 〈빅 쇼트〉 같은 영화들이 이룩한 눈부신 성취와는 아쉽게도 멀리 떨어져 있다. 일단은 조지 클루니와 줄리아 로버츠가 연기하는 두 주인공 캐릭터 사이의 무게 배분에 실패했다. 프로듀서를 연기하는 줄리아 로버츠의 무게감이 뒤로 갈수록 더 짙어지다보니 이야기의 중심이 되어야 할 인질은 어느 순간 영화에서 실종되어버리고 만다. 그 때문에 실시간 인질극이 갖는 장점은 거의 상실되어버린다. 그러나 가장 큰 문제는 따로 있다.

〈머니 몬스터〉의 가장 큰 문제는 이야기에 있다. 주인공은 문제를 해결하기로 마음먹는다. 진실을 수집해 대중에 알리고 인질범의 억울함을 풀어주기 위해 프로듀서와 협력한다.

그런데 〈머니 몬스터〉의 수수께끼를 푸는 열쇠는 주인공의 추리도, 프로듀서의 용기도, 어느 누구의 두뇌 싸움도 아닌, 그저 등장인물 한 명의 양심이다. 그 양심이 발화되기 위해 어떠한 합리적인 배경이나 맥락이 존재하는 것도 아니다. 그저 그 인물은 우연히 착한 사람이었던 것이다. 이는 이야기의 극적 구조와 완결성에 심각한 장애로 작용한다. 모든 수수께끼를 푸는 유일한 키를 누군가의 양심에 맡겨버린 결과 이야기는 매우 편리하게 마무리된다. 동시에 영화는 너무나 얇은 완결성과 문제의식을 가진 쉽고 편리한 이야기로 전락하고 만다.

그러나 〈머니 몬스터〉의 이야기가 갖고 있는 중대한 결점이 단점으로만 작용하는 건 아니다. 이 영화의 실책은 역설적으로 또다른 진실 하나를 드러낸다. 즉 지금의 현실에서 구조적인 문제로 전락해버린 경제범죄를 단죄하는 건 완전히 불가능하다, 개인의 양심에 기대는 기도하는 마음 이외에는 어떠한 해결책도 존재하지 않는다, 라는 (이 영화를 만든 사람들이 기대하지 않았을) 문제 제기에 이르기 때문이다. 이는 〈투 빅 투 페일〉과 같은 영화의 메시지와 닿으면서 다시 한번 현실세계에 대한 열패감을 끄집어낸다. 그들은 범죄를 저질렀지만 그들과 경제를 따로 떨어뜨려 인식하는 건 불가능하다. 그들이 곧 경제이다. 고로, 그들을 단죄하는 건 불가능한 일이다. 그들은 실패하기에는 너무 큰 존재들이다.

그들은 범죄를 저질렀지만
그들과 경제를 따로 떨어뜨려 인식하는 건 불가능하다.
그들이 곧 경제이다.
고로, 그들을 단죄하는 건 불가능한 일이다.

그들은 실패하기에는 너무 큰 존재들이다.

평범성

포도주를 먹는다 생각하고 먹어라. 교수가 말했다. 교수가 내민 병에는 동료들의 인분이 들어 있었다. 인분을 먹고 인간이 되라는 게 교수의 주문이었다. 그는 먹어야 했다. 그가 당한 고통은 인분을 먹는 것에서 그치지 않았다. 그는 수시로 동료들과 교수에게 얼차려를 받았고 얼굴에 비닐봉지가 씌워진 상태에서 호신용 스프레이 세례를 맞아야 했으며 피부가 괴사할 지경에 이를 때까지 야구방망이로 구타당하기도 했다. 며칠 동안 벌어진 일이 아니다. 그는 이 일을 지난 2년 동안 당해왔다. 교수가 지시했고 두 명의 동료가 동참한 일이었다. 교수는 경찰 조사에서 이렇게 말했다. 내게 악마가 씌었던 것 같다.

우리는 이런 일을 마주했을 때 대개 다음과 같은 질문을 떠올린다. 왜 당하고 있었을까. 동료들은 자신보다 나이가 어린 여자였다. 충분히 폭행을 제지할 수 있었다. 그러나 그는 그러지 않았다. 하지 못했다.

우선 권위와 위계에 의한 것이라 생각해볼 수 있다. 교수는 해당 분야의 권위자였다. 과거 지방 대학에 제자를 교수로 채용하게 하는 등 영향력을 행사해왔다. 피해자 또한 교수를 통해 그렇게 될 수 있으리라는 희망을 가졌을 것이다. 그러나 지난 2년 동안 이어진 지속적인 폭행과 구타, 그가 느꼈을 끔찍한 모멸감, 더불어 생명에 위협을 느끼게 만드는 상황들을 고려해보면 충분한 설명이 되지 못한다.

피해자는 각서 때문이었다고 설명한다. 교수가 자신의 가혹 행위를 발설하는 것을 막기 위해 수십 회에 걸쳐 1억 3천만 원에 달하는 지급각서를 받아왔다는 것이다. 이유들을 살펴보면 전화를 제때 받지 않았다, 마음에 들지 않는다는 식의 말이 안 되는 것들뿐이다. 각서는 법적으로 효력이 없다. 그러나 그는 이것이 강제성을 갖고 있다고 믿었다. 교수는 네가 도망가면 네 부모가 갚아야 하고, 네 부모가 못 갚으면 너의 외할머니가 갚아야 한다고 말했다. 그는 이 모든 걸 철석같이 믿었다.

언뜻 이해가 가지 않는 상황이다. 어쩌면 먼저 떠올렸어야 하는 질문은 왜 당하고 있었을까, 가 아니라 왜 그런 짓을 저질렀을까, 였는지 모른다. 이 경우 가장 쉽고 간편한 답변은 늘 준비되어 있다. 교수가 미친놈이기 때문이라는 것이다. 가해자를 우리와는 전혀 다른 사이코패스로 완전하게 구별하고 나면 납득할 수 없는 서사의 구멍들은 아주 선명하게 채워진다. 그는 왜 피해자에게 인분을 먹이고 폭행을 하고 고문에 가까운 체벌을 가했나. 사이코패스이기 때문에. 간단한 설명이다. 그러나 과연 삶이란 게 그리 명료하던가. 이를 단지 사이코패스의 문제로 구분하는 것은 이 사건에 포함된 어느 불편한 지점들을 무마하고자 하는, 단출한 사고의 결과물일 수 있다.

영화 〈엑스페리먼트〉는 어느 심리학자에 의해 벌어진 실험을 다루고 있다. 연구원들이 면접을 통해 스무 명의 평범한 사람들을 모집한다. 이렇게 모집된 이들에게 간수와 죄수라는 역할이 주어진다. 이들의 일상은 24시간 카메라를 통해 관찰된다. 그렇게 14일만 지내면 상당한 돈을 지급한다는 것이다. 그렇게 12명의 죄수와 8명의 간수가 나누어졌다. 실험 1일째, 모두가 즐겁다. 간수도 죄수도 진지하지 않다. 그러나 시간이 흐르면서 분위기가 달라진다. 역할을 수행하는 과정에서 간수는 권위적으로, 죄수는 반항하다가 결국 순응하고 굴종을 견디는 방향으로 급격하게 변모해간다. 그리고 마침내 5일째. 첫번째 살인이 벌어진다.

올리버 히르비겔 감독의 〈엑스페리먼트〉가 국내에 소개되었을 때 가장 흔한 반응은 '비약이 심하다'였다. 간수와 죄수의 역할을 나눈 것만으로 어떻게 그렇게 짧은 시간 안에 폭력이 발생할 수 있냐는 것이다. 그러나 일부 극적인 요소를 제외하면 이것은 실제 일어났던 일이다. 〈엑스페리먼트〉는 1971년 스탠퍼드 대학에서 벌어진 심리실험의 내용에 기반한 영화다.

1971년 필립 짐바르도 박사는 모의감옥에서 간수와 죄수 역할을 맡은 이들이 어떻게 변화해가는지에 대해 연구했다. 일당 15달러를 받고 2주간 실험에 참여할 학생들을 모집했다. 24명의 참가자가 모였고 무작위로 간수와 죄수 역할을 나누었다. 간수들은 법과 질서를 유지해야 하며 죄수를 학대하거나 폭력을 가해서는 안 된다는 설명을 들었다.

　단 이틀 만에 폭력사건이 벌어졌다. 태도가 불량한 죄수들을 독방에 가두고 옷을 벗기고 소화기를 뿌렸다. 잠을 재우지 않고 얼차려를 시켰으며 폭언과 욕설을 쏟아냈다. 죄수들은 눈빛이 흐려지고 행동이 눈에 띄게 느려졌다. 한 죄수는 정신쇠약 상태에 빠져들었다. 나흘째에는 간수들이 죄수들에게 동물이 성교하는 동작을 해보라는 주문을 하기에 이른다. 짐바르도 박사는 더이상의 실험이 불가능하다고 판단했다. 실험은 다음날 중지되었다. 그들은 모두 평범한 학생이었다. 훗날 짐바르도 박사는 『루시퍼 이펙트』를 통해 다음과 같이 썼다.

　"일부 교도관들은 악의 창조자로, 또다른 일부 교도관들은 아무런 행동을 하지 않음으로써 악이 번성하는 것을 방조했다. 한편 정상적이고 건강한 젊은이들 일부는 죄수 역할을 하면서 정신적으로 완전히 무너져버렸고, 남은 생존자들은 좀비 같은 추종자가 되었다."

　인분을 먹인 교수와 인분을 먹은 제자는 그들이 만들어낸 감옥 안의 간수와 죄수였는지 모른다. 교수는 '그래도 되는' 그만의 감옥 안에서 자기 당위에 심취해 마음껏 폭력을 행사했다.

제자는 '그래야 하는' 그곳에서 교수의 일상적인 폭력과 너를 위한 것이라는 논리 앞에 정신이 완전히 무너져내렸다. 방점은 저들이 영화 〈엑스페리먼트〉나 짐바르도 실험에 참가했던 학생들처럼 매우 특별하고 유별난 사람이 아니라는 데 찍힌다. 저 감옥 또한 거기에만 존재하지 않는다. 지금도 어느 가정에, 어느 일터에, 어느 친구들 사이에서 스스로 간수와 죄수임을 부정하는 가운데 명백하게 존재하고 기능하고 있다.

요컨대 나도, 우리도 누군가에게 이미 인분 교수이거나 그럴 수 있다는 것이다. 누구나 그럴듯한 상황과 환경이 주어지면 사랑을, 혈연을, 우정을, 금전을, 위계를 빌미로 악을 행사한다. 그 자신만이 그것을 악으로 인식하지 않고 내가 반드시 해야만 하는 것, 혹은 선의로 인식할 뿐이다. 악은 특별한 사람들에 의해 자행되지 않는다.

한나 아렌트는 『예루살렘의 아이히만』을 저술하면서 악의 평범성에 대해 거론했다. 전범재판에서 목격한 아돌프 아이히만은 뿔이 난 악마가 아니었다. 평범하다는 표현이 아까울 만큼 평범한 사람이었다. 저 잔악한 아돌프 아이히만이 타고난 악마가 아니라는 데 한나 아렌트는 충격을 받았다. 아이히만은 그저 자기 자신의 끔찍한 행동을 객관적으로 살피지 않고 생각 없이 역할에만 충실했던 사람에 불과했다. 한나 아렌트는 그와 같은 상황 안에 있을 때 더욱더 '생각'을 해야 한다고 강조한다.

악의 평범성 개념은 아이히만의 말년 인터뷰와 새로운 연구 결과들을 통해 반박되거나 보충되고 있다. 그러나 위계와 시스템, 적극적인 동조자들이 발견되는 이와 같은 사건이 벌어질 때마다 악의 평범성 논쟁, 그리고 〈엑스페리먼트〉가 남긴 가장 중대하고 어려운 화두가 머리를 떠나지 않는다. '그래도 되는' 상황에서 '그렇게 하지 않는' 것 말이다. 인간이 인간답게 살기란 그렇게 힘들다.

누구나 그럴듯한 상황과 환경이 주어지면
사랑을, 혈연을, 우정을, 금전을, 위계를 빌미로
악을 행사한다.
'그래도 되는' 상황에서
'그렇게 하지 않는' 것.
인간이 인간답게 살기란 그렇게 힘들다.

정치적이다

살아가면서 모든 선택과 결정은 결국 정치적인 것이다. '정치적인 것'을 '부정한 것'으로 환원시키고 모든 종류의 비판적인 텍스트를 정치적이라 겁박하는 시도들은 가장 음흉하고 비뚤어진 형태의 협박이며 가장 저열한 수준의 정치다.

드센
사람

대중을 신문고로 착각해서는 곤란하다. 억울함이란 반드시 주관적일 수밖에 없다. 물론 주관적이라는 것이 무조건 거짓을 의미하지는 않는다. 다만 자기 입장에만 갇혀 있는 경우에는 나의 뜨거움에 젖어 심취하기 쉽다. 억울함을 호소하기에 앞서 나의 불만을 있는 힘껏 객관적으로 바라보고 타인의 시선으로 냉정하게 판단하는 과정을 거쳐야만 한다. 그러한 과정을 거치지 않은 호소는, 불의에 저항하고자 하는 다른 억울한 목소리들에 민폐를 끼치는 꼴이 된다. 드센 사람이 다 저렇지, 라는 선입견을 생산하기 때문이다.

동성애

여전히 동성애 반대의 근거로 레위기를 거론하는 가장 고루하고 극성맞은 기독교 근본주의자들조차 레위기에서 언급된 다른 '부정한 것들', 예를 들어 돼지고기나 여성의 월경과 출산을 죄라고 말하지는 않는다. 인지부조화의 좋은 예.

예수는 예루살렘 입성 후 넋이 나간 제자들에게 "네가 이 큰 건물을 보느냐. 돌 하나도 돌 위에 남지 않고 다 무너지리라(마가복음 13장 2절)"라고 말했다. 난 그가 한국의 대형 교회와 근본주의자들을 목격하면 지체 없이 도장깨기를 시작하리라 생각한다.

탈주하는
여자들

나는 언제나 세라 워터스의 소설 『핑거스미스』에서 이야기 말미에 석스비 부인이 보여주는 변화가 조금 이상하다고 생각해왔다. 『핑거스미스』에서 가장 무시무시한 사람은 이모부도 아니고 젠틀맨도 아니다. 석스비 부인이다. 그는 무언가를 그토록 오랫동안 계획하고 치밀하게 조종해 행동에 옮길 수 있는 사람이다. 그런데 키운 딸과 낳은 딸 앞에서 어떻게 그리 쉽게 허물어질 수 있단 말인가.

　　단지 키운 딸을 향한 모성애나 양심의 가책이 작동한 모양이라 여기고 넘어갈 수도 있다. 그러나 그러기에는 재미있게 잘 읽고 있던 이야기에 없던 틈이 큼지막하게 벌어진 것 같아 아무래도 개운치 않았다. 그 틈을 메워줄 다른 반전이 있을 줄 알았으나 남아 있는 페이지는 속절없이 동이 났다. 『핑거스미스』를 원작으로 한 박찬욱 감독의 영화 〈아가씨〉가 이 부분을 어떻게 바꾸고 개연성을 통제했을지 궁금했다. 영화를 보고 궁금증이 풀렸다.

애초에 그런 설정 다 날려버림.

시작은 원작과 같다. 배경만 일제강점기로 바뀌었다. 주인공은 고아다. 대부호인 이모부의 집에서 사는 그녀는 엄격하게 통제된 생활에 익숙해져 있다. 이모부는 희귀한 고서들을 수집하고, 귀족들이 모이는 날이면 그녀가 단상에 앉아 낭독을 한다. 그런 그녀의 삶에 백작(원작의 젠틀맨)이 등장한다. 백작은 주인공 앞으로 상당한 액수의 상속금이 있다는 것과 그녀가 결혼을 해야 그 돈을 받을 수 있다는 걸 알고 있다. 백작은 주인공을 꾀어 결혼하고 돈을 가로챌 심산이다. 이 작업을 수월하게 하기 위해 백작은 역시 고아이며 소매치기인 숙희를 하녀로 잠입시켜 아가씨 곁에서 생활하게 만든다. 두 여인은 급격하게 친해진다.

원작은 『올리버 트위스트』의 레즈비언 버전 같은 이야기였다. 박찬욱의 〈아가씨〉는 주인공들을 옥죄어 억누르고 있는 질서로부터 탈주하고 복수도 성공하는 연인의 모습을 그린다는 점에서 〈델마와 루이스〉 해피엔딩 버전에 더 가까운 모습이다. 중반까지는 익숙하게 흘러가다가 원작과 결별하고 갈라지는 시점부터 조금 더 경쾌하고 활기 있어진다.

중반 이후의 바뀐 이야기는 반전으로 이어지는 원작의 설정 하나를 버리는 대신 훨씬 간결하고 직선적인 느낌을 준다. 떠올려보면 박찬욱의 전작 〈스토커〉는 한 소녀가 '나는 누구인가'라는 문제에 대해 각성하고 어머니의 질서로부터 벗어나 세상 밖으로 탈주하는 이야기였다. 〈아가씨〉에서 주인공들은 이모부와 그의 은밀한 취미가 대변하는 남성적인 억압의 세계로부터 탈주한다.

　　조금 더 감독의 취향으로 다듬어진 게 분명한 낭독회의 풍경은 꽤 변태적이고 재미있다. 언뜻 피터 그리너웨이의 영화나 직접적으로는 파솔리니의 〈살로 소돔의 120일〉 같은 느낌을 준다. 이 부분에 살을 붙여 부각시켰다면 조금 더 논쟁적인 영화가 되었겠지만 등급을 받기 어려웠을 테니.

　　결국 〈아가씨〉에서 겉으로 보기에 가장 논쟁적인 부분은 성적 묘사 부분이 될 것이다. 이 영화에 남녀 간의 섹스 장면은 존재하지 않는다. 아가씨와 숙희 사이의 굵직한 섹스 시퀀스가 몇 차례 있고, 이 과정의 성적 묘사는 대단히 과감하고 생각보다 조금씩 더 길다. 그러나 그렇게 긴 묘사를 통틀어 딱히 성적 흥분을 일으키게 할 만한 구석은 거의 없다. 이 영화에서 포르노그래피를 향한 욕구를 챙기고자 했던 관객이라면 다른 걸 찾는 게 좋겠다(그녀들이 탈주하는 세계가 정작 남성-포르노그래피화된 야설의 세계다). 대신 그간 한국 영화에서 본 적이 있나 싶었던 자세나 표정들이 나와서 좋다(표정이 특히 마음에 든다. 이 영화에는 섹스 장면에 언제나 등장하는 재채기하기 직전의 표정 같은 건 없다).

<스토커>[2012]

<스토커>는 한 소녀가
'나는 누구인가'라는 문제에 대해 각성하고
어머니의 질서로부터 벗어나
세상 밖으로 탈주하는 이야기였다.

<아가씨>에서 주인공들은
이모부와 그의 은밀한 취미가 대변하는
남성적인 억압의 세계로부터 탈주한다.

<아가씨>(2016)

배우들의 연기는 역시 현장에서 잘 조율된 기색이 역력하다. 김민희의 일본어 연기는 생각보다 훨씬 더 좋다. 김태리는 연기도 비교적 안정되어 있지만 무엇보다 한국 영화에서 '못 보던 얼굴'이다. 좋은 얼굴이다. 그걸 영리하게 사용할 쓰임과 자기 길을 찾는다면 이건 좋은 출발이 될 것이다.

그리고 하정우 이야기를 안 할 수가 없는데, 두 가지다. 먼저 이 영화는 의외로 웃음 포인트가 많고 그 팔 할이 하정우 덕분이다. 역할의 능청스러움이나 악역으로서의 기민함은 원작의 젠틀맨보다 백작을 훨씬 매력적인 인물로 보이게 만든다. 자유도가 높은 캐릭터이기 때문에 그냥 혼자 영화 안에서 호객행위하며 신나게 놀았다고 볼 수도 있지만, 그럼에도 불구하고 영화 전체와 격리되어 따로 놀지 않는 선을 유지할 수 있는 건 배우의 능력이다.

다른 하나는 결과적으로 아주 달라져버린 캐릭터의 인상이다. 젠틀맨은 악랄한 인물이었다. 백작도 그렇다. 이야기가 한 차례 반전을 맞은 이후 백작이 아가씨에게 진심으로 사랑을 고백할 때 원작을 읽은 관객은 생각했을 것이다. 야 저놈이 나머지 반도 먹으려고 하는구나, 능글맞기 짝이 없는 놈. 그러나 영화가 끝나면 알 수 있듯 이야기는 원작과 달라져 있고 결과적으로 백작은 젠틀맨과 달리 꽤나 순정이 있는 존재가 되어버린다. 원작의 설정 하나가 증발하면서 두 여인이 탈주한 이후의 백작은 (소매치기 패거리가 그렇듯이) 자칫 이야기 밖으로 떠밀려버릴 운명이다. 영화에서 실제 그렇기도 하다. 그러나 백작이라는 인물 자체의 성격이 어느 정도 낭만화된 덕에 그의 운명을 그리는 후반부가 이야기 안에서 균형을 찾는다.

나는 〈박쥐〉를, 사랑하는 사람과 말 그대로 영원히 함께할 수 있게 된 연인이 누군가를 영원히 사랑한다는 게 가능하지 않다는 사실을 깨닫고 동반자살하는 이야기로 기억하고 있다. 그리고 그것을 마지막으로 박찬욱의 영화가 행복한 결말을 갈구하는 방향으로 선회했다고 느낀다. 〈스토커〉는 소녀가 성장하고 각성해 자기를 가둬둔 틀 밖으로 뻗어나가는 이야기였다. 〈아가씨〉에선 연인이 사랑하는 사람의 손을 꼭 잡고 세상 밖으로 나간다. 그들은 행복했을까. 왜 하필 그 시점에 상하이로 갔을까. 그러나 그들은 딱히 역사와 불화하지 않는 이들이니 어찌됐든 힘들게 얻은 걸 소중하게 여기며 행복하게 살았으리라 생각하고 싶다. 어렵고 힘들게 얻은 걸 까먹고 소중하게 생각하지 않는 사람들은 행복할 자격이 없다.

여기서는
그래도 되니까

왜 〈송곳〉은 〈미생〉이 되지 못했나. 드라마 〈송곳〉이 종영되자마자 가장 먼저 들려온 질문이었다. 그럴 만하다. 시작부터 〈송곳〉에 대한 언론의 관심은 이 드라마가 〈미생〉의 인기를 재현할 수 있을 것이냐에 맞춰져 있었다. 그리고 드라마가 종영한 이 시점에서 돌아보건대 시청자들의 호감과 상찬에도 불구하고 〈송곳〉은 〈미생〉만큼의 인기를 끌지 못한 게 사실이다. 그래서 다시 들려오는 이 질문. 왜 〈송곳〉은 〈미생〉이 되지 못했나.

그러나 이 질문이 가능하기 위해서는 한 가지 전제가 필요하다. 왜 〈송곳〉이 〈미생〉이 되지 못했는지에 관한 질문이 성립하려면, 먼저 '〈송곳〉은 〈미생〉이 되려고 했는가'에 대한 해석상의 합의가 먼저 이행되어야 하기 때문이다. 그러니까 〈송곳〉이

〈미생〉을, 아니 〈미생〉이 〈송곳〉을, 아니다 〈송곳〉이 〈미생〉을,
아 헷갈려.

〈송곳〉은 〈미생〉이 되려 한 적이 없다. 둘은 애초 전혀 다른
종류의 이야기다. 이 두 이야기에 관한 대중의 상반된 반응은 바
로 그 '다른' 점으로부터 출발하는 것이다.

〈미생〉은 청년실업과 비정규직 문제를 다루었다. 보다 정확
하게 말하자면 〈미생〉은 기성의 조직에 소속되길 열망하는 청년
의 이야기였다. 부조리해 보이는 어른들의 세계에도 합리적인
요소들이 존재하고, 그러한 합리성을 지켜내려 노력하는 어른들
이 있으며, 그들에게 인정받고 필요한 사람이 되기 위해 온 힘을
다하는 장그래가 있었다. 〈미생〉은 그런 장그래가 결국 어른의
세계를 이해하고, 화해하고, 인정받고, 소속되어, 자기 밥벌이를
하는 상사맨으로 거듭나기까지의 풍경을 다루었다.

〈미생〉은 충실하고 사려 깊은 취재에 기반한 훌륭한 이야기
였다. 〈미생〉의 가장 큰 장점은 균형감각이었다. 청년과 기성의
질서라는 두 세계 사이에서 어느 한쪽을 절대적인 선이나 악으
로 몰지 않고 균형을 찾으려 애썼다. '거기에는 그럴 만한 이유
가 있다'라는 것 말이다.

그러나 〈미생〉의 가장 큰 단점 또한 여기에서 기인했다. 현
실에서 전혀 균형을 이루지 못하고 있는 것을 애써 균형감 있게
다루려다보니 결국 기계적인 무게추가 기성의 질서 쪽에 더 실
려버린 것이다. 그러다보니 되레 균형감각을 잃고 거꾸로 어느

한쪽을 신화화해버렸다.

　이제 와 〈미생〉은 기존의 룰이나 관습, 시스템을 옹호하는 데 우리 시대 가장 효과적이고 강력한 콘텐츠가 되었다. 원작자의 의도와는 전혀 달리 〈미생〉이 정략적인 이유로 이쪽저쪽 진영의 정책에서 엉뚱하게 인용되고 이용되었던 사례를 우리는 한동안 지켜봐왔다. 오과장으로 대변되는 정직한 정규직 어른들의 세계에 소속되기 위해 장그래처럼 더 열심히, 치열하게 노력하라는 자기계발 콘텐츠로 호출되었다. 〈미생〉이라는 이야기에서 판타지는 장그래가 아니다. 〈미생〉이 창조해낸 가장 강력한 판타지는 오과장이다. 오과장이 대변하는 정직하고 합리적이며 안정적이고 다음 세대를 위해 양보할 줄 아는 어른의 세계. 그러나 그런 건 현실에 거의 존재하지 않는다. 이 '거의 존재하지 않는' 오과장이라는 판타지가 현실에서 확대 재생산되어 기존의 질서에 면죄부를 제공한다. 〈미생〉이 폭넓은 팬덤을 얻을 수 있었던 건 바로 이 판타지가 거의 전 세대를 아우르며 제공하는 안정감과 저런 세계의 일부가 되고 싶다는 소속에의 열망 덕분이었다.

　반면 〈송곳〉은 앞서 말한 종류의 안정감이나 소속감과는 거의 관련이 없는 이야기였다. 〈송곳〉은 성공하기 위한 미션을 수행하는 이야기가 아니다. 〈송곳〉은 단 한 번 성공의 경험을 얻기 위해 끊임없이 실패하는 사람들의 이야기다. 실패할 걸 알면서도 기댈 곳이 없어 소속되고 싶지 않은 곳에 소속되는 사람들의 이야기다. 저렇게 되고 싶다는 열망보다 저렇게 되고 싶지 않다는 공포를 먼저 느끼게 만드는 이야기다. 사실 이 공포는 자기부정에서 나오는 것이다. 한국 시청자의 대부분이 이미 〈송곳〉이 다루고 있는 현실 안에 있기 때문이다. 그럼에도 '저렇게 되고 싶지 않다'는 공포를 느끼는 건, 저렇게까지 절박해지지 않길 바라는 자기보호 본능 탓일 것이다. 알코올중독 아버지를 치료받게 만드는 것보다는, 그저 오늘은 밥상을 엎지 않기를 바라는 것이 더 편하기 때문이다.

〈송곳〉 또한 〈미생〉만큼 충실한 취재에 기반한 훌륭한 이야기다. 서사의 강약도 잘 조율되어 있고 근사한 순간들과 두 다리에 힘이 들어가게 만드는 지점들이 영리하게 배치되어 있다. 슈퍼히어로 소장님이 등장하고 그런 소장님의 좋은 점을 닮아가며 조금씩 자기 방식대로 성장해가는 주인공이 있다.

그러나 차갑다. 그리고 냉소적이다. "한국인들은 노조를 가질 자격이 없어"라는 프랑스인 지점장의 대사가 보여주듯이, 〈송곳〉의 서사는 분노를 느끼면서도 동조하게 되고, 통쾌함을 느껴야 할 지점에서 이상하게 누워서 침 뱉는 것 같은 기분이 들게 만드는, 시니컬하기 짝이 없는 방식을 취하고 있다. 사람들은 죄책감을 느끼고 싶지 않아한다. 죄책감을 느끼게 만드는 시민운동의 방식이 잘못된 것과 마찬가지다. 사람들은 바로 그 죄의식 때문에 불편한 마음으로 외면하기 마련이다. 나는 이러한 원작자의 서사 전략이 과연 영리한 것인지 알 수 없다. 그러나 적어도 강박적으로 안간힘을 다해 현실을 담으려 노력하고 있다는 것은 알 수 있다. 〈송곳〉에 대한 시청자의 반응이 대개 '좋지만 불편하다'로 귀결되는 이유는 실제 이 이야기의 내용이나 서사 전략 자체가 사람을 불편하게 만드는 것에 기반하고 있기 때문이다. 그리고 이 불편함은 바로 TV 밖의 세계, 현실 그 자체를 겨냥하고 있다.

문제는 TV 앞의 시청자가 현실을 실감하거나 그 정체를 정확히 인식하는 걸 과도하게 불편해한다는 데 있다. 드라마부터 예능에 이르기까지 TV 콘텐츠의 목적이 현실로부터의 도피라면 요즘처럼 그 목적이 정확히 달성되고 있는 시절은 없었다.

결과적으로 〈송곳〉은 〈미생〉만큼의 반향을 이끌지 못했다. 그리고 그것은 애초 당연한 일이었다. 〈송곳〉은 〈미생〉이 되려 한 적이 없고 애초 전혀 다른 방식과 시점으로 현실을 이야기했다. 이만한 드라마가, 이런 종류의 이야기가 다시 도래하는 데 얼마나 많은 시간과 노력이 다시 들어야 할까. 지금 한국 사회의 제일 큰 키워드는 '불편함'이 아닐까 싶다. 모든 종류의 불편함으로부터의 도피. 이 도피의 끝이 모두를 결국 어디로 이끌지 생각하면, 아득해진다.

지금 한국 사회의 제일 큰 키워드는
'불편함'이 아닐까 싶다.
모든 종류의 불편함으로부터의 도피.
이 도피의 끝이 모두를 결국 어디로 이끌지 생각하면,
아득해진다.

천하제일
제목무도회

TV프로그램에 관한 기사는 제발 프로그램을 보고 썼으면 좋겠다. 앞뒤가 맞게 쓰는 건 바라지도 않는다. 하물며 함량 높은 글은 감히 꿈도 꾸지 않는다.

제목에 낚여 읽어보니 막상 '프로그램을 보지 않은 자가 쓴 프로그램에 관한 기사'임을 인지했을 때 우리가 얼마나 배설물과 같은 뉴스환경에 노출되어 있는지 실감하게 되는 것이다. 그냥 기사 쓰지 말고 천하제일 제목무도회 같은 걸 열어서 대결했으면.

역사를
지배하는 자

나는 조지 오웰의 『1984』를 좋아한다. 언제나 좋아해왔다. 참 잘 만든 뻥이라고 생각했기 때문이다. 사람들은 『1984』를 헉슬리의 『멋진 신세계』와 더불어 디스토피아 문학의 정수라고 소개한다. 나는 『1984』를 침소봉대 문학이라 불러왔다. 오웰의 문제의식은 충분히 수긍할 만했다. 그러나 그가 그리는 오세아니아의 풍경은 너무나 우화적이다. 실수라고는 존재하지 않는 통제와 절대다수 시민의 완전무결한 무지라는 전제 아래에서만 성립 가능한 그런 시스템이 굴러갈 수 있다는 상상력 자체가 지나치게 순진해 보였다. 비유와 풍자란 대개 있는 사실 그대로를 있는 힘껏 최대한 부풀려서 반대 진영을 겸연쩍게 하고 입을 묶어버릴 요량으로 사용되기 마련이다. 가만있자 지금 이 말을 조금 더 근사하

게 비유할 문장이 있을 텐데 그러니까 이를테면,

떠오르지 않는다.

『1984』는 두 번 영화화되었다. 그러나 역시 1984년에 만들어진 마이클 래드퍼드 감독의 〈1984〉가 빼어나다. 존 허트가 주연을 맡았다. 리처드 버턴의 유작이기도 하다(그는 촬영 한 달 후 세상을 떠났다).

이야기의 무대는 오세아니아라는 가상의 국가다. 오세아니아는 빅브러더라는 인물이 통치하는 당의 지휘 아래 있다. 모든 집에는 스크린과 카메라가 설치되어 있으며 당의 선전이 쉴새없이 이어진다. 오세아니아는 유라시아라는 국가와 전쟁중이다. 방송에서는 끊임없이 전선에서의 승전보와 이번 달 경제계획이 초과 달성되었으며 시민 생활의 질이 향상되었다는 통계 수치가 흘러나온다.

오세아니아에는 골드스타인이라는 이름의 공공의 적이 있다. 그는 테러리스트다. 체제 전복을 추구하는 것으로 알려져 있다. 거의 매일 골드스타인의 첩자들이 발각되어 스크린에 비치며 자기 고백을 한다. 사실 거기 전쟁은 없다. 골드스타인도 없다. 이곳에서 전쟁은 승리가 아니라 지속된다는 게 중요하다. 이 전쟁은 지배세력이 자국민과 벌이는 싸움이다. 그 목적은 승리가 아니라 사회구조를 유지하는 것이다. 시민들이 증오를 투영할 대상이 필요하기 때문에 전쟁과 골드스타인을 만들어낸 것이다.

주인공 윈스턴 스미스는 이런 세상에 염증을 느끼고 있다. 그는 겉으로 당에 순종하지만 속으로는 이 모든 것이 비인간적이라 여기며 저항하고자 한다. 어느 날 갑자기 오세아니아의 적이 유라시아가 아닌 동아시아로 발표된다. "오세아니아는 동아시아와 싸우고 있다. 언제나 동아시아와 싸우고 있었다. 유라시아는 우방이다. 유라시아는 언제나 우리 우방이었다." 그 즉시 관련된 모든 기록이 파쇄되고 오세아니아는 줄곧 동아시아와 전쟁을 벌이고 있던 것으로 변모된다. 주인공은 구토를 느낀다. 그러나 결국 주인공은 사상경찰의 함정수사에 빠져 체포된다. 그리고 모두가 두려워하는 사상범 수용소 101호의 문 앞에 당도한다.

『1984』가 표면적으로 겨냥했던 스탈린주의와 나치즘은 사멸했다. 그럼에도 불구하고 『1984』는 출간 이래 거의 모든 시대에서 수없이 많은 사람들에 의해 호명되고 환기되어왔다. 『1984』가 담고 있는 통제의 욕구, 감시와 순종에의 욕망은 어떤 종류의 사회시스템을 막론하고 권력을 가진 자가 손 뻗기 쉬운 꿀물이기 때문이다. 그래서 그리 많은 이들이 수시로 『1984』를 끌어들여 현실을 지적하려 애써왔다. 나는 그런 측면에서 다소 냉소적이었다. 『1984』가 그리는 풍경은 어디까지나 극단적인 풍자다. 사실을 필요 이상으로 과장하면 그에 대한 대응도 필요 이상으로 과장되기 마련이고, 그러면 지지자를 모을 수 없다. 지지세력을 얻지 못하는 운동은 결기만 남고 이기지 못한다. 이기는 경험을 쌓지 못하면 이길 수 있는 상황에서도 이길 수 없다. 아니 뭐 『1984』씩이나 언급해가며, 식으로 생각하고 판단했던 것이다.

국정 교과서 논란 전까지만 해도 그랬다.

대통령과 당대표 최고위원이 국정 역사교과서에 목을 매는 건 두루뭉술한 신념 때문이 아니라 필요 때문이다. 1. 역사를 아는 게 입시에 별 도움이 되지 않게 만들고 2. 그나마 남은 기록마저 편의대로 재구성하는 것은 일본의 우익이 과거의 나치 정권을 참고해 이미 실행중인 장기 집권 프로세스의 가장 중요한 부분이다. 히틀러가 뜬금없이 아리안 민족의 우수성 나부랭이를 떠들었던 사실을 상기해보자. 근현대사의 사실을 지워내고 '자랑스러움'이라는 신화적 감정의 수사로 채워넣는 것. 거기에 시민의 시니컬한 무관심과 열광적인 광신도들이 합세할 때 파쇼는 완성된다. 그리고 파쇼는 반드시 바로 다음 세대에 끔찍한 경험을 안긴다. 오세아니아의 전쟁처럼 말이다.

부끄럽지만 정직한, 그래도 우리는 정직하게 이런 흑역사라도 남기려고 열심히 싸웠고 그래서 너희들은 우리보다 제발 조금 더 나은 세대가 되어달라고 있는 힘껏 외치는 근현대사 서술은 기성세대가 다음 세대를 아주 조금이라도 응원할 때 취할 수 있는 가장 효율적인 방법이다. 그리고 이때 자기 과거를 거짓으로 낭만화하지 않고서는 더이상 현실을 견뎌낼 수 없을 만큼 노쇠한 자들은 입을 다물어야만 한다.

'자랑스러운 역사'란 왜곡된 자화자찬이 아니라 그 모든 부끄러움에도 불구하고 실수를 거듭해가며 우리가 여기까지 왔다는 사유와 반성으로부터 얻어지는 것이다. 과거는 대개 창피한 것이다. 그것을 사실 그대로 돌아볼 수 있는 정직함만이 늘 위대

자기 과거를 거짓으로 낭만화하지 않고서는
더이상 현실을 견뎌낼 수 없을 만큼
노쇠한 자들은 입을 다물어야만 한다.
과거는 대개 창피한 것이다.
그것을 사실 그대로 돌아볼 수 있는 정직함만이 늘 위대하다.

하다.

어용언론과 정부는 지금의 역사 교육이 학생들의 자긍심을 고취하지 못한다고 말한다. 그러나 다음 세대를 정말 염려하는 공동체는 '민족의 자긍심'이라는 수사를 핑계삼아 과거를 미화하거나 편의대로 조작하는 대신, 우리는 이렇게 놀라울 정도로 한심했으나 적어도 그 내용을 정확히 남기니 부디 너희는 조금 더 잘해달라고 가르친다.

개가 자기 밑을 핥는 이유는 할 수 있기 때문이다. 이 모든 걸 그저 누군가 알아서 하리라 여기고 말면, 그럴 수 있고 그래도 되는 자들이 모든 걸 망쳐놓을 것이다. 국정 역사교과서를 막지 못하면 우리는 한반도 역사상 가장 한심한 기성세대가 될 것이다.

말하지 않은 것이 있다. 『1984』의 주인공 윈스턴 스미스의 직업은 기록국 직원이다. 당의 입장에 따라 과거와 현재의 모든 역사를 바꾸어 기록하는 일이다.

과거를 지배하는 자가 미래를 지배하며, 현재를 지배하는 자가 과거를 지배한다. 『1984』에 등장하는 유명한 문구다.

바꾸어 말하면, 역사를 지배하는 자가 미래를 지배하며, 현재를 지배하는 자가 역사를 지배한다. 지금 당장 이 나라가 오세아니아로 전락하지는 않을 것이다. 그러나 이 나라가 오세아니아처럼 전락할 수 있는, 그리고 지금의 정권이 빅브러더로 군림할 수 있는 조건들은 하나둘씩 차근차근 충족되어가는 중이다. 조건들이 완성되면 결과는 지체 없이 이어질 것이다. 그리고 그때는 어느 누구도 저항할 수 없다.

국정 교과서는 결국
모두를 망하게 할 것이다

역사는 유기체다. 역사를 기록하는 일은 철수가 시비를 걸어 철수와 영희가 싸웠다고 주장하는 자들과 영희가 덤벼서 철수와 영희가 싸웠다고 주장하는 자들이 입증 가능한 자료를 무기로 쟁투하는 과정을 거쳐 유기적으로 이루어지는 것이다. 여기 당대의 정치권력이 개입하여 기준과 방향을 제시하는 것은 근대 이전의 사회로 후퇴하는 일이다. 안 되는 일은 안 되는 것이다. 전혀 그럴 만한 일이 아닌 것을 좌와 우를 나누어 진영을 가르고 이 모든 게 흡사 동등한 수준의 입장 차이인 양 몰아가며 본질을 흐리는 게 모든 종류의 사안에 대응하는 요즘의 추세다. 지금도 똑같은 길을 밟고 있다. 그로 인해 국정 역사교과서 문제가 대체 얼마나 시급한 사안인지 현실감각이 떨어져가고 있는 것 같다.

첫번째, 역사에 대한 관심을 멀어지게 하고 두번째, 아예 역사 자체를 엄정한 사실의 기록이 아닌 감정의 언어로 바꾸는 것. 과거 파쇼 국가들과 현재의 일본이 걷고 있는 길이다. 같은 길 앞에 우리가 서 있다. 다시 한번 말하지만 누구에게나 보기 편한 역사는 역사가 아니다. 역사란 누구에게나 불편해야만 정직한 것이다. 역사를 모르는 공동체는 반드시 망한다. 국정 역사교과서는 결국 모두를 망하게 할 것이라는 측면에서만 모두에게 공정하다.

부끄러운
역사

한국의 역사학자님들 가운데 유독 심약한 분들은 어느 순간 "자라나는 어린 싹들에게 이따위 역사를 가르칠 수는 없어! 조작을 하자!"라고 흑화하는 것 같다.

망하는 나라의 특징은 역사를, 특히 근현대사를 가르치지 않거나 교과서에서 대충 건너뛰고 얼버무린다는 것이다. 입시에 영향을 끼치지 않는 변두리 학문으로 전락시킨다. 그래놓고 애들이 역사를 모르면 통곡을 하고 손가락질을 한다.

부끄러운 역사를 정확하게 배운 사람만이 '그럼에도 불구하고' 여기까지 온 저력에 대해 생각하며 국가에 대한 긍지를 갖고 우리 공동체가 같은 실수를 반복하지 않도록 노력할 것이다. 이건 중요한 일이다.

정체되고
병든 사회

갈등이 없는 사회는 없다. 한 사회가 젊어지고 있는 갈등의 양상은 다양하다. 그것은 단순한 의견 충돌일 수도 있고 위계에 의한 소통의 문제일 수도 있으며 이해관계에 따른 분쟁의 형태를 띨 수도 있다. 혹은 역사적 상흔을 두고 남겨진 자들 사이에 처리해야 할 사과와 용서의 문제가 될 수도 있다. 사실 갈등이 없는 사회란 그다지 바람직하지 않다. 벌어진 일은 벌어진 일이다. 중요한 건 어떠한 문제해결 과정을 거쳐 이러한 갈등을 '다루어내느냐'에 달려 있다. 더불어 그런 문제해결 과정이 사회 전반에 어떠한 학습치를 남기느냐가 중대하다. 거기서 한 사회의 수준과 격, 그리고 지속 가능성이 결정된다. 진짜 심각한 문제는 거기 갈등이 있는데 갈등이 없다고 치부되어버리는 사회에서 발생한다. 이런 경우는 일반적으로 과거의 가해자가 지금도 여전히 힘 있는 가해자로 군림하고 있으며 피해자는 자신이 피해를 입었다는 사실을 침묵으로 지워내야 하는 상황에서 발생한다. 지금 우리가 들여다볼 나라가 바로 그런 나라다.

수카르노는 인도네시아가 네덜란드로부터 독립한 이후 초대 대통령으로 취임하였다. 그는 권위적인 교도민주주의를 주창하면서 의회를 탄압하고 사실상 종신 대통령으로 군림했다. 그는 민족주의와 종교, 그리고 공산주의를 삼위일체로 하는 민족통일전선을 제창하면서 비동맹 중립외교를 펼쳤다. 그러나 그의 공산주의 독재정권은 군부 쿠데타로 인해 무너졌다. 권력은 수하르토에게 이양되었다. 그리고 이 과정에서 폭력에 의한 정권교체에 반대하는 시민들이 무차별적으로 학살당했다. 공산주의자라는 이유였다. 공산주의가 무엇인지 알지 못하는 평범한 소시민들부터 노동자, 지식인, 화교에 이르기까지 수많은 사람들이 죽임을 당했다. 재판 과정에 의한 것이 아니었다. 아무데서나 아무렇게나 끌려가 도살당하듯 생을 마감했다. 시체가 산처럼 쌓였다. 시체 때문에 하수구가 막혔다. 이렇게 살해당하고 실종된 사람의 수가 300만 명에 달했다. 그렇다. 300만 명이었다. 그리고 저 당대의 살인자들은 지금 인도네시아의 유력한 지도층이다.

조슈아 오펜하이머 감독은 애초 그 끔찍한 사건의 당사자들이 지금 어떻게 살아가고 있는지 카메라에 담고자 했다. 그런데 문제가 생겼다. 가해자들이 스스로를 범죄자라고 생각하기보다 역사의 질곡 위에 반드시 필요한 일을 했던 영웅쯤으로 생각하고 있는 것이다. 심지어 TV 토크쇼에서 당시 공산주의자들을 어떻게 쉽고 빠르게 대량살상할 수 있었는지 자랑하고 사회자는 그런 출연자를 상찬하며 박수를 보내는 지경이다. 이대로는 다큐멘터리가 완성될 수 없었다. 오펜하이머는 본래의 계획을 틀었다. 그리고 살인자들 가운데 몇 명을 주인공으로 해 당시 벌어진 일을 재현하는 영화를 찍어보자고 제안한다. 이들은 카메라 앞에서 얼마나 기술적으로 완벽하게 공산주의자들을 죽였는지 자랑하며 기뻐한다. 사후세계로 간 희생자들이 자신들에게 고마워할 것이라 여긴다. 공교롭게도 등장인물 가운데 한 명은 마지막에 이르러 자신이 한 일이 끔찍한 범죄일지 모른다는 생각에 괴로워한다. 물론 그 괴로움은 연기일지 모른다. 그리고 실제 연기처럼 보인다. 그러나 결과적으로 그 모든 것이 어우러져 아주 끔찍한 농담 같은, 거의 부조리극에 가까워 보이는 이야기가 완성되었다. 그 영화가 바로 다큐 〈액트 오브 킬링〉이다. 실제 이해 당사자들의 잔인한 연극으로 채워진 이 놀라운 다큐는 큰 반향을 이끌어냈다.

2015년 9월 국내 공개된 〈침묵의 시선〉은 〈액트 오브 킬링〉의 정직한 쌍둥이 버전이다. 비교적 정공법으로 만들어진 이 다큐는 피해자 가족이 가해자들을 만나 인터뷰하는 형식으로 만들어졌다. 물론 그렇다고 해서 이 영화가 담고 있는 인도네시아의 역사와 현실이 덜 끔찍하게 다가오는 건 아니다.

주인공은 출장을 다니며 안경을 맞추어주는 일을 한다. 그에게는 형이 있었다. 형은 별다른 이유도 없이 학살당했다. 그는 학살에 동참했던 사람들을 찾아가 안경을 맞춰주는 척하면서 당시와 관련된 질문들을 한다. 물론 그들은 〈액트 오브 킬링〉의 출연자들이 그러했듯 전혀 반성하지 않는다. 되레 왜 그런 질문을 하냐며 화를 낸다. 혹은 당시 자신이 어떻게 사람들을 효과적으로 죽였는지, 얼마나 많은 사람들을 죽여봤는지 자랑한다. 아이들은 당대의 가해자이자 지금의 권력자의 입맛에 맞게 가공된 역사를 배운다. 앞뒤가 맞지 않는 거짓말투성이 역사를 배운 아이들은 '그렇게 많은 사람들을 빠르고 기술적으로 죽여준 살인자들에게 찬사를 보내는' TV 토크쇼를 보며 자라난다. 청산하지 못한 과거를 가진 사회는 저런 악순환 속에서 질식사할 수밖에 없다. 이 영화가 비추고 있는 인도네시아의 현실에는 출구가 없어 보인다.

흥미로운 건 〈액트 오브 킬링〉에 비해 〈침묵의 시선〉에 등장하는 인물들이 비교적 더 위악적으로 구는 경향이 있다는 점이다. 한두 명을 제외하면 〈액트 오브 킬링〉에서 살인을 자랑하는 자들은 정말 그것을 자랑스러워한다. 그런데 〈침묵의 시선〉의 인터뷰이들은 상당수가 당시의 기억으로부터 도망치고자 하는 기색이 역력하다. 이들은 화를 내거나 눈에 빤히 보이는 위악을 드러내 보이며 비명을 지르듯 당시 일을 자랑한다. 피폐한 자들의 가장 편리한 탈출구는 자조와 위악이기 마련이다. 주인공은 집으로 돌아와 이렇게 촬영된 필름들을 틀어놓고 복기한다. 그 모든 것을 바라보고 있는 주인공은 단 한순간도 입을 열지 않는다. 침묵으로 가득하다. 다만 그의 눈은 특정한 감정으로 규정할 수 없는 복잡하고 참담한 빛으로 가득하다. 피해자로 사는 것, 아니 정확하게는 피해자인 채로 영원히 살아갈 수밖에 없는 것의 처연함은 문자로 표현될 수 있는 감정의 경계를 벗어난다.

죄의식을 느끼지 못하거나 죄의식을 위악으로 덮어버린 자들로 가득한 저 사회는 한국의 관객에게 강력한 기시감을 이끌어낸다. 과거를 청산하지 못한 사회라는 화두는 우리에게도 전혀 어색하지 않은 문제이기 때문이다. 가난을 대물림받은 독립유공자 자손들이 기초생활수급자로 살아가는 현실은 광복절에만 눈에 잘 띄는 뉴스 꼭지로 선보인다. 딱히 정치인이 아니더라도 우리 주위의 '정말' 많은 수의 사람들이 친일파 자손으로 남들보다 혜택받은 환경에서 자라왔다. "우리 할아버지 친일파라서 원래 집에 돈 많았어, 그래서 뭐"라는 위악 섞인 검은 웃음을 나만 해도 열두 번은 더 들었다. 제때 정리되지 못한 과거는 대를 이을수록 그렇게 현실을 더욱더 공정하지 않게, 아프게, 속절없이 병들게 한다.

사과와 용서가 정체된 사회에는 희망이 없다. 앞서도 말했다. 벌어진 일은 벌어진 일이다. 그건 누구도 바꿀 수 없다. 문제는 가해자를 승자인 채로 피해자를 패자인 채로 남겨두고 사회통합이라는 알량한 거짓말을 들어 침묵하고 지워버리는 태도에 있다. 〈액트 오브 킬링〉과 〈침묵의 시선〉이 공히 주장하는 건 청산되지 않은 과거를 짊어진 사회는 반드시 곪아 부패한다는 것이다. 정당한 심판을 피해간 가해자는 그 어떤 이유로도 자신의

<침묵의 시선The Look of Silence>[2014]

그의 눈은 특정한 감정으로 규정할 수 없는
복잡하고 참담한 빛으로 가득하다.
피해자로 사는 것, 아니 정확하게는
피해자인 채로 영원히 살아갈 수밖에 없는 것의 처연함은
문자로 표현될 수 있는 감정의 경계를 벗어난다.

행동을 정당화할 수 있다. 그런 자들로 가득한 사회에서 이해받을 수 없는 부조리란 존재하지 않는다.

〈침묵의 시선〉에 등장하는 학살 가담자 가운데 한 명이 특히 기억에 남는다. 그는 조용히 질문에 대답하다가 어느 순간 수가 틀리자 화를 내기 시작한다. 그리고 똑같은 대답을 되풀이한다. 왜 이제 와서 과거를 들추며 정치적인 질문을 하느냐. 자신을 겨냥한 옳고 그름의 문제를 '정치적인 것'으로 환원시키는 자들의 멘털은 늘 같다. 그들은 '정치적으로' 병들어 있다.

괴담의
시대

정보가 부족하면 사람들은 이야기의 빈틈을 납득 가능한 가설로 채우기 마련이다. 이건 너무나 자연스러운 일이다. 괴담을 만드는 사람도 문제지만 정보를 틀어막아놓고 그 빈틈을 채우려는 이야기들을 무조건 괴담으로 규정짓고 처벌한다는 건 더 큰 문제다. 밥을 주지 않으면서 공복을 법치로 다스리겠다는 것과 다를 바 없다.

이제 한국 사회는 아주 사소한 영역부터 공적인 영역에 이르기까지 비공개-괴담논쟁-진영논쟁으로 이어지는 공식이 완연히 지배하고 있다. 문제는 이게 먹힌다는 거다.

중립

프란치스코 교황이 한국을 방문해 다음과 같이 말했다.

"세월호 추모 리본을 유족에게서 받아 달았는데 반나절쯤 지나자 어떤 사람이 내게 와서 '중립을 지켜야 하니 그것을 떼는 것이 좋지 않겠느냐'고 물었습니다. 인간적 고통 앞에서 중립을 지킬 수는 없다고 대답했습니다."

가치관이 충돌하는 사안에선 균형을 찾아야 한다. 그러나 명백한 사실관계를 두고는 균형을 찾을 이유가 없다. 확실한 사실관계를 두고도 무게중심을 찾는다며 진영논리를 끄집어내는 사람들을 유심히 살펴보라.

그들은 용돈을 받았다.

확실한 사실관계를 두고도 무게중심을 찾는다며
진영논리를 끄집어내는 사람들을 유심히 살펴보라.
그들은 용돈을 받았다.

좀비

영화업계에서 좀비영화가 시들해진 건 이 소재가 의외로 다루기 까다롭기 때문이다. 좀비영화는 저예산으로 정치사회성을 풍자하고 드러내기에 매우 적합하다. 그러나 대개 흥행이 전혀 되지 않는다. 또한 많은 예산을 들여 재난 블록버스터를 만들기에 매우 적합하다. 그러나 재난 블록버스터의 소재로 이미 너무 익숙해서 새로울 게 없다는 사람들의 생각이 계산기를 두드리며 투자 대비 효용을 따지는 제작자들을 금방 포기하게 만든다.

사실 좀비영화처럼 다양하게 변주할 수 있는 소재는 드물다. 이건 애초 〈살아 있는 시체들의 밤〉을 통해 현대적인 좀비의 레퍼런스를 만들어낸 조지 로메로 감독이 좀비라는 괴물의 정체나 원리에 대해 명확히 설정하기를 거부했기에 가능했다. 우리가 지금 좀비라는 단어로부터 떠올리는 형태의 좀비가 탄생한 건 바로 이 영화부터다. 그는 인터뷰를 할 때마다 "나는 좀비가 어디서 왔는지, 왜 나타났는지 관심이 없다"고 말했다. 덕분에 '연구실에서 만들어진 것이다'부터 '신의 저주다' '무분별한 핵 실험으로 인해 탄생한 것이다'까지 다양한 해석이 덧붙었다.

〈살아 있는 시체들의 밤〉에서 조지 로메로 감독이 만들어낸 좀비라는 괴물은 기존 부두교의 좀비 주술 이야기에 뱀파이어 전설을 섞어서 나온 결과물이었다. 온전히 그의 머리에서 나온 아이디어는 아니었다. 리처드 매드슨의 『나는 전설이다』는 뱀파이어와 좀비 사이의 교두보가 된 기념비적인 소설이다(이 소설은 〈지상 최후의 사나이〉〈오메가맨〉〈나는 전설이다〉로 여러 번 영화화되었다). 조지 로메로의 '설정에 제한을 두지 않는다'는 원칙 덕분에 좀비영화는 '좀비는 살아난 시체다' '좀비는 사람을 먹는다' '좀비는 전염된다'는 세 가지 설정을 제외하고 누구든 가져다가 마음껏 변주할 수 있는 좋은 소재가 되었다. 게다가 싸게 만들 수 있었다. 조지 로메로는 주변 정육점에서 고기를 사다가 가짜 피를 바른 조연들에게 먹으라고 시켰다. 그것만 가지고도 극장 안의 관객은 끊임없이 소리를 지르며 경악했다. 이후 셀 수 없이 많은 좀비영화가 쏟아져나왔다.

문제는 누구나 가져다가 자기만의 설정을 가지고 새로운 이야기를 할 수 있다는 장점으로부터 불거져나왔다. 소리로 전염되는 좀비, 인간과 사랑을 나누는 좀비, 나치 좀비, 인간을 먹는 걸 괴로워한 나머지 자살하는 좀비, 뛰어다니는 좀비까지 수많은 영화가 등장했다. 그렇게 과잉생산되다보니 역설적으로 굉장히 식상하고 오래된 소재가 되어버리고 말았다. 관객은 더이상 좀비라는 소재만 가지고 영화를 선택하지 않는다. 〈28일 후…〉처럼 핀잔을 살 각오를 하고 뛰어다니는 좀비를 처음 등장시키거나 〈월드워Z〉나 미드 〈워킹 데드〉처럼 막강한 물량공세에 좋은 원작을 기반으로 한 탄탄한 이야기를 가지고 있지 않으면 흥행이 어렵게 되었다.

연상호 감독의 〈부산행〉은 이 장르에서 우리가 아직도 보지 못한 것들이 남아 있다는 걸 증명하는 영화다. 〈부산행〉이 한국에서 등장한 첫번째 좀비영화는 아니다. 한국의 좀비영화는 1980년대에도 있었고(〈괴시〉), 2000년대 들어서도 저예산으로 종종 만들어져왔다. 〈부산행〉의 강점은 좀비라는 소재의 신선도로부터 나오는 게 아니라 그것을 다루는 방식으로부터 나온다. 이 영화는 한국 사회의 다양한 갈등 양상을 부산행 열차 안에 투영하는 데 어느 정도 성공할 뿐만 아니라 무엇보다 굉장히 훌륭한 수준의 좀비 액션을 보여준다는 점에서 차별점을 갖는다.

주인공은 주식 펀드매니저다. 개미투자자들을 짓밟아가면서 꽤 성공했다. 별거중인 아내는 부산에 살고 있다. 딸은 엄마를 보기 위해 혼자서라도 부산에 가겠다고 조른다. 주인공은 딸을 데리고 열차로 부산까지 함께 가기로 한다. 주인공 부녀는 서울역까지 가는 도중 도시의 풍경이 어딘가 이상하다는 걸 감지한다. 이미 한국 전역에서 좀비 바이러스가 창궐한 것이다. 주인공이 탑승한 부산행 열차가 출발하기 직전, 좀비에게 물린 희생자 한 명이 재빠르게 열차에 올라탄다. 이 부산행 열차는 곧 아비규환의 지옥도로 탈바꿈한다. 이미 좀비로 변한 승객과 살아남은 사람들을 태우고 열차는 달려간다.

〈부산행〉에서 가장 돋보이는 건 좀비의 액션이다. 이 영화가 좀비를 통해 구현하는 액션은 〈월드워Z〉의 좀비떼 비주얼 위에, 만화 〈아이 엠 어 히어로〉에서 좀비들이 보여주는 동작의 합을 얹은 것 같은 모양새다. 이미 수없이 보아온 좀비의 존재감만 가지고 관객에게 좋은 인상을 남기기란 어려운 일이다. 〈부산행〉은 영리한 액션 운용을 통해 관객이 실제 공포를 느끼게 만드는 데 성공한다. 액션의 합과 동선에 관한 연출자의 높은 이해도가 이를 가능케 했을 것이다(연상호 감독은 본래 애니메이션 연출자다. 그의 애니메이션은 늘 인물의 움직임을 자연스러우면서도 기발하게 만들어내는 데 주력해왔다).

아쉬운 건 주인공 부녀를 제외한 다른 인물들의 드라마가 제대로 부각되지 못하다보니 부분적으로 이야기의 개연성에 문제가 발생한다는 점이다. 워낙에 빠르고 직선적인 이야기이기 때문에 그렇기도 하겠지만 조연의 감정선이 중요한 역할을 차지하는 대목에서는 어김없이 진행이 덜컥거린다. 관객이 그들의 결정이나 감정에 충분히 몰입할 수 있는 정보가 부족하기 때문이다. 배우들의 연기 탓으로 돌리는 관객이 있겠지만 사실 이건 이야기를 제대로 정리하고 완결해내는 데 실패한 감독의 책임이 더 크다. 거의 콘티 그대로 수정 없이 만들어진 영화라는 점을 감안하면 더욱 그렇다.

〈부산행〉은 긍정적으로든 부정적으로든 매우 대중적인 영화다. 누군가는 분명히 이 영화가 보여주는 후반부의 과도한 신파에 거부반응을 일으킬 것이다. "아빠 가지 마!"는 하도 많이 듣다보니 〈클레멘타인〉이 떠오르기도 한다. 그러나 〈부산행〉이 여름 관객을 겨냥한 15세 이상 관람가의 블록버스터 상품이라는 점을 감안하면 더 많은 사람이 호응하고 감동할 수 있는 지금의 꼴이 결국 옳지 않았는가, 하는 생각이 든다. 좀더 암울한 성인 버전의 이야기를 바란다면 애니메이션 〈서울역〉을 기대하는 편이 낫겠다. 아주 조금 앞선 시간대에 서울역에서 벌어지는 이야기를 다룬다.

영화의 중반, 객차의 문을 연 할머니의 선택이 계속 마음에 남는다. 최소한의 이성과 합리가 다수의 광기에 의해 지배당할 때 이를 그저 지켜보고 있을 수밖에 없는 무력한 개인이 선택할 수 있는 건 결국 자폭밖에 없는 것일까. 그런 맥락에서 나는 〈살아 있는 시체들의 밤〉의 마지막 장면을 변형한 것으로 보이는 이 영화의 마지막 장면이 너무 좋다.

우리는 언젠가 반드시 다시 만난다. 만날 것이다. 그러므로 당장 힘들고 어렵더라도 자폭하기보다 설득하고 싸워나가기를 포기할 수 없다. 요즘은 그렇게 원론적인 것들에 자꾸 마음이 간다. 우리 사회를 지탱해주던 가장 기본적인 믿음들이 세상을 더 많이 안다고 주장하는 사람들, 아직도 그런 걸 믿느냐는 사람들에 의해 수시로 훼손되어 버려지고 있다. 나는 그게 너무 슬프다.

우리는 언젠가 반드시 다시 만난다.
만날 것이다.
그러므로 당장 힘들고 어렵더라도
자폭하기보다 설득하고 싸워나가기를 포기할 수 없다.
요즘은 그렇게 원론적인 것들에 자꾸 마음이 간다.

이 시민들을 담기에는
나라가 너무 옹졸하다

뭐라 드릴 말씀이 없습니다, 이 일은 언젠가 꼭 갚을게요.

네, 알겠습니다.

전화를 끊고 나는 참 복잡한 심경이 되었다. 이상하다는 생각이 들었다. 프로그램에 진행자로 섭외가 되었다가 이후로 일이 잘 진행되지 않아 취소가 되는 경우는 종종 있다. 그러나 유독 한 방송국에서만 '이 사람은 안 된다'며 최종 결재 단계에서 일이 반복해서 엎어지는 경우는 그리 흔치 않다. 벌써 여섯번째였다.

〈SNL 코리아〉의 한 시즌에 고정 출연했었고 〈택시〉나 〈마스터셰프 코리아〉를 비롯해 해당 계열 방송사의 다른 프로그램들에도 나갔었다. 그런데 어느 시점 이후로 그렇게 된 것이다.

작가 일을 때려치우고 방송 일을 본업으로 삼겠다고 고민해
본 적이 없었다. 이미 내가 좋아하는 다른 프로그램들을 하고 있
으니 아무래도 상관없다는 생각이었다. 그런데도 찜찜한 건 어
쩔 수 없었다. 너는 어떤 이유 때문에 우리와는 일을 할 수 없다,
고 명시가 되면 서로 납득할 수 있다. 그러나 도저히 경위를 알
수 없는 모종의 이유 때문에 배제되고 있다는 건 당사자로 하여
금 생각보다 끔찍한 기분이 들게 만든다.

요컨대 자기 검열을 하게 된다는 것이다. 이런 상황을 맞게
되면 사람은 먼저 무엇을 잘못했길래 그렇게 되었는지 스스로를
살피기 마련이다. 물론 이러한 궁금증은 해결되지 않는다. 설명
이 없으니 알 수도 없다. 해답 없는 질문이 그치고 나면 이제는
주변에서 벌어지는 모든 일에 방어적으로 반응하게 된다. 자기
도 모르게 말조심을 하게 된다는 이야기다.

어느 날 작업실에서 인터뷰를 하다가 현 정권의 문화정책과
관련한 질문을 받았다. "내가 어떤 말을 하면, 어떤 글을 쓰면,
어떤 영화를 만들면 불이익을 받겠지, 라는 생각이 들게 하는 토
양 위에서는 어떤 문화도 자라나지 않는다. 멀쩡하던 영화제가
망가지고 모든 영역에서 자기 검열이 판을 치고 정권에 반하는
말을 했다가 언제 어떻게 국정원에서 마티즈를 보낼지 모른다는

인식이 팽배한 상황에서 '문화를 정책적으로 융성하겠다'는 말은 또다른 눈먼 돈잔치를 하겠다는 말과 다를 바가 없다. 그런 정책은 애당초 문화와는 아무런 관계가 없다"고 말했다.

인터뷰를 끝내고 혼자 앉아 있는데 아무래도 기분이 지저분했다. 일어섰다 앉았다 서성대다가 핸드폰을 집어들고 내려놓기를 삼십 번 정도 반복한 것 같다. 나는 마침내 결심을 했다. 그리고 흡사 〈그래비티〉에서 지구에 도착한 샌드라 불럭이 대지를 밟고 일어서는 박력으로 문자메시지를 보냈다.

기자님.
네.
마티즈 이야기는 빼주세요.

나는 그날 밤 너무 창피해서 술을 진탕 마시고 기절해버렸다.

이러다가는 내가 망가지겠다는 생각이 들었다. 그래서 저쪽에서 이유를 말해주지 않는다면 내가 이유를 찾아야겠다고 마음먹었다. 해당 방송사의 고위직과 친한 지인에게 사정을 설명했다. 그리고 이유가 뭔지 좀 알아봐달라는 부탁을 했다. 누구에게 부탁하는 걸 싫어해서 말을 꺼내기가 너무 힘들었다. 그런데 막상 답은 생각보다 빨리 돌아왔다.

〈국제시장〉에 비판적인 의견을 냈다가 논란에 휩싸였던 일이 문제였다. 당시 그 방송사의 모기업 회장이 수감중이었는데, 이런 상황에서 정권에 밉보이면 안 되기 때문에 아무래도 일단은 출연 금지가 된 것이라는 설명이었다. 일선 피디들은 그런 사실을 잘 모르니까 섭외가 자꾸 가는 거고, 최종 결재에서 엎어지는 것도 그것 때문이다. 좀 기다리면 해결될 거다, 라는 이야기가 덧붙었다.

짐작은 했지만 정말 그것 때문이라니 조금은 허무했다. 이전에도 개그맨 친구와 해당 계열 방송사의 프로그램을 하기로 했다가 잘 안 되었는데 그때 이 친구로부터 "형 여기 블랙리스트에 올라가 있다는데?"라는 말을 들은 적이 있었다. 그때는 그냥 웃어넘겼다. 대체 〈국제시장〉은 나와 무슨 악연이길래 사람을 이렇게 괴롭히는지 알 수가 없었다. 아무튼 이유를 알고 나니 마음이 가벼워졌다. 내가 원했던 건 오직 명쾌한 인과관계뿐이었다. 나는 그날 밤 두 다리를 다 뻗고 오랜만에 아주 잘 잤다.

이게 다 1년 전 일이다. 그동안 많은 일이 있었다. 몇 달 전 회장은 석방되었다. 정권에 레임덕 분위기가 감지되면서 내 출연 금지도 어느 시점에서 풀린 모양이었다. 나는 지금 해당 계열 방송사의 프로그램을 진행하고 있고 앞으로 몇 개 더 할 예정이다.

그리고 박근혜-최순실 게이트가 열렸다. 거의 전 영역에서 대통령과 비선 실세의 비리가 밝혀지는 가운데 정권 차원에서 해당 방송사의 모기업에 압력을 행사한 사실 또한 드러났다. 그룹 부회장을 물러나라고 지시한 정황마저 알려졌다. 정권에 비판적인 영화를 만들어 찍혔던 이 기업은 그래서 〈국제시장〉 같은 영화를 만들었고 계열 극장에서 그토록 소위 '국뽕 광고'를 틀어댔던 것이다. 지금은 그 '국뽕 광고'도 극장에서 자취를 감추었다.

지난 세 번의 촛불집회에 모두 참석했다. 지난 주말에는 100만 명이 광장에 모였다. 거기서 엄마를 만나 이런저런 이야기를 했다. 엄마는 "물러나야지"라는 짧은 말을 남겼다. 정권 퇴진을 목적으로 100만 명이 한 공간에 모였는데 아무런 불상사도 일어나지 않았다. 집회 해산이 선언되자마자 사람들이 일사불란하게 다 빠져나갔다. 쓰레기도 없었다. 진짜 이상한 사람들이다.

이 시민들을 담기에는 나라가 너무 옹졸하다, 라고 나는 생각했다.

어느 누구도 내게 사과하지 않았다. 하지만 상관없다. 나는 요즘 우리가 얼마나 훌륭한 공동체를 가지고 있는지에 관해 자주 생각한다. 한국의 역사는 '그럼에도 불구하고'의 기록이다. 식민지배와 전쟁과 독재자와 너무 많은 죽음의 기억을 가지고 있음에도 불구하고 이 나라는 망하지 않았다. 이 사람들이 모두 해낸 것이다.

"우리의 위대한 현대사를 부정하고 세계가 부러워하는 우

지난 세 번의 촛불집회에 모두 참석했다.
지난 주말에는 100만 명이 광장에 모였다.
거기서 엄마를 만나 이런저런 이야기를 했다.
엄마는 "물러나야지"라는
짧은 말을 남겼다.

이 시민들을 담기에는 나라가 너무 옹졸하다, 라고 나는 생각했다.
한국의 역사는 '그럼에도 불구하고'의 기록이다.
쉽게 좌절하거나 침묵하는 것처럼 보이지만
명백한 끓는점을 가지고 있다.
이 끓는점에 도달하면 우리 공동체는 반드시 일어나
잘못된 것을 바로잡고자 했다.
그리고 지금이 바로 다시, 그 끓는점이다.

리나라를 살기 힘든 곳으로 비하하는 신조어들이 확산되고 있다."

박근혜 대통령의 말이다. 분명히 망해도 여러 번 망했어야 할 만큼 잘못된 것들이 거의 청산되지 않은 후진 현대사를 '그럼에도 불구하고' 극복해내고 자랑할 만한 유산을 만들어낸 것은 대통령이 아니라 우리 공동체였다. 이 공동체는 언뜻 주위가 산만하고 쉽게 좌절하거나 침묵하는 것처럼 보이지만 명백한 끓는점을 가지고 있다. 이 끓는점에 도달하면 우리 공동체는 반드시 일어나 잘못된 것을 바로잡고자 했다.

그리고 지금이 바로 다시, 그 끓는점이다.

풍파를 견딜 수 있는
나이

박근혜-최순실 게이트는 건국 이래 최대 정치 스캔들이다. 사정기관 혹은 정치권의 자정 노력에 의해 밝혀진 것이 아니라 언론의 취재로 촉발된 상황이라는 점에서 미국의 워터게이트에 비견될 만하다. 사안의 중대성에 걸맞은 결말을 맞는다면 우리 사회의 가능성으로 기록될 것이고 그렇지 못하다면 흑역사가 될 것이다.

비선실세나 재단을 활용한 재벌과의 불법자금거래 등 행위는 과거 군사독재 정권에서도 있었던 일이다. 일종의 학습효과로 볼 수 있다. 그러나 안보와 외교를 비롯한 국정 전반에 걸쳐 비선 실세의 이해관계가 작용했고 국민의 세금이 그들을 위해 운용되었다는 사실은 자다가 벌떡 일어나게 만든다. 나는 정말 며칠째 세금이 아까워 밤잠을 설치고 있다. 우리 사회가 공동체의 수준과 미래를 대변하기 위해 뽑은 대통령이라는 걸 감안할 때, '그들이 무슨 짓을 한 것인가'라는 질문은 곧 '우리가 무슨 짓을 한 것인가'라는 질문으로 되돌아온다. 나는 안 뽑았는데요, 라는 말은 지금과 같은 때에 아무짝에도 쓸모가 없다.

박근혜-최순실 게이트를 둘러싼 이슈는 매일 하나씩 터져 나오는 모양새다. 관련한 새로운 이슈가 어제의 이슈를 덮는다. 자연히 이를 둘러싼 사람들의 말 또한 차고 넘쳐 쌓이는 중이다.

그 가운데 내 눈을 가장 오랫동안 잡아끈 건 이경재 변호사의 말이었다. 이경재 변호사는 최순실의 변호인이다. 그는 라디오 인터뷰 프로그램에 출연해 최순실의 딸에 대해 묻는 사회자의 질문에 다음과 같이 답했다. "지금 그 딸이 어느 정도 세월의 풍파를 견뎌낼 만한 나이 같으면 모르겠는데 이거는 아닌 것 같다. 우리 사회가 이해할 만한 그런 아량이 있지 않나."

이경재 변호사가 공안검사 출신으로 그 나이 때의 젊은이들에게 과거 무슨 짓을 했는지에 관한 이야기는 논외로 치도록 하자. 놀랍게도 나는 이경재 변호사의 말에 동의한다. 나는 젊은 세대가 세상의 풍파로부터 어느 정도 보호받아야 한다고 생각한다. 세상의 원리를 배우기 전에 현실의 아니꼽고 치사함을 먼저 경험하지 않아야 한다고 생각한다.

문제는 한국 사회가 단 한 번도 젊은 세대를 향해 그런 종류의 아량을 베풀어본 일이 없다는 데 있다.

풍파는 세찬 바람과 험한 물결이라는 의미다. 풍파를 견딜 수 있는 나이란 과연 몇 살일까. 한국 사회는 그간 시작은 힘든 게 좋다며 생존의 출발선 앞에 선 젊은이들을 세찬 바람 앞에 바람막이로 썼고, 험한 물결이 있을 때는 그 안에 수장시키고 사고라고 둘러댔다. 덕분에 젊은 세대는 이 사회에서 전에 없이 가장 방어적이고 수동적인 세대로 전락했다. 한국 사회에서 풍파를 견딜 수 있는 나이가 몇 살인지 정확히 산출할 수는 없으나, 적어도 젊은 세대가 앞서서 풍파를 견디도록 강요당하는 나이인 것만은 확실해 보인다.

나는 영화 한 편을 떠올렸다. 다르덴 형제의 1999년작 〈로제타〉다.

로제타는 열여덟 살이다. 어머니는 알코올중독자다. 그런 어머니를 부양하며 로제타는 이동식 트레일러에서 살아간다. 그녀는 공장에서 일했지만 인턴 기간이 끝나자 해고를 당한다. 돈을 벌어야 한다. 로제타는 버려진 헌옷을 수거하고, 그걸 어머니가 수선하면 다시 내다판다. 먹을 것이 부족하면 강으로 나가 물고기를 잡는다. 실업급여는 나오지 않았다. 인턴 기간이 너무 짧았기 때문이다. 다른 일자리를 구하는 것도 어렵다. 일자리 자체가 없다. 삶이 너무 버겁다. 이유를 알 수 없는 복통이 찾아오곤 한다. 그래도 돈을 벌어야 한다.

어느 날 로제타는 와플 가게에서 일하는 리케와 만나 친구가 된다. 와플 가게 사장의 도움으로 취직도 된다. 잠시나마 그 나이에 어울릴 법한 행복이 로제타를 아주 잠깐 스쳐간다. 그러나 착각이었다. 그 나이에 어울릴 법한 행복은 로제타에게 허락되지 않았다. 와플 가게 사장의 아들이 퇴학을 당하면서 사장은 로제타에게 나가달라고 부탁한다. 아들에게 일을 맡기기로 결정한 것이다. 사장도 그것이 부당한 일인 줄은 안다. 그러나 어쩔 수 없다고 말한다.

로제타는 트레일러로 돌아온다. 그녀는 완벽한 절망감을 느끼고 있다. 술에 취해 쓰러져 있는 어머니를 수습해 침대에 눕힌다. 마지막 만찬처럼 달걀 하나를 삶아 정성스레 먹는다. 그리고 밖으로 나와 무거운 가스통을 옮기기 시작한다. 이쯤이면 관객들은 그녀가 무슨 일을 벌이기로 마음먹은 것인지 짐작할 수 있다. 이때 리케가 오토바이를 몰고 나타난다. 리케가 로제타의 주위를 시끄럽게 빙빙 돈다. 로제타는 무거운 가스통을 붙잡고 낑낑대다가 바닥에 나뒹군다. 복통을 느끼고는 배를 붙잡고 흐느껴 울기 시작한다. 리케가 멈춰서 로제타에게 다가온다. 일어선 로제타가 리케를 바라본다.

로제타가 바란 건 그저 평범한 삶이었다. 그러나 평범한 삶이란 대개 대중매체를 통해 학습된 것일 뿐이다. 그리고 대중매체는 현실을 조명하는 데 게으르다. 혹은 겁을 먹는다. 시청자들이 스크린에서까지 현실을 보고 싶어하지 않을 것이라 생각하기 때문이다.

평범한 삶이 지상과제였던 날이 있었다. 그런 나에게 소규모 상영회를 찾아가 보았던 〈로제타〉는, 끔찍했다. 동시에 나와 같은 고민을 하는 사람이 여기도 있다는 위로를 받았다. 무엇보다, 로제타가 마지막 장면 이후 열심히 살아갈 것이라는 확신이 들었다. 지쳐 쓰러져 배를 붙잡고 울다가 마침내 두 발로 대지를 딛고 일어선 로제타를 보라. 그래서 나도 열심히 살기로 했다.

영화 〈로제타〉는 '로제타 플랜'이라고 불리는 벨기에 청년실업대책의 모태가 되었다. 벨기에에서 학교를 졸업한 후 6개월 이내의 젊은이는 누구든지 이 정책의 도움을 받아 취업할 수 있다.

지금 이 파국의 시대를 맞이해 우리가 가장 염려해야 할 것은 우리 세대가 역사에 어떻게 기록될 것인가가 아니다. 다음 세대에게 이런 나라를 물려줄 수는 없다는 절박함이 우선되어야 마땅하다. 이경재 변호사가 언급한 사회의 아량이란 한국의 젊은 세대에게 허락된 적이 없었던 덕목이다. 그런데 모든 종류의 규칙과 질서, 심지어 세대까지 초월해 군림했던 최순실의 딸에게 아량마저 가장 빠르게 베풀어져야 한단 말인가. 나는 풍파를 견딜 수 있는 나이가 아니라는 말 앞에서 로제타를 떠올렸다. 저 말이 최순실의 딸이 아닌, 우리 사회의 로제타들에게 먼저 향할 수 있는 세상을 물려주기 위해 무엇이든 하고 싶다. 정말 무엇이라도 할 수 있을 것 같다.

평범한 삶이 지상과제였던 날이 있었다.
지쳐 쓰러져 배를 붙잡고 울다가
마침내 두 발로 대지를 딛고 일어선 로제타를 보라.
그래서 나도 열심히 살기로 했다.

나는 풍파를 견딜 수 있는 나이가 아니라는 말 앞에서
로제타를 떠올렸다. 저 말이 최순실의 딸이 아닌,
우리 사회의 로제타들에게 먼저 향할 수 있는
세상을 물려주기 위해 무엇이든 하고 싶다.
정말 무엇이라도 할 수 있을 것 같다.

<로제타 Rosetta>(1999)

끓는점

하야에는 정치사회적 비용이 듭니다. 그러나 이 비용보다 중요한 건 헬조선이라고 불리는 우리 사회에도 참을 수 있는 부조리에 한계라는 것이 있고 바로 지금이 그 끓는점이다, 어른들은 어리석고 지쳐 있지만 이것까지 그냥 두고 보지는 않는다, 과거에도 몇 번 도달해본 적이 있었던 이 끓는점이야말로 이 나라를 위대하게 만들어온 원동력이었다, 그러니까 너희들은 노력해서 뭐하냐고 미리 포기하지 말고 열심히 최선을 다해 살아도 괜찮다, 라고 다음 세대에게 증명하는 일입니다. 이건 우리 공동체에 중요한 경험이 될 것입니다.

헬조선이라고 불리는 우리 사회에도
참을 수 있는 부조리에 한계라는 것이 있고
바로 지금이 그 끓는점이다.

우리가
싸워야 하는 이유

우리가 싸워야 하는 이유는, 열심히 일하면 그에 상응하는 보상을 받고 의지만 있다면 반드시 공정한 기회를 보장받으며 규칙을 지켜도 물에 빠져 죽지 않는다는 걸 우리 다음 세대에게 증명해내야 하기 때문입니다. 룰을 지키는 사람들이 더 행복한 나라. 잘못이 있으면 그걸 바로잡을 수 있는 저력을 가진 공동체. 그것이 우리가 다음 세대에게 물려줘야만 할 유산입니다.

나의 친애하는 적

ⓒ 허지웅 2016

1판 1쇄 2016년 11월 30일
1판 4쇄 2016년 12월 19일

지은이 허지웅 | 펴낸이 염현숙

기획·책임편집 이연실 | 편집 고지안
디자인 이효진 | 마케팅 방미연 우영희 김은지 강하린
홍보 김희숙 김상만 이천희
제작 강신은 김동욱 임현식 | 제작처 영신사

펴낸곳 (주)문학동네
출판등록 1993년 10월 22일 제406-2003-000045호
주소 10881 경기도 파주시 회동길 210
전자우편 editor@munhak.com | 대표전화 031)955-8888 | 팩스 031)955-8855
문의전화 031)955-8889(마케팅) 031)955-2651(편집)
문학동네카페 http://cafe.naver.com/mhdn | 트위터 @munhakdongne

ISBN 978-89-546-4343-6 03810

www.munhak.com

Forty Years in the AMAZON JUNGLE

Dawn in the Guapore Valley

Original Korean manuscript
Translated into English by
Hyae Yeon Churchill

SUNG JOON KIM

40 YEARS IN THE AMAZON JUNGLE
The Amazing Life Journal of a Jungle Missionary

by Sung Joon Kim

Published by SOF Publications
Copyright © 2009

ISBN: 978-1-889575-07-0

Unless otherwise indicated, Scripture quotations are from *The Holy Bible*, King James Version (KJV)

Printed in the United States of America

SOF Publications
296 NE Alpenview Lane,
Bend, Oregon 97701
Phone (541) 330-6684
email: sofpublications@sfmiusa.org

Contents

This is the area in Brazil where
Sung Joon Kim lived and worked for 40 years.

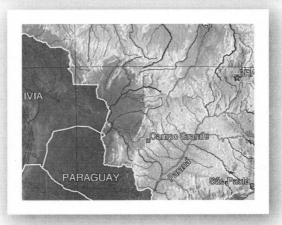

Detail of circled area above.

Foreword

ICONSIDER IT A PRIVILEGE to have the opportunity to write a few words in this book. In fact, I feel quite privileged to have had a very small part in encouraging Sung Joon on his way to the mission field. I myself had wanted to go to Brazil as a missionary, but by a series of circumstances ordered by God, my wife, Darlene, and I found ourselves in Korea for a few short years instead. We, along with coworkers, were led by God to conduct a missionary training session of which Sung Joon was a participant. Although several of the trainees were led into church work and some have high profile ministries, Sung Joon was led to an obscure place to bring the Gospel to men and women who were out of the way.

There are still an undetermined number of unreached people groups throughout the world. These, in the Bible, are called "nations" (*ethnos*). Jesus said, "Go ye...and teach all nations, baptizing them in the name of the Father and of the Son and of the Holy Ghost; teaching them to observe all things whatsoever I have commanded you; and lo, I am with you always even unto the end of the world." He also said, "And this gospel of the kingdom shall be preached in all the world for a witness to all nations; and then shall the end come." How fitting, then, that some should be called to the hard places, the obscure places, the habitations of illiterate and isolated tribesmen who make up the nations that still must hear "this gospel of the kingdom." When the work is done, the end will come. Praise God for men like Kim Sung Joon, the first Korean missionary to unreached tribal groups. He has blazed a trail, through obedience to God's call. Our prayer is that many will follow.

There are yet other tribes in other places that, without knowing it, are waiting to hear the Gospel, which the apostle Paul said is the power of God unto salvation to every one that believes it; and to receive the Scriptures that are able to make one wise unto salvation through faith which is in Christ Jesus. (2 Timothy 3:15). I trust that as you read the pages that follow you will be blessed, encouraged, and perhaps challenged. God is not impressed by our ability, nor is He hindered by our disability. He is simply seeking our availability.

Wishing you God's rich blessing as you read and enjoy,

—Dick York

Author's Preface

Professor Clymer laid his hand on my shoulder. "It was last year," he said, "during an 'Acts of the Apostles' class at the Bible School for jungle tribes. I asked them 'Who was the first person to come to your neighborhood to preach about the kingdom of God?' Paulito immediately raised his hand high and eagerly exclaimed, 'King. (Kim)'"

This caused me to think about the series of events that have occurred over the past forty years since I arrived here in the interior of Brazil.

It was long before Paulito was born that I first penetrated the Amazon Jungle. Last year he graduated from Bible school and began to spread the Gospel in the jungle that is his home, and in his wife's neighborhood, as well as to other adjacent tribes. He and his younger brother, who was his classmate, are now preparing to construct a church building for their own people to meet in.

I have spent most of my life in this mission site. It has been a long journey indeed. I have learned many lessons that have made me realize that the work of missions consists of endless hurdles and tribulations of various magnitude, relentless and repeated Satanic attacks, and, time and time again, making sacrifices without realizing they were sacrifices. It has required perseverance, commitment, and a right attitude.

Now I am in declining years. My wife has suffered homesickness from the very beginning. Until recently, she has suffered from severe depression due to nostalgia. At one time she even said that she would advise anyone who wants to be a missionary not to pursue that work. Yes, she is right.

Contrary to what she said, however, she has been strong, resilient, and has supported my work with everything she has. Whenever I made a trip into the jungle, she was left alone in the house, surrounded by an environment that, especially at first, was entirely foreign to her. She would fast and pray for me for days while trying to cope with her daily life and making provision for my next trip.

As fragile and empty as she seemed, she was like an inner tube, providing air pressure consistently enough to keep my big tire functioning. Together, we were invincible. God united us as an inseparably committed team that has continued effectively for over forty-five years.

Through the story that I am about to relate, I am going to share with you the happiness that we have experienced in God's work, and for which priviledge I thank the Lord from the bottom of my heart.

—Sung Joon Kim

Refreshing Encouragement

IT WAS THE MID-1960s and I was still in my homeland South Korea, preparing to go to Brazil – the land to which I felt God was directing me, the place that would one day be my mission site. I had just married and was working at various temporary jobs. One day, as I was collecting books and magazines from various dumpsters for the purpose of recycling, I picked up a worn-out *Reader's Digest*. The feature article captured my attention: "The Savage, My Kinsman." I was constrained to read it, and, as I did, I experienced such inspiration and encouragement that it seemed God had arranged, at this particularly awkward time, the precise means to refresh my vision for the work to which He was calling me. The content of that article was, in short, as follows.

On January 8, 1956, five missionaries died at the hands of Auca tribesmen on the banks of the Curaray River in Ecuador, South America. These men were aware of the potential danger involved with their effort to contact and carry the Gospel to this savage tribe. Their reputation for hostility to white men, and even to other Indians, was notorious. For months, the missionaries had made careful preparation to assure, as much as possible, a successful contact.

9

Nate Saint, a pilot with Missionary Aviation Fellowship (MAF), would find a way to fly them in. For several months, he searched the river banks for a possible place to land his airplane, a little yellow Piper Cruiser, near to where they thought the Aucas were.

In September 1955, they began to search the jungles for the Indians' houses. By October 6, they had located them and dropped their first gift to begin to cultivate their friendship. After nearly six weeks and several gift deliveries, they were encouraged by what appeared to be a friendly gesture, which they interpreted as an invitation to come down. By December 3, they had made their ninth gift drop. Nate had devised a way to lower gifts in a bucket while he circled overhead, and, by December 23, the Indians were reciprocating by placing gifts in the bucket for the missionaries to retrieve. It seemed that things were going well.

They found a sandbar on the bank of the river that afforded them almost two hundred and thirty yards of what proved to be a suitable landing strip. It was then determined, after much prayer, that January 3, 1956, would be "D" Day, the day they would enter "Auca Land." On that day, Nate began to fly the other missionaries and their supplies in to what they were now calling "Palm Beach." Jim Elliot, Roger Youderian, and Ed McCully established their camp and waited while Nate and Pete Fleming made repeated flights over the Auca village with a view of inviting the Aucas to come and visit their new friends at "Palm Beach."

For two days they waited; then, on January 5, the men on the beach, sensing that they were being watched, began to shout friendly greetings that they had learned in anticipation of this day. On January 6, they were surprised by a male voice responding to their greetings from the edge of the jungle. There emerged a man and two women, and what seemed to be a friendly relationship was apparently established.

January 7, expecting another visit and this time from perhaps more of the tribesmen, they waited in vain. No one came. On the morning of January 8, Nate made another flight over the village and reported excitedly that a party of Aucas was on the way to the beach. This they transmitted by radio to their mission base, arranging to call again at one o'clock in the afternoon to report how the contact had gone. That call never came.

At nine thirty in the morning, January 9, another MAF pilot flew over "Palm Beach." He reported by radio that Nate's little yellow airplane was on the beach, but all of the fabric was stripped from the wings and fuselage. There was no sign of life or any indication where the five men might be. A search party was immediately assembled to determine the fate of the five and to rescue any survivors that might remain. All were found, mutilated beyond recognition by the vicious attack of Auca lances. One of them was washed away and lost in the current of the river; the other four were buried in a common grave there in the land of the Aucas.

The wives had spoken together before the operation began, recognizing the possibility of their becoming widows. "What would we do?" they had asked one another.

"God gave us peace of heart, and confidence that whatever might happen, His word would hold," writes Elisabeth Elliot, wife of one of the martyrs. "We knew that 'when He putteth forth His sheep, He goeth before them.' God's leading [had been] unmistakable up to [that] point. Each of us knew when we married our husbands that there would never be any question about who came first—God and His work held first place in each life; it was the condition of true discipleship—it became devastatingly meaningful now."

There were many unanswered questions about what had happened on that beach, but "This much we knew," Elisabeth adds, "'Whosoever shall lose his life for my sake and the gospel's, the same shall save it.' There was no question as to the state of our loved ones. They were 'with Christ.'"

The quiet trust of those widowed mothers helped their children to know that this was not a tragedy. This was what God had planned. There were many around the world whose lives were changed by what happened at "Palm Beach." From around the world, letters of encouragement poured in to the five widows. Four of them stayed on in Ecuador, and plans were quickly formulated to carry on the work of the martyred men.

The Indians who speared the five men are Christians now. The New Testament has been translated into their language, and they are engaged in preaching its Gospel message. They are no longer called "Aucas," the meaning of which is "naked" or "savage." They are the "Waorani," a fearsome and warlike tribe no more but a people transformed by the Gospel of Jesus Christ. They have schools and a church and intercourse with the outside world. God has tamed the savage killer — brought him from darkness to light. The seeds of life planted by the sacrifice of five missionaries have germinated. "They that sow in tears shall reap in joy. He that goeth forth and weepeth, bearing precious seed, shall doubtless come again with rejoicing, bringing his sheaves with him" (Psalm 126: 5,6).

This is a true story. It inspired and encouraged me to be obedient to God's call. There are still vast stretches of jungle in South America where primitive tribes live in prehistoric conditions untouched by civilization. In such places, and under like circumstances, the possibility of a similar incident recurring is not unlikely. Therefore, significant sanctions against missionaries are in place in this vast territory. But it is here, nevertheless, that I play a minute part, for which I am so very thankful to our Lord.

—m—

Eternal Life

FIRST OF ALL, let me tell you something of what motivated me toward missions before I tell you the details of my life with an indigenous tribe in the Guapore Valley, one of the upper tributaries of the Amazon River.

I was born during World War II into a reputedly devout Christian family. Korea was suffering under Japanese occupation, which domination lasted thirty-six years. All Christian churches were enduring severe persecution. My grandfather was an elder of the church in a little town called Nam Pyeong, Na Ju County. He suffered much at the hands of the Japanese police. Because they suspected him of being a Korean spy, he was under constant surveillance. Instead of seeking asylum abroad or escaping to America, he stayed in his homeland, where he was able to help a female American missionary "Wha Re Yu" (her Korean name), who itinerated to little country churches in her sedan chair, by finding places for her to stay or giving her refuge in his own house.

During the occupation, he made a clandestine trip to the Korean Provisional Government, at that time in exile in Shanghai, China, to assist in the "Declaration of Korean Independence" movement. During that trip, he was arrested, sent to Daegu prison as a political criminal and tortured in unspeakable ways. After two years, due to grave illness, my grandfather was released and subsequently passed away.

His children became the object of ridicule at school because of his prison record and because of his Christianity. The Japanese teachers shamed them in front of the other children, mocking them with "Amen, Ramen, Giamen," which were the brand names of Japanese noodles. In spite of the ridicule that her children were made to endure, my grandmother refused to abandon her faith and raised her family to be faithful church-goers. As a result, I attended church every single Sunday with my mother even before I was born into this world.

I grew up this way until I was in high school, when I began to be filled with doubt. It was as though there was a dark cloud inside me, and I began to entertain many unanswered questions. Is God a living being? Was the universe really created by Him? Is there a heaven and a hell; if so, where do they exist? How could Jesus have died for my sin two thousand years ago, when I am less than twenty years old? How could this save me from sin? If God is almighty, why couldn't He save me without crucifying His own Son? And if He is almighty, why did He allow sin and disobedience in the first place? If the human race is His creation, aren't we His children? How, then, could He send people to hell even if they did something wrong? If God is just, how come wicked men prosper while good men suffer?

The questions multiplied. Where did I come from, and where am I going? This life is so full of sadness and difficulty, what makes us any better than the animals? *Reveal Yourself to me, so that I can feel You and believe You. Where are You?* As far as I know, the Bible was written by men; why should I believe that it is God's word? Where is the evidence? If the whole world is God's, why do I have to give to Him?

And so the questions continued to come. I could not find answers to any of them, and I was greatly confused. The foundations of my faith, which before this had been unchallenged, were now severely shaken, and I felt like I was in a maze. In my confusion, I concluded, "God does not exist." All this time I was religiously attending church. This life of pretentious religious protocol tormented me almost beyond endurance.

Moreover, my mother was so stern that she would not allow even the slightest deviation from her religious standards, especially on Sundays: "Sunday," she insisted, "is the Holy Sabbath Day. That means it is set aside exclusively to worship God — not to picnic with your classmates at Bek Yang Temple, not to go fishing, not to watch a volley-ball tournament, and not to spend money on ice cream bars or cookies, because that money should be given to God as alms." No matter what my growing body seemed to need, all of these things were somehow "against the Ten Commandments." I was living the life of a hypocrite, and I was uncomfortable, dissatisfied, and wretched.

On the other hand, I was struggling with another kind of question: throughout the ages, multitudes have become Christians. Among them famous kings, great politicians, intelligent scientists, scholars, and artists — all of whom must have at some time confronted God with their doubts — and they became His followers and worshipped Him. Am I smarter than them? Do I have greater wisdom than they have? *If so,* I argued with myself, *why are you in the shape you are in? You miserable little creature, why can't you improve yourself? Is this your only growth plan, arguing self-destructively every day?* I was losing my power to reason — to agree or disagree with any of these private discussions.

I was gradually coming to the realization that there was something wrong with my train of thought. Looking back, those tormented days were my opportunity to find God, to achieve a personal faith in Him apart from my family's tradition or some kind of ancestral belief. I had to find Him myself. Because I was the one who needed deliverance from the misery I endured, I must accept Him as my personal Savior.

But how does one find God? What shall I do? Where shall I go? I had no idea. I was still at square one. Nothing had improved. Several years passed this way until I was a college sophomore and an aspiring electrical engineer, but that aspiration was about to come to an end. My father couldn't afford my expensive tuition any more. The day that I was forced to drop out of college, I felt that my life was over.

My father was a school principal in a southern province, but during World War II he was sent to a school in Manchuria, far north of the northern peninsula, where the terrain stayed frozen most of the year. On August 15, 1945, the war ended. My family, on foot, and carrying our possessions in two small backpacks, started to move south. Crossing the dangerous northern mountain barrier into the Ge Sung area, where the North-South border line was established, we continued still further south until we reached our home town. When we arrived, the society was in chaos.

For five years, we, the Korean people, struggled to recover from the aftermath of World War II, but long before any recovery was accomplished, the Korean War broke out. At five o'clock, Sunday morning, June 25,1950, while many were still asleep in their beds, the morning peace was shattered by an invasion from the North. Thousands of North Korean soldiers, led by tank brigades, began to stream south until they had overrun the peninsula, except for one small portion of Gyeong Sang province. UN soldiers from sixteen nations were dispatched, and the Korean War began. The UN forces pushed the red army back north—beyond the Aprok river and Bek Du mountains—before being pushed back again to the south.

Four times in three years the battle lines pushed north only to be pushed south again. Finally, the North Koreans were pushed back beyond the thirty-eighth parallel, the capital city of Seoul was recovered, and the demilitarized zone was established. Once again, a war had ended, but tens of thousands of lives had been lost. What had survived World War II had been demolished down to the ground, the country ruined. Nothing was left.

Unlike the majority of the people, my parents were fortunate. Being teachers, they were able to make a living. They could earn enough money to raise their five children one day at a time. Sending them all to college was beyond their dreams. I was the oldest of the children, and it seemed clear to me that there was no hope for a good life. I decided I should either kill myself or, to survive, join one of the street gangs and live carelessly as a total ingrate. Either way, it seemed my life was over.

Somehow, though, deep inside me, the word "God" echoed persistently. It seemed impossible to free myself of it. I must resolve this issue for good! To do this, I determined to pray every night for a week. Frankly, that decision was not appealing to me, but there seemed no other choice than to have a showdown with God. I must either see Him or meet Him somehow. This would be the crucial factor that would determine my future.

It was late October. The weather was cold and windy. At ten thirty, the preliminary siren rang out, warning of the eleven o'clock curfew. I sneaked out of the house toward the little country church, which stood on a nearby hillside. The church door was open, but inside it was dark and quiet. The room was empty, devoid even of pews. It was as though I had entered a tomb. I walked all the way to the front and knelt down. I had a vague and uneasy feeling; I didn't know what to do. I had nothing to say except one little earnest prayer, "God, I'm a sinner. Please forgive me." I was wide awake all through that first night, repeating that one simple phrase. The next day, my mind was strangely filled with the words, "Repent and believe the Gospel." All day long, those words persisted.

The second night began with my confession. I tried to remember and articulate every sin that I had ever committed. The most painful moments were when I realized how ungrateful and silently rebellious I had been toward my mother, who had kept praying for me every day and caring for me so much. I thought about how offensive and irreconcilable I had been to my younger brothers and sisters. As dawn approached, I found myself weeping profusely. I felt excruciating pain and exhaustion from the devastating recognition that "I am a *sinner*."

Suddenly, words that I had read before in a Gospel tract came into my mind and spoke to my heart: "I have blotted out, as a thick cloud, thy transgressions, and, as a cloud, thy sins: return unto me; for I have redeemed thee" (Isaiah 44:22). I was totally engulfed in heavenly peace as I comprehended those words: "I (God) have redeemed (present perfect tense) you (me, Kim)." My sins have been blotted out! I have been saved! What a revelation! I was in shock, overwhelmed with a sense of tranquility and peace. It was as though all of my unanswered questions were suddenly resolved.

My desire had been to meet God, to see Him. Although He never visibly appeared, these words of His were more than enough to reveal Him to me. I was born again, and that verse became the pivot of my life thereafter. No need now to kill myself or join a street gang. My heart was filled to overflowing with thankfulness. *Dear God, thank you for allowing me this privilege of calling You my Father, my Holy Father.*

The third night, my prayer was simply praise and thanksgiving, the reiteration of one phrase: "Thank you, God, thank you." I was at peace. "Thank you, Lord, for finding me. Thank you, thank you!"

—◊◊—

Short Prayer, Big Response

I T WAS A BEAUTIFUL DAWN as I made my way home from my third night of prayer. It had been a night of thanksgiving to God. As I finished, for my last short prayer I said, "Lord, I need a job." It would be so nice to restart my life and get back into the process of learning.

Exactly one year earlier, I had written a letter to my high school English teacher, whom I had esteemed very highly. He had also been my Sunday School teacher. I wanted to communicate with him about my future. His name was Hahn Jae Ho, and several years before, he had moved to Daegu to work with a Christian Literature Mission, an organization that had a much needed influence upon a Korean Christian community devastated by war.

I was, at that time, attending Jeon Nam University College of Science. I was finding it extremely difficult to concentrate on any lectures during my electrical engineering classes, or on the mathematical formulas and calculations that filled the two blackboards at the front of the room. My mind was too preoccupied with worries: worries about my parents working so hard to raise my four younger siblings, who were fast approaching college entrance; worries about myself, the eldest son of a poor family, and where we would get the tuition for my next semester. I decided to quit school before my parents would have to take another loan from the Jo Han Bank to pay for my tuition. I would find a job and earn money to pay for my own schooling. In desperation, I found his address and wrote a letter to my old English teacher to see if there might be a position for which I could apply.

In his brief reply, teacher Hahn Jae Ho said, "It would be better for you to continue in your studies while you are in your critical formative years."

I wrote back to him, explaining my intentions. Some time later, in response to my explanation, I received a letter asking me to come to Daegu to take an admissions test because there was one opening in the editorial department, but I was to understand that the competition for that one spot would be very tough.

I went and took the test, sitting quietly alone in a basement room. The test was to translate into Korean two pages of a salvation story written in English by the renowned evangelist Charles G. Finney. There was no time limit, and an English dictionary was allowed, but what I was reading seemed totally different from the English I had learned in my high school textbook.

I knew my capacity — although I was willing and had done my best, I knew that I had not done very well. Hahn Jae Ho, however, said that he would send my answer sheet to Pastor Bob Rice, founder of the literature mission, who was taking a sabbatical in America. He expected that it would take some time, but he promised to notify me as soon as he received a response, whether it was a positive one or not. I thanked my old teacher, came home, and put it completely out of my mind.

One year later, the miracle of my conversion took place. At the dawn of the fourth day, after praying, "Lord, I need a job," I came back home from the church and was at the breakfast table, when the mailman arrived. He delivered one letter. It was from teacher Hahn.

I opened it and read, "Dear Sung Joon, can you come to Daegu? And prepare to stay over the whole winter."

I couldn't believe what I saw. I read it over and over again to make sure that I wasn't misunderstanding. It was definitely indicative of a long-term stay, not just a visit. I had a job! I was overcome by a surge of joy and a sense of gratitude, and any appetite for breakfast was swept away.

"Mother," I cried, "I am leaving tomorrow for Daegu. I have a job offer!"

Mother said, "Oh, really?" There was a pause, and then she burst into tears.

She was, no doubt, remembering the pain I had caused her. Looking back, I remembered that she had always insisted that I continue through college — or she would lose face as a parent. How would other parents view her, if she, as a teacher, educating other people's children, couldn't send her own son to college? My salaried father, far from being affluent, had managed to procure the entrance fee and the first semester's tuition for me with a bank loan, but the next year, with my younger brother coming up, it would obviously be beyond his financial ability. I understood my parents' predicament. Nonetheless, after I dropped out of school, I had developed an extremely defiant attitude.

"I knew it!" I had shouted at them. "I knew you couldn't keep up with my college expenses. I knew you weren't with me for the long haul, so I told you I would take a different route. Why did you mess me up? I don't want to live any more!"

I wouldn't eat, wouldn't talk, for almost a month. My mother had never stopped worrying about me. She hid anything sharp and any heavy cords. Whenever I opened the door, everyone in the family was wary of me. If I lingered a little too long in the bathroom, she would send my sister to find out why. "Big brother, are you there? Big brother?"

I had felt like I was under house arrest or confined to a psychiatric hospital, prison, and mausoleum all combined into one.

Obviously, it had been one long, exhausting year for my mother. On that merciful morning when the letter arrived, she saw the light at the end of the tunnel — the end of a long year filled with turmoil. She could not help but sob with the emotion of that moment. Her son had been saved! He had been saved spiritually and circumstantially. A double jubilation — salvation and a new job!

After breakfast, she busied herself preparing for my trip. She packed my underwear, winter clothes, my college uniform for a suit, and my father's worn-out leather shoes, which she polished till they shone. The next night, I took leave of my family. After an emotional farewell, I boarded a night train that would arrive in Daegu the following morning. Here I was, a fledgling, leaving the nest for good, nervous, filled with anticipation, and about to be exposed to the world on my own for the first time, where I would be trained and tested in many storms for years to come.

This was late October 1956, immediately following the salvation miracle that I had experienced in the Ham Pyeong church. I firmly believe that I got my first job as a twenty-one-year-old youngster not because of my performance — most certainly not — but by the grace of God. *Thank you, God. Thank you, indeed!*

I was filled with gratitude to my teacher, Hahn Jae Ho, for being instrumental in providing this first step, one of the many steps that would culminate in unyielding commitment to my mission in the Brazilian jungle, where I would work by faith in God, joyfully and without fear.

—ᕰ—

God's Calling

FROM THE TIME I WAS SAVED, I began to read the Bible. I would rise at three or four o'clock every morning and, alone in my small room, would read and pray, "God, You saved me by Your grace, so now I am at Your disposal. What would You have me do?" Several years passed this way. One day as I prayed, a question arose in my heart, *Should I become a missionary to another country?* I was perplexed by that thought, laughed at myself for thinking it, and brushed it aside.

My mother used to pray concerning me, "I beseech you, Lord, to accept my firstborn as an offering." Later, when I realized that she meant for me to become a minister, I was indignant and reacted strongly against such a prospect. I was not disposed to become a minister or a pastor. I considered these to be unmanly occupations performed by weak people. My mother, however, was motivated by what she perceived to be the meaning of Leviticus 27:28, 29: "No devoted thing, that a man shall devote unto the Lord of all that he hath, both of man and beast, and of the field of his possession, shall be sold or redeemed: every devoted thing is most holy unto the Lord. None devoted, which shall be devoted of men, shall be redeemed; but shall surely be put to death." It was evident that my mother had dedicated me, her firstborn child, unto God. To her, I was the "devoted thing."

But to me, there was no way that I would be a minister! And now, even worse, to be a missionary? I was not favorably impressed by the missionaries that I had seen. Their lifestyle was different from anything to which I or the people that I knew were accustomed. They preferred to reside in the suburbs rather than in urban areas where mingling with ordinary people would have afforded them a better understanding of the native culture. They had their chefs and babysitters and cleaning women, and they lived in "palaces" surrounded by high fences and guards. When they drove their luxurious jeeps down the dirt roads where ordinary people were walking, the people had to run away from the roads to avoid the clouds of dust and gasoline fumes that were stirred up. I used to wonder where they found gasoline in this petroleum-starved nation.

I perceived that missionaries would call on little country churches but would decline to eat the food that the country people had laboriously and lovingly prepared for them because it might be contaminated. Instead, they carried their own bottled water, sandwiches, and coffee. Nor would they stay overnight in the homes of the church people but would always return to their own homes, no matter how far it was or how late it might be. The attitudes of missionaries offended me and went against my grain. And now, I would become one of them? It was ridiculous!

Then, of course, there was one more thing: the thought was presumptuous that I was equipped to be a missionary. I had no qualifications. Furthermore, looking at the big picture, Korea was a poverty-stricken nation, devastated by two wars, and was a third-world country. I harbored some compelling questions: *As a Korean, where could I go? Who would support me financially? Could I overcome my cultural and racial inferiority and work as an equal with other missionaries?* Well, those were the realities, and I concluded that being a missionary was not a job that warranted my highest aspirations or hope.

During my daily prayers, the missionary thought persisted. The more I tried to suppress it, the stronger it became. I was anguished by it. I continued to pray until I found a measure of peace in deciding to wait and see what God's eventual timetable would be.

One day as I prayed, this outrageous thought entered my mind, *How about being a missionary to cannibals?* This was like jumping out of the frying pan into the fire! I was somewhat bewildered by the thought, but it reminded me of a cartoon I had seen when I was in grammar school. In it, a white explorer in Africa was captured by cannibals. They tied him to a post and lit a fire under him. After gleefully dancing around him for a while, they ate him. Remembering this cartoon was not troubling at all; in fact it triggered some adventurous thinking. *If I were there,* I reasoned, *I'm sure I could figure out how to avoid such a mishap.* And I was at peace. Without realizing it, I must have accepted the idea of becoming a missionary to cannibals, because from then on I was never troubled about the matter again in prayer. My direction was clear. At last, after six years, the issue that I have wrestled with since I was born again had been resolved: a "mission to cannibals."

I began to research through several books in the library to locate cannibals anywhere in the world. I learned that there were such primitive tribes in Papua New Guinea in the South Pacific Ocean, but missionaries from several countries were already working in that region to reach them with the Gospel. As I searched further, I found that there were still many unreached tribes scattered throughout the immense Amazon Jungle in Brazil, South America. *The unreached tribes in the Amazon Jungle,* I thought. *That's my destination*!

I now had a new subject for prayer. "How am I supposed to proceed with this task?" I didn't know where to start, because as far as I knew, no one had heard of "missions" in the Korean Christian community, which made it difficult for me to see how I could advance or get support through them. Generally, church activities in those days were limited to Morning Prayer, frequent "revival" meetings, "Church Growth Movement" to enlarge congregations, and receiving missionaries from foreign countries, but not sending missionaries. In a hundred years of Korean church history, no missionaries had been sent to other countries.

As a first step, I wanted to study through the Bible in an organized manner and in a short time. In every province there were three-year Bible schools run by foreign mission organizations, which trained assistant ministers. But these were gradually fading away and being replaced by four-year divinity schools that were more popular. In these schools, after that additional year of study, the graduates were qualified as pastors. I didn't want either of these outcomes. My desire was to be equipped solely by the Bible. I didn't need or desire a title.

I was looking in another direction. From one missionary, I had learned of two international mission institutions, the addresses of which he was able to supply. One of them was Wycliffe Bible Translators in Los Angeles, California. I sent a letter to them explaining that I was an Asian, very interested in mission work to unreached tribes, and wanting to know what were the qualifications for admission to their institution. When I had almost given up hope of hearing from them, their long overdue reply came. "We appreciate your letter...we require a four-year college degree followed by a two-year study of linguistics and anthropology and a one-year survival course in Mexico, etc...."

It seemed unlikely that I would pursue those qualifications if I must spend seven years as a scholar before starting my mission. Then there was the age factor — that mattered, and the financial burden mattered. So I gave up pursuing that organization.

Again, I wrote the same letter to the New Tribes Mission in Chicago. This time, the reply came very quickly and was very brief: "We are glad to receive your good letter. However, up to this time we have not considered an Asian missionary...you may write to us any time...." So they declined with thanks. In my perception, prejudice existed and probably would continue to exist in this organization. But instead of feeling sorry, I realized that God does His work in His way, not in man's way.

Now my questions became, *How did these missions start their work in new tribes? Could I start the way they did? Was their method, however they started, considered to be the most appropriate? Could there also be another good approach?*

I was confident that God's will would be different and His guidance variable according to the circumstances and the targeted area, and our individual faith to carry out His will would not be the same, either. God wouldn't ask one to go beyond the means that He himself was willing to provide. It seemed that would be God's formula. I was convinced that I would proceed alone, with God as my mainstay: "For by thee I have run through a troop; and by my God have I leaped over a wall. As for God, his way is perfect: the word of the LORD is tried: he is a buckler to all those that trust in him" (Psalm 18: 29, 30).

—∽—

Mission School

5

I HAD JUST COMPLETED my three years of compulsory military service. Shortly after coming home, I received a letter from Kees Glas, a Dutch missionary from The Netherlands, who was working with Worldwide Evangelization Crusade (WEC), a mission with headquarters in England. Some years before, I had tutored Kees in the Korean language. In his letter, he appealed to me to return to Daegu to tutor another WEC missionary who had recently come from England. Since Kees had been so successful with the language, the new missionary had opted to be tutored as Kees had been, rather than attend language school at Yon Se University. I hesitated because I was praying every day and, in spite of the fact that the Korean job market was still very poor, looking for a more promising job than that—one that would help me toward my mission goal.

Then my mother persuaded me with her advice. "Son, in the Old Testament it says not to ill-treat foreigners and travelers. This man came to this country in poverty at the risk of his life, and who are you to be unwilling to support him? Rush to help him, Son!"

"Yes, Mother."

So I hurried to Daegu to meet the new missionary. Derek Earl[1] was twenty-seven years old and a typical Englishman. He had

---

[1] From the early '70s to the present, Derek Earl has had a remarkable influence preaching the Gospel to the Korean Society of Nursing Assistants in Germany. Derek married a German girl, who also spent time as a WEC missionary in Korea. Since leaving Korea he has taught in the Bible College of Wales Korean Department and has continued to produce follow-up material in the Korean language, which is sent around the world.

graduated from a theological university in Wales, had passed the WEC missionary training course in Bulstrode, England, and now he was here in Korea. My first impression was that this was not going to be easy for either of us, but at the very least, my life in Daegu was started again.

One Saturday evening, Kees invited me to an evangelistic meeting for young people. He explained to me that there was a missionary who could teach the Bible in such an understandable way that he was reaching a large number of college students and foreign missionaries. Kees said that he himself had not heard such a wise and clear interpretation of Scripture even when he was in the theological University in Glasgow, Scotland.

I was thinking, *You are a missionary yourself, and you are introducing another one to me without hurting your ego?* It made me curious and filled me with anticipation, but all the time I was thinking, *Can any good thing come out of Nazareth?*

The missionary was holding the meetings at the YMCA in Daegu. The sign, if it had been in English, would have read, "Youth Rally," but in Korean it said, "Youth Revolution," which was a sensitive and somewhat challenging title, since Korea was still very unsettled following the military revolution led by Pak Jung Hee. As a result, there were Secret Service men from the Korean CIA in attendance. They were there to get a close-up look at this "revolution" and to make sure it was not something that would jeopardize the new government.

There were about one hundred and fifty eager college students crammed into the tiny auditorium, all exuding a sense of urgency. Dick York, a burly American missionary accompanied by an interpreter, opened the meeting and began to teach the Bible: "In the beginning was the Word, and the Word was with God, and the Word was God..." (John 1:1) — discoursing and quoting from memory other verses related to the text. The Bible study was fascinating, simple, and easy to listen to. I had never heard these things before.

Dick had been raised in Canada by his widowed mother. She was from England, born again in a Baptist church when she was a young girl, and had walked with the Lord for more than forty years. At the age of fifteen, Dick, during World War II, had left the godly home she had provided to serve in the U.S. Merchant Marine. He had broken his mother's heart by the profligate lifestyle he had embraced and was wasting his life as a "Prodigal son." His brother, five years older than Dick, and a church-goer all his life although saved only a year earlier, had been burdened for his younger brother's salvation and, intensely preaching the Gospel to Dick, had led him to Christ.

Immediately after he had received Christ, his brother asked him a question, "Dick, would you like to be perfect?"

Of course, the answer was an emphatic, "Yes!"

Second question: "Would you like to be thoroughly equipped for every good work?"

Again, the answer was eagerly affirmative.

"Then read these verses," said his brother, holding his Bible open to 2 Timothy 3:16,17. "Read them out loud."

Dick read, "All scripture is given by inspiration of God and is profitable for doctrine, for reproof, for correction, for instruction in righteousness, that the man of God may be perfect, throughly furnished unto all good works."

"That's it, Dick," his brother said. "The Word of God will make you perfect and equip you for every good work. Read it every day. Read it all your life. It will teach you."

From that day on, he began to read the Bible. He studied it every day and, as a result, began to preach the Gospel everywhere. Many of those to whom he preached were people like he had been, drunkards, drug addicts, and people of the street. From his home in Vancouver, Canada, he went to Eugene, Oregon, in the United States.

There he started a mission to minister to those ruined lives that plied the streets of that city. He started a radio program to broadcast the Gospel and to make known the work of the mission. The message and the ministry attracted the attention of a wealthy farmer and businessman, who began to involve himself in the ministry by supporting the work of the mission in various ways.

God made this man, whose name was Harry Holt, aware of the plight of thousands of orphans and mixed-blood children resulting from the wars that had ravaged Korea and the foreign armies that had been stationed there. God had then led him to do something about it. Subsequently, he spent his entire fortune to rescue those unfortunate children. He established the Holt adoption program known today around the world as Holt Children's Services. In the course of doing so, he observed the great spiritual need that seemed to be as great as or greater than the physical damage that war had inflicted upon the nation.

He sent word back to the United States, urging Dick to come to Korea and preach the Gospel in this needy land, but Dick was not convinced. After repeated invitations, Harry Holt persuaded Dick to accompany him to Korea for two months to see for himself the miserable conditions prevailing there. Two months turned into three. Then, upon returning home, Dick had been so haunted by the need he had seen there that he could do nothing else except return, with his family, to Korea to preach the Gospel.

Situating his family first in Pohang and then in Daegu, he traveled much, conducting Sunday services in U.S. Army chapels, preaching the Gospel in homes and in villages, doing personal evangelism, and trying to make disciples of the Lord Jesus Christ, all the while praying that God would allow him to disciple some Koreans for mission work. It was to that end that he and the missionaries with whom he worked conducted the meetings for college students in the YMCA as a step toward fulfilling that goal.

Through the "grapevine," I heard that they would start a missionary training program in late 1962. I felt sure that this would be a God-given opportunity for me, and I was excited about it. I understood that it would be a six-month course, and there were only two requirements: a true salvation experience and scriptural baptism by immersion. It was perfect for me. There was one potential problem: the students would be chosen, so participation would be by appointment. That could be another obstacle for me, but, as it turned out, I was called in, thank goodness, by the grace of God.

The first class consisted of eight men and three women. We assembled in a large Japanese-style house, which at one time had been government property. It had many large rooms with straw mat floors. It was surrounded by a spacious yard with many trees, but it had been vacant a long time and was in need of maintenance, so there was much work to do. The first day, we were engaged in a major cleaning project. Something went wrong, and somehow it was determined that I was at fault. It seemed serious enough to Dick that he told me I could not continue in the program.

What a blow that was to me! I had just entered and had been expelled already. I was completely crestfallen. At that time, Marlin Baker,[2] a missionary from Seoul, was also there. He approached me and said, "Brother Kim, I'm so sorry. It would have been nice if you could have trained with us."

I thought, "Wow, it's real! I'm out of this training program. What am I going to do?" I felt like I was standing at the edge of a cliff.

There must have been a discussion among the staff, because a little while later Marlin Baker[2] came back and, placing his hand on my shoulder, said, "Brother Kim, we have decided to let you continue as a student, so please, cheer up."

---

[2]*Marlin Baker went to Korea with Christians in Action Mission. After leaving Korea, he went to the Philippines for some years and now works in a prison ministry in Texas.*

I was extremely thankful and so relieved. It seemed imperative that I redirect my focus and concentrate, more than anything else, on self-discipline, which seemed to be lacking. "But He knows the way that I take: when He has tried me, I shall come forth as gold."

We had been cleaning and repairing the house for a week when one of the students, becoming impatient, asked when the training program would begin. The answer, surprisingly, was, "It has already begun."

We had all assumed that we would study as we did in the formal school system, but Dick opened a new chapter for us: the training went beyond textbooks and notebooks. He had been observing each student from day one. Living, itself, was the training, and everyday situations were the context in which that training took place. This confirmed why the regulations were so strict.

First, we had to use respectful language when addressing one another, regardless of age difference. In Korean tradition, respectful language is used when the younger addresses the elder but not the other way round. This was awkward at first, but this courtesy later became meaningful, and we understood that it was a biblical injunction eliminating foolish jesting and the vertical relationships with one another that are the norm in a Confucianistic society.

Second, punctuality: If we were late even one minute after the bell rang, we were not allowed to sit down at the table. That was designed to get rid of the "Korean time" concept, in which it is acceptable to be late, sometimes even as much as thirty minutes.

Third, we were to live by faith. No tuition was charged for the training. Each individual was required to be self-sufficient for everything, including bedding. We were not supposed to make our needs known to anyone but the Lord. For food, we were to put money in a box on the table and the two students who were assigned to kitchen duty were to use that money for food and charcoal (which at that time was our cooking fuel) for a week.

No one knew, or needed to know, who put how much in or when. This was designed to teach us to live by faith, responsibility, integrity, and caring for one another.

The daily agenda was as follows:

Rising time was not prescribed; it was up to each individual to rise as early as he wished. However, when the rising bell would sound, it was time for everyone to be up, square everything away, and be ready to sit down at the table when the breakfast bell sounded.

After breakfast we had a ninety-minute quiet time, during which the students dispersed and read their Bibles and prayed alone, using the opportunity to meditate and hear what the Lord had to say to them individually. We all liked these sacred moments and wished that our quiet time were longer. After quiet time, we cleaned and did chores according to an assignment chart. This was followed by a two-hour class time, in which the Bible was our text-book. We did not study books "about the Bible." The sixty-six books that the Scriptures comprise were our resources for instructing us how to live by faith.

After lunch, it was time to go out and preach. Oh, how I feared this time! What a conflict I experienced between my flesh and my spirit. The enemy was definitely against my doing this, and although I knew that it would be a win/win situation to go out and do battle with the "sword of the Spirit," God's Word, I nonetheless wanted to find an excuse to retreat from doing it.

With much trepidation, stuttering, clearing our throats, trying to reassure each other, we went out in pairs to designated areas. We would be in each of those neighborhoods seven times before the training session ended. In addition to that assignment, we had to self-train in personal evangelism, street preaching, child evangelism, village preaching, and preaching in hospitals and prisons. There were also the Saturday night evangelistic meetings and campus preaching exclusively to students. We trained in almost every facet of evangelism.

Upon returning and before dinner, as each team reported, we were overflowing with excitement. The scripture says, "They that sow in tears shall reap in joy" (Psalm 126:5). In our case, we went out to sow in fear, but we returned ecstatic with joy.

We didn't study how to preach; we went preaching. Experience is a wonderful instructor, and practice produces proficiency. After dinner, our time was relatively free. We filled it by completing homework assignments or following up on people to whom we had preached. At ten o'clock, it was "lights out," time to go to bed. *O, Lord, thank you!* I would rest, all right. Good mornings start the night before.

If there was one stressful issue in the training program, it was the individual interview that happened once a month. All of the carnal attitudes, hidden secrets, or errors were uncovered and talked about during that interview.

"Brother Hong, you have been reading books by candlelight in the closet at eleven o'clock at night. Why do you think that is good when there is a ten-o'clock 'lights out'?"

Brother Hong was a bookworm.

"Brother Pak, you have been sneaking in after lights out, climbing over the fence. Why?"

"Which is better to do: come home on time, or follow up after ten o'clock because of the hours the people I meet with work?"

Brother Pak was very bold.

Now it was my turn, and the interview went something like this:

"Brother Kim, were you able to put any money in the box last month?"

"No, I couldn't."

"Why were you not able to do so?"

"Because I didn't have any money."

"Why, do you think, you didn't receive any money?"

I had no answer.

"Did you ask God in prayer?"

"Yes, I prayed hard."

"Why, do you suppose, did God not give you money? Did you ask in faith?"

His questions were right; so were my answers. But at this point I did not see the solution. This whole process was to orient us to a walk of faith. Every consequence, it seemed, was attributable to faith or the lack of it.

Where is faith, and how does it come to me? That was the great question, and to me it was a very serious one. More and more often, there were days when we didn't eat because there was no food. One of the students dropped out and went home because he couldn't cope. In the beginning of the training session, we had plenty of hot steamed rice, kimchi, and bulgogi, favorite Korean dishes that may not be familiar to many who read this. One by one, as the training progressed, these things disappeared from our table. Perhaps lack of faith was everyone's problem.

What is "living by faith"? What does "living by faith" look like? How do we have to live to be able to say we are "living by faith"?

We must have entered the preliminary training stage. The Apostle Paul said, "I know both how to be abased, and I know how to abound." This must be the "abased" stage. "Everywhere and in all things," Paul continued, "I am instructed both to be full and to be hungry, both to abound and to suffer need" (Philippians 4:12).

One day, after having only a glass of hot water for lunch, we went out to preach on the street. Everyone was feeling weak, and our faces, as a result, were expressionless. I carried an accordion, which I played for accompaniment as we sang hymns. My Bible felt heavy and the accordion heavier. Ten of us stood in the middle of the Bang Cheon marketplace, ostentatiously singing Gospel hymns. I did not have to look around to see the rice cakes, roasted sweet potatoes, wheat bread, grilled chestnuts, ripe persimmons, apples, and roasted locusts. Nor did I have to take a big whiff to recognize the smell of barbequed ribs, barbequed snipe-fish, bean curd soup, rice cake soup, and seafood soup, etc. They were there, and I was fantasizing how they would taste. I was thinking that I was there to be tempted by the enemy just as Jesus had been tempted by the Devil after forty days of fasting. We have definitely chosen the wrong place!

I thought, "Perhaps someone will bring a whole batch of rice cakes to us because they are so moved by our preaching. Or maybe they will bring us a bunch of roasted sweet potatoes; or serve us each a bowl of hot noodle soup at the end of the day, since we have worked so hard in this chilly weather." The enemy was trying to hinder our preaching with all sorts of ideas.

As I spoke aloud, "Ladies and gentlemen…," and began to speak of Jesus on the Cross, I felt that the faces of those merchants, from whom I had been expecting so much, revealed frowns and sneers as they turned their backs on me thinking, "Is this what you do for a living? You young Jesus People have nothing better to do? Go to heaven by yourselves. Just leave us alone."

But I was encouraged to see that there were also some people around us who were all ears. They were showing interest in what we had to say. We were just about finished when a young man came up and stood next to me while both of my hands were occupied with the accordion and thrust his hand into my left pocket. I was startled, and turning my head to the left, I was looking into the face of a young man with a kind expression. Although I didn't have any money, my first thought had been that he was a pickpocket. On the contrary, he must have put something into my pocket. What could it be? I moved my left leg a little and could feel that something was in my pocket. Was it money? I wondered how much. I was anxious to know.

We introduced ourselves to each other when our street meeting ended, and I discovered that he was a sophomore in a theological seminary. He had admired our evangelism as he passed by and, stopping to listen, had felt impressed to give me all that he had. It could have been his bus fare for two round trips. I immediately gave the money to the two students who were currently on kitchen duty, and they in turn bought two large loaves of dinner bread, two containers of tofu, and a handful of green onions. Around our dinner table that evening we enjoyed a delightful meal of bread and tofu soup, accompanied with joyful shouts of thanksgiving.

The merchants in whom we had placed our hopes had turned their backs on us, but this poor theology student, just passing by, God had used to provide enough to meet our needs. God had blessed us with "the widow's mite." It was a remarkable lesson for us to learn that God's provision comes not from where we might anticipate but sometimes from a totally unexpected direction as incentive for us to trust Him when we can't see. "Now faith is the substance of things hoped for, the evidence of things not seen. For by it the elders obtained a good report" (Hebrews 11:1, 2).

(I wonder every now and then where that theology student is and hope that he has eternal life and that God has rewarded him abundantly.)

That was generally how the first three months of training went. For the second three months, we were to go out in pairs to an area of our choice and plant seeds of the Gospel by preaching to the local residents in hope of starting a new church. I deviated from the program and carried out my own plan. I wanted to go out alone without a partner because I thought this would best prepare me for my mission field, Brazil. I felt I needed practice for my unique project, so I studied carefully the details of the map of Korea and found the most remote and inaccessible spot, where I hoped to experience, for three months, God's leading and the power of faith.

Immediately after the first three-month segment of the training, I got engaged to be married. When I was leaving for my second three-month adventure, my fiancée came to see me off and handed me a little money wrapped in a memo paper on which she had written some Bible verses. That was the only money I had. My itinerary was from Daegu in Gyung Sang province to Je Chun in Choong Buk province by train, and then on to Young Worl, a coal mining district and the end of the rail line; from there by foot to the small and extremely isolated village of Jeong Sun in Gangwon province.

When I got off the train at Young Worl with my one small bag, I started walking toward the tiny village of Jeongsun. There was no road, not even a trail, and I had never been here before, but I followed a course that I had plotted on my map. I soon found myself climbing over an almost impassable mountain. Struggling up that steep and rugged mountainside, I thought to myself, *Only a crazy man would commit himself to something like this.* Insurgents lost and hiding in the Gi Ri mountains must have felt the same way, or North Korean spies infiltrating South Korea through these same mountains. But I knew that the Apostle Paul had endured much and had overcome all sorts of difficulties.

It was a long, rough hike through that mountainous wilderness. Around sunset, I passed through a valley where there were a couple of huts, and further down beside the river was a deserted tile factory. I would spend the night there. For supper, I drank some river water to fill my empty stomach, put on all the clothes I had in my bag in an effort to keep warm, and fell down to sleep on the gravel floor.

I woke at the dawn of a chilly morning. For breakfast, I drank more river water, after which I had a "quiet time" until the morning mist cleared away. Then I started walking again toward what appeared to be a cluster of about twenty huts, probably ten miles away and halfway up the mountain on the opposite side of the valley.

When I arrived at the small neighborhood, I enquired for the Village Chief. In the West, he would probably be called the mayor, or the representative. When I found him, I asked permission to stay in his village for three months, and I offered him all that I had, which was not very much. He showed me the tiny room where his children slept and said I could stay there. The floor was of flat, uneven stone, the cracks between them filled with dirt for mortar and covered with a thin hand-woven straw mat. It was so rough that lying on it made my back hurt.

A small dinner table was brought in for me. It was low, of course, because in Korea we sit on the floor, but the legs on this were unsteady, and, with the uneven floor, it was quite wobbly. If there had been soup on the table, it would no doubt have been spilled. Fortunately, there was just one bowl of steamed barley and grits and one indistinguishable side dish of what was either bean curd or hot-pepper curd. Whatever it was, I enjoyed it immensely. As they say, hunger is the best sauce. When I finished my supper, I informed my host that I would spend my time in the Word of God, without food from tomorrow on. He was taken aback.

"Are you sure?" he said. "It is Spring, and we are in the lean time of year—the poverty of Spring—so there is a food shortage. But how can you live without eating?"

I think he was suspicious that I might be on some kind of drugs.

At that time, the churches in Korea were booming with revival meetings, all-night prayer meetings, and much fasting. Some, perhaps much of it, I thought was the result of congregational peer pressure. Often there was boasting about how much of it was done, as though it were a measure of spirituality, a badge of faith.

As a student, I used to think that "prayer and fasting" was pretty extreme, and I would have been very reluctant to be a part of it. Now, here I was in a strange place for the purpose of preaching the Gospel but feeling very timid and not knowing what to do or how to start. I needed God's guidance. What Jesus had said to His disciples on one occasion came to mind, "This kind can come forth by nothing, but by prayer and fasting." So it seemed that to fast and pray was the best way.

My host's living room was the same as the children's room: the same rough, stone floor, the same straw mat. If his baby relieved himself on the floor, then my host would call to the dog, "Tsut tsut tsut, olreo reo reo!" The dog would jump up into the living room and lick clean the baby's excrement. It seemed handy to have such a dog, but because of him there were fleas in every fold of the straw mats. After a very difficult first night, during which I slept very little, I woke in the morning to find my white underwear stained with the fleas' discharge. It was a painful situation.

From that day on, I stayed in the room, read my Bible, and prayed. Then I would read more and pray more until it was time to sleep. Every morning, I got up, brushed my teeth, drank water, went to my room, and repeated the pattern. The first three or four days my stomach ached. My host would open the door every now and then and ask, "Aren't you going to eat something?" or "What kind of book are you reading?" or "Do you prophesy the future?" And then, one day, he said, "I hear that a North Korean spy has infiltrated into this area."

After about a week of fasting, my stomach pain went away, my mind became clearer, I wasn't hungry anymore, and, except for a little weakness, I felt extremely calm and settled. I was really expecting some kind of revelation, either through a dream or some inspiration from the Bible, but no such thing happened. "Perhaps," I thought,

"I am still too carnal or not earnest enough."

Again the Village Chief opened the door, and this time he said, "Yesterday we heard that several North Korean spies were detected in our marketplace, so twenty truckloads of soldiers were dispatched to secure the area."

North Korean spies used to come down frequently into these mountains, and this village had gone through a series of training to equip the people to deal with spies. The representative was suspicious that I might be one of them, and he seriously questioned me for a long time.

During all of this, I had a strange fleeting thought, *If your father should die, how could you return home in your weakened condition?*

My father was a fifty-three-year-old, healthy individual. Why would I even think such a thing? I guessed it was Satan's increasing opposition. He was making me worry about my father and, at the same time, bringing me under suspicion of being a spy. This was all to hinder my fasting and prayer.

The next time the representative opened the door, he said, "Young man, today I went to the Jeong Sun police station in the marketplace and reported that you are here in my house doing nothing but reading a book and refusing to eat."

He must have been concerned about what to do with my body if I died of starvation in his house, so I told him, "Tomorrow I will start eating; it's been two weeks. And I'll drop by the police station and talk to them directly."

The next morning, I ate a small breakfast, spent quiet time until noon, and then, after lunch, went with my host, his wife, and their twelve-year-old son to weed his field. I worked with a hoe for two hours and that was it—I was too weak to do more.

The next day was farmer's market day. I wrote a letter to the mission school in Daegu to inform them of my location, dropped by the post office to mail it, and then went to the police station.

The officer in charge was glad to meet me. He apparently thought I was OK, because he did not hesitate to give me permission to preach on the street in the marketplace but warned me not to criticize our government or say anything in opposition to it.

The market was reasonably quiet. I preached the Gospel aloud, although in a rather weak voice, handed out Gospel tracts, and, about dusk, returned to the Maedok neighborhood, leaving behind me in the marketplace a lukewarm response to the Gospel. I had heard that there was a small Methodist church in Jeong Sun at that time.

The next day, I had quiet time in the morning, visited several houses in the afternoon, and, at sunset, went to the cemetery to meet the children that were playing there. This area was apparently under the international airway because as I was watching them play, a huge airliner flew overhead. Suddenly, I asked a question.

"Children, who made that airplane?"

They looked quizzically at each other for a moment, and then one of them said, "Who else? People made it."

"How do you know?" I asked. "Did you see them making it?"

"Do we have to see it? We know without seeing it."

"Who made this shoe?" I asked, holding up one of my shoes.

"Some man made that, too."

"You're right. Man made that, too," I said. "You don't have to see it."

"And who made this?" I asked, grabbing a handful of grass and holding it up high.

"Nobody made that; it came by itself."

"You are wrong. It was made. There is no such thing as 'by itself.'"

"Well, then, who made it?" one of them asked.

I began to explain that "In the beginning, God created the heaven and the earth." To the words "God, His work or His will," the children seemed totally incomprehensive.

In this Maedok neighborhood, there were about ten children. To attend school, they had to walk a long way to Jeong Sun village, so they were absent from school more days than they were present due to the heavy rains and deep snow throughout the year. No one ever graduated. Fifth grade was about the highest anyone achieved. I invited them all to the Village Chief's house to study arithmetic and Korean. The parents were so excited about this opportunity for their children. Unfortunately, though, the children often had to work with their parents during the day, tilling the soil and tending their farms, and at night there was no light whatsoever by which to study. Consequently, most days, only my host's two children could study for a little while before dark. Nevertheless, the whole neighborhood was much appreciative of what little they got.

Several days passed; then, after lunch one day, I decided to visit a couple of huts that were down in the valley. I was walking very slowly, with my Bible under my arm and humming a hymn. It was a farewell hymn. For some reason, tears began streaming down my cheeks and I was feeling extremely sad. Suddenly, there appeared a red thicket. It was a wild raspberry bush, full of ripe berries! Although my time of fasting was over, my stomach was still not full, and I was yearning for some kind of fruit. Looking at those raspberries, I was surprised at how much I wanted to indulge myself, how thankful I was for them, and how long I had been without.

After eating the raspberries, I continued walking down to the valley, still humming over and over the parts of that hymn that I could remember.

I had no reason to be sad, but there were tears streaming down my face, and I didn't seem to mind this inexplicable sadness. As a matter of fact, I rather wanted to be in it for a while.

There were several huts scattered here and there along the

valley. All were miserably humble, and they were all vacant. The people must still have been working in their fields. At the last hut, however, sitting on the sunny side of her house was an old, feeble grandmother. I carefully approached, introduced myself, and tried to engage her with a story from the Bible. It was not easy to communicate; in fact, it was very difficult. She seemed afraid of me. Besides that, I was quite tired, too, which probably didn't help.

While I was talking to her, something caught my eye. It was a small cucumber vine, two or three feet tall, with several yellow flowers on it. At the bottom of it was a cucumber about the size of my little finger or smaller, with the flower still dangling on the end of it. Although I had just enjoyed an unexpected treat of ripe raspberries, I was still feeling hungry and weak. I had not had any vegetables since I came here. When I said goodbye to her and left, I was harboring a sort of silly thought, *I wish I could have had that little cucumber.*

It was nearly dark when I was climbing back up the mountain. Suddenly, I came upon a big cucumber about half the size of my hand lying right there in front of my foot! It had definitely not been there when I came down this way, and it wasn't really the height of cucumber season either. How did it come to be on this lonely trail? I was curious. I picked it up, and, sure enough, it was indeed a cucumber. I cleaned it off with my fingers and devoured it. It was delightful! I was so thankful that tears came. I didn't consider this little event to be a miracle, but I thought that this was the kind of life that should be maintained between the believers, God's sons, and their Father. I firmly believed that "faith is the substance of things hoped for, the evidence of things not seen," as it is written in Hebrews chapter eleven.

It was after dark as I drew near to the Chief's house, and his two sons came dashing out to meet me. "Teacher," they cried, "someone has come here from the marketplace to see you!"

Who could it be? I wondered.

As I approached the house, there was a stranger waiting for me, a young man who asked, "Are you Mister Sung Joon Kim?"

"Yes, I am," I replied.

"Then this is for you," the messenger said, handing me a telegram and then vanishing into the night.

The telegram was from the mission school in Daegu. It read, "Father deceased."

I didn't cry immediately, but I realized that this must be why I had had questions about my father during my prayer a few days ago and why I had been so agonizingly sad and tearful this morning.

The mission school did not have an address for me until I had written to them, so by the time I received that telegram, my father's funeral had taken place over a month ago. While attending a national school principal's conference, he had had a cerebral hemorrhage and fallen off his chair, dead. He had always felt so sorry about me being taken up with what he called "Jesus affairs" while he thought there were so many other responsibilities that the first son of the family should be attending to.

I decided to go to Daegu first and told my host that I would leave in the morning.

"I'm so sorry to see you go," he said. "I can't help you much. But here, take this please."

He handed me the whole amount I had paid him the first day. Until then, I had nothing for fare. I was very thankful and promised him that I would pay it back as soon as I reached my home. Later, I sent him a money order for double the amount, and he responded with a thank-you note. I felt sorry for having to depart from such warm-hearted friends and neighbors just when it seemed I was about to initiate my work there. I left that place promising that I would some day come back.

It has been forty-some years since I left, and so far, I have not had a chance to revisit. I wonder: has the Gospel taken root there by now? Has anyone been working there? Has someone from that neighborhood come forth to the work? Only God knows.[3]

The name of that place was East Maedok neighborhood, Jeon-sun County, in Gangwon Province, and the Village Chief's name was Joong Gun Kim. This is where I started the second three months of my six-month training course. It was truly an extremely valuable and rewarding time. It was a short but epitomizing lesson about my future work, strengthening my conviction about how God would work through me.

Nobody knew why I chose Gangwon Province to finish my course. What they may have concluded about me was that Brother Kim was a persistent, obstinate person.

My mother had sent that telegram to the mission school twice. The news of my father's death was a huge problem to them, creating a great deal of confusion. They had no idea how to find me or where to look. I was the first-born son; I was supposed to be the head of my father's funeral ceremony. But even my fiancée didn't know my address.

Maybe because of this commotion, I became a dropout once again. But the training I received from this mission school, from the time of my entering to the time of my dropping out, was invaluable—a second-to-none experience that only God could have provided. It has been a pivotal mainstay for me, even yet, after nearly forty years here in this Amazon jungle. It has been like a maturing blossom, and I'm eagerly looking forward to seeing its fruition. "Your body is crucified with Christ. Faith alone is your life."

---

[3]*During the two-week period of my fasting and prayer, I had expected something miraculous and spectacular from God. I didn't experience any special power of the Spirit, any amazing vision, hear any words or gain any special revelation. What I did learn was that it was a gift from God that I could cope with daily events—no matter how severe, devastating, or hard—peacefully, naturally, wisely, safely, and with a friendly attitude, no matter how foreign, frightening, or precarious the conditions might be. It was God saying, "My grace is sufficient for you. I am your everything." He let me know about my father's death in advance. He had me write that letter to inform the school of my whereabouts. He prepared my fare to return home when it was necessary. God proved His sufficiency to me.*

I am praying with my hands together, *Dear God, I'm so thankful for Your grace. You have done all things well. Thank you.*

"I am crucified with Christ: nevertheless I live; yet not I, but Christ liveth in me: and the life which I now live in the flesh I live by the faith of the Son of God, who loved me and gave himself for me" (Galatians 2:20).

Sad to say, but after the completion of two training sessions the mission school closed its doors in Korea. I truly wish it could be opened again. May God have compassion on my homeland.

—⟋⟍—

First to Taiwan

IT WAS SIX YEARS from the time I received Jesus Christ as my personal Savior until my mission site was confirmed, and another six years before I actually set out on the journey to my destination in Brazil. As a missionary prepares to be sent out, Satan finds ways to resist him by playing tricks and creating emergencies. God had reduced Gideon's army from thirty-two thousand to only three hundred to demonstrate His enormous power through that tiny minority. Satan therefore understands that God can work through one weak vessel. Of course he would try to prevent me from going out. This last six years was a period of preparation. To me, it seemed long and tedious, difficult and vague.

I was attending a small church. As soon as I announced my intention to go out as a missionary, there arose much opposition. "We don't have enough workers in South Korea. If you were to spend the rest of your life preaching the Gospel here, it still wouldn't be enough. Why in the world would you want to go to Brazil, of all places? It is so far away from Korea. Some other Southeast Asian country, maybe, but why Brazil? You must be talking in your sleep."

The biggest problem was financial. Although my wife and I were praying about it, we wondered how we could raise enough money for two airfares? And what about living expenses after we got there? It would be difficult to ask for help once we were there because we didn't know the language. If only we could acquire faith as a grain of mustard seed, then we could say to this mountain, "Move hence to yonder place, and it would move…"!

It was so impossible. No matter how much we could save out of our little earnings— my wife as a cleaning woman and me working odd jobs—it was all we could do to pay our rent and buy a few groceries. It was like standing on a cliff looking out at a chasm that couldn't be crossed.

Next, Satan began to plant all kinds of logical propositions in my mind: *Dick is in America now, but since he started the mission school, wouldn't he be willing to help to that end? The Bible says to be patient, so if you wait for a while, maybe he will send you a check or something.* Or, *Aren't there seven missionaries that you tutored in Korean? They wouldn't hesitate to help. Relax!* Or, *Maybe you could convert Byung Chul Lee, the multi-millionaire CEO from Daegu. Haven't you already started a Bible study once a week in the dormitory of his Jae Il wool fiber factory? It wouldn't hurt to ask. To him, the cost of airfare to Brazil would be as insignificant as a sesame seed.* Indeed, Satan was attempting to delude me with all kinds of carnal surmising, trying to trip me up and cause me to fall. It was a tough battle.

But while Satan was opposing me, the Holy Spirit was interceding for me. He spoke into my heart, "Letting you stand at the edge of this cliff is purposeful; it is not a trick. It is to cause you to stand on the rock of faith—to let you be strengthened and to advance by faith in God alone. Remember the Psalm you recited? '…and by my God I can leap over a wall.'" *Yes, that's it!*

One day, I was coming home, tired and thirsty from a particularly hard day of labor. As I rode my squeaky old bicycle past a produce stand with beautifully displayed apples, I thought, *I wish I could have one of those apples.* Apples are the chief agricultural product of that area, and Daegu apples are nationally known as "the best" That day they looked particularly good to me. When I arrived at my house, there on the step, in front of our locked front door, was a fruit basket containing thirty-some beautiful Daegu apples! No one, not even our landlord, had touched them. I thanked the Lord with tears.

On another day, there was a bushel sack of rice waiting for me, and with it, a white envelope containing enough money to cover our living expenses for a whole month! I couldn't imagine who in the world knew what we needed and when we needed it. It seemed that God was working on our behalf when I was only thinking about it, even before we asked! He was sending signals to us, in various ways, that He had been continually caring for us. Yet there we were, blocked, because we couldn't see through the eyes of faith. When would I ever eradicate worry and learn to rest like a child in the bosom of God? I wished I were there! How I wished!

During those six years, I married, learned by practice all I could about the aluminum business, woodworking, plumbing, electrical, general maintenance, first aid, agricultural chemistry, etc., and prepared for everything else that I thought I would need on the mission field. I also recalled the things I had learned in my Boy Scout days and some music and foreign language study as well.

My plan was to serve independently at my mission field, which I perceived that the Apostle Paul had done, as the sole player of all the instruments — the drum, the chimes, the triangle and the cymbals — and working to make a living as well, since I wouldn't be getting any support from the church or any mission institution (which, at that time, had not yet been born in South Korea).

Reading in the book of Esther, I was impressed with the phrases, "...I also and my maidens will fast likewise; and so will I go unto the king, which is not according to the law: and if I perish, I perish" (Esther 4:16). I was perfectly at peace as I rested in that same decision, *Yes, if I perish, I perish. I will cope with it.*

One night, there was an elderly, white-haired missionary in attendance at our evening meeting. His name was Horace Williams. He was on the staff of WEC mission in Fort Washington, Pennsylvania, but previously he had been a missionary in mainland China for forty-five years. He had gone to Taiwan soon after Chiang Kai Shek, his nationalist Chinese government in tatters, fled with the remnants of his armed forces before Mao Tse Tung's Communist hordes to Taipei. Horace Williams had recently established an Oriental WEC in Taiwan. He was visiting WEC missionaries working in Asia and was seriously recruiting Asian candidates to be missionaries to the Orient. When we were introduced, he demonstrated tremendous enthusiasm, asked me many personal questions, and obviously wanted to grab me. He was very emphatic that I should join WEC.

"But I am planning to go to Brazil," I said, "to work with unreached tribes."

"We have WEC in Brazil, too," he responded. "Although we don't work with tribal groups there, if you were to use WEC as a channel, it would make it easy for you to leave Korea. As soon as I get back to Taiwan, I will send you an invitation letter so that you can start the departure procedure. Once you get to Taiwan, you can stay there for a year and prepare for the Brazil trip. I will help you as much as I can."

It was a stunning breakthrough! I was in shock. His promise was so reassuring that I thoroughly rejoiced in the Lord.

At that time, the Korean government was not encouraging Koreans to go abroad for any reason. The restrictions and the red tape were extremely time consuming, and the corruption of government officials was encountered on every hand. Even though it was difficult, I managed to complete the emigration application procedure without having to resort to the shameful practice of offering bribes, a custom rampant in our country, which was relatively closed to Western civilization. Ironically, while undergoing the process,

I began to feel as though I were already contacting primitive tribesmen. It seemed that Satan was setting traps at every corner.

For almost a month, I traveled back and forth to the capital city of Seoul, where I had no relatives with whom to stay. When I finally received our passports, I can't describe the exhilaration that I felt. It was immeasurable and probably surpassed anything that a young lawyer might experience upon passing his bar exam. I handled my passport every day, thanking God for what He had done for us. I had almost worn it out before our departure day arrived.

My youngest sister was born again on April 20, 1963, through the message of John 1:12,13: "But as many as received him, to them gave he power to become the sons of God, even to them that believe on his name; which were born not of blood, nor of the will of the flesh, nor of the will of man, but of God." After she was saved, she told me that she wanted to be a missionary, too. She had been recently employed by Eun Suk, a very famous private grammar school in Seoul. When she heard the breaking news about our going, she was excited—so much so that she paid the airfare for both of us to Taiwan all by herself! In addition to that, she paid our living costs while we were in Taiwan, airfare for both of us to Brazil, and provided most of the cost of living for our first year in that country. All in all, about 98 percent of our finances came through her.

We were now thankful to God that there had been no monetary support from the various sources to which Satan had suggested we look. "Render unto Caesar the things that are Caesar's, and unto God the things that are God's." I didn't know how my youngest sister could accomplish such an undertaking alone, but it seemed obvious that God intended, almost miraculously, to supply our needs through her.

In that private school, her income was skyrocketing. She was receiving more than a college professor. Fifty children in her class were from the families of CEOs of major industries, entrepreneurs, congressmen, doctors, etc., and their parents were willing to invest in their children's education, since "today's good schooling is tomorrow's good career." Besides her salary, each of those parents were voluntarily giving her extremely generous pay envelopes each month. Children in Korea were, and still are, their parents' "social security system" for their golden years, so you can understand those parents' zeal for the children's education. Sixth graders used to study sixteen hours a day to prepare for the entrance exam to prestigious middle schools.

Three years later, the government abolished the entrance exam for middle schools in order to relieve the children of that burden, and replaced them with a lottery system. Accordingly, the booming private school industry diminished and so did my sister's support.

"And the children of Israel did according to the word of Moses; and they borrowed of the Egyptians jewels of silver and jewels of gold, and raiment: and the Lord gave the people favor in the sight of the Egyptians, so that they lent unto them such things as they required. And they spoiled the Egyptians" (Exodus 12: 35,36). As it is said here, we received what we needed by the grace of God, literally before we asked. He employed all sorts of practical methods, beyond our imagination, to keep things going for us.

For the last forty years, we have been learning that it is God's gracious will that we be not too poor to thank Him and not too rich to appreciate Him. In Proverbs 30:8,9, Agur the son of Jakeh said, "Give me neither poverty nor riches; feed me with food convenient for me: lest I be full, and deny thee, and say, 'Who is the Lord? Or lest I be poor, and steal, and take the name of my God in vain.'" He gives us every day our daily bread, like the widow's oil that was never exhausted. He has kept us from being soiled by greed. Whatever comes is all right, as long it is God's will. Hallelujah!

A twelve-year period would be less than a nano-second on God's calendar, but to us, it was a long time to wait and to be trained (although His training will continue for the rest of our lives). Finally, we could reaffirm, "Yes, he has called us!" April 5, 1968, was our departure day. I was trembling with anxiety. Our luggage consisted of two bags, one handbag, and one briefcase. The contents of my briefcase resembled a small library: Korean, English, German, Portuguese, and Chinese dictionaries, several important documents, a Bible (containing its 66 books), which was my basic textbook, a map of Korea, and a world map—all together, almost eighty editions.

I had made sure there were no unpaid bills and that I had left behind no human relationship problems or unresolved conflicts. I parted friends with all of our church family. I was confident that all four of my younger siblings were mature and independent. My mother, who used to pray, "Lord, accept my firstborn as an offering," had gone to be with the Lord three years after my father passed away. My mother-in-law had become a Christian shortly after we were married. She bade us an amicable farewell: "God will take care of my jobless son-in-law," expressing her faith and confidence in God. So now, having taken care of everything that was our responsibility, there were no loose ends and we were free to go.

The next day at Kimpo airport, we greeted the many people who came to see us leave: my youngest sister, who voluntarily became our sole supporter, my other sister and brothers, my aunt, and Missionary John Cook and his wife from Child Evangelism Fellowship in Korea. John used to come to Daegu from time to time to teach child evangelism to the students in the training program. Missionary Derek Earl came, too. When he shook my hand and said,"God bless you," he left a folded twenty-dollar bill in my palm. There was a coupon attached to my passport, allowing me to exchange up to three hundred dollars at the Korean Exchange Bank. I didn't use it; I didn't have that much money to exchange. These twenty dollars were all we had to manage our world for a while, and that was a gift of grace.

We boarded a small China Airline Boeing 727. This was my first flight. The interior was beautifully decorated, the flight attendant was polite, and there were only about ten passengers on board. I felt like this was the "wagon" that God had sent to carry me on my journey, like the wagons that Joseph, the ruler over all the land, had sent to carry his father, Jacob, on his journey to Egypt. God only does marvelous things.

Soon we were airborne. Looking down on my country, the earth looked brown. The Japanese had chopped down all the trees and carried them to Japan, and the trees that had been planted since were still too small to make the land appear green. We had lost a rich treasure in our forests, and the sight saddened me. We should have planted at least one tree before we left, in memory of this day. Today is Arbor Day. That was my last impression of my homeland: war and the ensuing poverty. How sad.

About two hours later, an announcement came over the intercom in Chinese, which was somewhat familiar to me, followed by the same information in English: we were approaching the Taipei Airport.

During the great East-Asian war, under Japanese rule, my parents were sent to Manchuria and were compelled to teach Japanese to Koreans living in a Korean town located in Gilim Sung Bansuk Hyun yuntong San Changpang Go. I lived there six years, from the age of four until I was ten, during which time I learned some Chinese by osmosis. During the time of my compulsory three years of military service, so as not to waste that time, I studied English industriously, learning by heart the whole conversation textbook. It turned out to be especially useful, and I feel very fortunate.

Horace Williams and his wife were waiting for us at the Taipei Airport, and with them was the chairwoman of the Chinese Church, Reu tai tai. They greeted us enthusiastically. Suddenly we were surrounded by a totally different culture. We were hearing a different language and, with some apprehension, as new trainees, we were entering a different lifestyle.

Taiwan is a subtropical country lying on the tropic of Cancer. It felt as though we had stepped into an oven. The color red was everywhere and on everything; even the taxicabs and the gates of the houses were red. And just inside the gate of every house was a little table with a statue of Buddha, which remained lit twenty-four hours a day. I was impressed that this land was permeated with idolatry.

My country, Korea, was still very limited in industrial production at that time. TVs and refrigerators were yet to be produced. Tourists from Japan had to bring their own tissues because Korea was not yet producing even the most basic products. But here in this huge island, material riches were in abundance, and a vibrant economy was evident everywhere. Even though Taiwan was politically opposed to mainland China, the atmosphere was peaceful; there was no sense of war. It was quite a contrast to my homeland. I felt intimidated and insignificant.

At the same time, I wondered if the people would feel any need for the Gospel. How could it penetrate such a society as this? How many missionaries or churches or believers in God would there be, and what kind of activities would they maintain? I was thankful that my immediate reaction seemed appropriate for someone who was a missionary candidate.

Taiwan has been known for frequent earthquakes and hurricanes. Several years ago, as a category-five hurricane, strong enough to wipe out the entire island, was approaching, schools, railroad stations, and government buildings throughout the entire country were closed. President Jang Ge Seok broadcast an urgent appeal to the people to pray to God. The storm changed course ninety degrees, and the island was spared. God is worthy to be praised!

I met a female Swedish missionary who was a member of China

Inland Mission (CIM). Every Thursday afternoon, she conducted a Bible study with First Lady Song Miryung and the wives of government members of the Cabinet. Yet she showed not the slightest hint of pomposity. Her humility made her look all the more great.

I also attended the monthly national preachers' conventions, prayer meetings with foreign missionaries, and churches that met in plain houses unlike the ostentatious Korean church buildings. I could tell that in Taiwan the marvelous power of the Word of God had silently penetrated the society, affecting the demeanor of the people in every walk of life. That encouraged and vitalized me. I was sure that the number of people who served God and had not bowed the knee to Baal was well over seven thousand. God would know for sure.

—⁂—

Waiting Game

IT WOULD BE DIFFICULT to graft Korean "Bali-bali" (quick, quick) onto Chinese "Man-Man-Dee" (slow, slow). It would disrupt both of them because they are so contrary. I would say that this would describe, in a general way, the difference between the Chinese and the Koreans. It would be impossible to change their cultures, so it would be best to utilize the positive attributes of both. The Bali-bali people would be disciplined or modified by placing them among the Man-Man-Dee people, and vice-versa.

God uses such methods, at times, to teach and correct His chosen individuals. I presumed that we were in just such a situation and later learned why God had not kept us in Korea for this additional year. He had designed a more profound blueprint for us. In addition to the twelve years we had waited and trained in Korea after my call to missions, it was integral for me to spend another year to further instill self-discipline. I needed to amend my error-prone disposition. I used to rush into things on my own without waiting for the Holy Spirit to lead. If I had stayed in Korea one more year, I would probably have worked hard at this or that trying to prepare airfare to Brazil and whatever else I thought I needed, and that year would have flown by like an arrow shot from a bow. I would never have learned the principle of patience. It was in God's plan to endow us with something intangible during this year in Taiwan—a time of discipline and waiting.

It was hot and muggy every day. I didn't need to learn much Chinese, but Portuguese was a necessity. I couldn't find a Portuguese tutor, so I purchased a book of basic Portuguese and audio-taped my efforts every day. I was concerned, however, about picking up strange pronunciations, due to the difference between Portuguese-Portuguese and Brazilian-Portuguese, much like the difference between British-English and American-English. That made me vacillate whenever I thought to study harder.

We stayed in an apartment with Horace Williams and his wife and two young WEC missionaries. One was from England and the other from New Zealand. They all had their hands full, but we had nothing to do—no lawns to mow, no wood to chop, no napping. Living aimlessly every day, I felt suffocated, like a dog on a leash.

I went out one day to a reasonably quiet street to distribute Gospel tracts. With a smile on my face, I offered one to a passer-by. He glanced at it and declined, saying, "Buyo (I don't need it)."

I tried to give one to a young man who asked, "Sermer, sermer? (What is it?)."

I said, "Wer sungei nen (I'm giving you a gift)."

He took it reluctantly, but when he saw the words "Wer Mernder Joo (Our Lord)" and "Wer Mernder Yaso (Our Lord Jesus)," he refused it and handed it back to me.

Another day, a young person took one, proceeded a short distance, and dropped it on the street. So far, no one had accepted a tract. I returned home, feeling like a failure after trying hard but unable to deliver even one tract successfully in this place where idolatry had captured the minds of the people. I was convinced that it would not be easy to bring these people to God with Gospel tracts alone.

After spending several unproductive months this way, one day

I received a letter from Kees Glas in Daegu. In it, he said he wanted to introduce me to his wife's brother-in-law, Gustavo Bringsken, who was currently a tribal missionary in Brazil. I was ambivalent—feeling glad, yet feeling sorry. Why had he not mentioned this to me while I was still in Korea? What was the purpose of this belated news?

When Kees was single and I was a youngster away from home, we had rented a house together. Our Korean tutor/foreign student relationship had grown into an inseparable friendship. Many heated arguments had welded our relationship.

"So you didn't do your homework yesterday? OK, we don't study today until you finish it." Or, "You don't want to study? Fine, I'm going home."

Then, invariably we would patch things up. When Kees would complain about Korean customs or say that this or that were no good, I would rebuke him,

"We don't need a missionary like you in Korea. Go back to where you belong."

The more we argued, the closer we became and the more we came to trust one another, as though arguing was the means of purifying our relationship. We couldn't cement that bond without it.

Kees used to say, "Sung Joon, you are my best friend in the whole world."

I would reply, "Really? You didn't have a best friend in the Netherlands? I think you're giving me 'soft soap.'"

The day that I left for Nonsan training camp to fulfill my mandatory military duty, as all Korean males must do for three years, he came to the bus station crestfallen, with tears on his face, and looking so sad because he was on the verge of losing his best friend for three long years. It was at a small town called Sunsan. As the bus pulled away and I watched Kees' receding figure grow smaller and smaller, I felt that same sorrow myself. Our friendship would be forever, until death would part us. My mother used to tell me not to mistreat foreigners and travelers. This foreigner had found me as a friend, a tutor, and a co-worker for the long run.

I learned that Kees had written to Gustavo Bringsken immediately after our departure date was confirmed in hopes of helping us with our immigration to Brazil and to discuss what the demand was in that locality for those of our profession. At that time, the ineptness of the postal service in Brazil was notorious. For example, a telegram sometimes took more than one year to be delivered. The German mission to which Gustavo Bringsken belonged was headquartered in Vila Bela, which was like the end of the earth. There was a twelve-hour time difference from where we were in Taiwan. I understood the difficulty in communicating.

Gustavo informed Kees that there was a demand for workers there and that we should expedite all the documents necessary for entering Brazil. Upon hearing this news, I sent our documents to Kees in Daegu, Korea, which he forwarded to Gustavo's mission headquarters at "the end of the earth" in Brazil. Adding official papers requesting the registration of foreigners, Gustavo then sent them on to Caceres, a major city in Mato Grosso State, from there to Cuiaba, the state capital, and then by way of Campo Grande, another city in the postal link, to São Paulo, and finally to Rio de Janeiro to be processed—all in all, a journey of over three thousand kilometers. The mail was transported by bus from city to city, and the connections were not always reliable. The roads were unbelievably rugged, being red dirt, clay, or gravel, except for the last six hundred kilometers. Even under perfect circumstances the trip would take four days and four nights, which was seldom the case. It usually took much longer.

From the immigration office in Rio de Janeiro, those documents traveled to the Korean consulate, then to Wycliffe headquarters before being mailed back to us. They finally reached us after several months, through the determination and collaboration of several mission agencies and the missionaries involved. Indeed, almost a whole year had passed!

The one-year visas allowing us to stay in Taiwan were about to expire. We needed to have them extended before applying for our Brazilian visas, so I made a visit to the Korean consulate. As I entered, I noticed that it was very quiet and there was only one consular official present. He notified someone that I was there, and soon the consul came out of another office, listened to me explain my situation, and said, "This passport was issued with the stipulation that the purpose of your trip was 'training.' You are not allowed to go from here to another country. You need to return to Korea within the term specified." With that, he disappeared into his office. The consular official that had been alone when I arrived looked uncomfortable, as though he were thinking, *It might be possible.*

Here I was, a novice traveler abroad, rebuffed by my own consul, who was commissioned with the power and the obligation to facilitate the needs of his countrymen. The office was not busy, yet he showed no intention of taking time to reconsider or even discuss the matter. It was painful for me, and devastating. My first thought was to demand an audience with our ambassador Sin Kim, whose office was upstairs in this same building, but I calmed down and decided it best to come back in a couple of days.

"How did your interview go?" Horace Williams asked when I returned home.

"We have to go back to Korea before our visa expires," I replied.

"What? That can't be," Horace said, struggling to stand up because of his age. "Let me go back there with you."

We left immediately for the consulate, which was not far away. When the consul came out of his office, Horace asked, "He can't go to another country with this passport? When I invited him here, it was understood that his coming was specifically to prepare to go to Brazil. Now he has to apply for his Brazilian visa, but the expiration date here is too close for comfort. Can it be extended for just fifteen days?"

"Oh, is that right?" the consul said, smiling. "One moment please." Taking our passports he handed them to the officer whose demeanor just a short time before had signaled me that there might be hope. After a brief moment of quiet conversation, he signed them and nonchalantly gave them back to me as though nothing had happened just a short time before, when he had rejected me out of hand. I didn't feel thankful. I rather felt cheated and couldn't condone his previous adamant refusal. It gave me an indelibly unpleasant impression about our diplomats abroad.

Horace Williams suggested that I participate in the missionaries' prayer meeting the following evening to meet Dr. Dale, a missionary doctor from England. He owned a small clinic and had been the primary doctor of the Brazilian consul general. I had met Dr. Dale before, and he was aware that we were waiting to fulfill our calling to missions in Brazil. He was so glad that we had obtained our papers to enter Brazil, gave me his business card, and told me to show it to the consul general.

The next day, my wife, Jae Sun, and I visited the Brazilian consulate. Each of us held over twenty pages of documents. It was quiet as we entered the reception room of the consulate, where one middle-aged female consular agent was on duty. When she recognized Dr. Dale's business card, she promptly telephoned the consul general. Almost immediately, with quick steps he descended the stairs from his office. Smiling, he said, "Hello, my name is Castro. Come this way, please." And he led us upstairs to his office.

In his office, he offered me his business card, poured us some Brazilian coffee in small, gold-trimmed porcelain cups and observed, "Do you know that Brazilian Indians have faces that resemble yours?" Then he began to converse very frankly.

"I was born in the state of Amazon," he said, "and my father is a businessman there, with a large ship that travels up and down the Amazon River." It was apparent that he was from an affluent family. When I presented him with our thick stack of documents, he regarded them indifferently and said, "I don't need these. They are not necessary. You need to go to the Taiwan University Hospital and get a general medical check-up." Without a glance at my documents, he gave them back to me.

I had heard that people with conjunctivitis or tuberculosis were prohibited from entering Brazil, which concerned me greatly because I had had conjunctivitis when I was young and even yet suffered from chronic bronchitis. It took a whole week to get the check-up. When we returned to the consulate, the consul general greeted us pleasantly, scrutinized the results of the physical check-up and the accompanying x-ray film, then handed them with our passports to the consular agent and said something to her in a low voice. She looked surprised, stared for a moment at the consul general and then at us, where we sat unpresumptuously on the other side of the room. She beckoned us to approach. The consul general signed our passports and, handing them to us, said, "God bless you. The airport officials at Rio de Janeiro will ask for this x-ray film. Good luck." Then he shook our hands and bid us farewell.

We left there gleefully. I was curious and opened my passport. The red stamp inside read "Visto Permanente" in Portuguese. I didn't understand what it meant, and I showed it to Horace Williams. He, too, appeared shocked, and almost shouted, "This is not a regular entrance visa. It's a permanent visa! Sung Joon, I'm so happy for you!"

Much later, after we had reached Rio de Janeiro, we attended a meeting of Wycliffe missionaries. Several of them reacted similarly, commenting, "I've been here a year waiting for just 'registry of foreigner' papers. How did you get a permanent visa even before you entered the country? This has to be a miracle of God." They said it was unprecedented.

I realized that this was the innovative way that God had chosen. By detouring us through Taiwan and placing the right people in our path, He had delivered us from the notorious red tape of the Brazilian government and freed us from the confusing chore of immigration documentation. "He knows the way that I take." *Dear God, thank you so much.*

—∾—

Toward Brazil

THIS WOULD BE THE FINAL STAGE: we were heading for Brazil and anticipating life-changing experiences. Horace Williams assisted us greatly by planning our trip's itinerary. From a travel agency, he had found out the fares from Taipei to Okinawa, and from there to Guam, then Hawaii, San Francisco, and, finally, Rio de Janeiro. Then he accompanied us to the American consulate to obtain transit visas so that we could visit Dick York briefly en route. He recommended this rather indirect route because Cathay Airline (CAL) offered a 50 percent discount to missionaries between Guam and Hawaii, which represented a considerable saving. Horace willingly assisted us in every way that he could, with no expectation of reward but because he loved God. I was impressed with his excellent example of a godly missionary spirit.

I posted two international letters: one to Dick York at his old address (the only one I had), informing him of our departure date and our time of arrival in San Francisco, and one to Gustavo at the Brazilian mission headquarters "at the end of the earth," informing him of our arrival time in Rio de Janeiro. In that letter I suggested that we could find our way to Vila Bela ourselves. In fact, that would have been almost impossible.

We had the same amount of luggage that we had leaving Korea. As we were leaving Taiwan, I became very sentimental about the many people with whom we had become involved and who had supported us so solidly in so many different ways. I didn't want to leave them. Yet, as one whom God had chosen to be a soldier, I knew that I should not be overcome with sentiment. I didn't want to cave in to emotion, because at this juncture it seemed essential for me, as it had been for Joshua's twelve spies, to run to the battlefield with undivided attention.

I had heard that when a trained spy is sent into the enemy, they cover his eyes until he reaches the designated front line. I felt that God had trained us with our eyes wide open and that He had just covered our eyes to push us into the airplane. I had no idea where Brazil was or how to get there, but this airplane was supposed to take us.

Here is the big picture. We were going to Brazil, where we had no relatives, no knowledge of the country, and we did not speak the language. Our ignorance about knowing what we would do when we arrived there was justified. It was reassuring, however, to know that we had found favor with God and that we were in the center of His will. I glanced over at Jae Sun, sitting next to me on the airplane, and her countenance was peaceful, too.

It was dusk when our Japan Airlines plane landed in Okinawa. This had been the scene of bitter fighting between Japan and the United States in one of the major battles of WWII. But now everything seemed clean and orderly, without the slightest vestige of war. We found our way to a tiny little inn, where we were greeted by a Japanese man.

"*Hi iratshai* (hello, welcome)."

"*Heaga arimaska?* (Do you have a room available?)," I asked.

"*Hi, dozo* (Yes, this way please)."

So we spent a night in Okinawa.

The next day, we flew to Guam. Late in the afternoon, we arrived at a small, unimpressive airport terminal. The few passengers that had been on board our flight soon dispersed, and my wife and I were alone in the small waiting room. When we stepped outside, the place seemed deserted except for a few natives' huts here and there. Then a man approached and asked, "Do you want to go to a hotel?" When we affirmed that we did, he drove us in silence to a Holiday Inn.

It was a surprisingly large building. After checking in, a guide led us to a separate building, which seemed quite far from the main entrance. He opened the door of our room, turned on the air conditioner and hurriedly left us. The appearance of the room raised concerns: *Is this room in the process of being remodeled?* On one wall and the bathroom walls, the insulation was covered with a plastic moisture barrier, and all of the plumbing was exposed. The room was unattractive, unpleasant, and dismal. I thought our ethnicity may have something to do with our assignment to this room. (At that time racism was still evident in American society.) We showered and went to bed. *Dear God, thank you for leading us safely to this point.*

Although we were from a poverty-stricken, non-westernized, third-world country, and maybe few Koreans had been here before us, we wanted to make a good impression about Koreans. So we used only two of the eight towels provided, only one bar of soap out of the four that were there, setting it aside after each use and leaving the other three untouched. We cleaned the bathroom and made the bed up just the way we had found it, leaving our footprint light and conveying our heartfelt appreciation for the room, even though it was apparently unfinished. I hoped that by doing that, we would project our intention to live at peace with everyone and leave behind us a sense of national pride.

May God have compassion on my homeland.

The next morning, we flew from Guam across the Pacific to Hawaii, the land of dreams. This would be a once-in-a-lifetime experience. We landed in Hawaii at eleven o'clock Friday night. So now what are we going to do? I had had cash for the trip, but it had been largely consumed by taxi fares to and from hotels. I had a two hundred dollar check in my briefcase, but there would be no banks open on Saturday, and at eleven o'clock Saturday night, just twenty-four hours from now, we would have to board another flight to San Francisco. Well, there was no choice — we had to take another taxi. I asked the driver, "Could you take us to a really inexpensive inn?" He drove us to a little Japanese hotel about twenty minutes away.

The Japanese owner, who spoke only English, asked me, "How long are you going to stay?"

"We will leave tomorrow night," I said, "Our plane leaves at eleven o'clock."

"That will be forty dollars," he said, "in advance."

I paid him the forty dollars, but that was all the money I had left. The next morning, I contemplated our predicament. We had no money for a taxi, so we had to make some adjustments. I told my wife, "We have to leave very early this morning to get to the airport."

It was still early when I told the hotel owner, "We're leaving now."

Without saying anything, he gave me twenty dollars back. I was so thankful!

Right in front of the hotel was a waiting taxi. I got into the front seat next to the driver, who was an elderly, white-haired oriental man. His ID card displayed on the dashboard read, "In Chan Yang, 64 years old." I supposed he was Chinese, but he turned to me and asked, "Are you Chinese or Korean?"

"I'm Korean," I said.

"Why didn't you talk to me in Korean?" he scolded, pointing to his name on the ID card.

"Oh," I said, "I'm so glad to meet another Korean. My name is Kim Sung Joon. My wife and I are on our way to Brazil as missionaries."

"Oh, is that right?" he said. "I used to be an elder in a church. But now I'm too busy earning a living and chasing women." He spoke in a mixture of English and Korean. "Now I don't go to church anymore."

I began to explain the fundamentals of the Gospel to him and to admonish him that the fear of the Lord is the beginning of wisdom.

"Maybe I should go to church again," he said. And then, "By the way, do you know my brother?"

"No, I don't," I said. "Who is he?"

"He is Dr. Yang Yoo Chan."

"The former Korean ambassador? Yes," I said, "I remember. He was ambassador to the UN in the early days of this Korean government."

"That's right," he said wistfully, "He is rich, but I am poor."

When we reached the airport, the meter read "$18.00." I had heard that in America we were supposed to pay a tip, so I gave him the twenty dollars that I had gotten back from the hotel owner and told him to keep the change.

"No, no, it's all right. It's free," he said, shaking his hands vigorously.

I was thinking, *Is it because we look so poor? Or because we are Koreans also?* He helped us to unload our luggage and with a hasty "good-bye," he left.

I rejoiced in the fact that I still had some cash. I thanked God that our twenty dollar bill would provide us an emergency

fund, should we have an urgent need along the way. We roamed
around the airport all day long, just drinking water to satisfy our
hunger. Then we came upon a fish pond and, looking in, we realized there were a lot of coins in the bottom of it. What a blessing
from the Lord! Making a kind of spoon from a soda can and a
stick, I retrieved enough of those coins to provide us with a meal
and snacks for the rest of the day. But that day had its perplexi-
ties as well as its blessings. When we wanted to use the public
restrooms, we found all the little doors were locked. It took us a
while to realize that one must insert a quarter. It's fun to think
back on that now, but it seems kind of ridiculous, too.

The day wore on, and finally it was time to board our Pan-
Am flight for San Francisco. Shortly after boarding, food was
served, and what a palatable and satisfying meal it was! Soon our
weary bodies succumbed to drowsiness, and we slept till dawn.

We arrived in San Francisco in the early morning. From
Taiwan to San Francisco, we had traveled from dawn to dusk for
several days, crossing many time zones, and we were suffering
from what some call jet lag. I was dazed and felt like I could use
several days just to rest.

When we entered the airport terminal, it was busy, with
crowds of people coming and going, brushing shoulders with
each other just like on the famous Myeong Dong street in Seoul.
We made our way through the crowds to the baggage claim area.
Suddenly, my wife cried out, "Look! Here comes Missionary Dick
and his wife, Darlene!"

I was surprised and delighted. It had been four years since
we had seen them last. We embraced enthusiastically, hugging
one another tightly for a long moment.

"This is a miracle," I said.

"Sung Joon, it's so great to see you," Dick responded, "We left
Oregon yesterday and spent last night in a hotel here. Let's claim

your luggage, have some breakfast somewhere, and then we'll go directly to Oregon."

Here I was, actually on my way to the mission field as, I suppose you could say, Dick's first protégé from South Korea. This would mean more to him than just meeting an old "dropout." It would be evidence that a part of his vision had been realized. And maybe "dropout" would be an inaccurate portrayal of me: I would become, God willing, a messenger of God's kindness, a minister of reconciliation.

We drove eleven long hours, arriving in the city of Bend, Oregon, sometime after sunset. It was cold, even in late April; cold enough that they could have snow flurries. Twenty-some guests were already gathered in the York's home, awaiting our arrival, and they welcomed us warmly. We shared a wonderful time, singing hymns, sharing our testimonies, and just worshiping God together.

For the next week, we were busy every day, attending morning Bible studies, a Christian workers' prayer breakfast, ministering in the missionary training center, visiting the Christian school, and attending church services.

At the end of the week, we returned to San Francisco to resume our flight to Rio de Janeiro, from this point, just thirteen more hours. We would go wherever that airplane took us. As far as our future was concerned, God had covered our eyes. I couldn't even see one inch in front of me, and there was nothing I could do about it. We were entirely in God's hands. Whatever might lie ahead, we would approach it in faith. Everything that had happened until now seemed like a dream. We seemed so far removed from the past and not able even to imagine the future. It was like being in a fog.

Finally, our grueling journey ended at the Rio de Janeiro airport. But now a different kind of journey would begin.

There would be no one to meet us. It was highly unlikely that Gustavo would have traveled three thousand kilometers from "the end of the earth" in Vila Bela. There was no need to rush, and we were the last passengers to disembark, so we rambled unhurriedly toward the terminal building. The crowd of people waiting to greet the new arrivals slowly dispersed. One by one, they welcomed their arriving parties and disappeared, until only one middle-aged white couple remained. They were obviously waiting for someone, and they looked toward us. We were tired and walking slowly, when I jokingly said, "That white couple is waiting for us."

"Yeah, right," my wife said, pouting a little.

I slightly waved a polite greeting to them, as strangers do when they catch each other's eye. They acknowledged it and returned the greeting with a wave. Then they disappeared as well.

As we passed through customs, I presented our x-ray films to the immigration officer, who appeared stand-offish and spoke no English at all. Although that went all right, I now realized that we were in big trouble. We could not communicate in the local language! I had thought that I could find my way to Vila Bela myself and had even written in my letter to Gustavo that this was my plan. I had intended to do so, but I had obviously underestimated the problem it would be.

As soon as we exited the building, we were surprised to see the middle-aged white couple approaching us. He extended his hand and, in very clear English, inquired, "Are you Mr. Kim?"

I was so happy and relieved, I must have smiled from ear to ear.

"My name is Olaf Ellis," the man said, "and this is my wife, Elizabeth. You are going to stay with us until the procedure of foreign registry is over. Don't worry about anything; you're going to be all right." It was beyond our imagination. God had sent us angels!

Olaf's father had been sent out as a missionary from a Brethren Assembly in England and had worked in Brazil until the day of his death. Being born in Brazil, Olaf possessed dual citizenship. He followed in his father's footsteps, serving the Brethren church in Rio de Janeiro while also representing Wycliffe Bible Translators in Brazil. Olaf's role was almost indispensable, facilitating entry and exit procedures for the mission as missionaries came and went. In his home, everything was done in the style of the English, systematically and economically; even the food was English. When I showed him my visa he said, "Oh, this is a permanent visa! I'm so glad. This procedure is going to be very easy,"

As he predicted, our permanent papers were issued expeditiously in a month, and we were told, "You may go now." We were permanent residents of Brazil and free to proceed to our destination at "the end of the earth." Olaf Ellis did not abandon us but finished all the preparations for our trip. He purchased two bus tickets to Cuiaba, the Capital of Motto Grosso State. One bus left every day, and it would be a two-day trip, but from there we would still have to travel another six hundred kilometers to reach our destination at Vila Bela. Olaf provided me with a simple map, giving directions to a missionary's house at the end of the first day's leg of the journey and also directions to the Wycliffe Bible Translator's office in Cuiaba, where we would arrive at the end of the second day. He also telephoned them in advance to confirm our coming. So our trip had been thoroughly arranged, and I couldn't express how thankful we were to be the beneficiaries of such selfless hospitality.

Now I felt as though God had uncovered my eyes, thrusting me into my mission field, the interior of the Amazon jungle. Here, I would be on one of the upper tributaries of the Amazon River, close to the equator. From this point on, I knew I would be physically and mentally challenged, but I would have to focus

on the work even if communication should be minimal or if I
should find myself without material supplies or support. I knew
that could be a possibility, but we were prepared to live by faith.
I really felt as though I were in Peter's situation: "...the angel of
the Lord ...smote Peter on the side, and [woke] him....When they
were past the first and second [guard post] they came unto the
iron gate that leadeth unto the city; which opened to them of his
own accord: and they went out, and passed on through one street;
and forthwith the angel departed from him. And Peter [came] to
himself..."(Acts 12:7-11).

Once we had found favor with God and were in His will,
what in the world could oppose us? Jesus spoke to the waves and
the wind, "Peace. Be still."

—◊◊◊—

Into the Interior

SITUATED ON THE EAST COAST, São Paulo is the southern metropolis of Brazil. About seventeen hundred kilometers (one thousand twenty miles) northwest and very near the equator lies the city of Cuibá, with a population of three hundred thousand, the seat (capital) of Mato Grosso State. Approximately six hundred kilometers (three hundred sixty miles) west of Cuibá, near the Bolivian border is the Mato Grosso (The Great Jungle). In this jungle, on one of the upper streams of the Amazon is the small village of Vila Bela (Beautiful Village), with a population of about fifteen hundred people.

Unlike its name, this place had little of aesthetic value. It was dirty and poorly maintained. The cultural standards of the people were extremely low, and there was no apparent interest in social norms. Under Portuguese colonization, black slaves had been imported to this region from the African Congo to work in the gold mines and still made up 98 percent of the population. Moreover, the necessities of life were extremely expensive due to the torrential rainfall that inundated the area for six months of every year, transforming the only access into an eighty-kilometer-wide marsh and totally isolating the town.

Midway between Cuibá and Vila Bela lies the small city of Caceres, which we reached without difficulty, but to travel from Caceres to Vila Bela was problematic. It was now November, the beginning of rainy season. The road was almost impassable and there was no public transportation. Fortunately, we had an opportunity to catch a ride on an old truck. We had only two pieces of luggage, which we threw on the truck and then joined many other people who were crouching on top of the luggage and the cargo.

The truck was a dilapidated affair that looked more than ready for the junkyard. It had no license plates, only one headlight, the driver's side door was obviously from some other vehicle, because the hinges didn't fit and it was another color. Each time it was opened or closed, it had to be readjusted by the ropes that held it in place. Incredibly, the vehicle moved, albeit at a snail's pace. Indeed, it kept moving for about three hundred kilometers, rattling and squeaking relentlessly. It seemed like this journey would go on forever. Time was no longer a factor. I was thinking, *Am I being exiled? No wonder this area is called "the end of the earth."*

Needless to say, we arrived. It was so hot and humid that we found ourselves showering six times a day just to survive while we acclimatized. (In this torrid region, trees grow without seasonal circles — it's that hot.) Around our rented hut were countless baby snakes, which drove our chickens crazy and made us very vigilant about where we stepped. One day, while digging dirt to repair a wall, within one square yard by eighteen inches deep, I uncovered four poisonous snakes. They hide in the dirt in the daytime and come out at night when it's cool. Our outhouse was a three-sided hut built with dirt walls. Imagine seeing a snake about two feet long crawling around in that space looking for a mouse or a frog while you are in the process of answering nature's call! Think about the immense consternation in such an unforgettable moment!

Day and night we moved around through clouds of mosquitoes and fought with all sorts of harmful bugs that cause infections — and especially malaria. Plasmodium parasites are spread by female mosquitoes and are treated by different drugs, depending on the species of the parasite. There are a couple of species that cause malaria in humans, including in temperate zones, but the strain that occurs principally in tropical areas was becoming increasingly resistant to treatment. We heard that many people were losing their lives to hepatotoxicity (liver damage) due to some of the medicines that were being used. I myself suffered with malaria five times in one year and was dysfunctional for nearly the entire year. I had paid my dues for my valuable jungle membership.

We also endured *karapato* (tropical leeches) that live in the jungle's fallen foliage. They would bury their heads under our skin, suck the blood, and dangle like bloated soy beans on our skin. Another annoying pest was *mukuim* (jungle chiggers) that live in the green grass. Their bites caused a painful itch that would last for more than three months. We were experiencing jungle life, totally immersed in the overwhelming and merciless superiority of nature. All sorts of creatures imposed great and rigorous hardships upon us. One thing I learned for certain: no matter how many hardships we endured, and no matter for how long, we never became accustomed to these unfathomable difficulties.

This little jungle town was our mission headquarters. Seven missionary families lived here: four from Germany, two from the Netherlands, and one from South Korea (us). Some of us were engaged in missions to the general Brazilian population; the rest of us were occupied in tribal ministry. In our daily living, as far as conveniences were concerned, there were enormous deficiencies: no electricity, no refrigeration, no electric fans, and no hospital. Consequently, ice water existed only in our dreams, petroleum lamps were used for light, and each person was responsible at times to play the role of pharmacist or doctor to his own family. But everyone had his own specialty, and the degree of interaction, cooperation, and helpfulness was indeed beautiful. One person was a mechanic, another a teacher, another a farmer. Sometimes, and in some areas, our talents and abilities overlapped, which created competition among us.

I had my share of all of these virtues and vices.

Among us, Portuguese was used as our official language, but German popped up a lot in private conversation. Our denominational backgrounds differed: Pentacostal, Baptist, Mennonite, Lutheran, and Brethren, but through the grace of God we worked harmoniously together and maintained a rich and significant communion among ourselves.

According to law, in order to work with Indian tribes, a permit issued by the Bureau of Indian Administration of the Department of Home Affairs was mandatory. During the year that I had to wait to acquire that permit, I studied Portuguese on my own and helped with the mission to the local Brazilian population, which was not easy, by any means. Minute clusters of people lived far from each other, and there were no established roads between them to facilitate transportation. We had to walk to visit them, and if I happened to return home after dark, the concern of being attacked by snakes or leopards was terrifying. One missionary was riding a horse when it suddenly collapsed under him after having been bitten by a snake. The missionary laboriously made his way home, leaving the horse where it fell and carrying the saddle on his back. A postman, passing through the jungle on horseback, was attacked from behind by a leopard. He fell from his mount, and the terror-stricken horse took off, leaving him to make his arduous way home on foot, bleeding and holding his gun in his hand to defend against any other predator that might attack.

I learned from those reports. Whenever I went out on horseback with other missionaries, I carried a gun with me in preparation for that terrifying moment, and I kept my baggage light, just in case I might return on foot. We would ride all day long without seeing any evidence of the presence of another human being. We would be constantly alert until we discovered a little cluster of people living in some improbably remote place. These people were characterized by an uncanny wild look, and they all carried weapons. They would lead us to some stable-like room where we would spend the night preaching and teaching hymns to the tune of Gustavo's guitar and my accordion. The room would be thick with smoke from slowly burning dried horse manure to repel all sorts of harmful insects. There were still plenty of mosquitoes, however, that braved the repugnant smoke in search of our blood. Usually five or six neighbors would gather in the room and respond to our proceedings approvingly, smiling through sinister moustaches. Apparently, they appreciated our visits, because they always asked us to come back again.

Around the town of Vila Bela, there were many small streams — tributaries of the Amazon River — and these streams were frequently traveled by *canoas* (canoes). The narrow, five-meter-long (sixteen feet) canoa is just right for one person, but we contrived to maximize its usefulness by placing one person at the front, one at the back, and our luggage in the middle, which almost made it sink. We would go upstream in kind of an "s" course all day long. At some spots, the stream would be virtually obscured by floating tropical water plants, such as water lilies or great duckweeds, and we had to cut open a passage with our machetes. Sometimes, as we paddled through those narrow openings, water moccasins would dart over my paddling arm. Camouflaged by their cryptic coloring, they were not spotted easily. I used to get goosebumps when I recognized what that subtle movement was, which would remain long after the snake was gone.

As we paddled deeper into the jungle, the further upstream we went, the more numerous became the bats, mosquitoes, and cobwebs. Sprouts, saplings, and trees hung over the water; kiririki, a giant, tropical pampas grass, cut into our skin at the slightest touch, and intertwined with all of this were thorny vines, the name of which I do not know. We managed to penetrate and overcome all of these obstacles. When the streams became too overgrown for us to maneuver our canoa, we had to jump dispassionately into the water — clothes, shoes and all — and pull or push it through. Very few committed, tenacious pioneer types would endure such merciless hardships just to prove something to themselves or to satisfy their ego.

Whenever we paddled in these waters at night, myriad baby alligators' eyes along the water's edge would shine like bright blue stars as the beam of our flashlight found them. It was as though hundreds of penetrating eyes had been set to watch us through magical binoculars. It was a strange and eerie phenomenon. Sometimes I would try to catch a really small baby alligator for fun, but it's probably a lot safer not to disturb a mother alligator or try to kidnap her babies.

There were usually no alligator attacks around the town, due to the human traffic, but farther downstream, where the water is stagnant, I heard that a three- or four-meter- (ten-to-thirteen feet) long alligator, with only its eyes visible above the peaceful water, followed a canoa, then suddenly went under the boat, and, using its ironclad tail, turned it over, wreaking much havoc. A weapon such as a gun for defending oneself against the secret dangers of this jungle would be almost useless. To keep going through such a horrible adventure, to keep fighting against the awesome, capricious nature of this jungle, it would be quintessential to have either the tenacity of purpose, the devotion to life as a pioneer, or the conviction that this is absolutely the will of God, along with a heavy dose of tactfulness and endurance.

Besides all of this, there was hunger, overwork, discomfort, and miserable sleeping conditions, just as in war, the reality of which I realized every day. It was because God was my mainstay that I embraced with deep thankfulness these remarkable, unmitigated challenges in this world of indomitable wonders.

—m—

Where Is My Workplace?

IN NOVEMBER, 1970, I was informed by the Department of Home Affairs Indian Administration that I had permission to contact Indian tribes. I was excited and much encouraged by that news. Gustavo and I decided to make an aerial survey to determine on which area I should focus. The day I boarded the mission's Cessna 170, which is a small four-place aircraft, the sky was blue and the weather beautiful, in spite of the fact that the rainy season had already begun.

I was emotionally exhilarated and uttered a prayer of thanksgiving as we took off, dragging a cloud of red dust from the airstrip, which lay on a hot plateau across the stream from Vila Bela. Finally, after praying to God for years, my dream of taking the Gospel to the tribes was about to come true!

We had flown over this area many times, seeing nothing but the boundless expanse of this dark green jungle that had existed here unchanged since the creation of the earth. The Amazon River, with its many dark secrets, wound its tortuous way through the vastness of this foreboding wilderness, gradually gaining width and volume as it went. There were no signs of people—just ominous silence.

Beneath that silent canopy, however, there was the ceaseless activity of alligators, serpents, panthers, and innumerable varieties of other wild beasts: blood-sucking killer bats, poisonous spiders, scorpions, venomous wasps, infectious mosquitoes, noxious insects, and a multitude of other demonic creatures. Besides that, many forms of diseases, nourished by the thick shade and tropical moisture, made this jungle even more notorious. That must have been the reason that this area was known as "the green hell." In this green hell, descendants of Adam had lived, generation after generation, in human misery beyond our ability to imagine, alienated from civilization, without hope for the future, and certainly with no answer for the reason of life in this world.

I realized afresh that our omnipresent God had predetermined to send his soldiers through hazardous and faith-testing missions to these naked and grossly uninformed illiterate jungle savages living at the end of the earth that they might hear the Gospel of eternal life at least once.

We had flown for about twenty minutes and traveled about one hundred kilometers, when we spotted a clearing in the jungle. From our altitude, it was merely a dot, but clearly there was a hut in the middle of it. We descended and circled the clearing, but we saw no one. As we continued to circle, about ten men, all of them naked, crawled out of a small opening and began to jump around. One of them aimed an arrow at the airplane.

As I concentrated on watching them and taking several pictures, I felt a strong impulse to descend right then and talk to them. We made a low pass. With what to the Indians must have been a deafening roar, we almost touched the top of their hut, apparently frightening them nearly to death, because they scrambled to hide themselves inside their house.

Gaining altitude again, as we flew toward the equator, Gustavo, the pilot and chief of our mission headquarters, said to me, "It would be nice if you could take charge of working with them."

I couldn't respond immediately. I was thinking that there would be some urgent preliminary issues to deal with. Judging from what I could see from the airplane, it would be a good two-day hike from the nearest *fazenda* (a pioneer farm cut out of the jungle by white settlers) to the Indian territory that we had just spotted. Walking alone into this unfamiliar dangerous jungle, which had been totally closed to the outside world, would be an extremely foolhardy undertaking. Chances were ten to one that even with a compass I would be lost in the middle of that jungle. Furthermore, to insure a successful penetration, I would need a lot of preparation and supplies, including drinking water, food, first-aid supplies, some way to defend myself against fierce animal attacks, etc. At this point, I didn't have any of those things, even if I'd had the courage to implement this venture. I also needed a viable plan to engage with these wild and possibly savage Indians, who would be without the ability to communicate. I was not negligent in asking God to give me such a plan—in addition to more wisdom and courage—and to fill my empty Korean hands with suitable resourcefulness.

We flew another forty minutes, about two hundred kilometers, before we landed at our destination, a deserted, grass-covered strip somewhere in the middle of the jungle. This area was said to belong to the Jillu fazenda and was designated as a future subdivision for residences, but as yet there was not a single residence or any sign of development. I had heard that this fazenda owner intended to chase the Indians away. He had razed their huts with a bulldozer while they were away hunting for several months and then had constructed this airstrip in their place. It is actually unlawful to purchase lands where Indians reside; therefore, fazenda owners reportedly chase them out, kill them with poison, or simply file false documents stating, "No Indian Inhabitants." In this case, the Indians had returned from hunting, rebuilt nine huts not far from the airstrip, and reoccupied the area.

Ironically, on the same day, at almost the same time that we flew in, an investigative group consisting of four missionaries from the South American Indian Mission (SAIM) and one Indian guide had arrived in a station wagon to survey a possible site for a tribal mission.

While we were there, about forty Indians had quietly advanced upon us. None of them—whether men, women, or children—wore even a stitch of clothing. They had an innocent look about them as they tumbled about in the dirt. They obviously did not know what a bath was. They chatted and giggled, as they tried to rock the airplane and, out of curiosity, tapped the station wagon with their bows. Then they jokingly threatened us to see how we would react. If we remained calm and self-possessed, they would consider us safe and approachable. If, on the other hand, they should detect in us an air of fear or defensiveness, they would consider us dangerous opponents. Of course, I kept a smiling countenance, not because I was afraid, but because my heart was fully with them. I would have been thankful to God for this moment even if I would have suffered a wrongful death at their hands while endeavoring to bring the Gospel to them.

I was told that this "Wanairisu" tribe had killed two missionaries and had thrown their bodies into the Amazon River several years ago and, until recently, had killed civilians on occasion. Nevertheless, I wanted to begin a great adventure and work with this Wanairisu tribe. Before we left that place, a temporary agreement was reached between the two missions: the Wanairisu would be the responsibility of our Brazilian mission, while the Alantesu, spotted earlier during our flight, would be that of the SAIM.

On our return flight to Vila Bela, I was truly overwhelmed by this huge moment, this tremendous sense of belonging: *This is my work place, with the tribe in whom I will invest the remainder of my life, to bring them to God.*

—ɯ—

11
Moving

ACCORDING TO THE MISSION POLICY, in order to sustain the headquarters, every missionary was obligated to contribute one-tenth of his income. Whoever used the airplane would be responsible to buy the gasoline and pay for the related expenses for each round trip. As an independent missionary without financial support from my home church, it was a financially awkward situation. Being from a poverty-stricken country with no mission institution or church back home to support me seemed a major handicap. I sincerely believed that I could not depend exclusively on our mission headquarters' plane indefinitely. I needed to develop another route over land to tackle the problems in the Indian area. To meet this challenge, we needed to relocate to Várzea Grande, a suburb of Cuiabá, the State Capital. Finally, after five years, I severed my relationship with the mission headquarters, due to financial hardship. Here is the message I want to put forward: *I am an independent missionary, a pioneer, a leader. I need to follow the Lord's leading, even if alone.*

To get to the Wanairisu tribe would mean seven hundred kilometers toward the equator on a state road and then another seventy kilometers eastward through the jungle. This last seventy kilometers, I was told, would be so nasty that it would add many days to the trip. Jae Sun and I didn't have our own vehicle. I spent a lot of time collecting information about that part of the jungle and what plausible transportation was available, equipping myself for the journey, and praying for God's special guidance before working my way into the jungle, where I knew I would be tested. I also remembered to get my immunization shots for yellow fever and some other diseases.

I decided not to postpone my departure another several months until the end of the rainy season: If not now, when? So, on January 18, 1971, I began a solo trip without an exorbitantly expensive guide or any reluctant civilian companionship. Before leaving, I had things to attend to: straightening up all sorts of family affairs, writing my last will and testament, and leaving for my wife detailed instructions on where to look for me in case of an accident. My wife would stay behind in our one-room rented house. It was a solitary place in a remote neighborhood in what was to her a totally strange and foreign country. There was no one to check on her and no one for her to visit. For her, this was neither more nor less than what she had expected. Basically, in her mind, she was committed to being a missionary wife, whatever that might mean. Nonetheless, her face betrayed her great anxiety and concern at this time.

At eight o'clock the following morning, I boarded a long-distance bus to Porto Velho, toward the border of Peru. I was planning to stay for one month with the Wanairisu Indians. I had no idea what was in store for me. The bus rattled like an empty truck as we traveled the state road that stretched across the seemingly endless wilderness. Every four hours, day and night, the two bus drivers took turns driving. At dawn we stopped for an hour at a shabby filling station near the entrance of the Guapore Valley for gas, an engine check, and, for those who were continuing on, breakfast. But this was my stop. I got off the bus.

From this point, I planned to hitchhike on a truck destined for one of the fazendas scattered here and there in the Guapore Valley. I was told that this would not be easy, because an area one hundred and fifty kilometers further on, where the Guapore River (one of the upper tributaries of the Amazon) forms the border between Bolivia and Brazil, had been placed under restriction to foreigners. "Besides," I was told, "the truck drivers, in order to protect themselves, will be very reluctant to tell you where they are going."

I spent the entire day anxiously waiting for the opportunity to hitch a ride. For my meals, three times that day I ate a little bread. Because there was no lodging available (and even if there had been, it would have been too expensive) I entered a run-down warehouse, closed my eyes, and spent the night.

The next morning, the filling station owner showed his good will to me by introducing me to a truck driver who was hauling a load of logs and other supplies to the Zillo fazenda. The truck did not have a deck but rather a ladder-type frame with some planks laid over it. On these were stacked all sorts of provisions, on top of which many loggers rode as passengers. There was absolutely no room for me or my two pieces of luggage, but this would be my only chance for several days, so one way or another I had to find space on that truck. I was like a war refugee escaping with the last departing refugee truck. It wouldn't matter how many times I fell off during the seventy-kilometer ride over the rugged jungle road. I had to be on that truck!

The driving was wild and relentless. The driver cared little whether his passengers were human beings or livestock. We were tossed about violently, holding tightly to one another, shouting at times for fear of being thrown from the vehicle or because we were being splashed repeatedly by muddy water as we crashed through huge puddles. Whenever a piece of luggage or cargo fell off the truck, he would brake abruptly, adding to our consternation.

At one point, the truck plunged into an especially deep puddle and became buried in the mud. We were stuck. Everyone got off and began to dig under the truck. They chopped down nearby trees to place under the wheels. Raising the truck with a jack, they pushed and pushed, struggling to liberate that vehicle. I helped aggressively, as though it were my own truck. I didn't even mind being drenched in dirty water and covered head-to-toe in mud—but it was an extraordinarily horrible trip!

Human nature is the same everywhere. People, in general, tend to be aloof, which had been the case in this situation. After the incident that I have just related, everyone on the truck, seeing how I had participated, became very friendly with me. *Yes, I'm a missionary, a fisher of men. I have wholly embraced the gift of life that God gave me; I want to live it daily and invest it into the restoration of the lives of others.*

At first they spoke evil of my slanted, oriental eyes. "Are your eyes open or closed?" they would ask. Even the black people would stretch their big eyes with their fingers to make them look slanted and sneer at me. I learned to laugh with them and at myself. Although I was unable at first to impress them favorably as an Asian, I determined that I would overcome that handicap and rise above it at every encounter by letting my inner person shine through. Finally, after five hours we reached a fazenda in the middle of the jungle. This was my immediate destination.

This fazenda appeared by no means to be a safe place. It was a frontier pioneer farm; several small huts covered loosely with palya leaves were scattered randomly along the banks of a small river. I saw many wild-looking men, both black and white—loggers, I presumed, with their axes and tree-falling equipment, but armed with guns and knives in their waistbands and looking like some kind of militia. I had heard that there was, now and then, a murder in this male society, where liquor, allegedly forbidden, was plentiful.

As soon as we arrived, everyone on the truck scattered in all directions, and I was left alone with no place to go. Suddenly, a cloudburst sent a downpour of rain. Not knowing what to do, I simply stood under the eaves of the nearest building. The foreman, whose name was Lewis, seeing my predicament, invited me inside to join him in a late lunch. He remembered how hard I had worked to free his truck from the mud on the way here. The simple lunch was only a little sandwich, but it tasted like royal food to my hungry stomach, especially in this remote isolated place. I was truly thankful to him and to God.

That night, through the kindness of one of the supervisors, I slept in a *hagy* (hammock) slung inside a rather leaky hut. From this point to the Wanairisu area, to which I had previously traveled by plane with the survey party, would be another twenty-six kilometers—about sixteen miles. There was no transportation of any kind, and not even a road but only an obscure jungle trail. There were no options; I was resigned to the fact that I would be alone on foot, carrying my heavy luggage through this no-man's jungle.

I had brought with me provisions for a month. This included five kilograms of rice, one kilogram of powdered milk, ten cans of meat, one kilogram of Indian sugar, one kilogram of candies, a small amount of salt (no hot pepper, although necessary), matches, a lighter, six batteries, a flashlight, pain relievers, fever reducers, antibiotics, a couple of syringes of penicillin, simple surgical instruments, first-aid supplies, a Bible, writing materials, a camera, soap, clothes, a military mosquito net, a one-man camping tent, a hagy, a sleeping bag, a dagger, an axe and sword in one, a military shovel, a gun, bullets, and two cooking pots. Although I tried to reduce weight and bulk as much as possible, altogether my load weighed over thirty kilograms (sixty-six pounds), which I carried in one backpack and one front sack.

Early the next morning, I drank a cup of Brazilian coffee for breakfast before setting out. The Brazilians in the fazenda kept telling me, "That's a long way to go.... That won't be easy all by yourself...." They seemed to leave their sentences unfinished, but their expressions implied, "You will be attacked in that jungle, and that will be the end of you."

I had heard that there were many leopards living in this tropical forest. I had also heard that a party of armed Bolivians had come across the river to collect rubber and were killed by black leopards that attacked them from the trees. I didn't let these things bother me too much. I kept telling myself, *You are a motivated man. Don't stop. Keep going. Don't abandon your mission. Pursuing what you believe God called you to do is the most important project you have worked on so far in your life.*

By early morning, no rain had fallen, but the atmosphere was saturated with moisture, and a heavy mist prevailed. The deeper I penetrated the jungle, the darker, quieter, and more frightening it became. I observed various shapes and sizes of paw prints left by animals whose names were unknown to me. I saw giant snake skeletons. At one point, I was startled by a sudden sound like wind overhead. Looking up, I saw a countless number of monkeys passing by, jumping from tree to tree. The sight struck terror in my heart as I thought, *Are they being chased by some fierce animals?* I imagined being attacked from behind by a leopard at any moment.

As I continued walking, the dark, foreboding jungle seemed endless, and the pack I was carrying became increasingly heavy, until it seemed my shoulders would break. My army boots became so cumbersome that my feet nearly refused to move. From time to time I drank a little water. I consumed almost two liters, and I made two cups of thick milk for my lunch. Suddenly, there was a downpour of rain, and I was drenched. I sat down to rest and…*Where did they come from?* Ants, moths, other insects, detecting the smell of sweat, were all over me in an instant! I had no choice but to quickly get up and continue walking. I walked forward with my gun in my hand, constantly looking backward over my shoulder. I got chills up my spine, sensing that animals were stalking me in the shadows and would surprise me at any moment.

Why am I walking here? I wondered, *surrounded by this jungle, one of earth's wonders and a symbol of the greatness of the creation of our omnipotent God.* At every step I was bombarded with thoughts of, *How fragile human life is! How helpless, and how insignificant I am before the overwhelming power of nature!*

If a leopard should attack me, he would drag me into a tree and hang my body over a branch before eating me. Vultures and innumerable crows would participate in devouring me, and ants would take care of whatever was left. I would disappear from this world without a trace. So, every now and then, I took a picture of myself, just in case....

Through years of self-indoctrination I had convinced myself that I possessed, in my own strength, sufficient backbone to keep going, whatever the circumstances might be, but in this helpless moment of truth, I came to the end of myself and was passionately hungry for God. I took off my straw hat, put my luggage down, wrung my hands and folded them together, and, falling on my knees prayed once, twice, three times..., four times, in a desperate denial of any ability of my own. Confessing my helplessness and total dependence upon the Lord, I prayed, "Dear God, you have brought me to this point. I am and will be totally in Your hands. Amen." Even as I was praying, I trembled at the thought of a poisonous snake crawling on me or a leopard's sudden attack.

Finally, at dusk, an even darker jungle raised additional concerns: *How am I going to spend the night? How will I make a bonfire in this wet jungle in this rainy season?* I was filled with anxiety, but I could not dictate to my body; it was too exhausted, soaked in sweat, and hungry. Both of my shoulders were in excruciating pain, and my toes were numb. I was in a terribly vulnerable state, both physically and psychologically.

At that crucial moment, an amazing thing happened. "Cock-a-doodle-doo!" I was shocked to hear a rooster crowing in the distance. *That is a domestic fowl! Is there a residence somewhere nearby? I don't remember seeing any residence when we flew over this area.* The crowing continued. I was encouraged, revitalized. *Surely if I can go just a little farther I will reach the place where those chickens are.* I started walking again...and I kept walking. I didn't know how far I had walked, but I was becoming disheartened seeing nothing but endless jungle.

I had to find a suitable place to sleep, but I was becoming obsessed with that ceaseless cock-crowing. I continued walking, in hope of finding the place with the chickens...again, the crowing in the distance...again and again. I kept walking, but now I was discouraged and doubting.

Suddenly, I burst from the jungle, and a wide-open space came into my view. I couldn't believe what I was seeing: it was the airstrip where we had landed before! At that moment, I was overwhelmed with joy, saturated in thankfulness. "Oh, God! You saved me. Oh... God...!"

Then I remembered: just before leaving home, I had read in the Bible, "And they journeyed: and the terror of God was upon the cities that were round about them, and they did not pursue after the sons of Jacob" (Genesis 35:5). That was it! That was how I had passed safely through the jungle. God had kept all of the enemies from pursuing me!

As God had "opened the mouth of the ass..."(Numbers 22:28-35) to reprimand Balaam, and as he had used a cock-crowing to make Peter repent (Matthew 26:69-75), so God had led me through the jungle by allowing me a sign of hope, a subtle tool that restored energy to my weary body. He didn't allow me to sleep alone in the jungle but kept me walking by utilizing the jungle cicada's shrill chirrup that had sounded to me like cock-crowing! I was in awed amazement when I realized what God had done for me.

I had heard that there was an old man living in a hut near this airstrip, keeping watch over a generator that belonged to the fazenda. As I reached the midpoint of the silent, deserted airstrip, I could see a hut that looked like it was ready to fall down, and there was the old man, standing there watching me, his face expressionless.

"Hello," I said, approaching him. "My name is Sung Joon Kim."

"Oh meu Deus! Em fim mandou um homen para mim! (Oh my God! You have sent a man for me at last!)"

Hearing him, I could understand how lonely he had been. Before I could respond to him further, throwing my luggage down, I collapsed on the ground. After a short while, I pulled myself together, explained to him the purpose of my trip, and asked if I could stay with him.

"Oh, sure you can, gladly. But those Indians you came to see live about ten miles from here. They passed by this way about a half-month ago to go hunting somewhere. I'm sure they didn't leave anyone behind. And when the whole group goes out like that, they usually don't return for two or three months."

Listening to him, I felt devastated. I had come all this way and braved death a hundred times in the jungle. I was so disappointed that I couldn't meet them after all of this effort. In case they returned sooner, however, I decided to stay around for at least half a month until I had consumed half of my provisions. The thought of going back made me very uneasy. I really didn't want to make that trek again. "Dear God," I prayed every day, "let me get a ride on at least a horse cart going back." But even as I prayed, I knew there would be no such thing as a horse cart in this jungle.

Being harassed day and night by noxious insects was a constant misery. At night, they managed to persistently get inside the mosquito net. Under such circumstances, my patience was sorely tried. During the day, I spent my time reading the Bible and telling Bible stories to the old man.

One day, I made a field trip to investigate the Indian area. Their neighborhood seemed deserted, and all nine huts that I found there were vacant. I scratched in the bonfire ashes with my finger.

They were cold. Will they ever come back? I was impatient, and fidgeted for days. As my provisions began to dwindle, I thought there would be no other way out but to return the way I had come.

"I need to start preparing to go back," I told the old man one day.

He looked fixedly at me in silence for a while, and then he said, "Once a month, a small tractor comes from the fazenda with my month's rations. It's almost that time, so can you wait just a couple more days?"

I was really excited to hear that news because I had been praying many times a day, every day, for a ride, if only in a horse cart. I learned later that his story was a fabrication; there was no such tractor. His food and supplies were delivered by courier on foot. He just wanted to keep my companionship for a little while longer.

On several mornings, I went out and lurked under the trees with my gun, hoping to shoot a passing deer to supplement our food supply. One morning, while I was out there, I heard what sounded like a motor far away. "Whump, whump, whump."

Am I hallucinating? Maybe it's bees. I strained my ears to listen. Yes, it was definitely the sound of an engine of some kind. That must be the tractor the old man mentioned!

I was excited. I wanted to immediately abandon what I was doing and pack up my luggage. Then I noticed that the sound had stopped. There was no more sound…. Nothing. Nothing at all.

I began to think, *Tractor? What tractor was he talking about? I have not seen any tracks on the way to this place. And logically, no matter how large, there is no fazenda that would use a tractor to make a fifty-kilometer round trip to carry small rations for one person. That would be a disproportionate expense.*

I had been deceived by an illusion. It was demoralizing.

—ᨆ—

The Carriage of God

I FELT SO DEPRESSED that I lost all interest in hunting. Then
I heard it again! This time it seemed closer. It was a unique
mechanical sound — not a tractor or a motor vehicle. Suddenly,
I saw it. A small object was approaching, flying very low. It
appeared to be a dark green helicopter, and, as it approached, I
could discern the emblem of the Brazilian Air Force.

It must be on the way to the Bolivian border on patrol, I
thought. But it looks like it might make a sudden landing on this
airstrip, and if it does, I will ask for a ride to Cuiabá. As it continued its strange, low flight toward me, I became very perplexed,
and my first inclination was to think, *Military personnel are not
going to like the idea of a civilian bearing arms.* So I went dashing
toward the hut to hide my gun. Surprisingly, the chopper set
down right in front of our hut before I had time to get inside to
hide it. The door opened, and I watched in awe as Gustavo led
six people out of the helicopter: two civilians and four Air Force
personnel wearing dark pink uniforms.

What is going on in this uninhabited jungle? I thought. *I have no
clue. Am I dreaming?*

I ran to them and shook hands with all of them in turn: first Gustavo, who was smiling broadly, then the anthropologist, the primary doctor for the Indians, the wing commander, the lieutenant, and the sergeant.

One of them said, "You are Korean, right? When we took our helicopter training in America, thirty Korean air force personnel trained with us."

It was truly a moving moment for me in this remote jungle, still impossible to believe.

Gustavo explained that in his determination to find me, he had flown six hundred kilometers westward from Vila Bela to my house near Cuiabá, had gotten detailed information from my wife, and had then flown to the fazenda, where he had inquired as to my whereabouts in the middle of the jungle. During the aforementioned time that the engine noise had stopped, the chopper had landed at the fazenda twenty-six kilometers back, where I had spent the night before I had launched out on my jungle trek. At that time, about two hundred loggers were felling trees. When they saw the military helicopter landing, they were thunderstruck and fled in all directions, randomly throwing their guns and daggers away, and hiding themselves in the jungle.

Gustavo went down and asked the foreman, Lewis, "Have you seen a Korean missionary named Kim?"

"Yes, he spent the night here," Lewis answered. "He said he needed to go twenty-six kilometers in that direction and walked off into the jungle all by himself. Nobody knows what happened to him, but the rumor around here is that he's Japanese and that he's running away from a murder charge. Is he a Korean?"

So they had taken off again to resume their low-altitude flight toward the area where they thought I should be.

Gustavo was eager to leave immediately for Vila Bela.

An epidemic of measles, which to the tribes can be life threatening, had broken out among the Sarare Indians. All were suffering, some were dying. Sixty-some children and adults, male and female, had been flown from the jungle to Vila Bela by the Air Force transportation office under a disaster declaration and were now under the charge of a German missionary named Gerhart. Doctors and nurses had been mobilized from as far away as São Paulo and Brasilia in a massive relief effort, but they were still short-handed and struggling to meet the need.[4]

Hurriedly, I bid farewell to the old man, who had now become my friend, leaving the remainder of all my provisions with him. When I boarded that helicopter I was deeply moved to tears. There was no limit to my thankfulness to God. I was so impressed by what He had done for me! I had been praying for a ride on my return trip, even on a horse cart. God had sent His carriage—a sophisticated flying machine—and His coachmen, highly trained in America to fly me to safety. God had responded to my cry in His own incomparable way, a way that I never would have imagined, even in my three-year military career nor in my wildest dreams. Whatever His reason, He had sent this Brazilian Air Force helicopter to this remote, uninhabited jungle just to pick up me, one person!

God did not allow me to be defeated or to remain depressed, but He kept me safe through my initial trip into the jungle. It had been a dangerous adventure, from which I barely escaped with my life. But He protected me on the way home, transporting me in the safest way. Flying out of the jungle in God's chariot was, to me, the most exciting thing on earth.

---

[4] *Ever since these Indians have come in contact with civilization, they have begun to suffer with infectious diseases such as measles, which to them are not insignificant afflictions but serious, often life-threatening maladies. Sad to say, but we are bearers of germs.*

This was one of the many powerful, life-changing experiences that my life has comprised in the jungle, from the beginning until now. God has been leading me by means of many situations to the fullness of faith in order to accomplish His will. I believe this is why God has me on this mission, and it is what assures me that God is with me in it. *Dear God, thank you so much!*

The Jungle Tribe Alantesu

THE AGENT of the Brazilian government's Department of Home Affairs Bureau of Indian Administration sent me a mandate to be in charge of the Alantesu tribe, not the Wanairisus, which I could have approached from the convenient airport where the helicopter had picked me up.

We had seen the Alantesus from the air during our survey flight and knew that they occupied a densely covered area that was nearly fourteen kilometers into the jungle and almost completely surrounded by water. My task seemed even more complicated now because of the issue of penetrating this new area. I had to reevaluate my plan, because I was reluctant to go alone into this part of the jungle, where there was not even a trail. An even greater difficulty was that there was no affordable civilian guide available to accompany me. I needed a comprehensive plan in order to overcome these problems.

My wife and I had been attending a Brazilian church near our home. One day, we met a visiting missionary there, a young man named Florentino. He mentioned that he was looking for a companion to accompany him on an evangelistic trip across the Guapore River into Bolivia. I knew that this was God's response to the prayer I had been praying for over a month. God was opening another door for me!

As both of us had in mind to go in the same direction, we began to discuss and plan our trip together. For the first fifteen days I would accompany him to Bolivia, where we would work together; then, on the way back, he would accompany me into the jungle of the Alantesu for another fifteen days, and we would share the expenses.

Florentino had been a member of another German mission group and owned an old Jeep. This seemed to me to be a tremendous advantage, for which I thanked God. (The fact is, though, I lost track of how many times that old vehicle broke down during our fifteen-hundred-kilometer round trip. By the end of the trip, we both had become world-class mechanics. Fortunately, just before I left Korea, I had completed a six-month motor-vehicle course at a community college and had received excellent grades.)

Before we started our journey, there was something I needed to know. In an area roughly the size of the northern half of the state of Florida, twelve Indian tribes were scattered, widely dispersed from one another but all speaking languages with the same root, Nambiquara. Seven missionaries (three from the U.S., two from England, and two from Germany) from three different mission organizations had been working among them for several years, each missionary working with one tribe. I would be the first Asian to join this select group for the evangelization of this region and was on the brink of entering my work place, the Alantesu. I needed to know how to greet them. So I paid a visit to a missionary named Menno Kroeker of a Bible translation mission to learn how to say "How are you?" in their language.

He said, "There is no such greeting in their society, but you had better memorize, *Wihisannawa* (I am a good person)."

What a strange and awkward greeting, I thought. It was not what I would have expected, but, nevertheless, I learned it by heart.

In the Indian's world, there was no need to inquire about any-one's well-being because, regardless of their state, they conducted themselves as though they were lords of creation over everything in the universe, perfectly free and natural beings. If they only knew Jesus Christ as their Lord and Savior, they could live the rest of their lives in this doomed world by faith as God's people. What a won-derful thing, if they could know the peace of heaven while strug-gling with the difficulties of life in this world!

Florentino and I drove about eight hundred kilometers over very rough roads to the border of Bolivia. Leaving the Jeep on the Brazilian side, we crossed the Guapore River on a ferry boat and stayed in a riverside village, where we held a very successful evan-gelistic campaign in Portuguese. The people of this village made their living by crossing the Guapore River to harvest rubber in the Brazilian jungle, so they were bilingual, speaking both Spanish, the common language of Bolivia, and Portuguese, which is the language of Brazil. Both languages are very similar.

According to our original plan, we then headed for the Alan-tesu Indian area. Detouring two hundred kilometers further over extremely rugged road, we reached a huge fazenda named Estrela do Guapore, a pioneer farm registered with the Department of Home Affairs Bureau of Amazon Region Development. From there, we were within fourteen kilometers of the Alantesus, whose clearing we had seen from the airplane some time before.

I asked one of the civilians, "Do Indians show up around here?"

"Well, it's very rare," he answered. "But occasionally, it seems, they sneak in to within about five miles from here to hunt. You can try their pathway and find out."

The Indians were very wary of outsiders and loath to contact them, which made me uptight and a little anxious, but, by the same token, I was eager to get to their location with my companion.

We spent that night at the fazenda, prayed together at dawn, and stepped into the jungle. As always, the jungle seemed quiet and threatening. We advanced carefully and quietly for about two hours and were soaked in sweat. Both of us were feeling hungry, so we decided to take a break and make a cup of milk for our breakfast. Florentino then wanted to take our picture. I stood with my backpack while he hung his camera on a tree branch about four meters in front of me. He was going to set the automatic shutter and then stand beside me for the picture. He was adjusting the focus when he suddenly froze with fear, his eyes wide and his face terror-stricken. I sensed the danger and turned to see what had so frightened him. What I saw startled me as well. There in front of me, stark naked, stood two well-built Indians, each holding a handful of arrows.

Wearing no clothes and no shoes, Indians, like the animals, can steal silently through the jungle. It is the manner in which they hunt.

I managed to control my shock. I smiled and, without thinking, spat out, "Wihisannawa (I am a good person)!"

I wasn't sure if they understood me, but they showed us quiet, smiling expressions, which we took as gestures of peace. It was indeed an encouraging encounter that filled us with relief. Until then, I had never realized that a smile could be so important and could have such a powerful effect. In a world without language, communication was still possible through gestures of civility. I had just learned the true value of a smile from the face of a stranger — of all human beings, an Alantesu Indian, and of all places in the world, in the Brazilian jungle,

By gestures, without spoken words, I explained to them that my friend and I were trying to follow the path to their neighborhood. It was a moment of sincerity but also of suffocating anxiety. They seemed to understand me and responded with gestures that indicated they were going to another path, pointing to the top of the trees, to hunt monkeys. Then, pointing to where the sun would be at three o'clock, they indicated that they would return at that time.

They also gestured that it would be all right for us to go into their neighborhood. It was like trying to decipher a dream, but it was so crucial that this conversation between four dumb men be understood and interpreted correctly.

I was so pleased to see that our first possibly dangerous encounter was proceeding favorably. Hallelujah! I quickly opened my backpack and offered them a handful of candies I had prepared. I peeled the paper from one and ate it in front of them to demonstrate that it was not poison.

We were invigorated by that experience, and when the Indians left we started walking again. After about two hours, the dark jungle in front of us appeared to be dazzlingly bright. We had come to a wide-open area where all the trees had been cut down. It was the Indians' garden. Their living area could not be too far away, so we began to call out sounds like "Oh—ee... Oh—ee," to signify our presence. We continued this while walking for another hour. As we drew near to their area, I began to worry with every step, not knowing what imminent danger may be about to happen. Are they aiming their arrows at us from behind the foliage?

We finally arrived at their living area without incident. It was a wide, round, well-leveled field surrounded by five huts with thatched roofs, the eaves of which nearly touched the ground. There were no Indians, just an ominous quiet. We put our luggage down in the shade beside a creek and then watched for any movement in the area while we cooled ourselves down in the shade. It was at once evident by the many bones, large and small, scattered everywhere, that their mode of living was by hunting. It was also evident by the human excrement everywhere that they relieved themselves all over the place, attracting swarms of flies.

Suddenly, from the tiny openings in each hut, stark-naked, unarmed men began to emerge, followed by about twenty women and children, who must have been watching us surreptitiously.

They sat around us at some distance, with great curiosity showing on their faces. Because we had come in on the same path by which their chief had left earlier in the day, they must have guessed that he had already met us. Careful not to display any fear, I smiled at them, took out of my backpack a two-kilogram container of sugar, dissolved it in the creek water they brought to us in a wooden bowl, added cherry flavoring, which I had brought for just such an occasion as this, took a taste myself, and then passed it around to everyone else. They enjoyed it, smacking their lips and giggling at each other. The drink was not valuable merely as a beverage — it had negotiating power. It spoke for us who could not speak. It was a powerful means of communication.

It was already way past noon. We had to hurry to get to the place that we had seen from the airplane. I explained to the Indians, with elaborate and allusive gestures, why we had to go further. *Did they understand me?,* I wondered. I assumed that they were trying to tell me that there would be no one there; all of the Indians had moved down here. At any rate, I needed to do a field survey. As I picked up my luggage, about ten of them, adults and children, indicated that they were ready to follow me. I was very thankful, because then there would be no concern regarding direction, fierce animal attacks, drinking water, food, or spending a night, if these "kings of the jungle" accompanied me through the forest.

By the time we entered the shade of their regularly traveled jungle path, I had begun to feel very hungry. I took out a container of steamed rice, which I had prepared the day before for the present day's journey. As I opened the lid, I asked Florentino to pray and ask God to bless our food. He and I closed our eyes and thanked the Lord. They, all the while, were muttering to each other, tittering, and, I am sure, observing us very closely. When we had prayed, I asked each of them to bring a tree leaf, onto which I divided the rice very evenly, a spoonful for each of us. Although it was not much to eat, it allowed us to come one step closer to getting acquainted, which, at this point, was my singular objective.

After walking more than four hours through the rough, dark, jungle trail, I was extremely tired and hungry. It was after sunset when we finally reached our destination, the hut that we had seen from the airplane. As I had anticipated, it was empty. The inside seemed very confined and dismal, and there were too many fleas on the sandy dirt floor to sleep inside. I decided to sleep outside in the field. I collected many sticks, laid dried banana leaves over them, and spread my sleeping bag on top of the leaves. I crawled into my bag without washing up or removing my clothes, except for my army boots.

I couldn't sleep because I was too hungry and thirsty, so I got up again. Searching the dark area for something to assuage my thirst, I found a puddle that had formed by a fallen tree. I made a cup from a leaf and drank and drank until my thirst was quenched. Then I crawled into my sleeping bag again.

One Indian man who had made a bonfire for the evening vigil lay down next to me with his dirty, smelly head next to mine on my sleeping bag; another lay down diagonally, using my tired legs as his pillow, moving his filthy fingers back and forth on my bag. My head began to feel itchy. *Have those lice crawled onto my head from his?*, I wondered. But I didn't push them away, because I thought maybe this was their way of expressing friendship.

I couldn't use my mosquito net, so I sprayed insect repellant on me. The Indians were captivated by the fragrance. One of them asked for the spray, and when I gave it to him, he began spraying it all over his body, even though he didn't need it. Another rushed over to take his turn, profusely spraying it on himself, then another and another. I had planned to use it for at least fifteen days, but it was going to be used up tonight. *What am I going to do tomorrow?* Since childhood, my life had been so regimented with saving,

saving.... I now concluded, however, that it would be much more significant to let it be wasted in the pursuit of their hearts. Tomorrow is tomorrow, I'll cope with it then. These are the hardships incident to pioneering, but those Indians are going to come first, and I will go the extra mile to that end.

I had left my flashlight above my head, and they played with it with enormous curiosity. One of them shined it everywhere, turning it on and off; another took it from him, turned it on and off, on and off, giggling and laughing; another one...on and off...on and off, then another. The battery wouldn't last more than tonight, and I had brought no extra batteries. How am I going to protect myself from spiders and poisonous snakes at night? I was becoming anxious; but then I realized that I had already given up my life to the will of God. *Don't let it upset you*, I told myself. *Don't be small. Pour yourself out for them.* God had chosen me to show His greatness, and I wanted to shepherd them and nourish them to spiritual life. *To get the job done, stay in rapport with them and practice radical humility. Quit fighting against it, and just go with the flow.*

I was so tired that I finally fell asleep amid thoughts that, despite the kind, yet uneasy, atmosphere so far, they might barbeque me on that well-burning bonfire!

All of a sudden, someone shook me awake. I opened my eyes, and the awareness that I was still alive made me thankful. One of the Indians gestured to me that he wanted to use my flashlight. I had given up, so I gave it to him and went back to sleep.

I don't know how long I had been asleep when another one of them woke me again. In his dirty hands, he brought me two sweet potatoes and a small, whole fish that had been baked in the ashes of the bonfire. The potatoes were broken open and covered with dirt, sand, and charcoal, and the fish they had caught from a pool, using my flashlight, was cooked unscaled and undressed and covered with dirt and sand.

I was still woozy with sleep and had no desire to eat anything, especially such dirty food, but I quickly realized that it was out of their hospitality that they had prepared this special food during their night vigil. I accepted it graciously, turned around and roughly scraped off any unwanted stuff with my fingernails, and put it into my mouth. It was too gritty to chew and not very tasty to me in my sleepy state, so I simply swallowed it.

Now I have swallowed it. What if I develop appendicitis out here in the jungle?, I worried. *That issue, too, I will cope with in the morning.* And I went back to sleep.

Waking in the morning, I was drenched with condensation from the jungle's humidity, but I was extremely thankful to God for letting us spend the night without incident. For the first time in my life, I had a flash of awareness of how precious was one more day of extended life. When I went to wash my face at the same puddle from which I had so voraciously drunk the night before, to my horror, it was literally black with hundreds, perhaps thousands, of mosquito larvae! *Think positively,* I told myself. *Last night's mosquito soup quenched your hunger. It happened! Get over it.* So I didn't vomit.

Florentino had a good night's sleep, too, in a hammock hung between two trees not far from the hut. I had a cup of milk for my breakfast, read the Bible while waiting for the morning dew to evaporate, and learned several of their words: "*Hyattatte* (What is it?)," "*Ayaosu* (water)," "*Yingyasha* (Let's go)." I listened to them, repeated the words to myself, memorized them, and systematically recorded them in my notebook.

After that field survey, all of us returned to the Indians' present place, where we had stayed briefly the day before. By gesturing, I asked the man who seemed the most senior for permission to build a hut for myself. He readily gave me permission to build on a spot about fifty meters away from their living area on the edge of the jungle. First of all, I cut the trees, eliminated the roots, leveled the ground, erected posts, and then the Indians brought the leaves of trees for making a roof. It soon became a small wall-less hut, good enough to provide shade. When I told them my wife would accompany me on my next visit, they all seemed very pleased.

My original plan had been to stay for fifteen days, but I had encountered too many deterrents that had caused me to rethink my decision: my food supply was exhausted, the weather was extremely hot, what little water was in the foul-smelling creek was undrinkable and unfit for bathing, and the stinging insects were unbearable twenty-four hours a day.

"I will come back with my wife next month," I signified to them by pointing to the moon as I drew a circle with my arm. I left that place after staying only five days.

My first meeting with the Indians had been a very successful milestone, and the experience I had gained would be put to good use. The Omniscient God had been with me during this time, and it seemed there was only constant victory wherever I looked.

He caused me, an ordinary man, to discover extraordinary abilities, and I had experienced peace and a sense of well-being that only God can produce. *Dear God, You are my solution, You are my provider. Thank you so much.*

—⚏—

One Month Later

14

WHILE RECUPERATING AT HOME, I familiarized myself with the vocabulary I had recorded in my notebook and prepared gifts for my second trip: sugar, candies, clothing, matches, knives, hatchets, fishing rods, scissors, bowls, pots, fragrant soap, etc. For my wife and I, however, what I packed for a month's supply was minimal. It was a hard decision for a woman to penetrate the jungle for a month. The fact that at that time we had very little financial support and our mobility was severely limited by the lack of any kind of vehicle for transportation made her decision to accompany me very difficult indeed. Nevertheless, she decided to go, we found a ride, and set out together on our seven-hundred-kilometer journey.

After two days, we arrived at the fazenda Estrela do Guapore. From there, with our luggage on our backs, we walked six kilometers into the dark jungle. At that point, while we were resting, I warned my wife to adapt, adjust, and be resilient to what she was about to encounter in the jungle. Everyone — men, women, and children — would be completely naked; she should remain calm, relaxed, and not show any attitude that would agitate them. I wanted to be sure that our actions would be coordinated. It was her first experience in such a circumstance, and she appeared stressed and anxious.

We finally reached their neighborhood. Suddenly, a young Indian man jumped out of nowhere acting as though he were about to knock my head off with a large club he brandished above his head! Terrified, Jae Sun let out a loud, shrill scream and ran to hide behind me. I, too, was taken by surprise. Although this event was totally unexpected, I managed to stand my ground and smile. The Indian stared at me for a moment, then threw his club away and chuckled, as if to say, "Just kidding." We had narrowly escaped. How thankful I was!

I later learned that establishing the first contact with the Indians was most critical, since they were on strict guard against outsiders and frequently killed them, assuming that they had penetrated their domain in order to harm them. Once the outsider had contacted them, the Indians would test the newcomer by threatening him abruptly with a club, as they had done to us, or by aiming an arrow at him, or by holding him by the arm and pretending to bite him. If the outsider reacted to them by drawing a gun or a knife, or if he demonstrated extreme fear, they would mark him as being "dangerous." If I had been marked that way, it would mean failure, because I would lose all access to them. I could not afford such a mishap. For the first three years I was subjected to such testing. Each time, by God's grace, I was able to react properly and remain stable. Every time that I passed the test, my relationship with the Indians was strengthened — so much so that now I test them from time to time, just for fun!

Civilized people often have the misconception that Indian tribal people are incompetent and of a low intelligence. On the contrary, it seems to me that they possess a high level of intelligence and that they can discern an outsider's attitude without verbal communication. Their sense of sight, hearing, smelling, and power of intuition are comparable to those of wild animals, far superior to those of ordinary people who, in the jungle, would be by comparison as fools. If one acted as if he knew something, it could be a huge mistake. But if one conceded his inferiority before them—if one yielded the palm of victory to them—he would gain their compassion and be able to mingle with them easily. *Humility accomplishes everything. Practice radical humility.*

Jae Sun and I entered the hut that I had built the previous month and were confronted by myriad insects and lizards crawling everywhere. Our furniture was a bed made of sticks, crisscrossed to make a flat surface. Her kitchen was a log upon which she set her pots and bowls. In the middle of the hut, we made a bonfire of sticks on which to cook our rice. With great curiosity, the Indians watched us continually. Before dawn, some of them would creep silently in and, like dark shadows, keep a silent vigil. Being unaware of their presence, upon arising we would be surprised. Their faces were always of severe countenance, and we had no common language with which to communicate with them.

When we brushed our teeth, they stared at us, liberally squeezed the toothpaste from the tube to taste it, and rubbed their dirty fingers freely on our toothbrushes. When we cooked, they sat watching us, helped themselves freely to our food, enjoyed it, and went out and bragged about it to the other Indians, a couple of whom would rush in and look around for food that they, too, could enjoy. Feeling sorry for them, we would cook more rice. They enjoyed it and went out to brag, a couple more would come in, and the scenario would continually repeat itself.

All day long, from early dawn until late at night, we had no privacy at all; personal quiet time was literally impossible. They took turns like guards. Our month's supply of rations was exhausted in just a few days.

My wife and the Indian women shared characteristics common to women—"the girl stuff." They gathered around her, smiling, saying things we could not understand, touching her long hair, holding her arms and gently shaking them, treating her as though she were a real, live doll. Their acceptance of each other seemed genuine. A concrete connection seemed to have been made.

Every afternoon, the Indians would go to the creek and jump in the water, the men upstream, the women, according to their custom, in a less favorable spot downstream. One day, my wife took charge of the women, leading them to the spot upstream where the men usually bathed, shouting and gesturing to the men to go downstream. The men, looking confused, smiled sheepishly and rambled on downstream to bathe where the women usually went. The women splashed and laughed and seemed to love it. My wife shouted to the men even louder, "Go farther, you don't have to see us!"

The men, as if to say, "What's this all about?" jumped up and down, showing off their male attributes to the women: "Look at it, all of you look at it!", they chuckled and consoled themselves, though obviously thinking, *If the women assert themselves this way, it's going to be difficult....*

Jae Sun managed to keep food in the pot by bringing in pumpkins, sweet potatoes, dried corn, etc., from the Indian women. Nevertheless, many nights we couldn't sleep—we were simply too hungry. She adamantly insisted, "We have to stay for at least one full month because getting here was such a difficult trip." When we talked, we frequently said things like "When we get home, let's treat ourselves to beef bulgogi (a favorite but somewhat expensive Korean dish), steamed dumplings, grapes, apples, strawberries, all sorts of other fruits," and so on. But once we got home, of course, the reality was that we couldn't afford to indulge ourselves with such gourmet foods, and we would be tired and willing just to relax in our home for a while.

While in the jungle, every day at dawn Jae Sun and I would kneel and pray inside our mosquito net. One day, one of the

Indians, after observing what we had done, asked, "What did you do?"

Pointing to the sky, I explained to him very ineptly, "I talked to my God."

Later in the day, when there was more light, it was our routine to read the Bible together. The same Indian, pointing to my Bible, asked, "What is that?"

I tried to make him understand, "My God is talking to me through this book."

Although I am sure he didn't have the slightest understanding of what I was trying to convey, he nodded as though he did. At least he demonstrated a good attitude and accepted what we were doing, whether or not he understood it. Our preaching had begun: our lifestyle represented preaching without the means of language.

Although this jungle ministry was, for my wife, physically challenging to the extreme, I was very pleased that I was able to introduce her to the Indians from the beginning. Starting together as a team ultimately proved to be the key to forming an unguarded and totally friendly atmosphere between us and the Indians. Again, God had given us an advantage. The Holy Spirit was working in us, through us, and for us, whether we realized it or not.

In contacting and continuing to work with the Indians, the most important thing was to earn their trust. Otherwise, the consequences would be insurmountable: we would be ostracized and in constant life-threatening danger. Nor would we have an opportunity to learn their language, their real names, the locations of their relatives or their enemies, or about the poisons they used, either by ingestion or by smearing on their arrows. We would have been thoroughly isolated.

Ever since I passed the "club test," I have lived among them as one of their tribal members, speaking congenially with them and acknowledging one simple truth, that this is their awesome and much-appreciated gift to me. It was impossible even to imagine that I could sleep alone securely, snoring peacefully among these wild, unreachable, and primitive Indians; that I could dwell with them in their dirty, smoke-filled hut, wreaking of obnoxious odors; that I would endure, day and night, all kinds of harmful insects, sitting shoulder to shoulder with these disorderly and unhygienic savages, eating their food, which could hardly be called food—some would think it barely qualified as pig fodder—mingling with them, laughing at what they laughed at. Spending time with them, by God's grace, was an exotic life of indelible satisfaction.

I gained quite a large vocabulary, enough to communicate with them in everyday situations, and, within six months after my original contact, I was able to start teaching them the Portuguese alphabet (Portuguese being the Brazilian national language). Although intellectually still beyond them, I regularly read them a chapter of the Portuguese Bible, taught them a hymn, sang it together, and prayed together in a "daily chapel."

They had lived until now in a world without literature without feeling any deficiency. For them, there was no need to write letters, read newspapers, or inquire about world events or the nation's economy. Obviously, it would be challenging to overcome illiteracy, but I planned to teach them diligently until they could read the Gospel message.

God's creation is a multi-faceted diamond, but it is desecrated. The story of Jesus, the Redeemer, is the most fascinating truth. The lives of mortal men who live only for the moment are utterly meaningless, but Jesus is the Master of life.

I wanted them to learn the eternal words of God. "So then faith comes by hearing, and hearing by the word of God" (Romans 10:17). Only the Word of God from the Bible will pierce their hearts, touch their souls and bring them into the kingdom of God through Jesus Christ.

I was determined to help this Alantesu tribe to become literate and to have biblical knowledge coupled with true spirituality before the life that they only thought to be real came to an end. This was the principal thing above everything else in my life. It was my ultimate goal. It was, and still is, my mission.

—⁓—

15
Curious Literature

ONE DAY, while they were gathered, Quinto, the most promi-
nent middle-aged Indian man in the group, announced, "I will
embrace that man as my father," and he has assisted me ever since.
He has been a tremendous help to me, a true companion bolstering
my activities.

As time passed, a tentative contact had been established
between the fazenda residents and the Indians. Quinto came to me
one day and said, "Let's go to the fazenda and bring back some
sugar; I want to have something sweet to drink. Come on, Quinna
(Kim), come on!"

It was Quinto who was asking me. I knew I couldn't refuse
him and cause him to be disappointed, but I was reluctant to waste
nearly an entire day. The distance was only about six kilometers
through the jungle, but I would have to get ready and cover myself
suitably for travel on the jungle paths, and besides, the weather was
extremely hot and muggy.

I pondered for a while what would be a pragmatic solution to
this problem. Then I decided to write a letter to the secretary of the
fazenda: "Dear Antonio, this Indian's name is Quinto. If you would
do me the favor of selling him two five-kilogram bags of sugar on
credit, I will stop by and pay you for it on my way home.

Thank you, I appreciate it very much. Missionary Kim."

I folded the letter and gave it to Quinto (who had become my son) saying, "If you give this to Antonio, he will give you the sugar."

Late in the afternoon, Quinto returned sweating profusely, beaming all over, and carrying two bags of sugar. They made their sweet drinks and, all of them looking delighted, obviously enjoyed them immensely.

Quinto then proceeded to tell every Indian he saw, "Quinna (Kim) drew something on the paper and gave it to me. When Antonio saw it, he just gave me the sugar."

It was evident that in all of Quinto's life he had never seen such a miracle: one little drawing on a piece of paper had been transformed into ten tangible kilograms of sugar. Inwardly, it had affected him deeply (for over twenty years after that incident, even to the present time, Quinto has struggled tenaciously to master the Portuguese alphabet). This sugar episode became the chief topic of conversation among the Indians for a long time.

One day, one of the Indians asked me when I would be going home again. Then he asked for a pen and a sheet of paper. I had no idea why he wanted them, but I gave them to him anyway. He took them to his hut and the next day brought me the folded paper. Speaking with passion, he said, "I wrote the next time you come, I want you to bring me one medium-size knife and several fishing rods in various sizes."

I wondered how he had written that and unfolded the paper. It was indeed strange writing: it looked like rows of wiggly noodles had been lined up in curious fashion on the page. He explained the message in detail, earnestly pointing at each line.

"Oh, is that so?" I mused, and then I translated it into Korean on the back of the sheet: "One knife, medium size, and several fishing rods in various sizes." (I complied with his demand on my next visit.)

As I looked at his letter, it captured my attention. I felt that his spirit, his soul, was in those carefully drawn wiggly lines. I could grasp his mind, the thoughts that he had explained to me from the indecipherable letters he had drawn. At that moment, I realized that the Bible had been written with the same intent—to reveal the mind of its author. In the Bible lives the power of the Holy Spirit which will lead us into all truth; the author himself deciphering for us its meaning; giving us new freedom, new power, new life, and faith that will enable us to see Jesus Christ as our Lord and Savior.

His words go so far! If you read them and believe them, they will lead you to eternal salvation and, ultimately, to perfection.

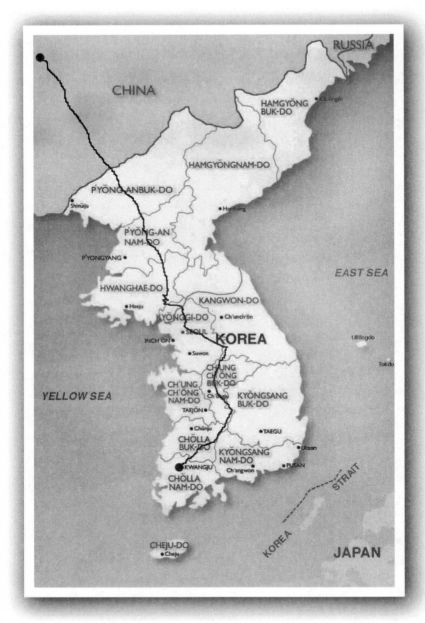

This map depicts the journey the Kim
family travelled by foot from Manchora to
their home in Kwangju after WWII.

This is the first physical contact Sung
Joon had with the Alantesu. They are
standing in front of a typical Indian house.

Sung Joon (wearing the hat) with Indian
youngsters on the "farm." The Indians burn off
an area to create a field for planting corn.

Young men return from hunting.

After the hunt, villagers prepare these pigs to eat.

The Village folk.

The whole group.

Even in this rough field, the corn grows,
and it looks like they have a good crop.

A mother multi-tasking, jungle-style.

Jae Sun and
Sung Joon
with their
new friends.

Thank you, Lord, for this food.

Jae Sun enjoys a moment with an Alantesu woman
and her puppy. Heavy loads are carried long distances
using these jungle "basketpacks."

Sung Joon with the Indians.

Jungle schoolhouse.

Sung Joon built benches and desks and set up a classroom in the jungle to begin the education of the children.

Sung Joon teaching Quinto to read.

The Bible school student returns to the jungle village
to teach another Indian to teach others also.

Some of the women in the prison were
transformed by the Gospel.

A Bible student with his father.

The guards allowed the new
believers to be baptized.

The men in the prison received the Bibles eagerly.

Bible School students come home to teach
their siblings and the children of the tribe.
"Teaching others to teach others also."

Sung Joon and boys enjoy a lesson together.

" Snakes and snails and crocodile tails?" These boys
enjoy their puppy, and play with a baby croc that has
been temporarily spared from the cooking pot.

Newborns are taken to be washed in the river.

Jungle trails are hip-deep in water
during the rainy season.

These two seem happy with the piranha and
the waterfowl they have captured.

The children's choir presented the Gospel at many unusual venues to the glory of God.

This is a common problem on the many primitive roads that lead into the fazendas. Travel is difficult, especially in rainy season.

The gold mine was God's provision.

These are the grandchildren of the Indians that
Sung Joon first encountered forty years ago. Their
children will grow up in the light.

Young Indian believers being baptized in their
declaration of commitment to a God their
grandparents never knew.

The Brazilian Air Force helicopter that
Sung Joon considered " God's chariot" to bring
him safely out of the Jungle.

Marriage and Birth

FROM BIRTH TO DEATH, during the normal course of life, everyone reaches the culmination of youth and the time to marry. Even though Indians in the jungle live as animals without clothes, that does not mean that they are driven by their instincts to mate randomly. In fact, their morals are very strict in this regard.

When their children reach puberty and undergo physiological changes, the parents and the community as a whole begin to search among their tribal members for a bride or a groom, as the case may be. Intermarriage is taboo. Their family tree is handed down by word of mouth. It is common knowledge that so-and-so is someone's uncle, aunt, cousin, or grandfather. In some cases it is very difficult to find a suitable prospect in the immediate tribe: one fifteen-year-old boy had to wait for a five-year-old girl to grow up in order to marry.

A few years ago, several of the men had walked for three days to the location of another tribe that spoke a different language and, under cover of darkness, kidnapped a young woman to be a bride. As a result, war erupted between those tribes and has continued for years. In recent days, missionaries are trying to mediate the quarrel between them about this issue concerning women, and the animosity is gradually dissipating.

Traditionally, the parents of two families promise to become relatives, and, at a suitable time, two of their children will marry. The decision is made jointly by the parents and the children: the parents agree, and the children are in accord. Before the marriage, the young man visits the girl's parents, and then the bride-to-be is placed in solitary confinement in a separate hut without food for one month. (I have wondered why she must go through such a long transition period of near-starvation, but I understand that her mother often sneaks some food to her surreptitiously.)

When the days of confinement are over, the young man offers gifts to the girl's parents according to their specifications: it may be building a hut or making a certain number of arrows, etc., and then he takes the girl with him to his own neighborhood. The people of both communities provide game animals for a party that lasts several days, the bride and groom are officially recognized as a couple, and they vanish into the jungle for their honeymoon.

These Indians have existed in this jungle with no mentor, no education, and isolated from civilization for centuries. It causes one to wonder: "Where did this regard for the sanctity of marriage come from? Where did they learn the propriety of moral behavior?" I can only acknowledge that "conscience" has been instilled in every generation since the creation. God created sex, God created marriage, and he placed it in man's heart to observe the fundamentals that He has established: "So God created man in his own image; In the image of God created he him; male and female created he them. And God blessed them, and God said to them, 'Be fruitful and multiply, and replenish the earth and subdue it'" (Genesis 1: 27-28).

Being fruitful and multiplying are God's blessing upon us if we follow the dictates of our God-given conscience. It will only bring us happiness if we don't ignore or denigrate the principle of marriage. The same rules apply inevitably to this Indian world as well.

The Indians' main diet consists of game animals, fish, corn, manioc—no other vegetables whatsoever, almost no fruits, and no spices. There is no variety in their nutrition, and their regimen is irregular. They eat whenever they feel hungry regardless whether it is day or night. I presume the Indian female's unique physiology is attributable to this insufficient regimen: they do not have regular menstruation. When they have their cycle, it is a very small flow for a very short time. They are never aware of the beginning of a pregnancy or the due date of delivery. The Indians have no sense of numbers, of birthdays, or of age; no idea of holidays, of seasons, or even the fact of twenty-four hour days. They live simply and comfortably without any restriction or consideration of time. Their system of counting is binary: one (*kanakanacha*), two (*haari*). It is impossible for them to repeat "haari" fifty times to count to one hundred. They count items haari by haari (two by two). When they finish counting, they don't know the number of the pieces; they only know if the amount is odd or even.

Back to the subject of pregnancy: the woman neither loses her appetite nor gains weight appreciably. When the moon has changed several times, they simply guess that the time must be approaching. However, even then the woman continues to carry out her regular duties—going into the jungle in search of food, or making baskets at home, etc.—until the first signal of pain occurs. The husband then restrains himself from venturing too far from home to hunt but stays nearby to assist when the time comes for his wife to give birth.

When her labor begins, he massages her stomach as though he were kneading bread dough and continues until he is exhausted, at which time another man takes over, and then another, etc., until the delivery is over. I could never tell whether this massage is advantageous or abusive, both to the mother and the baby, but it seems to be a painful procedure stemming from ignorance. The whole neighborhood, men, women, and children gather round and attend until the end. Strangely, childbirth seems always to occur at night by the light of a bonfire, and there are always several women ready to lend a hand. The baby is expelled on the bare ground, just like an animal. The women wipe it clean with their dirty hands, than clean their hands with their own hair. They tie the umbilical cord with a wisp of dried cornhusk before they cut it off with their fingernails. They lay the baby on the ground next to its mother so that she can breastfeed it, and they bury the placenta about fifty centimeters deep in the ground with their hands. The baby is already covered in dirt and shivering, and the delivery is complete. Sometimes the mother goes immediately to the river to wash herself and her newborn.

To me, the whole process is horribly unhygienic and unimaginably dangerous, but to them, it is very natural — not ugly or shameful, just a normal event — the same as their ancestors and all of the animals of the forest have experienced for centuries. By the very next day, they have forgotten about it, and everything returns to normal, as it has always been.

Have you ever wondered how a human baby would survive if it were treated from birth as a baby wild animal is treated, with aggressive exposure and unhygienic conditions? What would the survival rate be? Such a question may sound hypothetical and unrealistic, but in fact it is happening every day. The young mother, from the first day, carries her baby on her back everywhere she goes, bathes it in the river, holds the same river water in her mouth and feeds it into her baby's mouth, chews her food finely and transfers it into her baby's mouth, and also feeds it upon her breast. For a while, the baby grows well, but the mortality rate the first year is frighteningly high due to diarrhea, colic, and dehydration.

What is an even greater wonder is that some survive these unclean conditions. Those that do, with their apparently superior genes, not only survive but dominate their environment, prevail, and overcome. Thus, they continue to exist as a people, generation after generation, by nature's method of selection.

There is no such thing as kindergarten for these children; they simply learn from their mother's bosom as babies, follow their mothers about as toddlers, and become accustomed without complaint to difficulty and danger. They "subdue, and have dominion over every living thing that moves upon the earth," as the Bible says. The children are totally obedient to their parents, and their parents never punish them physically but continually show them gentleness and acceptance. They lack civilization, but they are never lacking in trust, which is exercised among their family members, all being honorable men and women. I have learned many lessons by reading my Bible and also by my observations while living among the Alantesu.

These children are not perfect, of course. They fight with each other, steal things, covet, and lie, but at the same time, it is evident that each one undeniably has a conscience as one of God's creation. The clarity of conscience in man has never been altered or obscured in the thousands of years since the creation until the present because "God created man in his own image; in the image of God created he him...." *My mission is focused on this beautiful, relevant, and real component: the conscience in man. There is a lot of work ahead of me, but I intend to continue to pursue it until I see the difference that can be achieved by the power of the Holy Spirit.*

Food

EATING IS A BODILY FUNCTION and one of God's gifts to us. I am thankful to God that for me it is one of his greater gifts: I eat almost too well; so much so, in fact, that some folks speak ill of me. They don't know the reason that I eat as I do. I look very healthy, but in fact I am not.

From my childhood I have suffered from a disease that for many proves fatal. The many physicians with whom I have consulted have agreed with the prognosis: "incurable" chronic bronchitis due to a lack of mucolytic enzymes in my body. At every seasonal change, I experience a series of symptoms: heavy mucous, coughs, bronchial catarrh, bronchitic expansion, and bronchopneumonia. I have taken numerous x-ray treatments, antibiotics, and compound medicines, without realizing any help from any of them. I have even tried Chinese acupuncture therapy, all to no avail.

Ultramodern biomedical science's "gene replacement therapy," "stem cell research," etc., may come up with something to make a difference; but even so, it would take thirty or forty years before I would receive any benefit from it, so I may just as well forget about that, too. Actually, I gave up on taking medication or seeking therapy several years ago. I don't know why I have not had "faith" to be healed. I guess I was just taking a chance or hoping something would happen when I attended meetings to be prayed for or when I visited a "faith healer" to have him lay his hands on me and pray for my condition.

One solace, however, is that I strongly believe that God planned my life just the way it is. If I were granted perfect health, I might be energetic enough to waste my life pursuing my own desires. God created a "brake system" in me so that I would "drive safely," avoiding my reckless will; then He endowed me with the gift of a great appetite to control my condition without medicines. If I skipped even one meal, I would realize that my reservoir was empty, my energy consumed by the fight my body wages against my unhealthy condition. Furthermore, in the Chinese almanac, I was born in "the year of the pig," which may explain why I have that animal's appetite! Isn't that great? In addition, God was careful to see to it that I would have no difficulty living with the jungle Indians and eating their food. All I have to do is eat what they eat.

The Indians prepare their food in the same simple style in which they live their lives: no frills, just naked and natural. The ground is their table and their plate. Fortunately, they don't eat their food raw, they cook it—but not over the fire. They cook it underneath the fire, in the ashes and with no seasoning whatsoever. That's their style: dirty and tasteless. For many, it would be hard to identify as food.

It didn't take long for the Indians and me to become friends. One day, as they were talking among themselves, it seemed evident that they were making plans to go hunting for the express purpose of serving me. Soon the men left for a monkey hunt while several of the women went out to their garden spot to bring back a basketful of *mandioca* (manioc). First they made a bonfire, adding several sizeable logs so that it would burn strong and hot. When they returned, they buried their mandioca in the ashes underneath the fire. After a time, they retrieved the cooked mandioca: steaming, skins broken open, totally covered with ashes and dirt within and without, and laid them in a pile on the ground.

Soon afterward, the men returned with several game monkeys. They gave them to the women, who burned off the hair over the fire, cut open their stomachs with bamboo arrow heads, which they used as knives, removed the intestines, and laid them aside; then binding the eviscerated carcasses with vines, they buried them in the ashes underneath the fire. After about an hour and a half, they turned them over and buried them again. Meanwhile, they buried and cooked briefly the intestines they had previously laid aside at the edge of the fire. Without eliminating the contents of the colon the women ate them, sharing them with their children. They rubbed their bloody fingers in the dirt and then wiped them off with their hair, their natural brushes, every now and then wiping their noses with the palms of their hands.

As I watched, one of the children relieved himself nearby. His mother, one of the cooks, cleaned her child by rubbing him with dirt, covered the dung with a handful of sand, picked it up and threw it away, wiped her fingers on her hair, and then went back to her cooking with those same hands. Finally, when the smell of cooked monkey signaled that they were done, the women dug them up. The cooked monkeys appeared to be smiling, their shriveled lips baring whitened teeth, their fingers and toes shrunken. The women tapped the cooked monkeys on the ground, breaking the heads off, which they gave to the men, who waited eagerly to devour them. Next they pulled off the arms and legs, divided the breasts into small pieces, put them all together into a mortar and pounded them until the meat and the bones were crushed indistinguishably together. Then they added the mandioca that had previously been cooked and piled on the ground and continued pounding, spitting occasionally on their hands as they worked. I sat watching with the other Indians while the food was being prepared. It was indeed quite an interesting process.

Apparently, it was done. The women wiped the sweat from their foreheads with the palms of their hands, made several balls about the size of their fists out of the pounded dough, sent them to several huts by the hands of their children, gave one ball each to every child, and, that being done, made one bigger ball and, smiling, presented it to me!

Although their hands must be clean by now, I needed to decide quickly what to do. Even though I am "King of the omnivores," this did not appeal to my appetite. But it took them all day to prepare it; and they did it for me, their guest. Was there any way that I could refuse it? If I did, they would be saddened, disappointed, and probably offended. I would have to deal with the consequences of that later on, and I didn't know what those consequences might be. On the other hand, if I ate it, I would no doubt suffer from diarrhea caused by some tropical amoebae and be sick for days. I was in an awkward situation, and this called for a split-second decision. My mind kicked into high gear, reasoning, *In many generations of eating this food, these Indians have never been in trouble as a result, and they are the same human beings as you are. You claim to be omnivorous! You said that you consider your life an offering! You know that wherever you go, the local food is suitable for that locale. This ball of food has carbohydrates, protein, minerals, and vitamins. Eat it. The end!*

So, smiling back, I immediately received it, and everyone, looking very pleased, stood watching me. First of all, I scraped off several pieces of charcoal as big as soy beans, broke off a small piece, and put it into my mouth. It was far grittier than I had even anticipated. I couldn't chew it, so I just moved it around in my mouth, picking out the pieces of charcoal, bones, hair and sand, and, still smiling, just swallowed it. I put on a pretty good act, as though I were in a restaurant sampling strange food, concentrating, looking thoughtful, saying "Hmmm, it's different; it's quite tasty," and finally, smiling as if to say, "It's all right." Well, at least my countenance didn't give me away.

It had a burnt taste. In fact, it tasted as it looked, burnt. I was barely able to finish it, but I managed to smile throughout the ordeal. The Indians watching me, however, thought that I found the food quite presentable. Assuming that I had enjoyed it greatly, they made me another! "*Woongku Sannawa* (I'm full)!" I said, rubbing my tummy and declining with much thanks. I was indeed thankful that I had a legitimate excuse to decline this time around.

Since the time of that first monkey ball, I have become accustomed to their food enough to look forward to it from time to time, and I think they appreciate my attitude. They would sometimes feed me a steamed giant maggot, a cooked lizard, an alligator, or a mole, etc. One day, I insisted that we needed to try snake soup, so I went out with several Indians, and we caught a huge snake, about two meters long, that crossed the narrow jungle path in front of us. We boiled the meat in a large pot and drank the broth. I would ask them to make fish soup whenever they went fishing. I would season it with salt and drink it instead of water. Since it was sterile, having gone through the boiling process, it was much safer to drink than plain river water.

Whenever I cooked rice, we would all sit around, I would say grace, and then we would take turns eating from the pot, one spoonful at a time, with only one unwashed spoon and all of us sharing it. The Indians never brushed their teeth, but it didn't matter; I just didn't think about that. I simply looked to the Lord and saw myself rising above that problem.

I am grateful for the gift of today. To mingle with them and to share their food is an honor provided by the blessing of the Almighty Creator of the universe. God decreed in me: "You are omnivorous. You are blessed. You are powerful. You are healthy." That is at the core of my being.

"Behold that which I have seen: it is good and comely for one to eat and to drink, and to enjoy the good of all his labours that he taketh under the sun all the days of his life, which God giveth him: for it is his portion" (Ecclesiastes 6:18).

Yes, dear God; yes, indeed!

—m—

Hunting

I WAS VERY CURIOUS TO KNOW how the Indians hunt without the protection of shoes or clothing from the many dangers present in the jungle. I had a growing desire to accompany them on a hunting trip, but every time I suggested it, they adamantly declined my offer, even though it seemed to me that my gun would have been much more efficient than their arrows. Perhaps it was because they knew I couldn't maneuver through the jungle as quickly or as quietly as they. Perhaps they thought I would talk too much and too loud, trying to communicate or catch up with them. Or it may have been that my boots or the swishing of my water canteen would make noise as I walked. Maybe the smell of sweat on my clothes would send a signal to the animals of our presence; or if my clothes caught on a thorny vine, it would not only tear my clothes but would transmit an impact that would shake the trees and alarm the game they were hunting. The commotion, if I were there, would certainly be significantly detrimental to the success of their hunt.

One day, however, the opportunity came for me to accompany them into the jungle to track a tapir that they had wounded in a hunt the day before. The arrow had entered its flank, but it had managed to evade them and escape into the forest. It was almost unsettling to witness how intelligently and deliberately they conducted their pursuit through the jungle. About ten men, after walking through the jungle for over an hour to arrive at the place where they had shot the animal, began to search for the tapir's tracks, looking for traces of day-old blood on the accumulation of fallen leaves. I wondered how they could distinguish their tapir's footprints, which were made yesterday, from the countless tracks, old and new, of myriad other animals laid down on the cushiony jungle floor. I had no clue; it seemed totally impossible to me. As we advanced, the already minimal blood trail diminished. We came to a huge puddle of water. After careful visual inspection, they were able to determine where the beast had entered the water and also where it had emerged. The wounded tapir, or *anta,* as they called the calf-sized relative of a wild pig, could have wandered frantically in any direction, but they continued their pursuit confidently and relentlessly. Sure enough, about two hours later we came upon the dead anta, with the arrow protruding from its flank. Its stomach was bloated, and its intestines were already beginning to decompose.

All the while, four Indian women had been following behind the search party, unnoticed, each carrying a huge basket. Their duty was to do the heavy lifting. They would divide the carcass into parts and carry the meat home in their baskets. We all returned through the pathless jungle without the slightest uncertainty about the direction of our travel, backtracking much more quickly than we had gone outbound.

The question that was in my mind was, "How could they go into an unknown part of the jungle for the first time and backtrack with no problem whatsoever?" There would soon come a time that I would learn the secret of their incredible skill.

One day, when I went to their neighborhood, the whole area seemed deserted and eerily quiet except for one seven-year-old boy, who was in bed suffering from some mysterious illness. He told me that everyone else had gone out hunting.

"Do you know which direction they went?" I asked.

"They went that way," he said, pointing.

"Do you feel up to going with me to try to find them?" I asked. He replied that he could do that.

I thought it may have been too much to ask of a sick boy, but he seemed to have a hidden desire to join the group, and my presence seemed to inspire him to do so in spite of his condition. We reached the edge of the jungle, where he, after looking this way and that, went confidently forward. I followed him rather tentatively as he rambled about a little bit, touching this branch and that. Looking around, he would move on a little farther. Passively trusting this sick boy in this foreboding jungle gradually began to worry me. We might be completely lost, with him as my guide.

"Hey, how are we doing? Are we getting there?" I asked.

"They went this way," he answered.

A moment later he pointed out a broken twig dangling right in front of him. It captured my attention and I became actively involved in searching around for more such signs. There! Every five or ten meters I would find a little twig dangling, beckoning to us! They were brighter than street lights pointing us in the right direction.

"Monkeys can break the twigs, too," the boy told me, "but they can't make them dangle."

That demonstrated to me that the Indians' analytical ability is far superior to that of monkeys. For some time the boy and I were guided by the dangling twigs. Then I heard the sound of hubbub somewhere in front of us and began to smell smoke as well. The Indians had already killed two wild hogs, cooked their intestines, and were enjoying their feast.

I learned that every time the Indians walk through the jungle, they break twigs intermittently as convenient navigation aids. Not just individually, but as a people group, they have collectively overcome every challenge that the jungle offers. Their intelligence has developed in a manner eminently suited to conquer the world of the jungle and the hazards it presents. Their minds are agile and sound, and they function the same way we do in our cultures.

There is no tree in the jungle that has branches in more abundance than does this one: humanity. We are all branches of that family tree. The Indians are not related to the monkeys any more than we are. I have been in this jungle over forty years, long enough to know that monkeys don't evolve into men. To satisfy the theory of evolution, at some point there would have to be some striking evidence of that transformation. By now I would have seen some odd monkey-like men or man-like monkeys, either old or young. Until now I have not heard of or encountered any such phenomenon.

On one occasion I suggested to the Indians, "Monkeys are your ancestors, are they not?"

They burst into fits of laughter and made me a laughing stock saying, "Yeah, yeah, they may be your hairy ancestors. They are certainly not ours!"

I was made fun of and dishonored briefly as being a product of evolution myself. My goodness, all of this while I was pretending to be knowledgeable about such things!

—m—

Disease and Treatment

LIVING IN THE JUNGLE, the Alantesu have not been affected by such disorders as stress, high blood pressure, diabetes, cancer, psychosis, or venereal disease, which have been the consequence of the complicated lifestyle associated with "civilization." I don't know if it is solely because of their simple lifestyle or also because of their genetic makeup. They never brush their teeth, yet they never experience toothaches or middle-ear or sinus infections. However, such fatal diseases as malaria, yellow fever, and dengue, copious in their environment, are always lurking around them. It is difficult to readily distinguish one from the others because their symptoms are almost identical: high fever, chills (even if under warm blankets and beside a huge bonfire), or hemorrhage. There have been cases, when treatment was too late or poorly administered, that entire tribal groups have perished.

Yellow fever can be prevented for up to ten years by vaccination, but malaria and dengue are difficult to prevent. The only way to do so is to avoid mosquito bites, and could that be entirely possible in a jungle literally filled with mosquitoes of every size and shape? Both of these diseases cause loss of appetite and possible liver damage. Their treatment involves administering doses of vitamin B12 to promote red cell production.

One year, my whole tribe caught measles. Every man, woman, and child lay on the ground depleted, moaning in distress and burning with fevers, their entire bodies covered with red hives. I experienced an extreme sense of urgency: I need to preserve this tribe! I dashed to the Bureau of Indian Administration to acquire IV drips and IV antibiotics. When I brought them, I was inundated with many patients, all requiring my attention at the same time. With great concentration, I devoted my time and effort to taking care of the entire neighborhood by myself.

They had never seen or even heard of injectables. How could I explain to them the benefits they would receive if they would give me their arm and let me stick it with a needle? Or the relief they would get from watching IV drips going into their blood vessels one drop at a time for an hour? Or how they could trust that those drops were beneficial and not poisonous? One thing is certain: they must have felt that I was trustworthy. I was truly thankful to God for that.

Prior to each injection, I wiped the injection site over and over again with an alcohol pad. But as diligently as I tried, I could never wipe it completely clean because they had never in their lives used soap or warm water to wash the dirt from their bodies, even though they would jump in the creek from time to time to cool off. In the end, they all recovered without further complications, for which I was also thankful. It meant much to me, and it meant the preservation of the tribe.

From the beginning of my time here, there have always been at least a couple of Indians suffering from some minor or major ailment: headache, stomachache, diarrhea, a heavy cough, eye infection, cuts, boils or other skin diseases, etc. In Brazil, many good medicines are readily available without prescription, so I always keep various recent acquisitions in my medicine bag.

When I treated them, I wanted them to trust me and to be assured that what they were about to receive was not poison, because all of the medicines have a bitter taste. For high fever and headaches I would give them Novalgina (similar to extra-strength Tylenol). I would take one pill in front of the patient first, and then would give him two. For someone suffering from diarrhea, I would take one Imosec and then give him one. I made sure they understood that if this were poison, I would die first.

I was glad that I had taken the medicine first each time, because later I was to learn that whenever someone became sick among them, they immediately assumed that some neighboring Indians had visited and secretly sprayed *dinnare* (poison powder) on their food. Because of this belief, they harbored grudges against their neighbors and were constantly on guard against them, but they did not have doubts about my medicine. In fact, when they began to realize the efficacy of modern medicines (of which they previously had no knowledge), they began begging for them at the slightest signs of discomfort. "No, you can't have more," I would tell them. "It's like dinnare. You can die if you take too much."

The difficulty in administering medicine to them properly was that they had no concept of "three meals a day." Thirty minutes after a meal, or one hour before a meal, or two tablets every four hours— all of this meant nothing to them. As previously mentioned, there is no concept of time in their world; they eat whenever they feel hungry. Consequently, I had to chase patients down whenever it was time for their medication. There was no way that I could allow them to be responsible for their own medication.

On one occasion, the son of the chief (the oldest male tribal member) was sick. The boy, who was about seven years old, lay on his bed, extremely weak. His ashen face was haggard, and he appeared to be near death. His head was so red and swollen it appeared as though he were wearing a beret. It was large, soft, and mushy, obviously full of pus and infection and in need of an operation.

"Chief, I am going to have to open that up," I explained, "and press all of that matter out. It could be very painful, but I believe it will promote the healing process."

"Okay," he said. "Go ahead."

I came as close as I could to shaving his head with only a pair of scissors, then, with a match, I sterilized one corner of a razor blade and made a three-centimeter incision on the top of his head; immediately the exudates streamed out. I covered the opening with a clean handkerchief that I had and said to the boy, "All right, I'm going to squeeze hard. Hold me tight if it hurts too bad."

I pressed his head firmly with my palms from his ears upward, eliminating the torrents of pus. I cleaned it up and applied bandages to his head. That done, I took a penicillin syringe out of my bag, injected about one quarter of the antibiotic into my own buttocks in front of the entire gathering that was on hand to watch, and the rest of it into the boy's. He handled it very well, right to the end. It was a huge operation in that primitive jungle setting. I felt like I was working for *M.A.S.H.*

The following morning, the little boy, José, showed tremendous improvement. His eyes sparkled like stars! He was revitalized, restored! *Oh dear God, thank you so much!*

José was the boy who had earlier guided me through the jungle by following the dangling twigs. He symbolized for me the "incandescent streetlights of the jungle." I hoped that one day José could be a shining light to lead his people out of darkness and direct them to God's life-giving plan.

At the time of this writing, José's son Rafael is attending Bible school. Times have changed for this second and third generation!

—ɯ—

A Little Health Tip For Our Readers

As daily life becomes more complicated, more people—particularly women—are affected by depression. If severe, depression can lead to what some might call bipolar disorder (manic depressive syndrome) My wife has suffered from severe depression, from which I have also suffered. When my younger sister, a pharmacist, heard about it, she wrote me a letter:

> *Dear Brother: One of the transmitters and modulators of the central nervous system is serotonin. I strongly believe that bananas contain 5-HT, a serotonin-like substance, as well as abundant potassium. Prescription medicines for depression do not supplement 5-HT, but do adjust bodily function. The necessary nutritional ingredient only comes from food. I recommend one or two bananas every day as a great source of 5-HT, along with a lot of vegetables and fruits....*

My wife has completely recovered from depression by eating one or two bananas every day. She threw her expensive three-month supply of medicine in the trash can; our burden has been lifted!

"And God said, Behold, I have given you every herb bearing seed, which is upon the face of all the earth, and every tree in the which is the fruit of a tree yielding seed; to you it shall be for meat." (Genesis 1:29).

Dear God, you are truly our Provider!

Language and Evangelism

EVER SINCE THE TOWER OF BABEL, when "the LORD [con-founded] the language of all the earth: and from thence did the LORD scatter them abroad upon the face of all the earth" (Genesis 11:9), the history of languages continues in confusion and complexity to the present time. Every language involves varying degrees of difficulty, yet we are getting accustomed to managing the problem of communication as things stand. As an example of that, one interpreter working at the UN understands twenty languages and is able to facilitate communication between many people.

It seems, however, that God's will is different. He plans to keep us divided in this world for a while, rather than allowing us to experience total convenience with this world's secularism, He would have us surrender our lives to His eternal purpose and be united by the Spirit and by His Holiness rather than by one secular language.

It is not easy to learn a different language; it is even less easy to master it! But God used an ass, a mere beast, to open its mouth to reprimand Balaam with a human language. It's unclear how the ass learned the language or how long or how well he spoke it. Like the ass, if I could just speak some of my tribe's language, enough to make them realize that they were sinners and that they needed to repent and to accept the Lord Jesus, I would not only be satisfied, but also immensely thankful. This was my ultimate desire.

163

From my first contact with these tribal Indians, what I needed most was to learn their language. I had no desire to go through the usual process of learning the origin or history of their language, whether it is linguistically Ural-Altaic, or if anthropologically these people are of the Oriental Mongolian line, whose babies are born with a bluish spot on their buttocks. I wasn't interested in any such foolish detours, I wanted to cut to the chase and learn their language as their children do, from direct everyday living with them. It is a well-known and rather obvious fact that little English children can utilize the English language more fluently than can Korean college graduates with degrees as English majors.

Therefore, I kept a pencil and a sheet of paper in my shirt pocket at all times and started, from the very beginning, to jot down in Korean alphabet the first simple and easy words that I could catch when I heard them talk. I was able to write down most of the syllables that they pronounced quite accurately using Korean symbols (I couldn't write them in English or Portuguese that satisfactorily) and then I memorized them.[5]

My tribal Indians very much enjoyed my learning their language. Some of them were eager to teach me more; some even tried to teach me methodically. Sometimes they would look at my memo paper, touch it, and wonder, "How can he say the same things over in exactly the same way he said them before? What's on there?"

Wa weena ingkisatta (Where did your father go)?

Kayu wha ainari (He went hunting).

Iro ee hingini waaitii (When is he coming back)?

Wa sootti waatuwa (He is coming back soon).

---

[5] *Linguistics: I heard that some linguists in America and England used to practice pronunciation of languages by listening to Korean International students who were invited by them specifically for that purpose. Korean is believed to be one of the four most difficult languages but a model for language discipline because of its variety of expression, in pronunciation, and in honorary, normal, or lower prefix and suffix.(The Academy Korean Language needs to develop a method that would enable Koreans to write the pronunciation of th, r, l, f, v, and z.)*

It was an interesting language. In this way, within six months I had learned a considerable amount of commonly used vocabulary. At times, they seemed surprised and glad. "Since when does he know such words?" One day I repeated one of their jokes that they tell among themselves, and the men and the women, falling backward, nearly burst their sides with laughter. I followed suit and laughed too. I could feel the power that language has to bind people together. Language endows us not only with power but the opportunity to embrace other people.

One time, when a tribe that lived some distance away—a whole day's walk—came to visit and found that I was able to converse with them in their own language, they were delighted. "Quajatdisu (a cultured man) can speak our tongue, too?" I sensed that familiarity was being established immediately.

Another time, another tribe came to visit us from two or three days' walking distance. When I greeted them in their language, they were struck with admiration and extended to me an invitation to their village. I immediately accepted their invitation, and then, throwing down on the ground before them a sizeable chunk of cooked meat that one of my Indians had hung up to keep, I said, "*Yaittura! Dinnare yunnaa* (Eat, there's no poison)." I showed my generous spirit in the way that they do it, just as though I owned the meat that I had given away. In spite of my unreasonable act, the real meat owner looked glad and added, "Yaittura! (Eat)."

All of our guests seemed to envy our free and comfortable relationship.

"Darutt kainandu kana hattana aawa kottuwa (When you eat that up, we'll catch another one tomorrow)."

Even though I spoke impudently, thereby making a shambles of any social norm and a mess of the atmosphere (as I perceived by the glances), the actual undercurrent, in spite of my cheekiness, was warm, free, and genuine, with a unique and delicate feeling possible only in the jungle. It was pleasant, and I saw that "it was good."

When I came back to the jungle the next time, I brought several gifts with me for the real meat owner, just in case he harbored any bad feelings for what I had done, although he hadn't shown any signs of this. Even if he had, I suppose it wouldn't have mattered much.

Now it was time for me to evangelize them directly.

Actually, my evangelism had started from the first moment that I had made contact with them. It was my belief that evangelism should spring out of my everyday lifestyle. I impressed them with my cheerful, smiling countenance, quiet early morning prayer, reading the Bible, and singing hymns as my daily routine.

One day, I cooked rice in a large pot. We all sat down to eat, but they just sat there, waiting.

"Why are you just sitting there?" I asked, "Aren't you going to eat?"

"Well," they responded, "you say your prayer first."

They had come that far, but that was only a beginning. It was not the evangelism I wished to see, although I would say it was a process of reforming their daily format. From the beginning of my time there, every evening after sunset I sang hymns to them. They loved to hear melodious songs, which seemed strange to them, unlike their folk songs that were composed of nothing but rhythm. Every time they heard a hymn they were unsparing in their praise, saying "Ou!" or "Yai!"

Brazilian hymns were somewhat different than the Korean ones that I had known, and many of them became my favorites. Under the jungle's glittering starlight, surrounded by the picturesque quietness of the night scenery, with some of them sitting, others lounging or lying down comfortably around me, I sang with full-throated voice many of the hymns that I had memorized. I would select one stanza and sing it repeatedly twenty or thirty times, like playing a recorder, in the hope that they could learn by listening. Living in a world of timelessness, I was usually unaware of how long those night sessions lasted. Many times I tried to explain, as much as I possibly could, what that particular hymn meant, followed by what the creation story in Genesis meant. It was like teaching Sunday school to a group of children. They would listen with great curiosity. But still, this was not the evangelism I wanted to convey.

Well, then, what is evangelism? What was it that they must hear? It starts with sin and the law of God: "I had not known sin, but by the law: for I had not known lust, except the law had said, Thou shalt not covet" (Romans 7:7). Where there is no sin, there can be no redemption, no salvation from sin. To a people who live with the absence of any sense of sin, I must inculcate in them a knowledge of what God's law is and why He gave it so that they could be aware of sin, have compunction, repent of what is offensive to God, surrender their lives to Jesus, and find their way out.

With these Indians, isolated from world affairs, living in a small group and seemingly at peace, I couldn't pinpoint anything among them that would help them to understand sin. Although I speak loudly or even yell at times, they always speak softly. Young mothers never become upset or spank their crying babies—they just breast-feed them and comfort them quietly. There were no thieves among them, no murderers, no rapists, no adultery in spite of their naked lifestyle, and no divorce. But, even so, they don't always act like angels either. The Bible says, "All have sinned" (Romans 5:12), and "It is written, there is none righteous, no not one" (Romans 3:10). "All have sinned, and come short of the glory of God" (Romans 3:23). That is definitely true.

All through the first year I struggled with this issue: Where is the leverage point—the basic argument that would afford me the opportunity to define their sin in such a way that they could acknowledge it? How am I going to penetrate their hearts deeply enough to evangelize them if I can't find a way to define sin? How can true conversion be accomplished? With this line of thinking, I was buried under an enormous psychological burden. And so the first year passed, while I was becoming increasingly familiar with them and with their language.

One day, an amazing thing happened: one of the Indians told me a lie. Yes, that's it! I could tell him that his lie was deception, and that's sin. But I didn't know the word for "lie," and I couldn't figure out a way to ask them for their word for "lie." So I said to him, "*Waina tairi ko kohte yekinawa* (You talked to me bad)."

Did he understand me? I had no idea. There was no response whatsoever. He had no reaction, not the slightest remorse. It frustrated me.

I pondered this awhile and then decided that I would tell them a lie and see how they reacted. One late afternoon, some of the Indians went out for a stroll. It was mostly for leisure, but we were also on the lookout for monkeys to hunt. About ten of us were walking single file, and I was at the end of the line. Looking at the top of a tall tree, I shouted, "*Quaichai tau san nalle!* (There's a bird like a pheasant!)."

Everybody stopped and, looking up, asked, "Where, where?"

They are, of course, the ones who possess a superior sixth sense, and there was no way that they would have confidence in what some obtuse man like myself would say about something in the jungle that had escaped their notice. I was just standing there, smiling, looking up at the sky. Then someone said, "*Yi ha.*"

I assumed that "Yi ha" meant "a lie," so I quickly memorized it.

Later Tainangio, the Indian who had lied to me before, lied to me again. He was a habitual liar. This time, I responded, "Waina tairi yi ha nari."

He didn't even blink an eye—no reaction. Well, I had failed again to make him realize his sin.

One day, one of the little children came into my hut. Pointing to a bow that was hanging on my wall that one of the Indians had made for me, he asked, "Who made that?"

I said, "I did."

"*Kihatnira! Kihatnira!*" he mocked.

That's it! I thought. *That's the word for which I have been searching for over a year!*

The liar, Tainangio, was Quinto's brother-in-law, and Quinto was the one who had adopted me as his "father" early on and had revered me ever since. Tainangio's habitual lying was making our relationship a little awkward. Predictably, he lied to me again.

"Waina kihatnira!" I snapped.

I had nailed it. This time, Tainangio was visibly perturbed. His face turned red with shame. I was exhilarated! If I could teach them the law of God and help them to make the connection, it would be possible to make a significant change morally and spiritually. This was a small victory and a truly encouraging moment.

One thing I must be careful not to do is to emphasize only the *law* of God. They must also learn about faith and of God's grace because, "by the deeds of the law there shall no flesh be justified in his sight: for by the law is the knowledge of sin" (Romans 3:20); "Therefore we conclude that a man is justified by faith without the deeds of the law" (Romans 3:28). Once they had learned of God's law, the Gospel should immediately follow. An intellectual knowledge of the *mechanics* of the Gospel is not sufficient to save. There must be a comprehension of the *essence* of the Gospel.

Digressing from our story for a moment, let's consider what that means.

"What is the essence of the Gospel?"

The essence of the Gospel is that it is God's work. You can do nothing to save yourself. God does His own work in His own way.

One may ask, "When will God do what is necessary to save me from my sins?"

He has already done it. Jesus died for your sins, and "If one died for all, then were all dead" (2 Corinthians 5:14).

"But that was done many centuries ago; is it still valid?"

Yes. What God did once is valid forever. "[Jesus] offered one sacrifice for sins forever…[and] by one offering he hath perfected forever them that are sanctified" (Hebrews 10:12,14).

"Really," one may say. "I don't have to do anything?"

That's right. Jesus said, "Verily, verily I say unto you, He that heareth my word, and believeth on him that sent me has everlasting life and shall not come into condemnation; but is passed from death unto life" (John 5:24). To believe means to fully trust what Jesus has done.

"You mean, then, that my sins are gone?"

Yes, "For he [God] hath made him who knew no sin [Jesus] to be sin for us, that we might be made the righteousness of God in him" (2 Corinthians 5:21).

"But I seem to be the same as I have always been, am I not?"

Stop and think. Is your focus on you, or on Christ? You must focus on Christ. This is about what He has done for you. God sees what Christ has done, and He sees you through Christ: "Therefore if any man be in Christ, he is a new creature: old things are passed away; behold, all things are become new" (2 Corinthians 5:17).

"Is it this easy?"

Yes it is, because this is "not of yourself, it is the gift of God" (Ephesians 2:8).

As time went by, and I became more deeply involved with them, more accustomed to their environment, and my knowledge of their language broadened, I gained with unusual clarity an insight into the nature of their sins. I couldn't stress enough the importance of teaching them to comprehend the consequences of their sin and what miserable human beings they really are.

The twelve Indian tribes, including my Alantesus, who share the Nambiquara language, were scattered throughout a vast area of nearly 33,000 square miles. Among them lived a sorcerer who visited the sick, playing a tune for them to exorcise their sickness. He also performed funeral ceremonies, taking the spirit of the deceased to a place three days away and casting it to the bottom of a cliff. All people, without exception it seems, have a religious spirit.

One day, I asked Quinto, "What does *anyaokertisu* (spirit) look like? Does it resemble a human or a monkey?"

"It looks like this," he said, stretching out his arm and pointing to its shadow on the ground as he moved it about.

That reminded me of an incident in my childhood. We lived in the country. One moonlit night, I was walking with several friends of mine. One of us looked back and saw his own shadow. "Here comes a ghost!" he yelled in terror, and we all nearly ran ourselves to death. Strange, isn't it, that these Indians, living on the other side of the world, have the same sense of "spirit," or ghost, that we had as little children in Korea? As Jesus said, "A spirit hath not flesh and bones..." (Luke 24:39); we know that spirits exist.

Let me tell you one more story:

When I was still living in South Korea, one of my Christian friends confided in me that his neighbor had invited a witch to come and perform an exorcism of some kind. A number of people had gathered to watch the spectacle, and he had joined them just for fun. The witch, having trouble performing her exorcism, stopped and complained, "There's a Christian in this crowd!" So my friend quickly got out of there.

I was happy that he had told me that, because it is evident that we Christians have the God-given power to hinder the devil and rebuke him in the name of Jesus. We don't have to scream or create a spectacle; our status as God's children is sufficient. There is no need to try to demonstrate our power. It is the Holy Spirit alone that exercises undeniable power. Elijah said, "If the LORD be God, follow him: but if Baal, then follow him…hear me, O LORD, hear me, that this people may know that thou art the LORD God, and that thou hast turned their heart back again. Then the fire of the LORD fell and consumed the burnt sacrifice…and…the people…said…The LORD, he is…God; the LORD, he is…God" (1 Kings 18:16-39).

A sorcerer, or a witch, is called *paje* in Portuguese. These pajes are gone now from the Nambiquara area. That is likely due to the missionaries' vigorous and sanctified activities throughout the region. The more powerful they seemed to be in the eyes of the people, the weaker they have proven to be in the light of the truth.

In the beginning of my activities with this Alantesu tribe, we had many visitors from neighboring tribes, and among these were pajes. On one occasion, I was awakened in the middle of the night by a jarring cacophony — an uproar coming from another hut. It was a strange, discordant sound that somehow cast a chill over the night air. I got up and crept unobtrusively into the back of the assembled crowd to observe what was going on. A woman was seated in front of the crowd and two men were performing some kind of spectacle over her. Red-eyed, perspiring profusely, frantically waving their arms and twisting their hands, they were singing wildly a dissonant duet, while all the people, under great apprehension, scarcely dared to breathe. After just a little while, the two men said, "It's over." Abruptly, they stopped what they were doing, sat down, lit up cigars, and began to make small talk with the people. They addressed me, too, apparently trying to convince me of something that I did not comprehend. I returned to my hut and lay down. Soon I heard the disturbance start again but this time much more quietly.

In John 10:34, 35, "Jesus answered them, Is it not written in your law, I said, Ye are gods? If he called them gods unto whom the word of God came, and the scripture cannot be broken...." The pajes, because of my presence, must have lost their power even though I was just sitting there doing nothing.

Whenever I cared for the sick, I would pray, holding their hand or putting my hand on their head while administering or injecting medication. I would explain to them that the good *anyaokertisu* (The Holy Spirit), which was dwelling in me (and could also be in them), would give us joy, heal our sicknesses, release us from the fear of death, liberate us from everything that would bind us, and endow us with the ultimate spiritual freedom. He was God (Portuguese: *Deus*), who had created all things in the universe. In the Nambiquara language, He is called *Tawansunne*. At the same time, I tried to make them understand that the other anyaokertisu (spirit) makes us behave immorally, kill other people, get sick, and fear everything.

The foregoing incident with the pajes was their first and last visit to my Alantesu tribe since I have been here. To this day, the practice of exorcism for the sick or the dead has completely disappeared. Although they still cry for the dead for several days, the atmosphere remains calm and comfortable. This change has come about without my effort to educate or reform them. It has occurred by itself, for which I am very grateful.

Recently, two of the tribe's children died and were buried in the middle of their yard without markers, as is their custom. One day, however, I saw that there were two little crosses standing there. Although that made me feel somewhat glad, I have restrained myself from making any comments about the crosses. Some day, though, I will make some biblical exposition on the significance of the cross; but at this point, they are probably just mimicking what they have seen in some Brazilian graveyards.

It is safe to say that Brazil is fundamentally Catholic. Unlike other Christians, they love to decorate their burial grounds with expensive paraphernalia, such as huge marble crosses or statues of the Virgin Mary to give them the appearance of cathedrals. Obviously, there is a huge difference between decorating a gravesite and serving God in the Spirit. I want my tribe to engage spiritually in true worship and to be hungry for something more nourishing to their soul and more truthful than secular or religious materialism. To nurture them in understanding this aspect of their lives is the one overriding issue that I must address in addition to all other existing issues. How do I overcome that and convert them to comprehend the spiritual reality of the intangible?

Every Christian must be aware all of the time that in this fight against the evil spirits of this world there are stumbling blocks at every corner against true evangelism, the proclamation of the Gospel. This is particularly true on the mission field.

To continue this theme, from the very beginning of my experience in the jungle with the Alantesus, there was one man among them who always stayed aloof, like a drop of oil on the surface of water. Naturally, I noticed him. It was he that always officiated at every special occasion and performed various Indian ceremonies and traditional functions: singing and dancing through the night, holding banquets, compounding drugs for the sick, or playing the bamboo clarinet (an instrument designated exclusively for men) all night long in a separate hut. Women, if they should even see the bamboo clarinet, would get sick or die. This man played the role of a paje, so to speak, and, I supposed, had negative feelings about me.

He said to me one day, "In this separate hut are several bamboo clarinets that we have made as a gift for you. Wrap them in a cloth and take them to your hut, but be careful not to show them to women."

My wife and I enjoyed twiddling with them for a while and then put them away. As we anticipated, my wife was not affected by them at all. Their tradition was nothing but a gimmick to maintain male superiority and to suppress the women—just groundless male chauvinism.

One night, my wife and I were sleeping when we heard a little commotion outside. We were no sooner awake than all of the women stormed our hut. The men were to play the bamboo clarinet that night, so they had come to hide themselves with us, far away from the separate hut where the deadly clarinet music would be played. Since privacy doesn't exist in the jungle, we gladly received them so that they could sleep securely on the ground with their babies and toddlers. I deliberately took those five clarinets down from their storage place and began to talk to the women openly.

"*Yanghaana yaki dettuchenaa itisusohri kihatnira yalutnaa,* (Come here, and look at these bamboo clarinets. The men are telling you a lie. You won't die.)"

They had never before in their lives seen the bamboo clarinets. For them, this was a first! Some of them just tittered, some were agitated but tried to remain calm, and some glanced at the clarinets and quickly turned their heads away.

"Yutta (my wife, Jae Sun's, name) has seen them, touched them, and enjoyed them very much," I told them.

I tried to use that God-given opportunity to eradicate their superstition.

Many years have passed since that incident. Now the bamboo clarinet is an antique. There are not many left, and they are seldom played by a whole group; perhaps occasionally by a couple of men. It has completely lost its power over women. The paje-like Oyu, who gave me the bamboo clarinets, used to be afraid of the story of Jesus and coldly refused to listen, but that attitude has dissipated. He is friendly with me now, even playful, but he has not yet accepted Jesus Christ as his Savior. I am praying every day to my benevolent heavenly Father to let Oyu know the gift of the Holy Spirit before his life is extinguished.

My Spiritual Battle Continues

One day, one of my tribal Indians asked me, "Can you give me a piece of paper to roll a cigar?"

"You can use that newspaper there," I told him.

"No, I need a white paper without letters on it," he insisted.

"Sorry," I said. "I don't have any."

I soon found out the reason for his insistence. In an area about 150 kilometers from where I live with the Alantesus, there is another tribe called "Galeras," among whom the missionaries of the South American Indian Mission have devoted themselves. Even though the Indians were illiterate, the missionaries had left a Bible with them, explaining that it is the Word of God, which, hopefully, they would some day be able to read. An American anthropologist named Price, who claims to be an atheist, visited the Galera tribe, ostensibly to study them. Price belittled Christianity to the Indians, showing his obvious disdain for the Gospel and touting his atheism. One day, he persuaded the chief of the tribe to tear a page from that Bible and use it to roll a cigar, explaining that the paper is so thin and soft that it would enhance the taste of his tobacco. Normally, he would have rolled his tobacco in dried corn husks, but this time, either out of curiosity or intimidation, he tore a page out of the Bible, rolled his cigar and smoked it.

Did it taste better? Did it make him feel good? Perhaps it was coincidence, but he suddenly died the next day! In the prime of his life and in good health, out of the blue, he died. This news was disseminated to all of the tribes throughout the Guapore Valley, which, as I have already stated, is an area the size of northern Florida. Using paper with printed text has become a taboo for tobacco users ever since.

Of course, Price never visited the Galera tribe again. His entrance to that tribe has been blocked and his "research" hindered.

He paid a high price for a lesson because of his atheistic behavior.

One day, Barbara, wife and coworker of one of the missionaries who had been sent to work as a translator among the Nambiquara and had been there about five years, in seeming amazement asked me, "Kim, is it possible to know the history, traditions, manners, and annual customs of a tribe after a contact of only three months? I don't understand how some people can earn a doctorate after such a brief and superficial study."

She was referring to Price, who, as an exchange professor working for the Brasilia State University had been a freeloader at Barbara's tribal house while studying the Nambiquara language and extracting all sorts of information from her about the tribe. While trafficking in the Nambiquara area, his atheistic conviction had impelled him, by cunning and craftiness, to disrupt the work of the missionaries.

"I talked to him about the Gospel every chance I got," Barbara said. "I thought he had almost reached the point of accepting Jesus. In the end, he dodged and went his way."

Generally, Western missionaries live a considerable distance from the tribal areas, with all kinds of equipment to afford them a relatively "normal" lifestyle. Generators, wells with submersible pumps, propane gas refrigerators and ranges, wireless transmitters, and perhaps a runway for their light airplane, etc., all provide a reasonable level of comfort. Normally, under the auspices of their churches or mission boards, they build in areas where law enforcement is available, in order to have security in any circumstance.

My approach to missions was quite different. As an "independent" missionary, with no title or promised support from any organization, it initially took considerable effort for me to reach out to the Indian tribes. My conviction of God's call to the work so compelled me to actively spread the message of the Gospel that I penetrated the jungle on foot to reach the Indian neighborhood, carrying my equipment in my backpack on my shoulder. Presently, I don't have my own hut; I live with them in their huts. Their living conditions are horrible: always dirty and smoky, with chickens, puppies, pigs, and fleas everywhere. At night, clouds of cockroaches cover the Indians' huts; they get inside my clothes and crawl all over my body. They sting, and they stink when they are squashed. The Indian's table is the ground and the interior of their huts is like an antiques warehouse.

Still, being eager to be acquainted with their lifestyle and to learn more about their customs, I preferred to do it this way. As a missionary to the Indians, I wanted to work through effective human relations, not according to what passes as "acceptable" missionary work. No one here has done or is doing it exclusively in this way. I had established my own unique identity. This is what caused the anthropologist Price so much pain. In his "scientific" opinion, I was a corrosive mold to the Indian culture, which, he thought, should have been preserved in its original primitive form.

But all the Indian tribes in the Guapore Valley were fond of me, and the other missionaries came to have a very high regard for me, even telling me, "You are a most inspiring visionary with your strong commitment and accomplishments."

Even FUNAI (the National Indian Foundation) acknowledged what they called my "great effort, planning, and long hours of execution." They told me, "Kim, you work differently. You have the courage to take bold steps. We are transferred so often that we don't have time to accept any challenge at a practical level, and we have so little knowledge of their language."

One day, I received a telephone call from the State Administration Indian Hospital. About ten Indians, all emergency cases, were brought in by air transportation from one of the tribes in the Guapore Valley, and they were not easy to deal with. They pulled the IVs out of their arms, refused to take any medications, throwing them away. They hit the nurses and snatched syringes from them; they even tried to run away from the hospital but were brought back. The suggestion was made that if I could come and help the nurses for just three days, it would help.

People from many different tribes, all with different languages, were brought to this hospital, so only the most experienced nurses were used for this aspect of their service, but even so, this case seemed to be beyond their control. After discussing the situation with my wife, I headed for the hospital thirty kilometers away from my house.

I had never seen these particular Indians before, but as I talked to them, they sat up and, with surprised looks on their faces, began talking to me, to each other, and to the nurses all at once. The implications were that they did not like the hospital and wanted to go back home. They would feel better, though, they indicated, and things would be easier if I would stay with them. I thought that was a reasonable solution, so every two hours a nurse accompanied me as I administered their medicines.

"He needs this syrup."

"That man needs this medication intravenously."

"This shot is for that man, intramuscularly."

I soothed them, teased them, talked nicely to them, telling them they could go home soon, all the while administering their medicines individually. I literally worked a forty-eight hour shift on two-hour intervals and, when it was over, returned home with a happy heart. Everyone was satisfied.

Solving Problems by Cooperation

Some time ago, a FUNAI official, supervisor of the general affairs in the Nambiquara area, paid a visit to our house in his Jeep. His name was Fritz Torsdorff, a German Lutheran and a naturalized

Brazilian citizen. He had escaped from Hitler's dictatorial Third Reich as a young man during World War II and was working now for the National Indian Foundation.

"I have received a call from a fazenda in the Guapore Valley," he said, "complaining that the Wanairisu Indians have injured and killed about one hundred cows with their arrows and have stolen the metal roofs from the farm buildings. Is there any way that you could go with me to resolve this issue, Kim? Please?"

Fritz was in his fifties and totally illiterate in the tribal language. The Warainisu were the Indians that we had first seen from the air — actually had flown in to — and that I had originally wanted to work with. They had been notorious for their misbehavior. The trip accompanying Fritz would be a challenging fifteen-hour Jeep ride over a very rugged dirt road.

"Okay," I said. "I'll go with you."

I saw this as an opportunity not only to deal with an additional tribe, but also to establish a symbiotic relationship with FUNAI. (Because Fritz is a German working in the Brazilian interior, he receives from the Volkswagen automobile factory in Brazil a free new car each year when he trades in the old one.)

I have been reciprocated, and the impact of Fritz's help has been enormous. With permission informally granted by Fritz, in August 1974, a group of reporters from the *Jo-Sun Il Bo*, a Korean newspaper, were allowed to penetrate deeply into the jungle to visit my Alantesu Indians. During the months of October and November of that year, they reported, in a weekly feature article, a biographical sketch from an intensive interview they had with me about my work and the result of their trip into the Amazon jungle. The series was called "Korean Missionary Sung Joon Kim: His mission to a stark-naked tribe in the Amazon Jungle." The repercussion was far reaching, impacting the entire nation of South Korea. It led to the Korean government's decision for the first time to open the doors for Koreans to go abroad, and the Korean Christian society began to change its attitude toward missions, which, until that time were virtually nonexistent. It was also a wakeup call for rank-and-file Christians to cease from their passive participation in church and become active components of the church's mission. Without Fritz's assistance, what happened could still be waiting to be implemented.

Returning to our story: when Fritz and I arrived at the fazenda, the general secretary, the other officers, and the workers were all glad to see us, but the atmosphere was grim.

These Wanairisus were the descendants of Indians who, many years ago, had killed two missionaries and thrown their bodies into the Amazon River. Since I have been working in this region, they have killed two Brazilians that I know of and one worker who was employed in the early days of the development of this fazenda. Let me digress a moment and describe these two incidents.

A father and his fifteen-year-old son used to come to this area by canoe to collect rubber seasonally. It was one full day's trip from the upper stream near Vila Bela. They would bring their rations and stay in the jungle for several months at a time. The Indians would come to their tent and demand something to eat, or they would demand coffee or sugar. If the tent was vacant, they would sneak in and steal. One day, the father stayed behind to prepare lunches and to keep an eye on the Indians while his son went out to work. At lunchtime, the son returned, hungry and ready for lunch, but his father wasn't there. Not able to find him, he began to search frantically, calling, "Dad, Dad! *Where are you?*"

Coming to a pond, he saw that the water was crimson and his father was floating face down, his body stabbed multiple times by Indian lances. The Indians must have demanded sugar, of which the father and son had exhausted their supply. Because he couldn't comply, he died. His son, distraught with grief, rushed home and reported this tragedy.

In the other account, a man used to cut trees and haul logs from this region. He must have been alone, and being somewhat niggardly, he apparently flat refused to give in to the Indians' demands and they killed him.

The fazenda worker's case had been closed with the simple notation "disappeared." However, one day my Alantesu neighborhood received a visit from the Wanairisus. They spent several days hunting with us. Among them was Bibi, a man who enjoyed all sorts of indecent talk. His eyes were always sparkling with a wild look. He talked about such things as hunting a doe and mating with it. (The Bible addresses that: "Neither shalt thou lie with any beast to defile thyself therewith: neither shall any woman stand before a beast to lie down thereto: it is confusion"– Leviticus 18:23).

Then he said, "I went to the fazenda one day and asked one of the workers for a cigarette, but he refused to give it to me. I wanted to pay him back. So several of us went back to him and told him we had come upon the tracks of a herd of wild boars. We begged him to go with us with his gun. We led him deep into the jungle, where we suddenly turned on him and clubbed him to death. We stuck his body in the hole of a giant mole that looked like a large turtle, sixty centimeters wide and forty centimeters deep."

It was a stupendously horrible, premeditated act. I didn't have the heart to relate this story to the fazenda officers. If I did, it might have made things much more complicated, and that did not seem like a solution. Besides, it had happened many years ago, and killing Indians had not been in conflict with Brazilian law. (Currently, Bibi is feeble, in his fifties, has been totally blind for the past ten years, is housebound and waiting for his final day. He "sowed the wind and is reaping the whirlwind" —Hosea 8:7.)

Fritz and I listened to all the details from the fazenda's side of the story, and then we went in search of the spot in the forest in which the Wanairisu were temporarily staying. At the entrance to the woods, in a small open field, stood a hut loosely thrown together, insufficient to provide any protection from the sun or the rain. Four families were there, including Bibi's, laughing and playing. They seemed glad to see me, and I was glad too.

"*Ya taha?* (How have you been?)," I asked.

I helped myself to some meat they had in a small basket just as though it were mine, and they offered me honeycomb wrapped in a tree leaf to suck on. Naturally, I offered a little piece to Fritz. "Here," I said. "You taste it too."

He shook his head vigorously, wincing, and making a face, indicating either that it was not clean or that he just had no taste for it.

"*Waina sohri quajatdisu rai* (You are a cultured man—I mean, a white man)," I said to Fritz. At that, the Indians burst out laughing, and we all had fun talking to each other, except for Fritz, of course, who had no idea what I had said. He couldn't understand a thing.

Bibi's wife was holding a baby who looked to be about a year and a half old. I asked Bibi, "*Wa kiraat niha?* (Is this your baby?)"

"Yes it is," he replied.

"*Itirakoh tktatirakoh dettuna tuwa* (Let me see whether you are a boy or girl)."

Its male gender being obvious, I said playfully, "I like baby boys."

"We do too," they said.

And we all had a spell of laughing. Fritz, sitting next to me, had no knowledge of our conversation or what was going on, but he looked quite satisfied, his face beaming with a smile and watching me fixedly.

Generally, when the Indians visit those in other neighborhoods, the men, sitting down in the nude, interact with each other with remarks and gestures that would seem crude in Western culture, even obscene, laughing like children, pushing and being pushed, while the wives and children laugh happily. Through such playful antics they come to familiar terms with each other.

When the preliminary niceties were over, I began to talk to Bibi about the purpose of our visit. I gave him a piece of my mind: "What you did really put me in an awkward situation, Bibi," I scolded. "I know you can't do much about those dead cows now, but it's not a good idea to go to the fazenda and bother them like that. I highly recommend that you return the metal roof material that you stole."

"Oh, the tin roofs?" he said. "They're right there on the grass."

"Well, then, let's gather them all up and stack them by the side of the road," I said, "so that the fazenda people can retrieve them."

Immediately, all of the men sprang to their feet, went across the road, scrambled to gather all the metal sheets, and stacked them by the roadside. We were satisfied with their unexpected willingness to help us. Fritz took a picture of them.

"Kim and all of you, sit down in front of my Jeep and pose for a picture." Click! It was done. We thanked them heartily and took our leave.

On the way home, we stopped at the fazenda office and told them, "Your sheets of metal roofing have been piled up by the road, so you can go and get them with your tractor now."

At that time, FUNAI only had one office at the seat of their jurisdiction and no representatives overseeing the localities. Whenever they experienced an upheaval of any sort caused by the Indians, such as we had just encountered, they inevitably solicited help from the fazenda officers or from the missionaries, which turned out favorably for the missionaries.

Anthropologists Oppose

NOW A NEWER, STRONGER ISSUE EMERGED. As missionaries had been greatly involved with the Indian tribes and closer relationships had evolved, FUNAI had been giving support to the missionaries' activities because of the benefit FUNAI got from the reciprocal working relationship that had developed. This caused the anthropologists so much pain that they viewed missionaries as adversaries.

Based on their anthropological opinions, missionaries were causative agents of the destruction of their research projects. According to them, the Indians should not be civilized at all; the possible reformation of their lifestyle, by supplying them with clothing, matches, gas lighters, knives, pots, or medicines would be detrimental to the study of anthropology. Their primitive way of making fire by rubbing sticks together should be preserved, and the Indians original medicinal substances should be applied to sick Indians. Any attempt to change their customs should be considered revolutionary and destructive.

The International Society of Anthropologists began to make a desperate effort to intervene in Brazilian policy concerning Indian affairs in order to protect the Indian tribes as "endangered species" and preserve their primitiveness, which barely continues to exist and only in the Amazon jungle.

An ominous signal that the Brazilian government's intent to limit missionary activities was looming. I had foreseen such a trend and had made plans to survive such an anti-Gospel eventuality. From the beginning, after praying, singing hymns, and studying the Bible, I had incorporated a Portuguese class into my daily routine.

To the anthropologist Price, I was a detestable fellow who paid no attention at all to what he had several times forbidden me to do. I could see what he was thinking, *How could that scrawny, insignificant, baby-faced, slant-eyed oriental, with no backing from any organization, be so obstinate and difficult to deal with? Such a pain in the neck!*

In my humble opinion, he was merely an individual scholar, just as I was an individual missionary, but I was working with a morally defensible purpose and legitimate authorization by the government. His preferences or instruction were irrelevant to my work, and there was no way that he could control me, since I was determined to stand up for the values that I had espoused.

I had examined and evaluated my work so far. While working in accordance with the "Certificate of Permission" granted to me, I had brought many things to the Indians that could be "detrimental to the preservation of their old customs": clothing, knives, pots and pans, forks and spoons, matches, lighters, scissors, nail clippers, fishing rods, flashlights, hatchets, watches, mirrors, razors, salt and pepper, canned goods, cookies and candies, toys, balls, shovels, hoes, saws, wire, nails, hammers, guitars, tens of bicycles, and scores of shotguns. Besides all that, I had purchased an eighteen-year-old Jeep just before the world oil crisis in the 1970s, brought it in to the Indians, and taught them how to drive it. It would have been logical for Price to conclude that I was an abominable villain who, by greatly disturbing the Indians' lifestyle, had ruined his research material along with his career.

However, here is logic: If the intent of the anthropologists was to keep the Indians as primitive as they have always been, they themselves should not have intruded upon the tribes. Just contacting them in itself would have been immediately harmful to them, putting them on their guard, inducing psychological stress by taking their pictures, offering them cigarettes and lighting them with a lighter, and trying to communicate with words they could not possibly comprehend. The anthropologists had been exercising a corrosive influence upon their primitiveness by giving the Indians the hope of acquiring more and better "stuff" while at the same time withholding it from them. Furthermore, they acted as carriers of diseases from their civilized society to the Indians' remote domain, where victims were then kept isolated from the necessary cures.

The anthropologist believes that the Indian living in the jungle is an evolving species. If their intent is to stop the process of evolution and maintain the status quo, their efforts have very little significance. On the other hand, if they would develop a real scenario and isolate a monkey, experiment with various feeding and environmental conditions, establish the results with electronic data, and release the estimated time that a human being would emerge from the door of the cage, *that* would be an impressive study—a guaranteed Nobel Prize winner in the field of research! However, to obtain a doctorate degree, as Price had done, by submitting a dissertation composed from secondhand information squeezed out of missionaries who had already invested much energy to influence and alter the Indians' lifestyle, was inaccurate, plagiaristic, and hypocritical.

The purpose of the missionaries and their perspective on the Indian tribes is altogether different from that of the anthropologists. Whereas the anthropologist sees them as merely evolving animals to be studied, the Scriptures say they are descendants of Adam, created by God in His own image. They happened to settle down in the tropics, where they live in blissful ignorance and total isolation, without clothes and with little knowledge of other human beings.

Except for their environment, however, the Indians are of the same human race as we, the sons of Adam.

"And the LORD God commanded the man, saying,... but of the tree of the knowledge of good and evil, thou shalt not eat of it: for in the day that thou eatest thereof, thou shalt surely die" (Genesis 2:16, 17). Did Adam and Eve die that day? Physically, no. "The woman did eat...and he did eat. And the eyes of them both were opened, and they knew that they were naked...and [they] hid themselves from the presence of the LORD God...God called unto Adam, Where art thou? And he said, I heard thy voice in the garden, and I was afraid, because I was naked; and I hid myself" (Genesis 3:6-10).

God had said, "You shall die." Did Adam and Eve really die? Yes, to God. When their eyes were opened to evil, they became afraid of God. Their relationship to God was broken and their trust destroyed. Yes, they had died to God; they were driven out of the Garden and cursed, along with the serpent, because of their disobedience. You and I, the Indians, the anthropologists, the animal scientists, and everyone else are all cursed children of Adam, children of disobedience.

God wants to recover that broken relationship. He wants us to return and not be afraid of Him any more. He wants us to be His children, to dwell in His kingdom in purity. God has a plan to accomplish that, and His purpose shall be accomplished. This is the primary motivation in my working with this Indian tribe.

Price's anti-Gospel campaign continued. He picked one of his college students as his protégé and helped him to gain employment with FUNAI as a patrol officer in the Indian neighborhoods throughout the Guapore Valley. This young man, Silveni, tried to demonstrate a particularly generous spirit to the Indians every time he patrolled my Alantesu neighborhood. His ulterior motive was to sow dissention between me and my Indians. They told me, "Quinna

(Kim), when you were not here, Silveni came in and told us that God does not exist; there is no such thing. And he said, 'you don't have to learn to read.'"

Silveni threw down the gauntlet to me. He challenged me very directly, "Kim, you don't have to teach them how to drive. What if they have an accident and someone gets killed — will you be responsible for it? Are you going to buy them an airplane if they ask for it, and teach them to fly, too?"

"Look, Silveni! FUNAI may be just the thing for you. If you have a complaint against me, you'd better submit it in writing. Meanwhile, yes, I'll be responsible for their car accident. Yes, I would buy them an airplane, and yes, I would teach them how to fly. So don't worry yourself. You and I are of a different lineage."

It was a tremendous issue to have to deal with: me on one side, and an ever-broadening government on the other. Would that impact my confidence level? No, I had every confidence that my God would show me a viable solution on behalf of everyone involved, including Silveni.

On one occasion, I was suffering from malaria, too sick and weak to get home. Out of kindness to me, the folks at the nearest fazenda were treating me. At just that time, Price dropped by on his way to my Indian neighborhood and saw me lying in the hot sun, shivering under several blankets. My jaundiced face was yellow. The look of exultation evident on his face seemed to say, "Well, you got what you deserve, working in the jungle. Why don't you just die?" But he held his tongue, not saying a word.

I wanted to test his intention, so I said, "Being this sick, I don't think I can work with the Indians anymore."

Obviously, that was music to his ears! His prompt reply did not conceal the delight his evil spirit seemed to express, hoping that his wish was coming true.

"Oh, is that right? That's a good decision," he said. "I think it's very good. Your health is far more important than anything else. Very good decision!"

He was aware that throughout the Nambiquara region of the Guapore Valley, my Alantesu Indians were emerging as the model tribe for being violence-free toward white people or any fazenda workers and for being harmonious with other tribes and neighborhoods. They had shown great potential to be civilized quickly, which raised a huge threat to Price. For him, the Alantesu area became, strategically, the most critical point in his desperate fight to bring the work of the mission to a halt — and for me, it was just as critical that I defend this mission to the end, while bringing them along to a place of spirituality. It was going to be an incredible war. I had an idea that the society of anthropologists would come up with a strategy.

One day, as I was taking a break at home after returning from the jungle, Price visited me. I wondered how he had found me, living here with no electricity, no city water, in completely indigent, rustic seclusion. He must have been a smart man with plenty of cheek.

"Kim," he said, "I need your assistance."

He unrolled the map he carried in his hand and continued, "This is an ideal project. You see, if we gather the five tribes from the Guapore Valley and put them all together in one reservation on this plateau, it would facilitate controlling them and resolve some of the problems. [This would be comparable to gathering five tribes living in Jacksonville, Tallahassee, Tampa, Leesburg, and Daytona Beach and placing them in Orlando.] And we will designate that reservation as a national park, with an abundance of game animals so that they can maintain their primitive tribal life in a controlled setting. So, if your 'model' Alantesu tribe would initiate it, the other tribes would gradually follow suit. With our collaborative effort, this great 'Guapore Project' can be a success!"

I was stunned by the absurdity of the proposal. Dealing with Indians was one thing; arbitrarily moving them to a strange location two hundred kilometers away from their homes, without any preliminary study, would be quite another. It would incur an additional level of complexity. To me, that project was a mere daydream and obviously not going to be implemented.

Furthermore, the proposed area, which I had seen one time from the airplane, resembled an Arizona mesa—nothing more than a high, flat, riverless expanse. They could dig wells, plant trees, raise rabbits or goats in the long run, but could they raise Indians there? Could the Indians possibly adapt to life on that plateau and survive? From there, any place that would afford hunting or fishing would be too remote. The project would absolutely be a failure in every respect. The anthropologists, who wanted to preserve the Indians' natural life and study it, were the very ones who were proposing to destroy their natural environment. How about that! No matter how hard they might make it for me, or how dire the consequences, I would never feel any inclination to surrender my Indians to those anthropological atheists.

I replied to him politely, "That's a fabulous idea, but why did you think you could convince me that this proposal could succeed? Didn't you foresee that as a problem? Even if I were convinced that that would be the best solution, I'm in no position to commit to it so quickly. I would have to insist upon your discussing it with the missionaries from the South American Indian Mission and from the German Mission first."

Tension had been kindled, and Price left provoked, with a disappointed, unpleasant expression on his face.

This tension between us was not a new occurrence. Five years after I began working with the Alantesu, Price had begun to visit this Nambiquara area (the size of Northern Florida), mainly in the highlands beyond the valley, where the translation mission was

actively engaged. At that time, Fritz, the only FUNAI regional officer, was patrolling this area occasionally and supporting missionary
activity. Price, however, as an anthropologist, had a great interest in
the Nambiquara. He urged FUNAI to protect these primitive tribes
by limiting missionary activity in the region. This had created a
cold war between him and me. From the day we met, we had been
provoking one another. When I rejected his great "Guapore Project,"
it became obvious that he would have to change his approach and
come up with another scheme to retaliate.

My theory about anthropology is dictated by the Bible: it starts
at Adam and ends with Jesus. The anthropology that Price has been
studying begins with a monkey, ignores Adam, and ends with Price
himself. Beyond that point, there's nothing. When it's over, it's over
forever. Being born as a sinner and conducting research on other sinners who are naked sons of the original sinner takes them nowhere
and provides no answers or benefits for any of them.

The thesis of God's anthropology is the Bible. Its conclusion
has been presented to us with undeniable authenticity that we
can't challenge. We have to accept Jesus as our Mediator. Thus, the
true God of anthropology will fill our lives with ineffable blessing
for eternity. It is God's plan to give us genuine happiness in this
world by giving us a new revelation of truth, which most assuredly
includes heaven.

Several months had passed since Price's visit to my home. The
weather had changed, and the rainy season had set in. I was returning home after my usual month-long stay with the Indians. Suddenly, a group of naked Indians came into my view. Out here on the
highway! How can that be? I slowed down and finally stopped my
car by the roadside to get a closer look. It was the tiny "Waikisu"
tribe, the smallest in number of all the tribes in the Guapore Valley.
That straggling line of naked Indian men with full frontal exposure,

their dirty faces expressionless, carrying their bundles of arrows on their shoulders, looked neither left nor right but stared only at the ground directly before them as they trudged wearily along. They resembled a remnant of defeated troops fleeing in humiliation some distant battle field. Following forlornly behind them was a band of women carrying baskets.

Though this may have seemed natural to the anthropologists, to me it was inhuman, immoral treatment to allow these men and women to walk naked in heavy traffic, exposed to trucks and buses, on a dusty interstate thoroughfare. Looking at this spectacle, I personally felt humiliated and mortified. In the jungle, these Indians had been naturally beautiful, but on the street, no! The jungle had provided them a sanctuary. After ten or so Indians had passed, following the group in a shabby outfit came the skinny anthropologist Price, stony faced and looking straight ahead. At the end of this sad column came a new 4x4 pickup truck loaded with children, luggage, and the invalids. The driver was Silveni, Price's protégé and now the FUNAI officer. On the door of the truck, the logo read, "Guapore Project."

They must have pushed the project through, with the government budgeting whatever was calculated to be necessary for its implementation; but the result had fallen far short of their expectation. Had they not understood the impossibility of that project? Now they were pitiably returning home. So far, they had two-hundred kilometers behind them and still had one hundred to go. It has been raining; now it's cloudy, I thought to myself. They are very fortunate today. Otherwise this area is a wilderness of nothing but scorching tropical sun. They should have a sense of gratitude to God, creator of those anthropologists' ancestors.

The grandiose Guapore Project, executed with ambition and bad judgment, had been branded a colossal failure, and the damage was historic. Price went back to America for good, after abdicating his powerful post in favor of his protégé. But his tricks were not over; he would exercise control from a distance. We missionaries understood that mission work and evangelism among the tribes would be a continuous spiritual warfare. Not long after Price's departure, Silveni, filling the dual roles of anthropology student and officer of FUNAI, showed us something about bureaucratic self-righteousness by harassing us in every aspect of our work.

I taught my Indians to work and to learn what civilized people do: "In the event that you visit the nearby fazenda, do not beg or bother the people there. Do not watch them eat at mealtimes in order to get free food. Instead, help them do their chores, such as sweeping the yard, weeding their gardens, chopping wood, etc."

The fazenda people considered this a proper education. My Indians have learned horseback riding to help the cowboys, have ridden on the fazenda's trucks and farm tractors to observe and learn their work; they have caught fish to exchange for bread, and exchanged game animals for sugar. All in all, they have established a good rapport with thirty-some fazenda workers, their families, and their managers, the fazendas' officers.

My Indians, who had lived with no sense of time, of responsibility, of order, or of regulation, required a considerable amount of social discipline and experience in order to adapt to civilization. Due to the continual expansion of fazendas in number and in size, knowing how to live in a civilized setting would soon be a prerequisite to their survival. One fazenda often covers as much area as two counties put together. On those premises, they have all sorts of heavy equipment, lumber mills, airplanes, and runways, etc. The proprietors of these settlements are entrepreneurs from several major cities in the southern coastal area. They receive industrial tax exemptions to encourage the development of enterprise as long as they reinvest an amount equal to those exemptions in further development. The enlargement of these proliferating fazendas will inevitably shrink the Indians' hunting grounds and press the tribes into confinement and eventually to extinction.

Game animals had diminished in number, and the Indians had to go further to hunt. At times, they would return empty-handed despite hunting all day long. Arrows had become inadequate, and I had to introduce guns and teach them how to use them. Even FUNAI had realized the changing situation and had come to the Indians' assistance. It was time to gain new insight and take the Indians' future into consideration — time to turn the page, to let them learn and advance to the next stage at the nearby fazenda. It was time now to meet their educational needs. Confining them like monkeys and treating them as objects to study would have been cruel and harsh punishment for them. If they were humans, they had rights! Those rights were not granted by other humans; they are inherent. The Indians, too, had the right to rise to their God-given potential.

Silveni, however, had applied a blind eye to this new trend. His total negation of the Indians' needs was ridiculous: "You don't have to learn to read; you don't have to work; the government will protect you; don't go to the fazenda (although it is only six kilometers away). Don't make contact with civilized people," he told them. "You will catch their diseases."

As if that were not enough, he would visit the fazendas and, as a government officer of FUNAI, would order them, "When the Indians come, send them away immediately. Don't give them anything — no food, no work, no rides; don't be friendly with them at all."

Some of the fazenda people were unhappy with him and irritated because he had been interfering in things that were none of his business. It had been rumored that he would be put out of the way. He was aware of that, of course, and was armed at all times, like everyone else in this lawless jungle.

Some of the other missionaries were getting along all right with Silveni. Those were the ones whose approach to their work was cautious enough to focus only on the regulations written on the "Certificates of Permission," and cautious enough, also, to reside full time far from the tribes they had been working with. My major difference is that I am more down to earth, and my approach to the work is different, based on my interpretation of the "Certificate." What is the real purpose of issuing the Certificate? Wasn't it to allow us to reach the Indians? Wasn't it so that we could do the greater good? By it, I have the ability to practice what I believe, and the essence of that is commitment.

The Guapore Valley, in particular, was a tense battlefield. There was a mysterious four-way war in progress between FUNAI, the anthropologists, the fazendas, and the missionaries. If you worked at all, you ran into unavoidable conflict with someone. My choice was clear: *I'm a soldier enlisted by God.* "For unto us a child is born, unto us a Son is given; and the government shall be upon his shoulder, and his name shall be called Wonderful, Counsellor, The mighty God, The everlasting Father, The Prince of Peace" (Isaiah 9:6). It seemed that I had been caught in a terrible dilemma, but in truth I enjoyed a heavenly peace bestowed upon me by the Prince of Peace, even as I was engaged in the fiercest of spiritual battles with the forces that oppose His government.

In this small battlefield, I had been under a dual attack. The battle was so relentless and the strikes so severe that I felt my resilience drained. I had struggled with all my might and the depletion of all of my resources to acquire building materials with which to build a church and a school in the Alantesu neighborhood. I had scarcely finished the almost impossible task of carrying it all in (lumber, metal roofing, etc.), when FUNAI confronted me with a new development.

"You can't build a modern building in the Indian territory.

Take all that stuff out of there. FUNAI is planning to build a school and send teachers in; until then, you are forbidden to teach the Indians. If any of them are sick, you, as an individual missionary, will not be allowed to take them to a hospital. FUNAI will do it."

I had no choice but to go to the fazenda and ask for help to retrieve all of those building materials. On the way out, I "lost it," as the saying goes. I could not have controlled my emotions to save my soul. The heavy weight of mortification brought forth unstoppable tears; I was inconsolable. The truck driver, Ito, tried to sympathize with me, saying, "What a ridiculous policy that is! It's unreal. It's destructive."

My Indians were not at all pleased, either. They reacted in total silence. I told Quinto, "Quinto, just let everything lie for a while, at least for several days, then go and ask Ito to help you bring all that stuff back again. You use it to build your own house instead of the hut you live in."

Silveni would think that this, too, was a mote in my eye, but it would be a real bombshell to him if he misused his bureaucratic power directly toward the Indians, because they would get even with him.

For FUNAI, victory was now within their reach. All they had to do was to block me from going into the Indian area altogether. It seemed that FUNAI was controlled by some distant entity with diverse connections.

Several months passed. Silveni was promoted to the central headquarters in Brasilia, the capital. From his new position, he would be empowered to impose his bureaucracy upon every tribe in Brazil, not just the Guapore Valley. Surprisingly, one year later he died in some unfortunate and unexplained incident.

Although Silveni had received a copy of the Bible from me early on, he and I had remained perennial adversaries. He had many opportunities to hear the Gospel from Missionary Edward of the

South American Indian Mission. Also, Missionary Gustavo of the German Mission used to give him many airplane rides and witness to him. But Silveni remained a might-have-been. He should have known that any sin would be forgiven him except his sin against the Holy Spirit and to reject the inspiration to do good.

—⟳—

Off Limits to Missionaries

THINGS WERE UNEVENTFUL FOR A WHILE. Then, as I had anticipated, in 1978, when my work seemed to be at its apex, all missionaries, and particularly those working in the Nambi-quara area, where Price had exercised so much influence, received an order from FUNAI that all Indian tribes were now "Off-limits." No reason was stated, but it was obvious that I would no longer have free access to my tribe.

Satan was apparently working furiously. All missionaries from the translation mission, the South American Indian Mission, the German Mission, and I, as an independent missionary, vacated the jungle tribal area. Some had left to go back to their homeland for good.

Soon after that, FUNAI employees were sent to every tribe to take up residence. They began their work in earnest and, using solar power to charge their batteries, established wireless connection with their headquarters. As the Korean proverb says, "A leper is the first to cross over when the new bridge is built." The missionaries had made the first move into the jungle seeking to contact unreached Indian tribes. They had risked losing their lives to break new ground and were now ready to perform rigorous and effective work. FUNAI had stepped in and exercised government authority to take over. Furthermore, the international anthropologists appear to be managing it.

Being at the center of this storm and completely dislocated indefinitely, I was troubled by inestimable emotional pain; this had become a huge problem. I knew that I couldn't resolve the problem by complaining about it, and I had too much work to do to allow myself to be distracted by it. I have never been big on quitting, and I didn't have a moment to lose. I would step back a bit and then move forward in prayer.

I didn't need to spend time wondering about the current situation; it was clear that FUNAI had launched this latest attack on the missionaries because of pressure from the society of anthropologists. As a result, the missionaries were in full retreat from their jungle posts. The translation mission remained in the urban areas and continued its work with the help of Indians who were allowed out by temporary permission. Part of the South American Indian Mission moved south to merge with an institution that had established a Bible school for Indians when government control had been relatively light. The German Mission had opened an elementary school by recruiting a Brazilian preacher and his wife to teach there unofficially. They were members of a Brazilian Pentecostal church near the tribal area and, as Brazilian citizens, had a definite advantage in case of any conflict with the government about regulations.

During this turbulent period, I had been thinking about my Indians continuously, "24/7," for over three months. I could stand it no longer. I made up my mind to sneak into the jungle to see how my friends were doing and to learn how FUNAI would react to my visit. For many years, I had spent one month with the Indians and one month at home. That had become my regular routine, but now I felt nervous preparing for this trip. After so many months, it seemed awkward — as if it had been several years since

I was there.

The moment I arrived in their neighborhood, the women and children acted as if I had been resurrected. They were so glad to see me! But the men all pushed me away angrily, saying things like, "Get away! Go away! Who told you to come here? What are you here for anyway?"

It meant that they had grown tired of waiting for me.

I responded to their charade, "Why are you pushing me? I can't go away. I don't want to go away!" And then, "Give me something to eat; I'm hungry!"

With that, we all laughed and were truly glad to see each other again, reminiscing together about "the good old days."

I explained to them that FUNAI had expelled all missionaries and ordered the jungle off-limits. "I can't come in here anymore. FUNAI employees will work here from now on."

"FUNAI is here already," they complained, glancing toward a tiny clinic building that had been erected since my last visit. Their dejection was evident by the sour expressions displayed on their faces. There at the clinic was the FUNAI officer in charge, a woman who was also a nurse.

Approaching her, I said, "Hello, I'm Sung Joon Kim, the missionary who has been working here from the beginning. I would like to stay here and visit for a week."

"No," she said abruptly. "You cannot stay that long...but let me check."

After contacting her headquarters, she said, "You may stay for two days. After that, on your way back you must report to FUNAI. The branch manager is expecting you."

"I will do that," I replied. "Thank you."

I was not at all happy about that, but what could I do? The spiritual war would continue, and I knew God would fight for me.

The day I was leaving, I felt sad, not knowing when I would

ever be back to see them again. As for the nurse, I deliberately wrote her name in large letters on the edges of the pages of a closed Portuguese Bible and gave it to her as a gift.

"Oh, thank you so much," she responded warmly. "I know there will be a school and teachers here in the near future, but in the meantime, it is so lonely, so isolated, in this jungle, with no one to speak Portuguese to and nothing to read. I was hoping for something to read, even a Bible. Thank you. Thank you so much!"

She seemed almost crushed. I realized how hungry she was for a Bible. At first she had been so cold and businesslike, but now she was probably regretting that she had contacted her headquarters instead of just allowing me to stay for seven days.

Giving Bibles away has been a major part of my ministry ever since I came to Brazil. I have given out many copies to people at filling stations, restaurants, and, on my long-distance trips, at check points along the way—and I have always received quite positive feedback from the recipients. Whenever I could afford it, I would place a large order with the Bible Hall for hundreds of copies and get an almost 50 percent discount. I never left on a trip without several copies of the Bible. I sincerely hope to deliver at least 100,000 copies before I die to the indigent people living in total isolation along the highways or in the deep interior of this vast and vacant country so that they, too, might trust in God.

Sadly, I left my Indians, being still very much attached to them. My next stop would be a visit to the FUNAI branch located in a small newly established city two hundred kilometers further from my home toward the equator. I was anxious to find out what trick Satan had contrived this time. When I arrived at the office, ten employees were busily taking care of their office duties. After a short wait, I was ushered into the office of the branch manager, whom they addressed as "Sergeant."

Brazil has been a country without gun control. Arming

FUNAI has made it more effective as part of the State Department in dealing with the Indians in the controlled jungle areas. Still, interviewing me with a fully loaded gun on his desk was an insult. It suggested that I might be a dangerous criminal. Had he pointed it at me, I would not have blinked an eye. I wanted badly to say, "Could you put that gun away while you talk to me?" but I bit my tongue and said instead, "I'm Sung Joon Kim. I understand that you have been expecting me."

"Oh, yes," he replied. "I have heard a lot about you and have wanted to meet you."

We shook hands with one another. Suddenly, he sternly said, "Kim, why did you go into the Indian area at this time? That is illegal! Why did you not ask permission beforehand?"

"Is it illegal for a father to visit his son?" I bristled. "That's not a legal issue. You don't have a case. I haven't visited them for months and without any explanation as to why. Aren't I at least entitled to let them understand why I haven't come? All of a sudden, without warning or reason, you ordered us out of the jungle and made it off-limits without giving us any chance whatsoever to explain anything or make arrangements. I delivered a lot of humanitarian aid to them, just as I have done in the past. Is that also illegal? Did I do anything wrong during the two days I was in there?"

I didn't want to make any apologies for my so-called illegal entry. I chose rather to confront FUNAI with justification of my action.

"Regardless," he said, "from now on you are prohibited from going there for any reason."

"That's fine. This time I went there to bid farewell to my Indians, and that's what I did."

I was on my way home now. Driving back alone over those nine hundred kilometers to where my sweet wife was waiting (often in prayer, enduring unrelenting loneliness in this strange foreign county), I worshiped God, reminiscing of my wonderful salvation even at this extraordinary time when it seemed that Satan had been able to block my work. I marveled, with spontaneous tears, that my heart was still filled to overflowing with thankfulness and genuine love for God! *Dear God, wherever you may lead me, you are my Shepherd. Thank you. Thank you so much!*

I took several days of rest, forgetting about everything for a while, as if I were on a long vacation. I felt physically refreshed, but now there was the need to be spiritually replenished. In fact, there was a lot of work to do, and I felt a great spiritual responsibility. What would be the very first thing the Lord would have me do? What is my plan of action? Come on, no doubt there is more to be done.

I knew, of course, that the church my wife and I were attending—a Brazilian branch of the European Moravian Church—could use more of our help. Still, when I closed my eyes, millions of sentiments and emotions competed with one another. I have not been disabled by not being able to work with the Indians anymore, I told myself. Such thoughts, however, constituted only a brief respite from my fury. This would be only the beginning. The impact that this was having on me made me more determined than ever to keep up the offensive, but passively, while living in this constant spiritual struggle. At this point, my mission would be to contend with one situation after another. God will give me the strength to work through anything.

The Lord seemed to be reminding me of the state of my faith eight years earlier, when my mission to the Indians had first begun. My daily routine in the jungle had included praying before dawn, reading the Bible at sunrise, living with the Indians, and learning their language throughout the day. At night I would sit in the yard with them, singing and teaching them hymns. The same routine would be repeated the next day, and the next, for a month.

Upon returning home, in addition to that same daily routine, I worked for our church and studied Portuguese. About a year had passed this way when I began to feel that my spiritual life was somehow becoming mundane. I couldn't understand this spiritual downturn, since everything around me seemed fine. I was spending a month in the jungle and then, during my month at home, I delivered sermons at church, taught Sunday school, listened to the preaching of others, studied my Bible, and worshiped in my home. I was doing everything a born-again person and a Christian worker is supposed to do. But something was missing. Should I back up and take a new approach in order to revive my intensity? Was there a reason for this spiritual stagnation? It was not clear to me where I was at spiritually. I longed to deepen my faith.

One day, when I was in the Word meditating on the Lord, something came to me like a drop of cold water on my forehead, alerting me: *You are neglecting evangelism.*

Yes, that was the answer! Until then, I had been on the *defensive*. I needed to go on the *offensive*, emphasize and train my skills to take victory over the enemy in this spiritual war, and maintain a vibrant and growing faith. So, what would my strategy be? What action would I take?

The following Sunday, I attended the morning service, had lunch at home afterward, took a break, as is customary in the tropics, and then made a visit, carrying just my Bible, to the only prison in the area. This was the first time I had attempted to evangelize alone in Brazil (Jesus had sent his disciples out two by two). The prison was built Mexican style. The building itself also constituted the fence, being built around the perimeter of a large yard in the center, with one opening for a gate.

As I approached the gate, the guard wondered what business

might be bringing this "Japanese" man to this place. "Sir," he said, "what is your business?"

"I would like to preach the Gospel to the prisoners," I answered.

"All by yourself?" he said, looking surprised.

"Why not? May I?" I asked.

"Well, if you like...."

The guard opened the iron gate for me and I went in. The yard looked spacious; a single tree stood in the center, with possibly ten prisoners lounging idly beneath it. The door to each of the surrounding rooms faced the courtyard, and all of them were standing open. About three hundred prisoners were in the place. Most of them were napping, while others were playing soccer in the hot sun. I hesitated briefly, not knowing how or where to begin under these circumstances. As I stood there pondering the situation, one of the men under the tree called with a loud voice, "Japonese (Japanese) guy, you must have come to worship! Let me gather some people for you."

He went from room to room, shouting to wake them up and ordering them to come out. But nobody came. It was simply too hot, and they were too sleepy. The soccer players were not interested. But the number of men under the tree was enough for me.

I started by saying, "I have been in Brazil for less than two years, and my Portuguese is not very good. I know that when we preach, we usually sing hymns and pray first, but I don't have any hymns memorized, and I can't pray very well either. So let me just read to you from Matthew twenty-four: 'Jesus left the temple and was going away...and what will be the sign of your coming and the end of the age?...for false Christs and false prophets shall arise and show great signs and wonders...heaven and earth shall pass away, but my words will not pass away... then two men shall be in the field; one will be taken and the other left…there will be weeping and gnashing of teeth.'"

After reading the whole chapter about Jesus coming back, I made a few short comments and said, "I am so glad to meet you all and I hope to see you again next week."

I was pleased that the procedure for entering the prison was so simple: no ID, no body search, and the prisoners had greeted me with a comfortable, nonjudgmental attitude. I came home elated. I was encouraged by this incentive to spiritual vibrancy but also feeling a bit sorry about the fact that I could not achieve what I wanted to because of my deficiency in the language. Even so, it was a moving experience. I had intended to start them on a journey through the Scriptures. Well, I decided, I'm going to have someone else accompany me next week.

Our church was pioneered by another German mission just a few years ago and consisted of only a few families. Each of them had nine or ten children, which made us rich in small children. We were poor, however, in young adults. Originally, two German nurses had voluntarily started a free clinic; from that work the church had developed. Consequently, we had an excellent supply of medicines from Germany. On one occasion I was able to administer Streptomycin (a patented antibiotic, which, at that time, was hard to find in Brazil) to the youngster living next door to our house who had been suffering from tuberculosis. He recovered completely after receiving injections for a couple of weeks. I was happy for such opportunities, but my desire was for evangelism.

That was the situation in our church: many children but no adult workers to accompany me. I pondered this situation for several days and then decided to visit a young Brazilian preacher who had been supported by a Swiss mission. He had graduated from a Bible school in Brazil run by WEC Mission. He lived in another neighborhood, but I was well acquainted with him.

"Hello, Mailton," I greeted him. "Would you be interested in evangelizing with me in the prison next week?"

"Oh really?" he said, "Wow, is there a prison here? Can we go inside? Kim, I would love to go with you! It will be a tremendous opportunity to preach the Gospel."

Late the next Sunday afternoon, which was much cooler than it had been the previous week, the two of us visited the prison. A different guard was at the gate, but he let us pass without a problem. There were more prisoners idling under the tree than there had been last week, and some of them looked sincerely happy to see me again.

"Hello, everyone," I began. "I would like to introduce you to my friend Mailton. He is a preacher."

As soon a Mailton stepped out in front of them, he began shouting loudly, "Hallelujah, hallelujah. Oh! Haalleuu…jah!" And he continued, preaching nonstop for about forty minutes, not once quoting from the Bible but occasionally punctuating his sentences with "O God. Oh, dear God. O God," as though receiving a personal blessing, and finally finishing in earnest prayer, "Amen, amen amen and aa-menn!" It was indeed a hot sermon, in keeping with the tropical temperature. They received it well. Everyone seemed glad, and we returned home praising God after having practiced our offensive move. Upon arriving home, though, as I thought about the afternoon, I felt somewhat deficient. It seemed obvious that I had not participated in the fight; I had just provided an opportunity for others to do so, although I suppose that wasn't such a bad thing….

One thing I had observed in our church was that everyone had natural musical talent. Although they had little opportunity to cultivate their music at school, when they sang hymns in church, everyone sang parts according to their pitch: soprano, alto, tenor, and bass; and they did so without urging or hesitation. They were good! Their harmony was very pleasing. When I was in a choir back in Korea, we used to practice all of our parts separately, over and over again, and we would still be worried that we might make mistakes. But here at our church, when there was melody, there were four parts naturally. For example, when those singing the melody sang, "As Jesus is beside me...," those singing the other parts beat the time, "...beside me..." in rhythm. Their music was not written — only the words were written, and the melodies had been handed down by word of mouth. I was impressed with the fact that the music seemed to originate within the singers.

The children, too, were good at playing the guitar without being instructed by anyone, just from listening to others play. In Brazil, the guitar is a very popular and convenient instrument in almost every local church. In my student days in South Korea, my mother allowed only two kinds of music: hymns and the songs our school taught us. She tried to keep us as far away from anything secular as she possibly could. For me to learn pop songs, which belonged to the street, was out of the question. Guitars were associated with pop songs, street music; therefore, guitar playing was forbidden in our home. Now, on the mission field, I regretted the lost opportunity to have learned to play the guitar when I was young.

Seeing their musical talent gave me the idea to form a children's choir. Within one week, we had a twelve-child choir, prepared with several evangelistic hymns, and we were ready. At seven o'clock one Saturday night, I took them in my Volkswagen van to the prison, where we found several guards posted at the dimly lit gate. They were surprised to see this group of children exiting the van and converging upon them.

"What's happening here?" one of the guards asked.

"We came here to evangelize," I announced.

"At night? No way. Not at night," said the guard.

"Well, then," I suggested, "perhaps we could just sing a few hymns right here without going inside."

"No, you may not. Everyone is in his room now."

I took a peek inside, and, sure enough, it was dark and the yard was deserted. Reluctantly, we turned around and left. On the way home, we drove to a small park located near a river that runs through the suburbs of the city of Cuiaba'. Once the rainy season arrives (between November and May), this area comes alive with a lot of traffic on this river that flows from Bolivia through Paraguay, Argentina, and finally to the South Atlantic Ocean.

I lined my children up in two rows in the middle of the park, instructed them to sing three renditions consecutively, and stepped into the crowd to assess the response. Standing on the street in public for the first time, they looked a little shy. I encouraged them with a big smile and, looking at me, they performed amazingly well! I noticed, though, how shabby they all looked — like a bunch of war orphans. *It's imperative that I improve their appearance,* I thought.

When they finished singing, I stepped out in front of the crowd.

"Thank you so much for listening," I said. "As you just heard, are we not what we are before God? We are sinners before God. But God loves us so much that he sent His Son to be our Redeemer. Accept Him! Show Him your repentance and total surrender. God always blesses those who place their trust in Him. Here are some Gospel tracts for you." I delivered a tract to each one, and my little choir sang two more hymns before we said "Goodnight" to everyone.

Most working people there enjoyed leisurely weekend evenings outdoors until late. This allowed my choir, after they had finished their homework, to sing to large crowds in the evening. There were a great number of places where beer was sold. We visited these bars and sang evangelistic hymns. Some in the crowd responded by drinking a toast to us or cheering heartily or saying, "Come join us for a beer!" The barkeepers did not seem opposed to our coming. The bar girls listened to our hymns all the way through. Some of them said, "Don't you feel ashamed, singing in a place like this?" No, my children didn't feel ashamed at all; they felt glad to be singing and believed it was what God wanted them to do.

We routinely visited several bars on a Saturday night. I would buy each choir member a cold Coca-Cola to encourage them. They looked good, so bright and clean in the uniforms that they now wore. The barkeepers never refused when I asked if they would like to listen to these children singing hymns. As soon as the children began to play their guitars, the bartenders would turn down the music in their establishments, the patrons would try to sit up straight, button their shirts, and listen to the words of the hymns. The majority of Brazilians were pious Catholics, who tried to show respect for religion. They would listen as the children sang:

> When you come to the end of life's labors,
> When death comes to stand by your side,
> What end will your destiny favor?
> In what home will your soul then reside?
>
> Today a choice you are given
> Life or death; which one will you choose?
> Jesus Christ wants to free you for heaven.
> Tomorrow your life you may lose.
>
> You search for peace in this world
> In pleasures that pass like a breath;
> But then they will not satisfy you
> In that final hour of your death.
>
> After you've toiled for your living
> You will reach the forked road at the end
> Death or eternal living;
> What will your choice be, my friend?

This hymn was sung sadly, beautifully expressing the Father's concern. Some barkeepers would give candy to each of my twelve children in appreciation, saying, "Come back, kids, you hear?" Some guests, having put their beer bottles down, applauded thunderously. Others would ask, "What church did you come from?" Then we would deliver our Gospel flyers to them and leave. On our way home in the van on those Saturday nights, we'd give thanks to God. "Thank you, Lord, for filling our hands and our hearts with blessings. Praise the Lord O my soul! Let the work of your kingdom be accomplished."

23
Treasures Temporal and Eternal

METAPHORICALLY, many believers in the homeland may think of the mission field as a greenhouse bringing forth new tender plants, which they help, by giving and prayer, to maintain. In reality, for those sent out, it would be the opposite. The missionaries have been called out of the greenhouse and planted as individual plants in a field, where they experience exposure to the severest of weather: droughts, storms, conditions frigid and steamy — a whole different spiritual reality. They must survive the ordeal of trials, pain, suffering, and disappointment, while, at the same time, discovering the most remarkable hidden spiritual treasures. Here, in a real sense, you are on your own. You have the opportunity to learn to endure and to grow and to propagate. Now I am crossing a bridge; it's a one way bridge: nothing will distract me. It is said that Rome was not built in a day; neither will the work of mission be instantaneous.

Even though the mission to the Indians had been made off-limits, I was now busy with my children's choir, striving to maintain a level of spiritual energy. I wanted to work, to create another life.

I knew there were other ways to help people find God's love and sought to channel my energy to an alternate outlet. I took action, and those strong efforts produced fruitfulness and life: the congregation of our church was enlarged, a daughter church was established, the requests for evangelistic meetings in remote villages escalated. Living in constant communication with God was truly a blessing to me.

Let me tell you of two more events that occurred, before I return to my narrative about the tribal work after my expulsion from the jungle.

One day, one of our church members came from his home fifty-five kilometers away to tell me that the Bureau of Development of the State of Mato Grosso was selling lots to indigent people for a trifle in order to develop a particular area. He suggested that our church should purchase one.

I went with several brothers from the church to survey the area, thinking that perhaps we could build a conference center for the church. The size of each lot was ten hectares (about twenty-five acres). The price was six hundred dollars per lot and could be paid in four payments of one hundred and fifty dollars over the course of a year—obviously, very cheap. But the land looked like a gravel pit—a useless, acidified, bone-dry wilderness, with no creeks nearby. The price would be attractive to poor people, but what could they do with it if they bought it? They couldn't plant anything.

It was disappointing. It was too far out and also unsuitable for a conference location. One brother, nevertheless, said he would just go ahead and buy one, simply because he couldn't beat the price, and he strongly urged me to buy one too. It won't be easy to sell later, I thought, but after pondering for a while, I decided to buy the one adjacent to his and went to the Bureau of Development to register my purchase. The first payment would be due in three months. I marked the boundary of my lot and forgot about it for a while.

Several months passed, when the brother who had bought the lot next to mine was transferred to another city and had to move.

"Kim," he said, "would you consider buying my lot? Please?"

My economic situation was not that great, but I didn't want to leave him in the lurch, so I obliged. Now I had become the owner of fifty acres of wilderness. After a year, the lots were paid off. One Sunday, I took some of the church members in my van to the neighborhood in which my lots were located to have fellowship with some of the believers in that area. While there, I was informed that people who were engaged in alluvial mining had come to the area and were looking for the owner of the lots. My informers thought the property should be guarded. Otherwise, the gold prospectors might indiscriminately mine my property, and they were armed outlaws, killing if provoked and attracting prostitutes.

That worried me. What could I do? As far as I could see, there was no immediate solution to the problem. Another major issue was that I didn't want to lose the potential profit from my property. It would be out of the question to build a hut and stay there as a virtual prisoner just to guard my land and be separated from my mission. I didn't have enough money to hire someone; besides, who would volunteer for such a risky job? I could see no solution to this problem. I had no options from which to choose. I was so frustrated and bewildered that I could hardly bear it. At this point, Satan was really trying me again. My children's choir was going so well, they had such momentum; but on the other hand was this troubling situation. What was the best question to ask myself? The best question would be, *What is the wisest thing to do? Nothing! Nothing whatsoever. Just pray.* "Dear God, let us know the collective wisdom of the church. Please, give me strength to deal with this."

One day soon after, a dump truck pulled up in my front yard. The driver looked familiar. When he stepped out of his truck, I saw that it was Aristide, a distant relative of one of our church members.

At one time, we had regional fellowship in his house when he lived in a nearby city.

"Oh, Aristide," I greeted him enthusiastically, "it's been a long time!"

"Yes, indeed it has," he said. "By the way, is that twenty-hectare (fifty-acre) gravel pit in Canga yours?"

"Yes it is. Why?" I asked.

"Well, a lot of alluvial miners are drifting into that area. Would you let me have the mineral rights on your lots? I already tested one truckload of gravel and it produced four grams of gold dust! That's very profitable land. Generally, two grams of dust out of four metric tons of gravel would be considered good. I'll put a mobile home on the place and live there with my family and hire a couple of trust-worthy helpers. Every week I will bring you 10 percent of whatever I produce. I believe that God will bless us. So how about it? Would you like to do that? Please?"

He was speaking from his heart and acknowledging God even in this kind of business. I wanted to ask, "What are you going to do when the temptation of profiteering arises?"

Suddenly, I was astounded by the realization that God had sent the solution to my problem. If Aristide were to do something dis-honest, that would be between him and God. It wasn't my concern to protect my interests. I should feel responsible for his sake to pray that he would not fall into temptation if he were tempted to do so. In that case, he himself would run to Jesus for help. It is a fact that materialism can make us extremely selfish. *Dear God, set us free from the trials of materialism.*

I had not appreciated the value of my property while liter-ally walking on gold! To use an allegory, it's like failing to realize or appreciate God's grace while every day enjoying the benefits of His bountiful provision. God was planning to save my gold from the outlaws in a most convenient manner and to use it for His good pleasure at the same time.

"Sure, Aristide," I finally said. "You have the mineral rights on my land."

"Thank you! Thank you very much," he said. "I'll set up my mobile home and get things ready to begin work the first month, and I'll meet my obligation."

"Fine," I agreed. "That will be a good first step, Aristide."

Then he added, "And could you visit me once a month with the brothers from the church to hold a regional evangelistic meeting? I'll gather the other miners, too."

This new development pleased the church members very much.

I declared, "I want to announce to you all that I will donate 100 percent of the income from the gold to our church, and I'll give you a weekly progress report on the project."

The first week, I received seventy-three grams of gold. At thirteen dollars per gram, the total was nine hundred forty-nine dollars. I was receiving gold? It was outlandish to me! It was difficult to believe that it was coming from my own land. It was beyond my imagination that I could touch gold from a mine on my own property and witness the production process, which involved the most tedious, difficult, dangerous, and time-consuming manual labor.

Gold mining is an incredibly labor-intensive process. After digging and loading the rock and gravel onto the dump truck, it is hauled to a distant riverside, where it is dumped into a wooden flume consisting of several steps. The gravel and rock is flushed with water. At each step, various sizes of rock and gravel collect, which are scooped into an aluminum cone shaped like a Vietnamese straw hat. This is swished around in the water in a circular motion, like a centrifugal machine, after which only the heaviest material remains in the center of the container. A drop of mercury is added, which attracts the gold dust. The conjugated mercury is isolated and evaporated by heat from a welding torch, leaving only the few grams of gold that have been attached. When enough gold has been collected, it is melted again to be made into pure gold ingots. I can now appreciate why "gold" is used to define superlatives such as a "heart of gold," a "voice of gold," etc.

Once they have uncovered alluvial soil, they survey the exposed strata and follow the vein of calcite or goldstone to a depth of as much as fifteen meters. The tunnels they create are narrow and dangerous. The miners could be killed or buried alive, should the opening collapse. If they find water, they have to pump the water out before continuing. Occasionally, when a worker comes upon a nugget of gold, he will swallow it or hide it in a body cavity in order to steal it. Gold, wealth, money — these things affect the human mind in different ways, producing covetousness.

In order to promote the production of fifteen tons of gold nationwide per year, the Brazilian IRS taxes only 10 percent of gold production. Consequently, this area has been eroded by excessive and uncontrolled digging, so now the Bureau of Environmental Management has ordered the curtailment of all alluvial gold mining in order to prevent further damage and to protect the sea from mercury contamination through runoff.

Aristide mined my ten hectares of land for seven years, netting us thirty-five hundred grams of gold. The adjoining ten hectares was sold for another thirty-five hundred grams of gold. That seven thousand grams of gold provided enough money to facilitate several projects. We were able to purchase two lots adjacent to the church and expand the premises three times. Besides enlarging our building, we constructed additional buildings, including an auditorium. We had a telephone connected, which was unusually difficult and expensive in those days. We purchased a thirty-acre plot about six kilometers away, with a creek running through it, ideal for a conference ground, where we built a cultural hall in which we conduct four training conferences a year and which we use for a training camp for our young people. We built another church further inland and four branch churches around us. The massive increase in the power of our church to reach out in totally unexpected ways was a confirmation of God's blessing. It was a miracle — a fulfillment on this mission field that I can remember with great joy. Moreover, it had a tremendous impact on many of the Moravian Brethren throughout Brazil. They came to visit our church to enjoy spiritual refreshment and to rejoice in God.

At our gold mining operation, there were no killings, no violence, and no street women in all of those seven years. God's grace was evident. His watchful eye was over all of it.

One day, I went with several of the brothers from the church to a small town thirty-five kilometers away to investigate the possibility of evangelizing at a women's prison. There were a couple of male guards posted outside a high double fence. Except for those exterior guards, all of the others were women. The atmosphere of the place felt strange. We set about to find the officer in charge. Upon finding her, we introduced ourselves.

"Hello. We are from the church. Would it be possible for us to come each Saturday afternoon to evangelize in the prison?"

"Surely, yes," she responded unequivocally. "This place needs a service like that. In the past, we had visits from a nearby Pentecostal church. Twenty or so men and women came as a team for a couple of hours each week. They were pretty noisy, and it didn't seem to help a lot. But we don't even have their visits any more. They must have had some kind of internal conflict.

"There are a lot of other churches in the city," she continued, "but none of them seem interested. However, a Catholic Father comes once a month to say Mass."

Even as we were speaking, a riot erupted in the prison. The

shrieking of women's voices and the violent shaking of latticed cell doors shattered the peace.

"Listen to that," the officer said. "Taming them is not even remotely possible. They fight each other fiercely, making a glorious mess of this place. They urinate in the cleaning buckets and try to immerse their opponent's head in it. When we try to make them exercise, they respond aggressively. They won't work. They curse violently and use abusive language toward us: 'We didn't come here to work. That's your job!' They throw their food trays away, 'What kind of food is this? My family pays taxes to this country! Give it to the pigs. I don't want it.'

"They are extremely trying to us. They absolutely run wild, far worse than men prisoners; even punishment by solitary confinement for a few days doesn't help."

Then she called one of the guards and said, "Would you give these people a tour of the facility?"

The facility was two sections, each consisting of a spacious center with cells facing each other on the perimeter. A high fence blocked any breeze, and the concrete buildings were heated by the tropical sun all day long. Even though the doors and windows were latticed, the place was hot. I would say it was like a preliminary hell.

In this no-men's land, all fifty-two women prisoners wore nothing but thongs, unabashedly lounging around naked. I felt unsettled by this anomaly, which was quite different from the nakedness of the jungle Indians. A most shameless woman approached the latticed door of her cell before which we were standing. "Are you all Christians?" she asked.

Then, jeering at us, she turned around and began to gyrate in a most lewd manner. One of the elders in our company, in sheer embarrassment, fled the scene. That was his first and last visit to the prison.

She continued her disgusting presentation, as if to say, "You are Christians, right? But don't you like it, too? You men are all the same. *Nothing.*"

She continued what she thought was a seductive dance, casting sidelong glances of invitation into her cell. It was an undignified spectacle, a very uncomfortable observation that made me want to leave. Satan was pointing his knife at us before we even started working. It was like Joseph with Potiphar's wife:

> Now Joseph was taken down to Egypt, and Potiphar, an officer of Pharaoh...bought him...The LORD was with Joseph, and he became a successful man; and he was in the house of his master the Egyptian...his master's wife cast her eyes upn Joseph and said, "Lie with me." But he refused... she caught him by his garment...but he left his garment in her hand and fled...she told her husband saying, "the Hebrew servant came in to me to insult me; but as soon as I lifted up my voice and cried, he left his garment with me and fled out of the house...and Joseph's master took him and put him into prison...the LORD was with him; and whatever he did, the LORD made it prosper. (Genesis 39)

The first Saturday came. Two couples from our church accompanied me. We decided that day to simply deliver a Bible to each of the prisoners. First, we wrote each of the guard's names on several individual Bibles and presented one to each guard as a gift, with our best wishes, which seemed to please them. Then we went into the premises. Because of some misdemeanor, all of the prisoners were confined to their cells that day, which was a benefit to us in dealing with them. We visited each cell in order to acquaint ourselves with their names and faces and to present each one with her own Bible, inscribed with her own name, as a souvenir. That took two hours. Now each prisoner owned a personalized Bible, whether she was literate or not. We returned home with great satisfaction in what we had accomplished that day.

The two couples who accompanied me were in their thirties. We decided to form a permanent team, and the next Saturday we visited for the second time. This time, we brought guitars with us. The women guards were happy to see us and escorted us to the first section of the prison, where the prisoners who wanted to participate in our evangelistic meeting were assembled in the center space. No thongs were in evidence. They wore short-sleeved tops with skirts or pants and were sitting decently, waiting for us. Upon our arrival, one of the women prisoners volunteered, "We read the Bible last week and worshiped God by ourselves!"

I was more shocked than pleased to hear that news. Who would have thought that there could be believers among them, considering what we had seen on our first visit? Their sudden change of behavior in one week could have lightened the burden placed upon the guards. First we sang a hymn in Portuguese:

You, weary soul, be not discouraged. Wait for God —
He's on the way to help you. Repose, trust God Almighty.
Oh, weary soul, be aware, God has special love for you;
Wait on God.

The beautiful melody and caring words seemed to have a powerful effect and moved the listeners profoundly. Most of these women were connected to the wrong side of society. Confused, living in horrible mental chaos and continual crises, they had committed crimes — some obvious, some hidden — and so far have had no real opportunity to discover the Guardian of life.

When the meeting ended, they came close to us to shake our hands and even hug us (quite different from what Koreans do. For me it was a little awkward), and saying, "Oh this was so good! Please keep coming; we enjoyed the meeting so much. We hope to see you again. Please do come back!"

We were very blessed and greatly encouraged by this improved outcome. On the way home, I realized afresh how blessed I have been to have a life as a follower of Christ.

It had been a month since we started visiting the women's prison. The guards were grateful for the change that had transformed the atmosphere in the place. Having finished our meeting that day, we were about to leave when a woman approached with tears in her eyes.

"I want to have Jesus in my heart," she said. "How can I do that?"

"Oh! Really!" I exclaimed, "What you must do is acknowledge that you are a sinner before God, believe that Jesus' life was sacrificed for yours, and that through that sacrifice on the Cross, your sins have been washed away. Know that you are clean through what Jesus did for you, and accept Him into your heart."

"I did that already!" she said, a bright smile lighting her face and her eyes sparkling with tears.

"That is so wonderful!" I exclaimed. "That's total surrender. Let's pray. Dear God, thank you so much for setting this prisoner free, for allowing her everlasting consolation."

Her name was Marisa. She was born into a devout Catholic family as one of sixteen children. She was a single mother with two sons, eleven and seven years old. She had left her sons with her mother and had been engaged in trafficking drugs throughout Bolivia with her younger sister. They were caught and sentenced to twelve years in prison. She had so far served five months. Her face was beautiful, her behavior the opposite. She was the mastermind of all sorts of unrest: fighting, abusing the guards, and literally acting like a crazy woman.

But one morning, she was changed — metamorphosed into a fair lady, as Jesus had changed the water into wine in a single moment. She began to read the Bible quietly and alone and began telling the story of her conversion to the other inmates. She began treating the guards kindly and with respect, and she wept with remorse and repentance for her sons and her mother, and she began to repair her relationship with the world.

As she began to set a new pace and others followed her example, the prison itself was changed into a place of decency and faith. Whether the warden was present or not, the place was in order. The guards became our friends. Marisa's sister Rita accepted Jesus Christ as her Savior and was converted. More and more inmates made up their minds to follow Jesus, and newly arriving inmates were influenced by this new atmosphere.

Many months had passed in this fashion, when one day Marisa said, "I'm getting out of this place next week. I am already sorry when I think that I may not see you again!"

Although that news should have been an occasion for great happiness, I was on the verge of tears over losing her. I knew I couldn't say, "Oh no, Marisa, you need to stay here longer…!"

Drug dealers and murderers were supposed to serve twelve-year sentences. However, Marisa's meritorious attitude since her conversion had been reported daily to the corrections office, and, due to her merits, she was going to be released after only eleven months. The court had apparently decided that there was no reason to confine her longer under human law when she had been so obviously forgiven under divine law and now had a conscience that was free of offense.

On the day that she was released, everyone was in tears. Several reporters from local newspapers and TV stations were on hand to interview her. She spoke into their microphone, "There is so much evil out there, and my involvement in it landed me in this prison. But out of evil came good, because I found Jesus here. I have been forgiven and have found heavenly peace. I hope I can convey the message that I am leaving this place spiritually rich. When I walk through that gate, I'm going to walk with my Savior in His way."

These were incredibly interesting remarks and were disseminated throughout the region by the media. Her sister Rita was also released one month later. She left her address and telephone number with me, requesting that we visit her family without fail. This was one of the fruits of our labor with which God comforted us during the short time of our exile from the jungle. Hallelujah!

Even as we were rejoicing over this good outcome, another dark cloud of challenge was looming. After Marisa's enthusiastic interview had been televised, the Catholic priest paid his once-a-month visit to the prison to say Mass. The inmates, however, did not voluntarily attend, saying that the Mass was simply ritual and was "flat." The warden was upset about this new mood, and, because she sensed that inevitably there would be pressure from her superiors, she used her power to intervene.

As I mentioned earlier, Brazil is fundamentally Catholic. When the priest showed up, he was to be treated with due respect. The iron gate was to be opened in advance, and the people were to stand erect and pay homage to him as he passed by. But for us Christians, it was a different story. As men, we were taken by the male guards, the women by the female guards, to be searched in separate rooms to the point of humiliation because unscrupulous people had begun to abuse Marisa's story. Posing as Christian ministers, they had contrived to bring in guns, knives, saw blades, and cell phones, hiding them in Bibles, loaves of bread, condoms, and even women's bodies, causing all kinds of upheaval in the prison.

On the positive side, if we were willing to be subjected to the humiliation of a body search, we could not possibly be held responsible in the case of an outbreak of rioting. For that reason, we gladly submitted to it. What's more, the guards knew who we were, of course, and feeling sorry for us, would sometimes simply go through the motions. Still, the warden had turned a cold shoulder to us.

Suddenly, every church had formed a team to evangelize prisons, some equipped with video equipment. Even the Seventh-Day Adventist Church wanted to come in. When the prison administrators couldn't find enough time slots for all the churches desiring to participate, they bundled them and allowed them to all come together during our assigned time. Then the State Department of Justice made a new regulation that only licensed evangelists who had completed a special twenty-four-hour training course by the Justice Department would be allowed in. In twenty years of prison ministry, this was the first time I had encountered the license issue.

Even so, we were determined to continue our mission to the prison and went to the Department of Justice to apply. We were shuffled from one office to another, until someone eventually told us, "There is no training this year—maybe next year, but it is uncertain at this point, so if you will leave us your address and telephone number we will contact you later."

I knew that this was Satan's trick to close the door to our evangelism after Marisa's TV interview. The warden had suffered an exceptionally blistering reprimand by her superiors and was finally transferred. When I went to see the new warden to ask permission, her one-word answer was cold and succinct, "No."

Some time later, I came across one of the guards on a downtown street: "Oh, I'm so glad to see you, Kim! Why don't you come to the prison anymore? None of the other churches come anymore either. The inmates are waiting for you!"

I answered simply with a smile, "If that is God's will!"

The possibilities of work in Brazil are endless. So are the hindrances!

—〰—

24
To the Jungle Again

IN THE EARLY YEARS, the State Department Bureau of Indian Administration had encouraged the missionaries' tribal work because the Bureau had an inadequate budget and a shortage of manpower to regulate the Indians, and they realized that there were not many that would make the sustained sacrifice that missionaries do. However, the international anthropologists were displeased to see that the primitive tribes, the sole objects of their academic research, were being civilized by the missionaries. The irony was that the anthropologists could not further their research without indirect help from the missionaries. They received from the missionaries the information they used to make their reports about the Indians' daily life. They lived at the local missionary's house for several months at a time to learn about the history and the customs of the Indians in order to gather material for their dissertations, yet they loathed the missionaries' activities among the tribes. They constantly urged the government to preserve the tribes' primitiveness. Consequently, the Bureau began to issue permission for only one year at a time, and it contained very restrictive requirements:

· Must be inoculated against numerous maladies.
· Must be free from any infectious disease.

- Must avoid activities that modify Indian customs.
- Must not propagate any religion other than that of the Indians.
- Must submit regular activity reports.
- Must submit copies of any pictures taken.

Looking at the requirements, one would have to question whether this was permission to work or a restriction to prohibit working. What would the outcome be? Would my presence be condoned by the Bureau or punished by the judicial system? Obviously, they could nullify my permission at any time they please.

The Wycliffe Bible Translators (WBT) changed their name to Summer Institute of Linquistics (SIL) and agreed with the Bureau that they would engage exclusively in the study of the Indian languages as linguists, not as missionaries. In my case, I could make no such guarantee. As an independent missionary, my work was in jeopardy. This would be the most important subject for prayer.

Currently, Milton, the husband of my Indian "granddaughter" (adopted) has undertaken to send their two daughters to Bible school, but at the time of the conflict I have just described, he was just a lanky little orphan nicknamed "Yalante" (Beanpole). I cared for him very much and considered adopting him as my son so that he could continue as my successor in the case that I was forbidden further contact with the tribes. I filed an application for adoption with FUNAI but was denied.

"Sorry," I was told. "Unless the law changes, it is legally impossible."

I waited for a while and then resubmitted my application. This time I was told, "That is not within the jurisdiction of this office. As a matter of fact, it is an unprecedented request. You will have to go to the highest authority, the Ministry of Home Affairs Bureau of Indian Administration. They are located in Brasilia, the Capital."

I rode the bus nineteen hours to Brasilia and, upon my arrival, waited one whole day before being granted an interview with the Bureau chief, a General Mello, who had been sworn in during the military revolutionary regime in 1964. When I was finally admitted to the office, the director was away from his desk, so his assistant met me.

"Good morning, sir," I said, introducing myself and the reason for my coming. "I would like to adopt an Indian orphan. I would also like to enroll two Indian boys in the public elementary school. I will rear them as my own and be their guarantor."

Lowering his voice, he said, "Kim, to tell you the truth, we don't want Indians to be educated. The more educated they become, the more problems they cause. And the more likely they are to protest against the government."

I was amazed by such a shockingly bold answer coming from such a high office. It was unbelievable! Is this what is actually happening out there? If that was the official reason for denying education to the Indians, it signified that the responsible parties were violating their trust to an astonishing degree. Government stimulus funds for education of the Indians were obviously meant to educate Indians, yet they were always dissipated by intervention and manipulation through mathematically inexplicable ways. There was no designated authority to investigate or regulate the handling of these resources. The Indians had been victimized.

I returned home, feeling dejected and with no apparent result from my effort. I had learned from this fruitless project why the nation has remained a "third-world nation" despite its vast area of arable land and abundant natural resources. I knew that, in spite of all this, I should be thankful to be allowed to stay and work in such a place. I will take it as it comes and remain hopeful about it.

I was eaten up with curiosity about what had happened to my

Indians since the "off-limits" order. It had been almost six months since my exchange of words with the manager of the FUNAI office. His last words had been, "Regardless, from now on you are prohibited from going there for any reason."

"Fine," I had responded. "I went to bid farewell to my Indians, and that's what I did."

Since that conversation six months previous, I had been busy concentrating on the affairs of our church. One day, I came home and my wife said to me, "There was a telephone call from the branch manager of FUNAI. He simply said that you can go into the Indian area. No other words — no explanation. That's it!"

I was dumbfounded by that news. I didn't know what to think. He had arrogantly threatened me, with a loaded gun on his desk, saying, "Regardless of anything, from now on you are prohibited...." Now he's changed his mind to allow me to go? Is this a trick? Is there something here I need to be careful about?

Although it was good news, I felt anger building up in me. This guy had thrown cold water on the acceleration of my work. Was there some brilliant achievement in his effort to diminish the Indians at the expense of my life's work? Was that why he had brought it to a complete halt by applying such an array of deterrence? And now he wanted me to reenter?

For six months I had been trying to discern whether God wanted me to change my battle plan and become involved in some short-term project that would yield only a handful of crops rather than a long-term one. Everything that had happened in the jungle seemed vague now. It was as though I were in a sabbatical year. I no longer felt a yearning to be in the jungle. By that time, major changes could have taken place in the Indian community: a new clinic, dispatch officers, a new school, new teachers, and lots of other new development supported by government funding. In the past, I had taken care of all of these areas by myself. I didn't know what I would be allowed to do— just evangelize? The branch manager had made a direct call to me without the formality of any written document. Was there something significant about that, which I should understand? I couldn't conclude anything with certainty. Besides, the great distance of seven hundred kilometers, inconvenient transportation, and lack of communication with the Indians in the jungle contributed to my nearly complete ignorance of their circumstances and what was going on there.

What if they let me stay there only a week instead of a month? It won't be easy to make frequent trips, either.... My state of mind was one of undeniable dismay. Like a broken bamboo stock, it had lost its resilience. The anthropologists had frustrated the work of the missionaries, reducing the mission field to a vacancy where no one could easily get back on track.

Once again, I was moved to pray for the tribal mission. Is there a higher test than happiness? Yes, there is. It is thankfulness. I intended to pray until God renewed in me thankfulness. I was in no hurry.

As I closed my eyes, many words flooded my mind. "Being confident of this very thing, that he which hath begun a good work in you will perform it until the day of Jesus Christ" (Philippians 1:6). Yes, He is the one who designated this place for me. He began the work.

"For a just man falleth seven times, and riseth up again" (Proverbs 24:16). Yes, the righteous man, after each fall, is made to rise up again, like a tumbler. If I start to dig a well I am supposed to dig without giving up until I find water. My turnaround had begun.

Dear God, thank you for the necessary stimulant, for renewing my spirit. I was bent but not broken. I will bounce back and stand straight again. The dismay was temporary, it was a trespasser — it didn't come to stay. Thank you so much for restoration. Thank you!

I had been busy with church work: leaders' meeting on Monday night, prayer meeting on Tuesday night, Wednesday night service, regional fellowship on Thursday, Bible study on Friday night, youth meeting on Saturday night and, of course, Sunday services. Meetings, without skipping a day for six months, made it seem like six years since I had been involved with the jungle mission. I needed to rekindle my mission to the Indians without neglecting my mission to the church. This dual purpose would double the busyness of my life. "Having then gifts differing according to the grace that is given to us, let us use them:...he who gives aid, with zeal..." (Romans 12:6-8). Yes, by His power, I would be able to do it by faith and with a keen mind!

Since FUNAI officers had been placed in the Indian neighborhoods, my job would be somewhat diminished. There would be no need for me to be away from home for over a month at a time. I would stay only a week at a time and concentrate on evangelization, thereby avoiding conflict with the FUNAI personnel and, at the same time, keep up with my church responsibilities.

I had to have my vehicle serviced for the trip, prepare various gifts for the Indians, and adjust my mindset for the unfamiliarity of the jungle all over again. Arriving at the fazenda, I was surprised to see a new road cut into the Indian neighborhood from a totally different direction. I proceeded rather fretfully to their location, only to find, upon my arrival, that the place lay in ruins. It was as though a tornado had swept through: the door was torn from the clinic; chairs tables and beds were broken to pieces and scattered about. However, there stood a newly erected schoolhouse that resembled a large airplane hangar. Nearby loitered a lonely and forlorn-looking young man. Right next to the building was an Indian family, appearing listless and downcast. Approaching them, I asked, "Where is everybody?"

"Several of them went out hunting," one of the family members replied. "Most of them went to see Quinto a couple of days ago. He lives in the deep jungle. It takes a couple of days to get there and come back."

"Oh," I responded.

Then I approached the young teacher standing next to the building and introduced myself: "Hello, I'm Kim."

"Oh, yeah, I know who you are. They talk about nothing but Quinna (Kim)."

"Is it all right with you if I stay here for a week?" I inquired.

"Sure. They've been waiting for you, and that's okay with me."

"Thanks," I said. "By the way, how is everything with you?"

"Well, the Indians are okay," he said, "but it's difficult to control them. They don't like to come to class or to study. All they want to do is hunt. When I applied to FUNAI for this job," he continued, "the conditions seemed excellent: twice as much salary as in the city schools, food and housing paid. It sounded great. But life out here is too monotonous. It's lonely, and there's no future. I'm leaving next semester. The nurse that was working here before I came left for the same reason." Then he informed me, "If you want to go to Quinto's house, you can get there by car now. There's a new road, but it's pretty narrow."

I gave the teacher a copy of the Bible as a gift and then headed to Quinto's house with an Indian guide. I found them all in the middle of the jungle, with an abundance of food and twittering happily among themselves. They were glad to see me, and their first question was, "Quinna, Quinna, how long are you going to stay?"

"For about a week," I replied.

"That short again? Stay for a month, will you?"

They plied me with cooked meat, mangiokas, *mamao* (papaya), and we talked long into the night. We had so much to catch up on, and we needed to bridge the gap between us right then and there. It felt comfortable and familiar again, just like the old days.

"We don't like FUNAI. We don't need them," they insisted. "They go to the city and stay there for days. They don't care about us, and we feel the same way about them. We don't support them. The nurse left, so we destroyed the clinic and threw away the wireless stuff with the solar batteries. One day, the local branch manager of FUNAI came to see us, and all of our men confronted him with arrows and clubs. We demanded, 'Why are you coming in here? We don't want FUNAI, we want the missionary! Because of you, Quinna doesn't come anymore. If you don't go away, we'll kill you!' We shouted at him and pushed him. He turned pale with fear and said, *'Tabon, tabon!'* (fine, fine), and he got in his car and fled. We haven't seen him since then. He hasn't come back."

Now I understood why he had given me permission to return. At one time he had laid his gun on the desk, as though making a boast of it to me. But when he showed up in the Indian neighborhood, he was almost shot by Indian arrows. Pretty ironic!

He had acknowledged that FUNAI alone can't subdue the "Alantesu" tribe without "Quinna." He knew that I was the Indians' best hope, no matter what FUNAI does, and that I could make a real difference for them because they prefer me. He probably struggled a while before he finally decided to call me, which was no doubt a matter of self-defense. If his incompetence to handle one tribe were known by his superior, he would likely be fired or relegated to some lesser position. He would rather issue his informal order for me to continue my work and then quietly ignore my visits to the jungle Indians in order to finish his term well and not jeopardize any possible future promotion. He would not interfere too much with my work, either, at this time, since that would raise another problem for him if I should step away.

The outcome was that in the six months since the "off-limits" mandate to the Indian tribes of the Nambiquara was issued in 1978, I was the only one allowed to enter the jungle Indian neighborhood.

It was a miracle! I was very thankful to God. At the same time, I felt a tremendous responsibility to protect and preserve the earlier contributions that the other missionaries had made in the rest of the tribes. Those missionaries knew where my heart was, and virtually every one of them encouraged me whenever we met. "Kim, we are praying for you. The commitment you have made to the Indians is remarkable. It is a great asset!"

The FUNAI officers also recognized my cooperation with FUNAI and that I wanted to be part of the solution. This earned me their support and the opportunity to work freely without interference from them. (In fact, at one time they wanted to hire me! I said no.) FUNAI learned one more lesson through that development: the Indians' opinions needed to be respected.

Accompanied by my Alantesu Indians, I visited four tribes in the Guapore Valley. I found that it was beyond the ability of one missionary to cover them all. The roads were too rugged and the distances too great. Moreover, my Alantesu were showing signs of dissatisfaction and jealousy about my visits to other tribes while spending less time with them. They were acting childishly. I greatly appreciated their bond with me, and I needed to be careful not to make them think that I was caring less for them. But there were the others, too.

To avoid a trap, I needed a revised plan. To meet the challenge of the changing conditions, I had to reorganize my activities. Otherwise, it wasn't going to work. I asked myself, *What is the right thing to do? It is to select the best prospect from each tribe and send them to Bible school in the city. Despite my repeated attempts, the earlier adoption project had failed. Then this is it! This is my best option.*

Since the mid-1990s the second generation of Indians had begun to resort to the fazenda, ride on their trucks to nearby cities, see new things, and emulate what they saw. That new trend frustrated FUNAI's efforts to control the Indians by their old methods.

Now they had to take the Indians to hospitals, shopping in the city, to work. The Indians had learned so many things: "Quinna, during our hospital stay, we enjoyed watching TV. We saw a man and woman hugging each other, kissing, playing on the bed. Women wearing almost no clothes were twisting their bodies and dancing. We know now what condoms are for and how to use them."

What they had seen was beyond their imagination. It infuriated me because, obviously, it could only get worse if they were not protected from such lewdness and temptation. I wanted desperately to insulate them and protect them against these distractions. I wanted them to be free from the dominion of the devil, lest they make complete fools of themselves. Oh, I wanted so badly for them not to violate the principles of Scripture! Some goals would be more important than others. But my most urgent goal was to make them yield themselves to God and enter spiritually into the Promised Land before they completely lost their way!

—∿—

Bible School

A FTER THE GOVERNMENT ORDER making the jungle "off-limits," the South American Indian Mission moved south to establish a Bible school for Indians. In the late 1990s, they established a branch of that school in Central Brazil, where we lived, in order to accommodate the Indians living there and in the North. We were fortunate in that respect, but for my Indians, there were some real obstacles to their progress. The Bible school had been founded to accommodate the southern Indians eighteen years and older who had been civilized and educated in the Portuguese language. On the other hand, my Alantesu had lived in isolation, without education, and not even knowing how old they were. Their knowledge of Portuguese was almost nil. Although all of the Indians in question belonged to the same Nambiquara tribes, those living in the highlands, an area as wide as three or four counties, where the Wycliffe Bible Translators had been working for years, had considerable advantages: the state road was nearby, affording them frequent civilian contact and the activities of the Army Corps of Engineers were vigorous in the area, contributing to their speedy civilization. These highland Indians entered the Bible school first, and some of them had even graduated. I felt frustrated, realizing that the opportunity was within a stone's throw, yet my valley Indians were unable to seize it because of their social inferiority.

One day, I made the sixty-kilometer drive to visit the Bible
school, which was a part of the South American Indian Mission
supported by American Baptist churches. The teaching staff was
made up of a new group of missionaries whom I had not yet met. I
introduced myself to the principal, a missionary named Wesley.

"Hello, Missionary Wesley! I am Kim."

"It's very nice to meet you, Kim," said Wesley. "We have all
heard much about you."

I immediately began to speak about the reason for my visit. "As
you may know," I began, "the Guapore Valley was the battleground
in which the anthropologists chose to wage their war to preserve
the primitiveness of the Indians for the sake of their research. The
trajectory of that battle brings us now to the issue of either moving
forward or facing declining intelligence among the Indians. One
problem we face is that the Indians get married before they reach
age eighteen. Missionary Edwards from South American Indian
Mission may know that, because he worked there before. I very
much want these Indians to attend your school. Would you consider
making it happen by changing the admission requirements? In that
case, I could gather the best prospects from each tribe and pay their
tuition myself."

I didn't have the money on hand, but I had faith!

"That sounds like an excellent idea," Wesley agreed. "It would
be especially nice to have students from tribes among which one of
our own missionaries has worked. I'll present three items for discussion at our next staff meeting:

1. To lower the admission age to fifteen.
2. Pre-school for two years to facilitate their learning the Portu-
    guese language and lifestyle.
3. Bible school for three years.

"I'll pray for you, Kim."

One week later, I received word from the Bible school that all the details were ironed out and giving me the information about what those details included:

1. Simple document of permission for the child to go to school with the signature of the parent or the chief of the neighborhood (to provide legal defense).
2. Mandatory residence at the student dormitory.
3. Estimated tuition: $190.00 monthly (roughly one-half of Brazilian minimum wage).
4. Students must bring personal bedding and nightwear, to be left at the school.
5. Students take individual responsibility for personal necessities.
6. Admission to be paid in advance at the beginning of the school year.

I selected five boys: three from my Alantesu tribe, one from the Wasusu tribe, and one from the Waikisus (belonging to the South American Indian Mission), and prepared the necessary documents. For each boy I bought a school bag, shirts, pants, shoes, underwear, casual outfits, blankets, bed sheets, toothbrush, toothpaste, razor, shaving cream, hand soap, bath soap, school supplies, and a Bible. Before we left for the school, I cut their hair and dressed them. Awkwardly beaming, they all looked like little actors. Their parents and neighbors alike, seeing them all dressed up in such stylish manner, happily envied them. I, too, could hardly believe that until now they had lived naked. My vehicle was filled with my five passengers and their luggage.

Here we go to study abroad, seven hundred kilometers from home, where people live a different lifestyle and speak a foreign language! On the way, we stopped for lunch at a Brazilian self-service buffet. Their discipline had begun, with table manners first: Don't put too much on your plate. Finish what you have on your plate before you go for seconds. Hold your knife and fork this way. Close your mouth when you chew. Don't make noises with your mouth. Don't spill. Don't drop food. Smile. Say thank you.

From now on, this was going to feel like torture until they got the hang of it.

We reached the school after a long, eleven-hour journey. Students from other areas were arriving at the same time. The principal and his staff were there to give us a warm welcome, register our boys, and show us to their assigned dormitory. All around us I heard nothing but Portuguese, and I hoped they could learn and communicate in that language adequately and soon.

At this school, there were one hundred and twenty students from various tribes representing thirteen different dialects. One of the students was from the lower Amazon area, from whence he had traveled three whole days by bus. This diverse body of students would represent a remarkable human resource in the future. It also signified that the Gospel, through these thirteen dialects, would penetrate some of the uttermost parts of the earth. As graduates of this school, their contributions to each of the tribes would be undeniably rewarded in the long run, and the Gospel would not be silenced.

Of our five valley students, one did not return for the second semester since he had been so tremendously homesick, the study had been too difficult, and the daily discipline overwhelming. This educational setback was not a surprise. The training was difficult indeed, there was no question about it.

I remembered how hard my wife and I had worked when we had Indian houseguests. In the early days of our mission work, when there were no local FUNAI or anthropologists, some debilitating disease had ravaged my tribe. I dashed to a fazenda to contact the state headquarters of FUNAI. They made two trips in a small airplane to transport my sick Indians to a general hospital, and I invited the remaining family members of the victims to my house. They lived in my house the same way they live in the jungle: they laid down in the dirt, washed their hands in the toilet because they didn't understand what a water faucet was, urinated anywhere outside, and poured buckets of water over their naked bodies because they thought the stream from the showerhead was too puny. We had to call them in whenever passers-by were shocked by their presence or laughed at them, looking over the barbed-wire fence. To keep them from being hungry, we cooked prodigious amounts of rice and fried fish, which they ate with their hands, picking the fishbones out with their fingers and then wiping their fingers on the bottom of their chair or on the table legs or in their hair. As a result, the whole inside of the house smelled of fish. Outside, it smelled of urine and attracted hundreds of flies. We followed them about and smilingly cajoled them in every blessed thing they did. "Don't do that, do it this way, not that way. It's better this way...." While we were trying so hard to enhance the Indians' understanding of civilized behavior, my wife and I had just about had it, both physically and emotionally.

In the jungle, they could enjoy hunting animals, catching fish, or picking fruit to eat, but in this town there was absolutely nothing to do: nothing to hunt, nothing to catch, and nothing to pick. All they had to occupy themselves was eating three times a day at mealtimes, taking naps in between, and going to bed at night. Their faces showed that they were suffocating with boredom, like a grandfather who had visited his son-in-law's house and wanted to get rid of all the useless flowers from the garden and plant lettuce there instead.

I dressed them with clothes and sandals to go into town sightseeing, but there was nothing of interest to see: no wild boars or deer—only uninteresting stuff, such as lots of people, lots of buildings, and lots of stuff in the supermarkets. They had no interest in any of that. They simply skulked around like dogs with shoes on, their faces devoid of expression. They did, however, attract the attention of children, who saw them as an oddity. I felt like the leader of a circus group.

I was reminded of many years ago in Korea. I had vivid memories of the year Korea was liberated from the Japanese. American G.I.s, cameras slung over their shoulders, walked the city streets with dozens of children following them and yelling, "Hello, okay. Chewing gum give me! Yankee, monkey, donkey!"

When I returned the Indians to their home in the jungle, the other Indians were curious about what had happened to them. "How was everything with you in the city?"

Surprisingly, they said, "That's not a good place to go. We were bored, hot, tired, and hungry."

Well, that was probably true. Although we served them huge meals at eight o'clock, noon, and six o'clock in the evening, with plenty of cookies and snacks in between, they couldn't eat continuously without regard for time as they do in the jungle.

Several years later, a girl from my tribe came home on vacation after four months at the Bible school. Although the Indians don't hug or even hold hands to express their emotions, when she saw her younger sister, unable to restrain her emotions, she burst into tears. Observing the tears flowing down her cheeks, I had difficulty swallowing my own tears. The Indians are tenderhearted people; they are part of one another. This girl had experienced how hard it was to live in a strange culture, isolated from her people. "Be it ever so humble, there's no place like home." I couldn't agree more.

Regardless, these young Indians have refused to give up what to them is an unbearably tough task. Each year, the number of student candidates increases. This year, seventeen valley Indians are studying at the Bible school. It has been my desire that at least five students from each of the five valley tribes would start through the Bible school curricula each year. If I could arrange in advance everything necessary to assure that future generations of valley Indians would have opportunity to study at the Bible school after my wife and I are gone, that, to me, would be one of the greatest validations of our mission to the Indians.

How am I going to arrange that? I don't know. But I have God's guiding hand, and if that is God's will, He will perfect it. Completion is up to Him.

Within the Alantesu tribe, the "Quinto" neighborhood has been the main force. During the school year, it is almost empty, it seems, since many of the young people have gone away to school. That number includes thirteen of Quinto's family members: two sons, two daughters-in-law (with their three children), one daughter, one son-in-law (with two children), and two granddaughters. Of the jungle families, he is most blessed. His home is sound, and in this he is well off.

As my work seemed to be advancing in a robust way, another huge and unsettling issue was stalking me. Two years ago, the five students from the southern part of the valley, where the German missionary had worked, had to quit school because they were no longer allowed to leave their neighborhood.

Unexpectedly, one day I received a call from one of them.

"Kim," he said, "I have heard that the Bureau of State Police has been investigating your work. They are going to arrest you and put you in prison because they think you are taking Indians out of the jungle and bringing them to the city. Please, Kim, be careful."

I thanked him for his call, but I actually didn't pay much attention to his warning. Several months ago, the principal of the Bible school, which I have mentioned before is run by South American Indian Mission, called my home.

"Kim, I have received an email from the Bureau of State Police, and it concerns you," he said. "They want to know whether you are a member of SAIM and whether you are extracting Indians from the jungle. In my answer to them, I explained the situation in detail. You need not voluntarily go to the Bureau to explain it yourself. Don't worry, just lie low. And Kim, we're all praying for you."

They were, I'm sure. In fact, the staff members of the Bible school had been happily marveling, "Kim! How can you afford the tuition for this many students all by yourself? My goodness!"

In retrospect, I remembered a casual conversation I had had with a new local FUNAI officer soon after the former branch manager had been transferred several years ago. While shaking hands and exchanging pleasantries with me, he had said, half-jokingly, "I've heard a lot about you. I've heard that many Indians are studying in the city. You must be taking them out of the jungle, eh?"

If I had really wanted to extract the Indians from the jungle, I would have had to go first to the local FUNAI branch office for application forms, then to their state office, and finally to the Supreme Bureau in the capital city, Basilia. These procedures then would have taken many months before I would finally have been informed of their inevitable decision, "Denied." I have been through their business procedures so many times, and I have always known the outcome before even starting. They are so predictable. Why would I even think twice about doing anything like that?

In reality, no one could take them away from the jungle anyway. The few Indians who left the jungle voluntarily, driven by some unknown self-impulse, show up wandering naked on the city streets, causing considerable discomfort to the populace. This has been attributable to FUNAI's incompetence in controlling the Indians. Some people, feeling compassion for these displaced Indians, have offered them clothes, food, or small jobs. FUNAI has been ignoring such frequent incidents.

My vision is to create an educational opportunity for the Indians so that, being trained, they could make a contribution to their own tribes, which would be a critical first step toward civilization. I had devoted my entire life to this immensely valuable project, yet they were trying to pick a quarrel with me on some pretext or other, either to demonstrate their bureaucratic power or because they simply had no understanding of what I was trying to accomplish.

The new FUNAI officer was aware that I had been given verbal permission to be in the jungle. I had been making verbal reports to him about school dates and who is on the student list, using as a messenger one of the students on the list. But the new officer and the new branch manager apparently thought that because of me they might get hurt some time in the future. So, wanting to curtail, or perhaps even block entirely, my activities in order to preclude any such possibility, they fabricated a document and submitted it to the investigating committee. With this document in hand, the Bureau of State Police, three years ago, began to surreptitiously follow me about, seeking evidence of wrongdoing.

It would make no difference whether such a matter were solvable or not—it would be unfavorable for the branch manager. By the way he was doing his job, he was unwittingly repeating the former manager's mistake.

When I related the whole circumstance to my Indians, it prompted an immediate reaction. Several of the young men dashed eighty kilometers to confront the branch manager of the local FUNAI.

"Is it true," they demanded, "that the state police are looking for Kim?"

"Well, I don't know for sure," the branch manager answered.

"Leave him alone," they warned. "Don't touch Kim!"

My forty-year mission to these Indians has been a long, tough journey, with much turmoil and many ups and downs and, I am sure, with many challenges still ahead. Yet I have absolutely no reason not to believe that God has been on my side. I have never stopped believing in my victorious God.

In February of this year, in the middle of summer vacation, a girl student from my tribe called my home from the fazenda.

"Kim! This morning five state policemen came to our neighborhood in two black state police cars," she informed me. "They were fully armed and in black uniforms. Their guide was the new FUNAI officer, and they were asking, 'Where is Kim? What does he do when he comes in here? When is he coming back? Does he do any bad things to you?'

"Kim, they even went into the next neighborhood looking for you! We told them to leave you alone. I'm praying to God for your safety. I got scared when I saw those black police cars and armed policemen. That's why I'm calling you."

This was an incredible warning, and the condition should be characterized as "severe." I had never asked them to pray for me, but the fact that on her own she said she was praying for me was an interesting remark! I was greatly moved.

My Indians were agitated over this matter and were acting like provoked bees in a disturbed hive. "All right," I said, "I'm coming in next week, and on my way home I'll drop by the police station myself. Thanks."

On the day that I stopped at the police station, I arrived during their lunchtime, and there was still about an hour before they would be finished. One lone guard with a revolver strapped to his side was monitoring the gate. Pretending naïveté, in order to acquire whatever information I could, I showed him my ID and said, "Hello, I'm Kim, the missionary that the state police have been investigating for the past three years. I work in the jungle with the Indians."

He listened nonchalantly, sitting with his hands folded behind his head. Since I had nothing to lose and absolutely nothing to hide, I began calmly and sincerely to explain all that I do, smiling all the while. I had been carrying several pictures in my wallet in case they would be useful at the numerous checkpoints encountered throughout Brazil. Included were pictures I had taken at my first contact with the Indians, in which they were completely nude, one when I was teaching them to read, one of me taking care of the sick, when I was playing and dining with them, and when I was tilling a field with them. There was also one of fifteen Bible school students, fully dressed and with broad smiles in front of their school, one with my own half-black adopted son, my daughter-in-law, my grandson, my wife, one of an evangelistic meeting at the women's prison (a forbidden area for picture-taking), and a picture at the men's prison, showing the inmates with the Bibles they had just received, cheering heartily behind their latticed gate.

I shared all of these pictures with the guard while I talked with him for more than thirty minutes, just as though we were long-time neighbors. He responded, "All right. I'll let you in as soon as the office reopens. Just wait over there."

It must have been getting close to the time, because men and women of various shapes and sizes were coming in, some pausing to speak with the guard. The guard himself went in and out three or four times, probably to report to someone about me. A short time later, I was ushered into an attorney's office.

"Welcome, Mr. Kim. Would you care for a cup of coffee?"

He then began to seek ways to discredit me. It was obvious that I was under his microscope. He questioned me in detail about a great deal of personal information: the year that I had received permission to contact the Indians, my activities, and the purpose for them, my financial situation, and whether I receive reward for my work, etc. Meanwhile, several important-looking officers came in out, asking to see the pictures. One of them said, "I need copies of these," and he took them with him.

Another rather statuesque officer, with a pistol at his side, came in and greeted me courteously with a Brazilian handshake.

"Senhor Kim." That's all he said, and he just left. But there was something familiar about him. *Have I met him before? Has he attended one of our evangelistic meetings in the regional church? He knew my name. Well, anyway, at this juncture, he seems to have the appearance of a potential favorable witness for me, the accused. Thank you, God!*

The attorney inquired about each of the fifteen Bible students in the pictures. He wanted each of their names. "Where is he now?... and where is he now?...And this one, where is he now?"

I answered all of his questions. "It's summer vacation. He is in the jungle...he's in the jungle also....he's in the jungle...in the jungle...in the jungle...jungle."

"May I have one of these pictures?" he asked.

After about two and a half hours, he handed me a closely written three-page report. "Read it and sign it, please." He commanded.

I took careful notice that toward the end of the report it concluded, "...it is a humanitarian mission." I was happy to sign it.

The attorney gave me a hearty handshake and said, "If anything develops, I will call you at home. Good luck."

During the two-hour drive back to my home I was feeling so relieved, thanking God, and singing at the top of my lungs, "Our God Reigns, Our God Reigns!" in tears.

I later learned that the new FUNAI officer was ordered to the State Police office twice. I was so thankful to God! I could not help but associate this incident with God's turning the Jew's misfortune into a blessing in the case of Mordecai (Esther 3-7).

Three years ago, a baptism-by-immersion ceremony was held at the Bible school jointly for seventeen students and the children of missionaries. Among them were four Indian students from my valley Indian neighborhoods. I was moved to tears as I watched them obey the Lord in this manner.

Early this year, a student couple from my Alantesu tribe, realizing that their sins had been washed away and that they had been cleansed, obeyed the Lord in baptism. It was the first baptism to take place in the jungle. It was an incredibly moving and blessed event, like the story in Acts 8:26-38: an Ethiopian eunuch met Philip on the way, returning after worshiping in Jerusalem. Along the road, they came to some water...and they both went down into the water, Philip and the eunuch, and he baptized him.

The seeds of the Gospel have germinated in the jungle neighborhoods. The days of grandeur, splendor, beauty, and the grace of the kingdom of God have dawned in this Guapore Valley!

"But ye shall receive power after that the Holy Ghost is come upon you: and ye shall be witnesses unto me both in Jerusalem, and in all Judea, and in Samaria, and unto the uttermost part of the earth" (Acts 1:8).

Yes, indeed!

—◊—

26
Toward the Sunset

TO A HANDFUL OF LOST SOULS, hidden away in the pitch darkness of the primeval jungle, far beyond the bounds of civilization, God's ineffable love has, for years, been trickling in. If you could look down from a spaceship and see the first light of the Gospel dawning on this dark valley, imagine how enraptured you would be! This is the picture God is drawing.

It feels like only yesterday when the jungle children first rummaged through my hair to see if I had lice like they did. They found a white hair and plucked it out. Now there are many white hairs and no need to pluck them. In this, the twilight of my life, they come out by themselves. If I could make a computer chip of one of those hairs, the monitor would depict my life, honestly lived, with all of the blunders I have made, from which, as a born-again Christian, I have learned so many lessons.

Most of all, it would reveal that by the grace of God I have lived a truly *happy* life. When I was conscripted by God and unexpectedly inserted into an undesirable jungle on the other side of the earth, I neither refused nor avoided that assignment, nor did I neglect, lose heart, complain, or regret any of it. God has made me the victor over numerous hardships. I always knew that it was not of myself. I felt that I was led by the Holy Spirit, looking at the world differently and interpreting things as working together for good.

The Holy Spirit makes it evident that God does His work by mobilizing His people and churches throughout the world. With collaborative effort and unified wisdom, we participate as individuals and as a team in God's inclusive work at home and abroad. Support and encouragement from every sector is what ultimately makes this remarkable achievement possible.

I certainly am not the star player—all who have contributed deserve recognition. It is a privilege for me to say to my supporters, colleagues, and friends, "Thank you, because you never gave in and never gave up. And thank you, God, for providing for us in such a way that there was always a little left over each month."

Now, unbelievably, I'm in my 70s, but the passion for the work to which God called me still burns within me as it did in my 40s. The body is growing old, but the spirit, the strength, the courage remains. I think I can work through my 80s, if God permits.

My Indians keep telling me, "Kim, you are not going to die. Please don't die! We don't want anyone else unless they are just like you. If you go, we'll cry a lot, a whole lot!"

I feel their love. I feel their sorrow. And I agree—I want my life to drag on so that I can continue to tangibly influence them. But again, only if that's what God wants!

The newly established city, Comodoro, which is eighty kilometers from our Indian neighborhood, covers a huge area, one-third of which belongs to the Indians. Many tribes are dispersed within a radius of one hundred kilometers from the city center. These tribesmen have contact with the Brazilian tradesmen and residents of the city. The importance of Comodoro, in my view, is that it attracts economic growth. If I could destroy the artificial boundaries to let our Indians' economy be a part of that growth, it would be a near-perfect situation. It is an excellent opportunity for the Indian and

Brazilian believers together to proclaim the Word of God in dynamic faith.

In order for the Indians to survive and succeed, hunting alone is not enough. They need to reevaluate. They need new strategies, new understanding of scientific and political realities, and new relationships with Brazilian society, so that the graduates of the Bible school might join in contributing to the role of Christianity in bringing about a tremendous transformation to the society.

Oh, yes, "The future starts from yesterday, tomorrow starts now." For me, this is the critical issue, an obviously significant one. I must identify the barriers, the differences, the ideal solutions, and the practical methods to seek after truth and build their faith while assuring that they are not outpaced and passed up by the world around them. I have nothing concrete yet, but this will be my next mission, and perhaps my last. It will carry me into my 80s, and perhaps beyond.

I have a long way to go, and it's already deep into the night.
The God who led me before will still lead me again.
In the bright morning after the dark night,
I, with all who have gone before, will meet my Savior,
Singing hymns. Hallelujah!

Sung Joon Kim
Jae Sun Yu Kim
Brazil, 2009

—⋙—

Adapted from Isaiah 52:7-12,
the following is one of my favorite songs—
a song of victory.

OUR GOD REIGNS

How lovely on the mountains are the feet of him
That brings good new, good news!
Proclaiming peace, announcing news of happiness,
Our God reigns, Our God reigns.

Ye watchmen lift up your voices joyfully as one,
Shout for your king, your king!
See eye to eye thee Lord restoring Zion
Our God reigns, Our God reigns.

Waste places of Jerusalem break forth with joy,
Ye are redeemed, redeemed!
The Lord has come and comforted his people,
Our God reigns, Our God reigns.

Ends of the earth, see the salvation of our God!
Jesus is Lord, is Lord!
Before the nations he has bared his holy arm,
Our God reigns, Our God reigns.

Depart depart, declare his name throughout the earth.
Say ye the Lord redeems.
And be ye clean, ye are the vessels of the Lord.
Our God reigns, Our God reigns.

We shall not go in haste, nor with the fear of men,
The Lord will go before.
Our rear guard is the Holy one of Israel,
Our God reigns, Our God reigns.